The Iconic Imagination

The Iconic Imagination

Douglas Hedley

Bloomsbury Academic
An imprint of Bloomsbury Publishing Inc

B L O O M S B U R Y
NEW YORK • LONDON • OXFORD • NEW DELHI • SYDNEY

Bloomsbury Academic

An imprint of Bloomsbury Publishing Inc

1385 Broadway	50 Bedford Square
New York	London
NY 10018	WC1B 3DP
USA	UK

www.bloomsbury.com

BLOOMSBURY and the Diana logo are trademarks of Bloomsbury Publishing Plc

First published 2016

© Douglas Hedley, 2016

All rights reserved. No part of this publication may be reproduced or transmitted in any form or by any means, electronic or mechanical, including photocopying, recording, or any information storage or retrieval system, without prior permission in writing from the publishers.

No responsibility for loss caused to any individual or organization acting on or refraining from action as a result of the material in this publication can be accepted by Bloomsbury or the author.

Library of Congress Cataloging-in-Publication Data
Names: Hedley, Douglas. Title: The iconic imagination / Douglas Hedley. Description: New York : Bloomsbury Academic, 2016. | Includes index. Identifiers: LCCN 2015034269| ISBN 9781441194633 (pbk. : alk. paper) | ISBN 9781441172174 (hardback : alk. paper) Subjects: LCSH: Image (Philosophy) | Imagination (Philosophy) | Art–Philosophy. | Imagination–Religious aspects. | Art and religion. Classification: LCC BH301.I52 H43 2016 | DDC 128/.3--dc23 LC record available at http://lccn.loc.gov/2015034269

ISBN: HB: 978-1-4411-7217-4
PB: 978-1-4411-9463-3
ePub: 978-1-4411-7607-3
ePDF: 978-1-4411-5191-9

Typeset by Fakenham Prepress Solutions, Fakenham, Norfolk NR21 8NN

For Werner Beierwaltes

Contents

Acknowledgements		viii
Prologue		xi
1	Images, Representation and Imagination	1
2	Human Nature and the *Imago Dei*	31
3	The Anagogic Image	59
4	Freedom and the Narrative Image	89
5	Symbol, Participation and Divine Ideas	119
6	Idolatry and Iconoclasm	149
7	Mythology and Theogony	183
8	Imagination and Revelation	217
Epilogue		257
Bibliography		261
Index of Subjects		293
Index of Names		299

Acknowledgements

I relished the great boon of a Templeton Fellowship at the NDIAS, Notre Dame during the academic year of 2013–14. My thanks to the John Templeton Foundation for their generous support of this project and the many opportunities they provided to engage scholars from so many disciplines. I am deeply grateful for the additional opportunity to host a Templeton Colloquium at the NDIAS. This proved to be a distinctive and fruitful opportunity to explore issues and topics in a manner otherwise unimaginable. Brad Gregory and Don Stelluto were excellent hosts. Grant Osborn and Caroline Sherman were invaluable in their support and my research assistants Sarah Lovejoy and Jack Yusko were exemplary. Billy Abrahams, Karl Ameriks, Robert Audi, Richard Cross, Celia Deane-Drummond, Augustin Fuentes, Stephen Gersh, Peter Holland, Tala Jarjour, Declan Kibert, Jonathan Marx, Christian Moevs, Vittorio Montemaggi, Cyril O'Regan, Gretchen Reydam-Schills, Denis Robichaud and Aku Visala were inspiring colleagues. I am indebted to the Center for Philosophy of Religion and the Departments of Philosophy and Theology and the Programme of Liberal Studies at Notre Dame. I am also deeply grateful to participants in the NDIAS mini conference on *Participation in God* at Notre Dame, 18–20 March 2014, especially Stephen Clark. Drafts of the book were presented at lectures throughout the US during 2013–14. In Chicago I benefited much from Willemien Otten, Jonathan Lear and Jean-Luc Marion, from Paul Griffiths at Duke, Charles Matthewes at Virginia. I learned much from discussion with John Kenney of St Michael's Vermont and John Bussanich at The University of New Mexico on Platonic themes and from Peter Hawkins on Dante. Various panels of the AAR Platonism and Neoplatonism section were both instructive and galvanising. I have profited immensely from discussions in the Early Modern Conversions Project at McGill led by Paul Yachnin, and especially with Torrance Kirby. At McGill James Bryson, Garth Green and Hadi Fakhoury have provided great stimulus. Charles Taliaferro and Jil Evans have been an inspiring philosophical and imaginative presence, as well as dear friends.

The Divinity Faculty at Cambridge has been a rich and warm environment in which to research and lecture. Not only am I thankful for a very collegial environment, but also for providing research costs. I am also grateful to the Divinity Faculty Library, especially Peta Dunstan. I wish to thank Tim Winter and various students at the Muslim College in Cambridge. The *rishi* Julius Lipner has been an excellent guru: I am deeply indebted to his vision and encouragement. I am grateful to my more recent colleague Ankur Barua and students of *Self and Salvation in East and West* and the *Imagination* paper. Special thanks also go to Catherine Pickstock, Garth Fowden, Rowan Williams, and Ryan Mullins. Jacob Sherman has accompanied this project from its inception. He read an early draft of *Living Forms* and was a colleague during the completion of the *Iconic Imagination*. Barrie Fleet, Simon Gathercole, Isodoros Katsos and all other members of the Plotinus seminar in the Divinity Faculty. David Goode, Philip McCosker, Peter Harland and Sophia Syddall have contributed in different ways to the completion of the book.

My debt to Clare College has been profound. I am very conscious of an intellectual debt to my colleagues in different fields, but I ought to mention the uplifting beauty of the Clare College choir and college evensong, where I learnt to reflect on the beauties of Cranmer and Coverdale with the aid of John Rutter, Tim Brown, Graham Ross. The Deans of Clare College, especially Nick Sagovski, who introduced me to Clare, Rupert Sheldrake, fervent admirer of Evensong, John Robertson and Nicholas Barrington have offered helpful advice.

I am indebted to the Cambridge Teape Fund for funding a research visit to Delhi in 2013. Most of the research for this book (and its two predecessors) was done in the Cambridge University Library, an inspirational setting with scholarly and supportive staff. My thanks to The Marion E. Wade Center at the University of Wheaton, Illinois for a visit to their collection. Some of the research was conducted at the Munich Centre for Advanced Studies (CAS) in the spring of 2012. I am grateful to James Vigus for inviting me and to Christoph Bode. I have also had the privilege of participating in the Montreal Early Modern Conversions project. The Classics Department at Dalhousie in Halifax, Nova Scotia, such an important centre of Neoplatonic scholarship and thought, has been a crucial presence in the development of my work and I feel grateful to Wayne Hankey, James Bryson and Evan King and to have such a strong sense of kindred spirits in the Canadian maritimes.

Hans Jakob Meier, Constantinos Proimos and Sylvanna Chrysakopoulou, Joshua Rey and Jolyon Mitchell have been sources of help and stimulus. Mark Wynn and John Cottingham have been very important guides and companions. Brian Hebblethwaite has been a continuing source of friendship, inspiration and support, as have George Newlands, Michael Langford, and Michael Allen. Sarah Hutton and David Leech have been indispensable. Alfons Fürst, Christian Hengstermann and Theo Kobush at the Origen seminars in Münster. David Brown and Ann Loades have been a source of guidance and inspiration in Durham and St Andrew's.

Sadly, I can no longer discuss 'the controlled imagination' of Austin Farrer with Basil Mitchell. Nor can I wander over to the beautiful rooms of the late George Watson in St John's College, where he would offer tea and lecture me with his stentorian tone, learned mischief and melancholy, regaling me with anecdotes and tales of Iris Murdoch or C. S. Lewis.

The Trialogue Group, especially Deborah Wilde and Michael Parsons, contributed much to my work in the last few years. My thanks to Helen van Noorden's seminar at Girton, and *The Friends of Coleridge*, Roger Scruton and Bob Grant, Jonathan Knight, Jan Rohls, Jörg Lauster Benedikt Aigner and John Rist. Margaret Barker, Geoffrey Rowell and Graham Davidson have continued to support my efforts. My thanks to Andrew and Nina Kroglund, Per Bjonar Grande, David Grumett, Russell Re Manning, Louise Hickman.

Peter Cheyne, James Vigus and Geoff Dumbreck read the entire manuscript. I am deeply grateful for their suggestions, though of course none of them bears responsibility for any errors and shortcomings in this work. A particular mention to Evan King for his assistance, especially during the final stages. Haaris Naqvi has been a most encouraging and supportive editor for this book as he was for its predecessor. Special thanks is due to my copy editor at Bloomsbury, Ronnie Hanna and the rest of the team.

My parents have been an abiding support and my sons, Clemens and Justin, have grown into men while I have been writing about the Imagination. And finally, my thanks to Teesta Austin, who endured more prose than her poetic soul should bear.

To the dedicatee, my debt is unfathomable.

Prologue

The human imagination has always been controlled by certain basic images, in which man's own nature, his relation to his fellows, and his dependence upon the divine power find expression.[1]

Why use the term iconic in relation to the imagination? Etymologically it seems a pleonasm. Icon is image in Greek and imagination has its etymological roots in 'imago'. Much 'imagining' has little or nothing to do with images. Nor it is clear that beholding an image, mental or physical, involves an essentially imaginative activity. The term is being used here wittingly as inviting a paradox. The ritual and restraint of the traditional Christian icon seems to contrast with the luxuriant excess of the modern occidental imagination. The Icon is the product of a hierarchical ancient structure of God, Man and Nature, and dedicated to 'the Lord's Glory'. The 'imagination', as the term is habitually employed in modern parlance, is the fruit of the Copernican-Romantic liberation from such ancient constraints. The use of the imagination in the modern sense serves to reinforce the Promethean dimension of a humanity liberated from the fetters of religion. Yet even the ancient icons presupposed imaginative activity. When the prophet Ezekiel or John of Patmos 'saw' the wheel rims of the divine chariot full of eyes and 'saw' the throne of God blazing with burning coals or lamps, this doxology or impression of 'the radiance of the Lord's glory' drew upon images of ancient Israel. The painter of icons in Byzantium or Orthodox Russia were meditating upon these singular and mysterious images, as did Dante in his *Comedy*. The greatest of the Romantics were deeply beholden to the imagination of the ancient prophets. Is this contemplation of the 'Lord's Glory' merely a fabulous aberration in the history of mankind?

If one considers the anthropological data, the imagination is clearly a crucial part of human nature. Evolutionary psychologists like Steve Mithen

---

[1] Austin Farrer, *The Rebirth of Images: The Making of St John's Apocalypse* (Westminster: Dacre, 1949), p. 13.

distinguish between mundane and the more exotic imagination, like beliefs in supernatural beings.[2] Religion is thus a spin-off of language. Language is of adaptive value, especially the cognitive fluidity associated with it: we can combine ideas in interesting ways and use metaphors. On such an account religion is a peculiar offshoot of important evolutionary strategies. In his recent book *Sapiens*, Yuval Harari offers an account of how, since 70,000 BC, mankind came to dominate the globe. His answer is basically simple. Humans could co-operate in ways that apes could not. The major reason lies in imagination or fictions. I agree, but for different reasons. While I assume evolutionary theory, I do not accept that it precludes the Divine. My starting point is the symbol and what relates to it. Platonists have long appealed to symbols, and in a sense this book – and its predecessors – is like Odysseus in the eleventh book of the *Odyssey* pouring blood to raise the spirits of the dead. 'Imagination' here is not a specific faculty or a module in the brain but an activity of the mind:

> Imagination – here the Power so-called
> Through sad incompetence of human speech,
> That awful Power, rose from the mind's abyss.[3]

Faculty psychology locks imagination into a false framework. The imagination defies any separation from reason, desire or sensation. The imagination as a mediating power – is not in any one 'place' and yet pervades the mind's activity and is, I shall argue, the 'locus' of revelation.

Samuel Parker, a severe seventeenth century Oxford critic of the Cambridge Platonists, admonished the Platonists for relying upon the imagination instead of rational argument. He chides the Cambridge Platonists for employing enigmatic and obscure images:

> as *Orpheus* represented his mysteries by Tales and Fables, *Pythagoras* by Numbers and Symbols, so *Plato* and his Followers have (in imitation of them) communicated their Notions by Emblems, Fables, Symbols, Parable, heaps of Metaphors, Allegories, and all sorts of Mystical Representations (as is vulgarly known). All of which upon their account of their Obscurity and Ambiguity are

---

[2] Steven Mithen, *The Prehistory of the Mind: The Cognitive Origins of Art, Religion and Science* (London: Thames and Hudson, 1999), pp. 70–1.
[3] Wordsworth, 1850 *Prelude*, 6.592–4.

apparently the unfittest signes in the world to express the Train of any mans thought to another: For beside that they carry in them no Intelligible Affinity to the Notices, which they were design'd to intimate, the Powers of Imagination are so great, and the Instances in which one thing may resemble another are so many, that there is scarce anything in nature, in which the Fancie cannot find or make a Variety of such Symbolising Resemblances; so that Emblems, Fables, Symbols, Allegories, though they are prettie *Poetick Fancies*, are infinitely unfit to express Philosophical Notions and discoveries of the Natures of things; and besides, seeing that they have left us with no key to these dark *Cyphers*, there can be no sure and constant way to unriddle what conceptions are lock'd up under them so that it does not only require a great deal of pains to frame conjectures of their meaning, but the surest we can pitch upon are withal so uncertain and ambiguous that they unavoidably leave us fluctuating in meer uncertainties.[4]

Even the great Aquinas complained about Plato's appeal to the imagination: 'Plato had a bad method of teaching, intending something other than the words signify, speaking figuratively and through symbols.'[5] Yet the symbol, for the Platonist, is not a metaphor: this is what I wish to stress in the *iconic* dimension of the imagination. The French thinker Alain Besançon views European history as shaped by the tension between 'two contrary imperatives' articulated by Plato as 'two incoercible facts about our nature: first, that we must look toward the divine, that it alone is worth contemplating; and, second, that representing it is futile, sacrilegious, inconceivable'.[6] The Christian doctrine of the Incarnation reinforced this. Platonists and Christians could agree on many points in relation to the icon. The iconodules in the great controversy in Byzantium appealed primarily to the Incarnation. One might say that Christianity coincides with a certain development of Platonism: *visibilia* do not constitute principal reality but are images of a higher perfect realm. This archetypal domain is of superior value to the visible image thereof and this principle should dictate and regulate the ethical and the political. This is the basis of the infinite value of the invisible human soul. Cudworth puts it well;

---

[4] Samuel Parker, *A Free and Impartial Censure of the Platonick Philosophie* (Oxford: Printed by W. Hall, for Richard Davis, 1666), pp. 68–9.
[5] Plato habuit malum modum docendi. Omnia enim figurate docebat per symbola, infundens aliud per verba quam sonent ipsa verba. See Thomas Aquinas, *Sententia libri De anima*, Book 1., C.8, n.107. See R. Pasnau, trans. *A Commentary on Aristotle's De anima*. p. 62.
[6] Alain Besançon *The Forbidden Image* (Chicago, IL: Chicago University Press, 2009), p. 1.

And this is the most natural scale by which the intellectual mind in the contemplation of corporeal things ascends to God; from the passive prints and signatures of that one art and wisdom that appears in the universe, by taking notice thence of the exemplary or archetypal cause, one infinite and archetypal mind setting his seal on all.[7]

The chapter *Images, Representation and Imagination* attacks the view prevalent among art historians that the artistic image should be seen as autonomous and divorced from transcendence. This view often confuses the transparency of the image to transcendence with degradation of the image. Sometimes this attack upon the legacy of Panofsky and his iconography relies upon an imperfect knowledge of the Platonic tradition. Our cursory analysis of the aesthetics of Plotinus shows, on the contrary, that transcendence, for the Platonist, need not diminish the significance of the image and in some sense requires it.

Human Nature and the Imago Dei considers the problem of human nature in relation to the dogma of the *imago Dei*, that man is in the image of God. Why are human beings unique? Darwinian evolution means that the image cannot reside in the particular properties of a unique species since any species has fluid boundaries. If so, where does the image reside? How can we envisage the sense of transcendence that is so distinctively human? The traditional doctrine of the *imago* was more varied and contested than sometimes assumed, and even more recently, it is not obvious how the biblical doctrine might be reconciled with modern anthropology. This is not just puzzling for the theologian since ideas of human uniqueness and special dignity have importance throughout the world.

The Anagogic Image reflects upon the relation of beauty to the sacred. Does this have metaphysical significance? In particular, is it coherent to envisage and imagine beauty as an image of truth and thus retrieve a theophanic sense of the world? Can beauty save the world as Dostoevsky claimed or does it, as Tolstoy averred, distract from the demands of the ethical?

In *Freedom and the Narrative Image* we explore the significance of images of freedom in narrative form with particular reference to the Christian humanism of C. S. Lewis's late novel *Till We Have Faces*, and the themes of

---

[7] R. Cudworth, *The True Intellectual System of the Universe* (London: Royston, 1678), p. 598.

shame, guilt and sacrifice. Genuine morality requires an imaginative narrative from which guilt and remorse cannot be readily expunged and the difference to mere shame explored.

Symbol, Participation and the Divine Ideas considers the images we live by as symbols in their proper sense and not as mere metaphors. The next chapter considers the doctrine of ideas as the background to the Platonic-Romantic doctrine of the symbol as representation of a higher reality at a lower level.

Idolatry and Iconoclasm concerns imagination and idolatry. Is monotheism itself a cruel idolatry of exclusion and oppression? Most great religions, and even enthusiastic iconodules, have prohibitions against idols as fantastic, dangerous and possibly demonic perversions of the sacramental. Is this outdated superstition and what is the significance of persistence of iconoclasm in political religion?

In *Mythology and Theogony* it is observed that atheists often dismiss theism as a ridiculous or monstrous aberration of human fantasy. The ubiquity of theistic belief throughout time and different cultures is at the very least an intriguing aspect of the human imagination. Even if belief in God is false, its prevalence and endurance demands an explanation. The belief in God is complex and enigmatic since all serious religion has quite properly a mythological dimension. In this section mythology is linked to theogony as the history of revelation in a brief excursion into comparative religion. The significant question is not just the relation between myth and logos but myth and history. Here we argue that there are certain stages in human history of imaginative attunement to the Divine: a coincidence of imagination and revelation. There is a divine history not as a Hegelian process of the unfolding of the *Weltgeist*, but insofar as human experience is transformed by narratives of the Divine in the history of religion: inspired imaginings of the divine presence in history.

Imagination and Revelation attests we note that it is easy to forget the importance of the aesthetic power of the natural world, a sense revived in the West by the Romantics. The holy mountain is an image of paradise, the celestial Jerusalem, the place of the heavenly banquet. The Feast is a distinctively human activity and a supremely important image of transcendence. We conclude with reflections upon the 'rebirth of images' (Farrer) in the book of Revelation.

Hans Urs von Balthasar, in his 'The Realm of Metaphysics in the Modern Age' (*The Glory of the Lord*, vol. 5), expounds what he views as the 'strategically wrong' theological development of the modern period towards an anthropologizing of metaphysics which he associates particularly with Bacon, Hobbes, and Descartes. Balthasar observes that 'remarkably enough it was from Descartes that the great English opponent of Hobbes, the leader of the Cambridge Platonists *Ralph Cudworth*, initiated his return to Plato, or better to that classical-Christian, ethical and aesthetic view of the world as a whole, which had nowhere in Europe been more deeply and more convincingly maintained, even up to the present, than in Anglican England … Christianity is here – and in an unbroken tradition from Cudworth and Butler, through the Oxford Movement (and its recourse to the Platonism of the Church Fathers), to the present with Farrer and Mascall – essentially the revealedness of the Glory of God' (290).

It is certainly true, as Balthasar suggests, that the Cambridge Platonists – especially the two most prolific and influential members, Henry More (1614–87) and Ralph Cudworth (1617–88) – were not content to let cosmology retreat into the background and make mankind the exclusive focus of glory. More was the first major channel of Cartesianism in England, yet he offered the first English-language critique of Descartes' *cogito*, and More and Cudworth resisted Descartes' (and Hobbes') banishment of teleology from the cosmos, and sought to preserve the Christian Platonic theophanic view of the world. While More and Cudworth adopted the framework of the Galilean-Cartesian programme, they were the first Englishmen to see the 'atheistic' tendencies of the New Science. Their significance can be appreciated in the light of the question of atheism. Atheism was not part of the imaginary of the antique or medieval Western world. Epicureanism was a minority position in antiquity and almost all the great philosophers accepted some form of deity and some version of providence. It is only with the seventeenth century and the emergence of a secular imaginary that atheism becomes a major, if not dominant, position in Western thought.

In an age of the 'Death of God', it seems puzzling to many why this theophanic view of the world exerted such a grip on the minds of artists, philosophers and poets of the ancient and medieval periods. Yet as Charles Taylor has eloquently argued, the process of secularization in the West is far more complex than many have hitherto imagined. Indeed, Taylor, with his own deep debt to the Romantics through Isaiah Berlin and Herder, speaks of 'social imaginaries' as creative and symbolic dimensions of the self-understanding of human society, but he does not explore the puzzling question of the ontological status of these imaginaries.

Is it still possible to envisage the Glory of the Lord? Notwithstanding a 'secular' age, is the iconic imagination a force withal? Part of the aim of the current work is the exploration of why Platonism remains a force in the realm of the imagination while chided and despised in the academy. The particular contribution of Platonism in the aesthetics of the modern world is an intriguing instance of the persisting power of art to sustain ideas that have been banished or marginalized in philosophy or theology. While philosophers and theologians were admonishing Plato's legacy in the twentieth century, art historians were presenting Plato's thought as the hidden key to the creative imagination of Gothic or Renaissance Europe. Moreover, many creative minds of the last century were deeply Platonic in their summoning of 'the lovely shapes and sounds intelligible' of what Coleridge calls the eternal divine language of the created realm. T. S. Eliot could draw upon the deep draughts of Platonism from the St Louis and Oxford of his youth, W. B. Yeats upon Plotinus, Berkeley, Blake and Coleridge; Kandinsky or Kiefer on more esoteric Platonism, while even a composer like John Tavener explored the Byzantine and Sufi traditions. Great artists have an uncanny and arresting capacity to mirror and articulate the culture and world they inhabit. Despite Darwin, Freud or Foucault, it is an imaginative abode still haunted by transcendence.

The key idea is 'participation'. Primarily, the concept is construed in terms of the Platonic doctrine of the Forms. The second sense is that of engagement or experience. While it is often claimed that contemporary culture is saturated by images, these images are essentially those of a world divested of transcendence. The images of the imagination in this work are icons of a greater reality. Contemplating such 'iconic' images of the sacred is not to indulge in harmless fantasy or escape from reality for a brief period. Nor are these images merely skilful devices to convey a content that can otherwise be conveyed conceptually. Rather, it is to encounter and to participate in a greater world. Such images participate in what they express.

1

Images, Representation and Imagination

In Bildern besteht der ganze Schatz menschlicher Erkenntnis und Glueckseligkeit.[1]

When we think with images, either in art or in religion, we are genuinely *thinking*. That's to say, we are coming more and more fully to 'inhabit' our humanity.[2]

In recent years, art historians have joined forces with philosophers to criticize the Platonic paradigm of the image. Panofsky, Wind or Gombrich viewed Platonism, especially Neoplatonism, as providing the meaning behind the images of great European art. The image, so the argument goes, became a signpost for transcendence; the image was dematerialized, even desexualized, and a means of disguising, for example, Michelangelo's homosexuality. In response to the highly literary Iconography of the Panofsky school, there has been return to the image, an iconic or pictorial turn. Here is a move to restore the image to its proper dignity and autonomy, rather than as a staging post to an immaterial idea. In this chapter, we will defend the Panofsky-Hegel-Plato view that the image is, indeed, best seen as the expression of spirit. Moreover, the rejection of transcendence will eviscerate rather than restore the image. Yet the appeal of crude materialism is often reinforced by what one might call 'Freshman' Platonism. This chapter will conclude with some observations about the image in Plotinus in order to distinguish his subtle theorizing about the image from crude stereotypes of the Platonist. This Alexandrian Hellenist was fascinated by the language pictures of the Egyptians, their

---

[1] Johann Georg Hamann, *Aesthetica in nuce* (Sämtliche Werke, ed. Josef Nadler II, Vienna: Verlag Herder, 1949–57), p. 197.
[2] Rowan Williams, *The Edge of Words* (London: Bloomsbury, 2014), p. 194.

hieroglyphs. He valued these as expressions of a non-discursive awareness that transcends habitual concepts. In this way, Plotinus was as sensitive to the problems of a misleading externalizing of ocular metaphors as many late twentieth century French avant-garde thinkers, albeit for different reasons. He was less concerned with reification as a mode of commodification than the requirement of the soul to become what it knows. He employs the beautiful image of people walking in a desert and taking on the colour of the sunlit dust surrounding them. Once we appreciate the value and role of images in Plotinus, it is easier to understand his powerful critique of both rationalism and reductionism.

What is an image? The word can refer to mental images or pictorial objects – e.g. the mythological image of Narcissus, or the ancestral *imago* of the imperious Roman aristocrat. What of the Veronica: the archetypal image of Christ, fabric which, according to legend, bears the image of Christ's face and thus a *vera icona*, one not made by human hands? One might consider the expressive power of architecture – the Parthenon or the Taj Mahal. Horace's renowned '*ut pictura poesis*' defines poetry as the re-presentation of images.[3] The poet's employment of the mind's eye is compared with the painter's imitation of nature. Certainly, the imagistic depiction in words is a key tool in the poetic device of *ekphrasis*: the vivid description of a particular object, like the Homeric Achilles' shield or the Urn in Keat's ode. Furthermore, one might consider the tradition of images as having a didactic quality for the unlettered: the *biblia pauperum*. Our historical being is shaped by *images* in myriad ways.

The emotional and motivational force of such images to mobilize tribes, nations and empires is incontestable. Images constitute a strident counterblast to the mechanical explanations of human history. Constantine's dream of the cross and the voice exclaiming 'In this sign you will conquer', or the Archeropoeitos image of Kamoulia from Cappodocia, which was used on the banners of the Byzantine army. One might think of the Venerable Bede's report of the conversion of England and especially St Augustine of Canterbury's encounter with Ethelbert, King of Kent (552–616): 'With them Augustine

---

[3] Rensselaer Wright Lee, 'Ut Pictura Poesis: The Humanistic Theory of Painting', *Art Bulletin* 22 (1940): 197–269.

went with carrying a silver cross and an image of our Lord and saviour painted on a picture.'[4] Or why should images generate such fury and violence: from the great Byzantine icon controversies of the eighth and ninth centuries, the iconoclasms of the Reformation, destruction of monuments and images in the English Civil war or the French Revolution up to – in more recent times – the destruction of the Buddhas of Bamiyan and the attack on the Twin Towers; the toppling of the Soviet statues? Pitiless acts of cruelty are often justified in terms of an archaic prohibition of sacred images (e.g. images of the prophet). The sacred and savage power of images, like the head of Medusa, is often invoked in modern political conflicts. It is often remarked that our era is a period of an unprecedented flood of images – the technology of the printing press, prints, photography and film. Walter Benjamin considered film to be the great art of the modern age. In the digital and internet age, with the rapid decline of print media there are questions about the erosion of critical judgement. Guy Dubord in his *La Société du spectacle* analysed the spectatorial nature of capitalist society and the prodigious influence of Foucault's exploration of the 'panoptic' surveillance structures of early modern civilization in his analysis of the proposed *Panopticon* of Jeremy Bentham.

Lying behind such intense recent debates concerning images is Weber's idea of disenchantment, where he states that the *stahlhartes Gehäuse* (steel-hard-structure) of the technological efficiency of modern society crushes the sense of enchantment enjoyed by our ancestors. This Weberian notion of disenchantment is often linked to Benjamin's highly influential idea of 'aura' and its loss through the mechanical reproduction of art itself in his *The Work of Art*. This 'aura' is the un-reproducible originality and authenticity of a work of art such as a painting. The photograph, so the argument goes, with its facility for exact and easy duplication loses the unique 'aura' of the painting.[5] The influence of Weber and Benjamin can be seen clearly in the work of the German art historian Hans Belting and his three-fold chronology of theology, art history, anthropology in his celebrated and much discussed opus magnum,

---

[4] 'At illi Augustinus et socii veniebant, crucem pro vexillo ferentes argeanteam et imaginem Domini salvatoris in tabula depictam ...' The venerable Bede, *Ecclesiastical History*, trans. J. E. King (Cambridge, MA: Loeb, 1930), 1.25.
[5] See James Elkins and David Morgan, *Re-Enchantment* (London: Routledge, 2008).

Bild und Kult, one of the most influential recent books in medieval and Byzantine history.[6] The basic dichotomy is cult and art. The ancient paradigm of the magical presence: the cult object that would be kissed, venerated and clouded in incense. We then have a move to art as the consciously reflexive illusionism of the Renaissance: the move from cult to art.[7] There is a stress upon genealogy here and Belting views the medieval as the era of the image as opposed to the subsequent era of art. Art history, like theology, tends to separate images from the body. Hence his *Bild* anthropology is conceived in opposition to both the theological paradigm of the magical cult objects and the rarified objects of 'art'.

The image has played a prominent role in much recent philosophy. Wittgenstein can say: 'A picture held us captive. And we could not get outside it, for it lay in our language and language seemed to repeat itself to us inexorably.'[8] Heidegger ominously associated modern technology with the world-picture *(Welt-Bild)*, the final product of an intellectual narrative that begins Plato's substitution of the problem of Being with onto-theology and develops through the mathesis of the Galilean-Cartesian approach to nature.

Iconic Turn vs Linguistic Turn?

'Les poetes sont des hommes qui refuse d'utiliser le langage.'[9]

Much of twentieth-century thought was shaped by the idea that inherited philosophical problems could be resolved or even dissolved by linguistic reflection. For Derrida *'il n'y a pas de hors-texte'* ('there is nothing outside the text or no outside text').[10] In another idiom, for logical positivists that meaning is determined by verifiability or analytic truth. The borders of the

---

[6] Hans Belting, *Likeness and Presence, A History of the Image before the Era of Art* (Chicago, IL: University of Chicago, 1994); *Das Echte Bild, Bildfragen als Glaubensfragen* Munich: Beck, 2006).
[7] 'Cult' derived, as Peter Cheyne has reminded me, from *cultus*, or reverence, which is the *eusebia* or *Theosebia* described by St Augustine (*The City of God*, trans. Henry Bettenson (Harmondsworth: Penguin, 2003), X.i).
[8] Wittgenstein, *Philosophical Investigations* (Oxford: Blackwell, 1981), §115.
[9] J.-P. Sartre, *Qu'est que c'est la literature?* (Paris: Gallimard, 1948), p. 17.
[10] Jacques Derrida, *Of Grammatology* (trans. Gayatri Chakravorty Spivak. Baltimore: Johns Hopkins University Press, 1997), Pt II, §2.

reality are determined by the limits of intelligibility. More recently various philosophers, art historians and cultural critics have announced a 'pictorial' or 'iconic' turn, a shift that explicitly breaks away from predominantly linguistic interpretations of reality. Does the pictorial or iconic turn supersede the 'linguistic turn'?

Images are ancient candidates for explaining the generation of meaning. There is an intuitively plausible basis for this assumption. Words have an overtly conventional dimension. It is otherwise with mental representations. An Englishman has to learn that the French call snow *la neige*. Presumably, the Frenchman has the same image of white stuff when he says *neige*. Mental images, on some theories – especially for empiricism from Aristotle to Hobbes and in Locke – explain how concepts can represent items in the world.[11] Under the influence of Kant, Coleridge objected to the 'idolism of the French' that the 'conceivable, must be imageable, and the imageable must be tangible'.[12] Aristotle presents words as marks of mental images.[13]

Consider ostensive definitions where a term is hard to define verbally, perhaps for children or foreigners, or because of the need for some specific and immediate perceptual acquaintance – as with a colour. There, a concept can represent an image of a basic perpetual kind, like a mental photograph. This seems to provide a neat and economical theory of how we grasp the meaning of words. However, many philosophers have argued that images in this sense constitute, in fact, a philosophical *ignis fatuus*. Wittgenstein has an example:

> If I give someone the order 'fetch me a red flower from that meadow', how is he to know what sort of flower to bring, as I have only given him a *word*?
> Now the answer one might suggest first is that he went to look for a red flower carrying a red image in his mind, and comparing it with the flowers to see which of them had the colour of the image ... But this is not the only way of searching and it isn't the usual way. We go, look about us, walk up to the flower and pick it, without comparing it to anything. To see that the process of obeying

---

[11] Olivier Boulnois, *Être et répresentation: Une généalogie de la métaphysique moderne à l'époque de Duns Scot* (Paris: Presses Universitaires de France, 1999).
[12] Coleridge, *The Friend*, I, p. 422.
[13] Aristotle, *De interpretatione*, 16a3.

the order can be of this kind, consider the order '*imagine* a red patch'. You are not tempted in this case to think that *before* obeying you must have imagined a red patch to serve you as a pattern for the red patch which you were ordered to imagine.[14]

The absence of interior images does not, Wittgenstein suggests, preclude the function and meaning of the concept. The proper work of the concept has little to do with any interior 'picturing'. Wittgenstein is pointing to the deceptive plausibility of the internal mirroring model. Far from a pictorial presence guaranteeing meaning, there is a rift between the image per se and any interpretation of its meaning. The recognition of the image is just as mysterious as the concept. Thus, the appeal to an image produces a regress.[15] The mind has to interpret whatever data it confronts, and an image requires a procedure of understanding.

The capacity to interpret an image requires the *logos*. St Jerome translated the Logos of St John with *verbum* but he could have used *ratio* or *intellectus*. The choice of '*verbum*' furnishes rather different connotations than the more rationalist associations of *logos*. For Philo, the Logos is the image of God εἰκών τοῦ θεοῦ and humanity is created 'according to the image' κατὰ τὴν εἰκόνα. Only a human being endowed with reason can 'get the picture', as we say colloquially. Higher apes perceive images but possess no *logos* with which to interpret these images creatively. Man can make machines, i.e. computing machines, with memories, as Kenneth Boulding observed strikingly, but we have not succeeded in 'building the simplest machine with a conscious image'.[16] That is still true.

---

[14] L. Wittgenstein, *The Blue and Brown Books: Preliminary Studies for the Philosophical Investigations* (Oxford: Blackwell, 1980), p. 3.
[15] For a lucid discussion see Simon Blackburn, *Spreading the Word: Groundings in the Philosophy of Religion* (Oxford: Oxford University Press, 1984), pp. 45–90.
[16] Kenneth Boulding, *The Image: Knowledge in Life and Society* (Ann Arbor, MI: University of Michigan Press, 1961), p. 46.

From Meaning to Presence?

Das Bild ist nicht Derivate oder Illustration, sondern active Träger des Denkprozesses.[17]

At the end of Shakespeare's play *The Winter's Tale* we have a scene in which the statue of the lost wife of King Leontes comes alive.[18] The statue closely resembles his wife Hermione and all are amazed by the artistry of the image. Paulina then summons the image into life:

> "'Tis time. Descend. Be stone no more.' (5.3.11)

In this play Shakespeare dwells explicitly upon the relationship between art and nature:

> his is an art /
> Which does mend nature, change it rather, but
> The art itself is nature. (4.4.6)

The philosophical poet and dramatist is presenting a reflection upon the nature of the image. The unlikelihood of the plot is remarked upon.

> That she is living,
> Were it but told you, Should be hooted at
> Like an old tale ... (5.3.115–17)

It is hard to avoid the assumption that Shakespeare is reflecting upon the power of 'living' images. He had lived through one of the great iconoclastic convulsions of English culture: the Reformation, where the 'magical' properties of images was one of the great disputes of the age. Leontes exclaims:

> O she's warm!
> If this be magic, let it be an art
> Lawful as eating (5.3.109–11)

---

[17] Horst Bredekamp, *Darwins Koralle. Frühe Evolutionsmodelle und die Tradition der Naturgeschichte*, (Berlin: Klaus Wagenbach, 2005), p. 24. 'The picture is not a derivation or illustration but an active bearer of the thought process.'
[18] A. D. Nuttall, *Shakespeare, The Winter's Tale* (London: Arnold, 1996).

We have witnessed in the last few decades the re-assertion of the autonomy of the image.[19] In thinkers like Gottfried Boehm and W. J. T. Mitchell the problem of presentation or representation of images has reignited. Such recent thinkers are drawing upon, and criticizing, a tradition evident in such eminent art historians as Warburg, Gombrich, and Panofsky. There is, perhaps, some reaction against the philological concerns of the founders of art history. Panofsky's Iconology accentuates the meaning rather than the form of art.[20] Some of the leading figures of the 'Iconic Turn' inveigh against the dominance of the interpretation of the image and stress the autonomy and objective power of the images. Most radically, Didi-Huberman questioned from a Freudian perspective the presumption of 'iconology' that the art work is composed of legible and intelligible signs.[21] G. Boehm asserts that what we grant to Logos, namely that it tells us about the world, must also be attributed to images. However images do not gain their meaning from 'iconic identity' with reality. He uses the term 'iconic difference', by which he means difference between figure and its background and the artistic representation and the model.[22] '*Bilder*' have, on Boehm's account, an autonomy and irreducibility to text. W. J. T. Mitchell's 'pictorial turn' depends upon a nuanced relationship between the mimetic and the role of conventions in artistic perception.[23] For Mitchell, the pictorial turn is a 'post-linguistic, postsemiotic rediscovery of the picture as a complex interplay between visuality, apparatus, institutions, discourse, bodies, and figurality'.[24] He writes:

> What makes for the sense of a pictorial turn, then, is not that we have some powerful account of visual representation that is dictating the terms of cultural theory, but that pictures form a point of peculiar friction and discomfort across a broad range of intellectual inquiry. The picture now has a status somewhere

---

[19] *Ideengeschichte der Bildwissenschaft*, ed. Jorg Probst and Jost Philipp Klenner (Frankfurt am Main: Surkamp, 2009).
[20] See Erwin Panofsky, *Studies in Iconology: Humanistic Themes in the Art of the Renaissance* (New York: Harper Row, 1962); idem, *Idea: A Concept in Art Theory* (New York: Harper Row, 1968).
[21] Georges Didi-Huberman, *Devant l'image* of 1990; English *Confronting Images* (Pennsylvania State University, 2009).
[22] 'Die Wiederkehr der Bilder', in *Was ist ein Bild?* ed. Gottfried Boehm (Munich: Fink, 1994), pp. 11–38, and 'Die Bilderfrage', ibid., pp. 325–43.
[23] W. J. T. Mitchell, *Iconology. Image, Text, Ideology* (Chicago: University of Chicago, 1986).
[24] W. J. T. Mitchell, *Picture Theory: Essays on Verbal and Visual Interpretation* (Chicago: University of Chicago, 1994), p. 16.

between what Thomas Kuhn called a 'paradigm' and an anomaly, emerging as a central topic of discussion in the human sciences in the way that language did: that is as a kind of model or figure for other things (including figuration itself), and as an unresolved problem, perhaps even the object of its own 'science'.[25]

Boehm stresses the significance of Heidegger's appeal to the art-work, and Gadamer's sensitivity to images as texts. Our nature is to interpret. Mitchell claims 'whatever the pictorial turn is, then, it should be clear that it is not a return to naïve mimesis, copy or correspondence theories of representation, or a renewed metaphysics of pictorial "presence".[26] In both the work of Boehm and Mitchell we can see the deep influence of philosophy upon their attempt to develop a theory of the image. This is perhaps not surprising within the continental tradition, where many leading philosophers like Schelling, Hegel, Nietzsche and Adorno were exceptionally well versed in the fine arts. Even Heidegger, whose first-hand knowledge of the fine arts was negligible, took great philosophical interest therein.

It is perhaps in the domain of metaphor that the analytic tradition has more to offer. There has been a well-established philosophical critique of metaphors since Aristotle.[27] Lakoff and Johnson[28] highlight the ubiquitous nature of metaphor. Not just the poets but most of us are metaphorical when we employ spatial prepositions for non-spatial affairs – 'in' hot water or 'in' dire straits and being 'in' difficulty. Happiness is 'high' and sadness is 'down'. We talk about arguments or illness in terms of warfare: fighting heart disease or demolishing an argument. Lakoff and Johnson distinguish between simple metaphors and structural metaphors. The latter are grounded in our embodied and experiential relationship to the environment. Various metaphors are integral parts of our reasoning: more is 'up' and less is 'down'. For example, military expenditure is 'escalating' or the revenue from oil is 'dwindling'. Such schemata usually need to be learnt within a culture and Lakoff and Johnson explore about fifty such schemata. We are not, of course, usually conscious of these inherited structural metaphors.

---

[25] Mitchell, *Picture Theory*, p. 13.
[26] Mitchell, *Picture Theory*, p. 16.
[27] Aristotle, *Topics*, (Organon V), 158b, 139b-140a, 133b: 'Every metaphor is indistinct'. See Nietzsche's early essay, *Über Wahrheit und Lüge im außermoralischen Sinn*.
[28] Lakoff and Johnson, *Metaphors we Live by* (Chicago: University of Chicago Press, 1980).

So what is correct in this position? It shows that language has deep roots in the imagination of the body. It also casts doubt upon any crude representationalism, i.e. language as a simple mirror of the world. The imagination for many thinkers in the Platonic tradition mediates between the body and the mind. Ibn 'Arabi, according to Henry Corbin, for example, views the imagination as elevating the mind to the isthmus (or Barzakh) between the sensible and the intelligible worlds.

However, there are serious weaknesses: especially in the penchant displayed by Lakoff and Johnson for a certain physiological reductionism wherein the mental is reduced to the bodily. Such a shrinking of the mental is problematic. Take, for example, the 'Copernican revolution'. Our world has been permeated since the seventeenth century by a vision of reality that bluntly contradicts our bodily experience. The earth is *obviously* flat and stable and the sun clearly goes around it, but we know that we are not the centre of the three-tiered cosmos of our ancestors. Yet the source is usually an image of the world. In the last few centuries the *image* of the earth as a globe rotating around one star within a galaxy of stars has seeped into general consciousness, regardless of individual knowledge of astrophysics or the details of four-dimension relativistic space-time continuum.[29]

Ever since the seventeenth century, the image of the solar system as a gigantic mechanism has been widely pervasive. A more nuanced view of the human being as a deeply symbolic and historical creature is required. We are body and spirit and the imagination is the unifying field of this duality rather than its dissolution. One might add that the philosophical tradition is replete with imagined scenarios and thought experiments: from Plato's Cave or the Winged Charioteer to Avicenna's flying man, Descartes's *genius malignus*, Hegel's Master-Slave Dialectic, Nietzsche's Madman, Rawls' Veil of Ignorance, Frank Jackson's Mary and Thomas Nagel's Bat.[30]

Richard Rorty writes of his choice of the title of his work *Philosophy and the Mirror of Nature*:

It is pictures rather than propositions, metaphors rather than statements, which

---

[29] See Kenneth Boulding, *The Image: Knowledge in Life and Society* (Ann Arbor MI: University of Michigan Press, 1961), p. 77.
[30] See Georg Bertram, *Philosophische Gedankenexperimente* (Stuttgart: Reclam, 2012).

determine most of our philosophical convictions. The picture which holds traditional philosophy captive is that of the mind as a great mirror, containing various representations – some accurate, some not – and capable of being studied by pure, nonempirical methods. Without this notion of the mind as mirror, the notion of knowledge as accuracy of representation would not have suggested itself.[31]

Rorty, in this justly renowned work, insisted that something distinctive happened in seventeenth-century philosophy and he associates it with notion of representation as 'reflection'. Philosophers like Descartes and Locke, he claims, began to compare the mind to a mirror that reflects reality. Knowledge, on this Cartesian-Lockean model, is concerned with the accuracy of such reflections, and the development of a technique of polishing the mirror to attain this knowledge. Rorty thinks that philosophers have been bewitched by philosophy as 'para-optics': the ancient paradigm of the mind as mirror coincides with a distinctly modern problem of consciousness. He claims that philosophers in the seventeenth century come to associate reflection with consciousness in a way that could make no sense for the ancients or medievals, especially because for Descartes, 'thinking' involves both sensation and intellection. Rorty insists that representative perception and a view of the 'inner space' of the mind, an 'inside' as opposed to an 'outside', marks a break with the tradition and generates the modern philosophical obsession with accurate representation.

Isomorphism between Language and World?

The idea that language may be transparent to the world is presented by Rorty as an accident of Western thought and its model of 'para-optics'. The Indian-Sanskrit term '*darshana*' with its root in the verb to see *drs* (as insight or philosophy) would suggest, however, that this is not limited to the West.[32] The Brahmins and the Buddhists debated vigorously whether language can be isomorphic with the structure of being. Is language a *picturing* of reality? For

---

[31] Richard Rorty, *Philosophy and the Mirror of Nature* (Princeton, NJ: Princeton University Press, 1979), p. 12.
[32] Diana L. Eck, *Darsán: Seeing the Divine in India* (Chambersburg, PA: Anima Books, 1985).

the Buddhists, language distorts the true nature of reality. Standard categories are fictions. The first person singular, the 'I' has a fake reference. Elizabeth Anscombe's familiar claim in *The First Person*, that 'I' is not a referential term has evident parallels in Buddhist literature.[33] The broader question is: can language be isomorphic? Does it in some way picture the world (like early Wittgenstein); or does it not (like the later Wittgenstein)? The Buddhists are content to find continuities between objects in the world and appeal to epistemological parsimony. We have no need to posit mysterious essences or natural kinds. Richard Rorty's own iconoclastic version of the linguistic turn was part of an attack upon a crude epistemological mimesis, and he appeals to pragmatic considerations:

> One is justified in believing that P (some proposition) if and only if one has engaged in the social practice of showing that one's belief that P sustains appropriate relations to the other beliefs of one's social community.[34]

In the background lies the rejection of the isomorphic model of language:

> If we see knowledge as a matter of conversation and of social practice, rather than as an attempt to mirror nature, we will not be likely to envisage a metapractice which will be the critique of all possible forms of social practice.[35]

Behind Rorty is Heidegger. In the decade following *Being and Time* Heidegger moved from his timeless view of the human relation to the world to a historical position in his *Die Zeit des Weltbildes*. Whereas in *Being and Time* he thought that concepts like 'subject' and 'object' distort our proper relation to the world (one that is more primordial and authentic), in *Die Zeit des Weltbildes*, Heidegger presents these concepts as applying specifically to the modern period, especially Descartes' foundationalism, a temper of mind that leads to the modern period that Heidegger diagnoses as the *Berechnung* (or calculation) of technology. Our access to Being and the gods (who mediate Being to us) has been closed off by modernity and its tendency to a rapacious and

---

[33] A view derived from Wittgenstein. See also David Pears, *Paradox and Platitude in Wittgenstein's Philosophy* (Oxford: Oxford University Press, 2006), Ch. 4, criticizing Wittgenstein's argument that 'I' is 'not a referential pronoun'.
[34] Rorty, *Philosophy and the Mirror of Nature*, p. 186.
[35] Rorty, *Philosophy and the Mirror of Nature*, p. 171.

controlling technology. He starts to use the term *Geschichte des Seins*. Thus, in a lineage akin to Hegel's history of the Spirit, the world of the Greeks, the medieval and the modern world are radically different worlds. 'Metaphysics' for Heidegger explains these shifts. Heidegger sees metaphysics as generating a baneful *reification* of Being. Modern thought, in particular, yet grounded in Plato's Cave Analogy, represents beings but fails to recognize the presence of Being.[36]

The idea of nominalism purging reality of abstract objects and ideas and the consequent disenchantment of the world was a chief principle of Blumenberg's philosophical 'metaphorology'. Deprived by God's hiddenness of metaphysical guarantees of the world, 'man constructs for himself a counterworld of elementary rationality and manipulability'.[37] Blumenberg developed the idea of Absolute metaphors – light of truth. Absolute metaphors fulfil human survival needs and function as self-assertion strategies. These absolute metaphors do not reveal reality but appease it. They serve to translate something unknown to something known. Blumenberg insisted 'The loss of metaphysics calls for metaphorics again on its own place.'[38] In his *Paradigmen zu einer Metaphorologie*,[39] Blumenberg argues eloquently for the irreducibility of the image to the conceptual: indeed, concepts are often 'condensed metaphors'.[40] Metaphors are, moreover, *Grundbestände der philosophischen Sprache*[41] ('foundational components of philosophical language'). It is in this context that he develops the idea of absolute metaphors.[42] Such absolute metaphors compensate for the failure of metaphysics. These paradigmatic metaphors may be modified or transformed over time but resist being totally 'dissolved into conceptuality'. In the *Paradigms* Blumenberg endeavours to demonstrate that 'absolute metaphors' have an inalienable role in predisposing

---

[36] Heidegger, *Platons Lehre der Wahrheit* (Bern: Francke, 1947) pp. 46ff., '*Seitdem gibt es ein Streben nach der Wahrheit im Sinne der Richtigkeit des Blickens und der Blickstellung.*' 'Since then there is the striving for truth is the sense of accuracy and orientation of the gaze.'
[37] Hans Blumenberg, *Legitimacy of the Modern World*, trans. Robert Wallace (Cambridge MA: MIT, 1985), p. 173.
[38] Blumenberg, 'Paradigmen zu einer Metaphorologie', in *Archiv für Begriffsgeschichte* 6, 1960, 7–142, p. 142.
[39] Blumenberg, *Paradigmen zu einer Metaphorologie* (Frankfurt am Main: Surkamp, 1997).
[40] Probst and Klenner, *Ideengeschichte der Bildwissenschaft*, p. 15.
[41] Blumenberg, *Paradigmen zu einer Metaphorologie*, p. 10.
[42] Angus Nichols, *Myth and the Human Sciences: Hans Blumenberg's Theory of Myth* (London: Routledge, 2015).

philosophical reflection: *Metaphern sind Vorgriffe* (anticipations), literally 'fore-graspings'. If he is correct, the consequences are momentous. He writes:

> Evidence of absolute metaphors would force us to reconsider the relationship between logos and the imagination. The realm of the imagination could no longer be regarded solely as the substrate for transformations into conceptuality – on the assumption that each element could be processed and converted in turn, so to speak, until the supply of images was used up – but as a catalytic sphere from which the universe of concepts continually renews itself, without thereby converting and exhausting this founding reserve.[43]

Blumenberg is a philosopher who wants to insist upon the ineluctably imaginative dimension of the human experience of the world. Imagination is not a poor substitute for the conceptual grasp of the world. Rather, the 'universe of concepts' is always relying upon resources provided by the imagination to engage with the world.

Paradoxes of Platonism: Image and Ascent

That uninhibited seventeenth century berater of the Platonists, Samuel Parker, was unflinching in his analysis of the faults of the Platonic school:

> All those Theories in Philosophie which are expressed only in metaphorical Termes, are not real Truths, but the meer Products of Imagination, dress'd up (like Children's *babies*) in a few spangled empty words … Thus their wanton & luxuriant fancies climbing up into the Bed of Reason, do not only defile it by unchaste and illegitimate Embraces, but instead of real conceptions and notices of Things, impregnate the mind with nothing but Ayerie and Subventaneous Phantasmes.[44]

In this passage we can see clearly the claim that the products of the imagination are not only in conflict with reason but stifle and distort the process of reasoning.

Coleridge, a deep student of the seventeenth century and its debates, is answering such a challenge when he retorts that 'It is among one of the miseries

---

[43] Blumenberg, *Paradigmen zu einer Metaphorologie*, p. 4.
[44] Samuel Parker, *A Free and Impartial Censure of the Platonick Philosophie*, 1666, pp. 75–6.

of the present age that it recognises no medium between the *Literal* and the *Metaphorical*.'[45] He is referring to the Platonic view of the *image* as instantiating or exemplifying its archetype. Should one not speak of 'metaphors we live by' but rather *images* to live by? The employment of 'metaphor' suggests the conventionalism of Rorty or even Blumenberg. Perhaps it is no accident that some of the greatest work of Iconology was done on the Neoplatonic tradition, where the truth of art is more than merely conventional – the Image points to its Archetype.[46] The image constitutes the presence of the transcendent divine mystery in and for the human mind through imagination. Once this is accepted, it is requisite to distinguish between the imaginative and the chimerical. In this special sense of Platonism, it is *Images* we live by but not exactly metaphors.

Part of the warp and woof of Platonic metaphysics is ascent from down the Cave in Plato's *Republic* and the vision of the Beautiful, the True and the Good in the *Symposium* and *Republic*. The special privilege of sight in Greek thought (as opposed to the verbal Hebrews, say) is a familiar theme that hides deep complexities. In the archaic world Homer speaks of θαῦμα ἰδέσθαι, *thauma idestai*, 'to behold a wonder' (*Iliad* 5.725, 10.439, 18.83, 18.377), with its connotations of divine beauty. Plato uses ἐκφανέστατον (*Phaedrus* 250d), that which 'shines out' for beauty. Plotinus draws upon this with his favourite model of the procession, creation or 'emanation' of the cosmos out of the transcendent Good as a shining forth (ἔκλαμψις, *eklampsis*) (*Ennead* IV.3.6.6; III.2.16.15; IV.5.61). Plotinus has a vision of eternity *through* the seen and the temporal. There is thus less of a gap between 'the lover of sights and sounds' and the philosopher in Plotinus than in Plato.[47] In *Ennead* I 3 (20), 'On Dialectic', Plotinus gives an account of the different stages of the musician and the lover and the philosopher. He is employing a Platonic theme. However, characteristically the theme is discreetly transformed. In Plato the *philosophos*,

---

[45] *The Statesman's Manual*, in S. T. Coleridge, *Lay Sermons*, ed. R. T. White (Princeton, NJ: Princeton University Press, 1973), p. 30.

[46] See Dillon, in Baine Harris, *The Significance of Neoplatonism* (Norfolk, VA: International Society for Neoplatonic Studies, Old Dominion University, Albany; distributed by State University of New York Press, 1976). See D. Watson, Images of Unlikeness: Proclus on Homeric σύμβολον and the Perfection of the Rational Soul, *Dionysius* 31 (2013): 57–78.

[47] Plato, *Republic*, V, 475d-e.

musikos and *erotikos* are three forms of the person but in Plotinus they are different agents. Furthermore, *Musikos* for Plato means refined or cultivated whereas for Plotinus it means musician in our sense (though meaning someone musical rather than composer or player). The lover and musician, on the Plotinian account, knows by acquaintance what they cannot describe in propositions.[48] The musician must be driven upwards by realizing that the beautiful sounds are images or 'ectypes' of heavenly archetypes. The lover, into whom the musician may be transformed, has to detach his love from one body to beauty per se and in particular must be able to learn the nature of ethical beauty. The philosopher is 'already winged', to use the imagery of the *Phaedrus*. The philosopher explicates what is already implicit in the musician or the lover. Here, the concern of the true philosopher is with contemplating the Ideas rather than logic or propositions (προτάσεις, *protaseis*) in the narrow sense. Dialectic is the most valuable part of philosophy, Plotinus tells us, because it deals with *ta onta*: real beings or realities.[49] Here we have an instance of the polemic between the schools. Whereas for Stoics, philosophy consists of propositional knowledge – for the Platonist it is knowledge by acquaintance – the *experience* we have of the realities of the ideas.[50]

Pheidias's magnificent statues of Athena on the Parthenon and Zeus at Olympia formed a paradigmatic part of the Hellenic 'imaginary'. At the very end of the Platonic Academy, when the goddess was removed from the Parthenon, Proclus dreamt that Athena asked for a place in his house.[51] After considering the example of the sculptor Pheidias, Plotinus suggests that we should 'leave the *technai* and let us contemplate those things they are said to imitate, which come into existence naturally as beauties'. For:

> all the forms we speak about are beautiful images in that world. Of the kind which someone imagined to exist in the soul of the wise man, images not

---

[48] Plato is more ambiguous: the implication of Plato's *Ion*, *Phaedrus* or *Symposium* is not that they *know*, but that they are *inspired*.
[49] 'ἀγάλματα δὲ οὐ γεγραμμένα, ἀλλὰ ὄντα'.
[50] For Plato, *dianoia* also is a form of *episteme*, though a lower one, and that descends from hypotheses in a geometrical and propositional, analytic manner.
[51] Marinus, *Vita Procli*, in Edwards, M. (trans.), *Neoplatonic Saints. The Lives of Plotinus and Proclus by their Students* (Liverpool: Liverpool University Press, 2000, pp. 58–115, §30).

painted but real. This is why the ancients said that the Ideas were realities and substances. (V8[31].5)⁵²

In this passage concerning the nature of the divine intellect, the identification of *agalmata* with *ta onta* is conspicuous. It is characteristic of Plotinus's deliberate yoking of paradoxical elements (e.g. the One as *dunamis* or as self-caused). *Agalama* or statue is an odd term to use in conjunction with *eikon*. It is not an obvious synonym and does not cohere readily with the dominant imagery in V.8 of the translucence of the Intellect (φῶς γὰρ φωτί) and harmonious interpenetration of thought and being. The word is used especially of sculptures of the gods rather than paintings: for Herodotus statues of men are *eikones* whereas those of gods are *agalmata*.⁵³ It is fitting for Plotinus, for whom 'the gods are majestic and their beauty overwhelming (Ennead V.8[31]3). The Ideas as gods are images of a non-representational and infallible knowledge.

The word is derived from *agallein* 'to praise or honour in particular a god – or that which adorns' (Homer *Il.* 4.144). By late antiquity the usage seems to be primarily as a cult image, especially a cult statue (as distinct from honorific images). Pausanias the geographer says that the *agalma* of Athena fell from Heaven.⁵⁴ Cassius Dio speaks of the images of Castor and Pollux as *agalmata*.⁵⁵ There is, however, not much archaeological evidence of veneration of *agalmata* of the emperor and in the mystery religions from the East like Mithraism. Christian works from the third and fourth centuries recount the destruction of such images.⁵⁶

There is a history of philosophical criticism of such objects. Heraclitus talks dismissively of those who pray to *agalmata* 'as if they are chattering to

---

⁵² Οὐ τοίνυν δεῖ νομίζειν ἐκεῖ ἀξιώματα ὁρᾶν τοὺς θεοὺς οὐδὲ τοὺς ἐκεῖ ὑπερευδαίμονας, ἀλλ᾽ ἕκαστα τῶν λεγομένων ἐκεῖ καλὰ ἀγάλματα, οἷα ἐφαντάζετό τις ἐν τῇ σοφοῦ ἀνδρὸς ψυχῇ εἶναι, ἀγάλματα δὲ οὐ γεγραμμένα, ἀλλὰ ὄντα. Διὸ καὶ τὰς ἰδέας ὄντα ἔλεγον εἶναι οἱ παλαιοὶ καὶ οὐσίας.
⁵³ Dieter Metzler, *Porträt und Gesellschaft: über die Entstehung des griechischen Portraets in der Klassik* (Münster: Wasmuth, 1971), pp. 157–9. Jeremy Tanner, *The Invention of Art History in Ancient Greece: Religion, Society and Artistic Rationalisation* (Cambridge: Cambridge University Press, 2006), pp. 55–7, 65–6.
⁵⁴ Pausanias, *Pausanias' Description of Greece with an English Translation* by W. H. S. Jones, and H. A. Ormerod, in 4 vols (Cambridge, MA: Harvard University Press; London: William Heinemann Ltd, 1918), 1.26.6.
⁵⁵ *Dio's Roman History*. Cassius Dio Cocceianus, eds Earnest Cary, Herbert Baldwin Foster and William Heinemann (New York, London: Harvard University Press, 1914), 59.28.5.
⁵⁶ Polly Weddle, 'Touching the Gods: Physical Interaction with Cult Statues in the Roman World'. PhD thesis, University of Durham, online, 2010, www.etheses.dur.ac.uk/SSS/

empty houses'.⁵⁷ Plato does call the created world a *to ton aidion theon gegonos agalma* in the *Timaeus* (37c). There is another striking Platonic precursor to the use of *agalmata* in the reference by Alcibiades to the satyr-like outward appearance of Socrates: 'Isn't he just like a statue of Silenus? [...] It's a Silenus sitting, his flute or his pipes in his hands, and it's hollow. It's split right down the middle, and inside it's full of tiny statues of the gods. Now look at him again! Isn't he also just like the satyr Marsyas?' (*Symp.* 215b).

Cult images in Rome were visible signs of invisible beings and indeed were an organ of communication with gods. They are places of divine presence after consecration. Cult images implied a relationship between human and the Divine: epiphany and enjoyment. Robert Parker writes:

> The gods loved beauty: one dedicated to them the loveliest objects that one could, and the word for cult-image, *agalma*, means 'thing to take delight in'. The gods were happy too to see performed in their honour many of the activities that humans most relished. Singing and dancing in a chorus was one basic form of worship, and competing at athletics was another. The great Panhellenic games and the great Athenian dramatic festivals had moved far from their origins, but remained religious ceremonies. One had to put on a good show for the god.⁵⁸

What should we make of Plotinus's use of such tactile images, objects that people touched and used in various ways? Plotinus has no interest in cultic objects per se. He has no concern for the supernatural materialism of the later theurgic strands of Neoplatonism. We are not merely spectators but drawn into the world of the images. They are icons not idols.

Plotinus employs the image of the cosmos as a mirror-reflection of the divine rather than as a picture or artificer's created model. The polished metal mirrors of the ancient world (*katoptra*) were murky by modern standards. Nevertheless, as A. H. Armstrong often remarked, the language of reflection suggests an intimate and unmediated relation of becoming to Being: the

---

[57] Heraclitus, B5 DK καθαίρονται δ' ἄλλως αἵματι μιαινόμενοι, ὁκοῖον εἴ τις εἰς πηλὸν ἐμβὰς πηλῷ ἀπονίζοιτο·μαίνεσθαι δ' ἂν δοκέοι εἴ τις μιν ἀνθρώπων ἐπιφράσαιτο οὕτω ποιέοντα. καὶ τοῖς ἀγάλμασι δὲ τουτέοισιν εὔχονται, ὁκοῖον εἴ τις τοῖς δόμοισι λεσχηνεύοιτο, οὔ τι γινώσκων θεοὺς οὐδ' ἥρωας οἵτινές εἰσι. *Heraclitus: Fragments*, edited by T. M. Robinson (Toronto: University of Toronto, 1991) p. 12.
[58] Robert Parker, 'Greek Religion' in *The Oxford History of the Classical World*, eds John Boardman, Jasper Griffin and Oswyn Murray (Oxford: Oxford University Press, 1986), p. 258.

closeness of the image to its archetype and thus the presence of the Divine in the physical cosmos. The lower is an image, shadow, dream or trace of the higher: 'sensations Here are dim intellections: intellections There are vivid sensations' (*Ennead* VI.7[38].7, 30-31). Thus, indeed, for Plotinus there is continuity between sense and intellect. Vision is not merely a metaphor for a Platonist. On the contrary, sensation and intellection belong on a continuum.[59] Plotinus seems to agree with Bachelard: 'The Imagination is not, as its etymology suggests, the faculty for forming images of reality; it is the faculty for forming images which go beyond reality, which sing reality. It is a superhuman faculty.'[60]

It is upon such a metaphysical basis that Augustine can say in his *Sermon 126* 'Look at what you see, and seek what you do not see', and link this to St Paul's reference in Romans 1.20 of the invisible things of Creation.[61] Augustine is drawing on the Platonic doctrine of creaturely participation in the Divine intellect: visible beauty and order point to its invisible source. Dante is also deeply influenced by this strand. Consider:

> That which dies not and that which can die are nothing but the splendour of the Idea which our Sire, in Loving, begets; for that living Light which so streams from its shining Source that it is not parted from it nor from the Love with which then makes the Three, of its own goodness gathers its beams, as it were mirrored, in nine subsistences, remaining forever one. (Dante, *Paradiso*, Canto XIII lines 52–60)[62]

Plotinus in *Ennead* V.8 [31] starts from the phenomenological question. What is beauty? He compares a block of marble with a statue. What distinguishes the two? The presence of mind or intelligence in the latter?

---

[59] As in book VI of the *Republic*.
[60] Gaston Bachelard, *Water and Dreams* (Dallas: Dallas Institute Publications, 1994), p. 16.
[61] '*Aspice quae vides, et quaere quem non vides*'.
[62] *Cio che non more e cio che puo morire
non e se non splendor, di quella idea
che partorisce, amando, il nostro sire:
che quella viva luce che si mea
dal suo lucente, che non si disuna
da lui ne dall'amor ch'a lor s'intrea,
per sua bontate il suo raggiare aduna,
quasi specchiato, in nove sussistenze,
etternalmente rimanendosi una.*

> Let us suppose, if you like, a couple of great lumps of stone lying side by side, one shapeless and untouched by art, the other which has been mastered by art and turned into a statue of a god or a man (εἰς ἄγαλμα θεοῦ ἤ καί τινος ἀνθρώπου).[63]

Plotinus is using the term ἄγαλμα for the initial aesthetic question – what makes an item beautiful in the case of two blocks of stone and – moves on to the nature of the intelligible world. The use of the same word *agalma* stresses the continuity between the physical and the intelligible cosmos and the thrill of beauty. It also fits well with the version of the Platonic anamnesis doctrine that Plotinus employs at this point: 'the soul, since it is by nature what it is and is related (*sungenes*) to the higher kind of reality in the realm of being, when it sees something akin to it or a trace (*iknos*) of its kindred reality, is delighted and thrilled and returns to itself and remembers itself and its possessions. What likeness, then, is there between beautiful things Here and There?' (Ennead I.6[1].2, 7-11). The soul re-cognizes beauty. The soul sees in beauty the intelligible and thus can find joy in it. The mistake of the Stoics is not the *association* of beauty with harmony but the *identification* of beauty with harmony. The soul finds itself in beauty, and hence the sense of at-one-ment with the experience of true beauty. Plotinus employs an analogy drawn from medicine:

> For illness strikes our consciousness harder, but the quiet companionship of health gives us a better understanding of it; for it comes and sits by us as something which belongs to us, and is united to us. Illness is alien [ἀλλότριον] and not its own, and since we are like this we understand ourselves best when we have made our self-knowledge one with ourselves. (V.8[31].4, 28-34)[64]

These statues or cult objects are not mere *representations* but are part of a complex interaction with the worshippers. Schefold famously wrote on cult

---

[63] Κειμένων τοίνυν ἀλλήλων ἐγγύς, ἔστω δέ, εἰ βούλει, [δύο] λίθων ἐν ὄγκῳ, τοῦ μὲν ἀρρυθμίστου καὶ τέχνης ἀμοίρου, τοῦ δὲ ἤδη τέχνῃ κεκρατημένου εἰς ἄγαλμα θεοῦ ἤ καί τινος ἀνθρώπου.

[64] νόσος γὰρ μᾶλλον ἔκπληξιν, ὑγίεια δὲ ἠρέμα συνοῦσα μᾶλλον ἂν σύνεσιν δοίη αὑτῆς· προσίζει γὰρ ἅτε οἰκεῖον καὶ ἑνοῦται· ἡ δ' ἔστιν ἀλλότριον καὶ οὐκ οἰκεῖον, καὶ ταύτῃ διάδηλος τῷ σφόδρα ἕτερον ἡμῶν εἶναι δοκεῖν. τὰ δὲ ἡμῶν καὶ ἡμεῖς ἀναίσθητοι· οὕτω δ' ὄντες μάλιστα πάντων ἐσμὲν αὑτοῖς συνετοὶ τὴν ἐπιστήμην ἡμῶν καὶ ἡμᾶς ἓν πεποιηκότες.
For other medical analogies, see V.9[5].10, 1-9; V.9[5].11, 13-25. I am grateful to Svetla Slaveva-Griffen for pointing out these references to me.
'It is more conformed to that Goodness and therefore more pleasing to it; for the Holy Ardour that irradiates all things is brightest in that which is most like itself.' Dante, *Paradiso*, Canto VII.

image as a living statue: *Das Kultbild ist der lebendige Gott selbst, und das Leben ist von göttlichen Kräften durchgestaltet.*[65] The striking and paradoxical use of *agalmata* in a philosopher who, no less than Heraclitus or Plutarch, is dismissive of any superstitious confusion of statues and deities, is a way of presenting the Forms as the plenitude and causal fecundity of the self-knowing of the divine mind. These forms are not primarily objects of abstract reflection but are the transcendent and invisible causal energies and powers that are the source of the myriad beauties and structures of the material world. Plotinus is describing the intelligible world that was 'never worthily sung by any earthly poet'. He nevertheless attains a poetic mood in his account:

> For it is 'the easy life' there, and truth is their mother and nurse and being and food – and they see all things, not those coming to be, but those to which real being belongs, and they see themselves in other things; for all things there are transparent, and there is nothing dark or opaque; everything and all things are clear to the inmost part of everything; for light is transparent to light. Each there has everything in itself and sees all things in every other, so that all are everywhere and each and everyone is all and the glory is unbounded. (V.8[31].4, 1–11)[66]

The intellect is constituted by the identity of being and thought. Or rather: the *being* of the Intellect is its self-relatedness. Intentionality is not, as it is among human agents, an aspect of particular and discrete substances. Rather, the substance of Intellect is determined by thought: its being is its thinking. The distinctive nature of this noetic domain – the intelligible world – can be made clear in terms of the part-whole relation. Whereas in the material world the individual is opposed to the whole, in the spiritual world the individual *is* the whole. The unity of mind is contrasted with composition and divisibility. The Intellect constitutes a reflexive act in which each part or Form reflects the whole. It is this relational harmony of absolute or divine thought that provides the paradigm for the beauty of physical objects.

---

[65] Karl Schefold, 'Statuen auf Vasenbildern', J dL 52, 1937, pp. 30–75, p. 33.
[66] καὶ γὰρ τὸ ῥεῖα ζώειν ἐκεῖ – καὶ ἀλήθεια δὲ αὐτοῖς καὶ γενέτειρα καὶ τροφὸς καὶ οὐσία καὶ τροφή, καὶ ὁρῶσι τὰ πάντα, οὐχ οἷς γένεσις πρόσεστιν, ἀλλ᾽ οἷς οὐσία, καὶ ἑαυτοὺς ἐν ἄλλοις·διαφανῆ γὰρ πάντα καὶ σκοτεινὸν οὐδὲ ἀντίτυπον οὐδέν, ἀλλὰ πᾶς παντὶ φανερὸς εἰς τὸ εἴσω καὶ πάντα· φῶς γὰρ φωτί. Καὶ γὰρ ἔχει πᾶς πάντα ἐν αὑτῷ, καὶ αὖ ὁρᾷ ἐν ἄλλῳ πάντα, ὥστε πανταχοῦ πάντα καὶ πᾶν πᾶν καὶ ἕκαστον πᾶν καὶ ἄπειρος ἡ αἴγλη.

What the language of the *agalmata* tends to stress, however, is the problem of the relation between intellect and ideas as really existent objects of divine thought. The Intellect is the One-Many – the highest form of unity that still includes plurality. And the imagery of the statues emphasises the reality of the many in the One-Many of the Intellect.[67] In the great *Ennead* VI.9[9] Plotinus is depicting the ecstasy of union with the One: which is said to be like the 'man who enters into the sanctuary and leaves behind the statues in the outer shrine' (VI9[9].11, 19). The agalmata are left behind in the final stage of Plotinus's ascent of the mind, but only at the very last stage.[68]

> All things of this kind there are like images seen by their own light, to be beheld by 'exceedingly blessed spectators'. The greatness and power of this wisdom can be imaged if we consider that it has with it and has made all things, and all things follow it, and it is the real beings, and they came to be along with it and both are one, and reality is wisdom there. But we have not arrived at understanding this, because we consider that the branches of knowledge are made up of theorems and a collection of propositions (V.8[31].4, 43–50).[69]

Those 'exceedingly blessed spectators' (*Phaedo* 111a3) 'a sight to make those blessed who look upon it'), should remind us of the mysteries. Happiness, as for Plato and Aristotle, is contemplation. Plotinus is invoking

> that blessed mood,
> In which the burthen of the mystery,
> In which the heavy and the weary weight
> Of all this unintelligible world
> Is lightened: – that serene and blessed mood,
> In which the affections gently lead us on, –
> Until, the breath of this corporeal frame
> And even the motion of our human blood
> Almost suspended, we are laid asleep

---

[67] See W. Norris Clarke, 'The Problem of the Reality and Multiplicity of Divine Ideas in Christian Neoplatonism', in *Neoplatonism and Christian Thought*, ed. Dominic J. O'Meara (Albany, NY: State University of New York, 1982), pp. 109–27.
[68] Thanks to Evan King for pointing to this passage.
[69] Πάντα γὰρ τὰ τοιαῦτα ἐκεῖ οἷον ἀγάλματα παρ' αὐτῶν ἐνορώμενα, ὥστε θέαμα εἶναι ὑπερευδαιμόνων θεατῶν. Τῆς μὲν οὖν σοφίας τὸ μέγεθος καὶ τὴν δύναμιν ἄν τις κατίδοι, ὅτι μετ' αὐτῆς ἔχει καὶ πεποίηκε τὰ ὄντα, καὶ πάντα ἠκολούθησε, καὶ ἔστιν αὐτὴ τὰ ὄντα, καὶ συνεγένετο αὐτῇ, καὶ ἓν ἄμφω, καὶ ἡ οὐσία ἡ ἐκεῖ σοφία. Ἀλλ' ἡμεῖς εἰς σύνεσιν οὐκ ἤλθομεν, ὅτι καὶ τὰς ἐπιστήμας θεωρήματα καὶ συμφόρησιν νενομίκαμεν προτάσεων εἶναι.

In body, and become a living soul:
While with an eye made quiet by the power
Of harmony, and the deep power of joy,
We see into the life of things.
(Wordsworth, *Lines Composed a Few Miles above Tintern Abbey*)

The Wisdom of the Egyptians

Plotinus is a product of one of the great intellectual powerhouses of the ancient world: Alexandria. From the conquest of Egypt in 332 BC by Alexander up to the suicide of Cleopatra VII in 30 BC, Alexandria was ruled by a Greek dynasty. It is the city of great intellects of the Hellenic world like Euclid or Galen: the greatest Greek city of late antiquity, and yet Egyptian. Ptolemy assumed the position of Pharoah – and there was a long tradition of reverence for Egyptian culture. In Plotinus we do not find reference to Egyptian but to Greek myths. Herodotus, however, claims the Egyptians are the most pious of all peoples and that they were the first to allocate altars and images and temples to the gods and the first also, he continues, who engrave figures on stone.[70] Egypt plays a role in Plato too – not least in Plato's *Phaedrus* (274bff) and where Socrates recounts the story of Theuth and the King of Thebes Thamus in which Theut showed the king the great arts, culminating in alphabetic writing, a *pharmakon* that Socrates regards as a remedy for poor memory, but which functions as a narcotic that diminishes the capacity for dialogue and argument. Plotinus is using *agalmata* for the sacred Egyptian hieroglyphs:

> The wise men of Egypt, I think, also understood this, either by scientific or innate knowledge, and when they wished to signify something wisely, did not use the forms of letters which follow the order of words and propositions and imitate sounds and the enunciations of philosophical statements, but by drawing images and inscribing in their temples one particular image of each particular thing, they manifested the non-discursiveness of the intelligible world, that is,

---

[70] Herodotus *The Histories*, book II, 37, 1ff, with an English translation by A. D. Godley (Cambridge MA: Harvard University Press, 1966), p. 319.

that every image is a kind of knowledge and wisdom and is a subject of statements, all together in one, and not discourse or deliberation. (V.8[31].6, 1–9)[71]

Plotinus is claiming that the knowledge of the Intellect does not consist of propositional attitudes to states of affairs that can be correct or false. Rather we are dealing with 'A concentrated unity (ἀθρόον), a representation in something else, already unfolded and speaking it discursively and giving the reasons why things are like this.' Plotinus prioritizes vision over discursive reflection; the immediacy of sight over the mediated.

The Greeks had been fascinated by Egyptian culture with its long tradition of 3,000 years – and its images of a very tactile afterlife. If one compares Egyptian and Roman deities – the Egyptian is more idealized – the Roman deities seem anthropomorphic. Plutarch's *On Isis and Osiris* discusses Egyptian images of the invisible. In this work, Plutarch attempts to steer a path between rank superstition and crass atheism. Plutarch claims that both Egyptian engraved forms and Greek statues were *ainigmata* that could mirror the divine. Isis, Plutarch claims, has a many-coloured robe because she represents the physical cosmos, whereas the diaphanous cloak of Osiris represents the noetic realm. His cloak was only worn once, which reflects the unique quality of the epoptic, or visionary, dimension of philosophy – that of pure immaterial truth. Thus Plotinus defends statues as useful models for the divine – even if the vulgar might confuse them with the gods Plotinus refers to the *Phaedrus* myth in the following passage:

> For this reason Zeus, although the oldest among the gods whom he himself leads, advances first to the contemplation of this god and there follow him the other gods and spirits and the souls who are capable of seeing these things. But he appears to them from some invisible place and dawning upon them from high illuminates everything and fills it with his rays. (V.8[31].10, 1ff.)[72]

---

[71] Δοκοῦσι δέ μοι καὶ οἱ Αἰγυπτίων σοφοί, εἴτε ἀκριβεῖ ἐπιστήμῃ λαβόντες εἴτε καὶ συμφύτῳ, περὶ ὧν ἐβούλοντο διὰ σοφίας δεικνύναι, μὴ τύποις γραμμάτων διεξοδεύουσι λόγους καὶ προτάσεις μηδὲ μιμουμένοις φωνὰς καὶ προφορὰς ἀξιωμάτων κεχρῆσθαι, ἀγάλματα δὲ γράψαντες καὶ ἓν ἕκαστον ἑκάστου πράγματος ἄγαλμα ἐντυπώσαντες ἐν τοῖς ἱεροῖς τὴν ἐκεῖ οὐ διέξοδον ἐμφῆναι, ὡς ἄρα τις καὶ ἐπιστήμη καὶ σοφία ἕκαστόν ἐστιν ἄγαλμα καὶ ὑποκείμενον καὶ ἀθρόον καὶ οὐ διανόησις οὐδὲ βούλευσις.

[72] Διὰ τοῦτο καὶ ὁ Ζεὺς καίπερ ὢν πρεσβύτατος τῶν ἄλλων θεῶν, ὧν αὐτὸς ἡγεῖται, πρῶτος πορεύεται ἐπὶ τὴν τούτου θέαν, οἱ δὲ ἕπονται θεοὶ ἄλλοι καὶ δαίμονες καὶ ψυχαί, αἳ ταῦτα ὁρᾶν δύνανται. Ὁ δὲ ἐκφαίνεται αὐτοῖς ἔκ τινος ἀοράτου τόπου καὶ ἀνατείλας ὑψοῦ ἐπ' αὐτῶν κατέλαμψε μὲν πάντα καὶ ἔπλησεν αὐγῆς καὶ ἐξέπληξε μὲν τοὺς κάτω, καὶ ἐστράφησαν ἰδεῖν οὐ δεδυνημένοι οἷα ἥλιον. Οἱ μὲν ἄρ αὐτοῦ ἀνέχονταί τε καὶ βλέπουσιν, οἱ δὲ ταράττονται, ὅσῳ ἂν ἀφεστήκωσιν αὐτοῦ.

From this fairly conventional light imagery drawn from Plato's *Phaedrus* to the remarkable image of men in the desert of the Nile region being suffused with such intense light so that they appear the same colour as the red hills on which they walk, Plotinus develops a wondrous image of contemplation:

> Zeus then sees these things, and with him any one of us who is his fellow-lover and finally he sees, abiding over all, beauty as a whole, by his participation in the intelligible beauty; for it shines bright up all and fills those who have come to be there so that they too become beautiful, as often men, when they go up into high places where the earth has a red-gold colour, are filled with that colour and made like that upon which they walked. (V.8[31].10, 24–31)[73]

Bathing in light while walking in the desert is an image of the transformation of the knower into the object of contemplation. We also have the themes of wonder (*thauma*) and epiphany. The experience of the beauty of the intelligible world is not of some irrational *mysterium tremendum et fascinans* but rather the sense of the order, lucidity and transparent beauty of the *nous*.

Images, Religious Experience and 'Spiritual Sensation'

It is a commonplace that Plotinus's theory of beauty has its proper place within a metaphysics of hierarchical unity. Yet perhaps our reflection about the term *agalma* suggests that it is not the word 'aesthetics' that is the problem but the term 'metaphysics'. In *Ennead* V8[31] we have a spiritual exercise that leads from the concrete example of the statue to its intelligible correlate in the intelligible world. One must not then suppose that the gods or the 'exceedingly blessed spectators in the higher world contemplate propositions, but all the Forms we speak about are beautiful images' (V8[31].5, 20f.).

In his *Idee und Probe alter Symbolik* (*Idea and Testing of Ancient Symbolism*, 1806) Creuzer refers explicitly to Plotinus's claim that the hieroglyphic symbol-language of the Egyptians is to be considered the most felicitous

---

[73] Ταῦτα οὖν ὁρῶν ὁ Ζεύς, καὶ εἴ τις ἡμῶν αὐτῷ συνεραστής, τὸ τελευταῖον ὁρᾷ μένον ἐπὶ πᾶσιν ὅλον τὸ κάλλος, καὶ κάλλους μετασχὼν τοῦ ἐκεῖ· ἀποστίλβει γὰρ πάντα καὶ πληροῖ τοὺς ἐκεῖ γενομένους, ὡς καλοὺς καὶ αὐτοὺς γενέσθαι, ὁποῖοι πολλάκις ἄνθρωποι εἰς ὑψηλοὺς ἀναβαίνοντες τόπους τὸ ξανθὸν χρῶμα ἐχούσης τῆς γῆς τῆς ἐκεῖ ἐπλήσθησαν ἐκείνης τῆς χρόας ὁμοιωθέντες τῇ ἐφ' ἧς ἐβεβήκεσαν.

expression of all philosophy. He directly quotes Plotinus's seminal treatise on the beauty of the divine Intellect (V8[31].5-6)[74].

Is the language of sensation merely metaphorical or does it refer to the perception of spiritual realities? Are terms such as 'seeing' and 'hearing' employed in a figurative manner to denote 'understanding', without placing any importance on the sensation? There are many passages in Plotinus which suggest just this. Later Plotinians have seen his work as describing spiritual sensation. John Smith (1618–52), perhaps the most eloquent Cambridge Platonist of the seventeenth century, in his first 'Discourse' claims that Divinity is 'a divine life' rather than a 'divine science'. Theology, Smith insists, is based upon 'Spiritual Sensation' which unites the will, intellect, and the affections. Spiritual sensation or 'intellectual sense' as Smith puts it. Smith knew the writings of Plotinus well although the language of the spiritual sensation is taken from Origen.[75] For Plotinus, the image becomes a vehicle of the experience of transcendence. Where conceptual and discursive thought fail, the image becomes an instrument of apprehension of the noetic realm. This model of the contemplative image is inextricably linked to a metaphysics of the cosmos as participating in its transcendent source.

Mirroring the argument of *Ennead* V3[49], John Smith claims 'They are not alwaies the best skill'd in Divinity, that are most studied in those *Pandects* which it is sometimes digested into, or that have erected the greatest Monopolies of Art and Science.'[76] Smith notes furthermore, 'We must not think we have attained to the *right knowledge* of Truth, when we have broke through the outward shell of words & phrases that house it up; or when by a *Logical Analysis* we have found out the dependencies and coherences of them with one another.'

Smith's claim that truths can be intuitively apprehended is not the rejection of philosophy. It is itself a philosophical consideration. The radical skeptic

---

[74] Benedetto Bravo, 'F. Creuzer et F. G. Welcker' in *L'impensable polytheisme: Etudes d'historigraphie religieuse*, ed. Francis Schmidt, (Chippenham: Editions des archives contemporaines, 1988), pp. 375–424, p. 384.
[75] See John Dillon, 'Aisthêsis noêtê: a doctrine of spiritual senses in Origen and in Plotinus', in *Hellenica and Judaica*, eds Caquot, Hadas-Lebel, Riaud (Leuven: Peeters, 1986), pp. 443–55.
[76] John Smith, *Select Discourses* (Cambridge: Flesher, 1660), p. 2.

fails to recognize that some truths, especially those of an ethical and religious nature, are immediate and do not require justification.

Plotinus's preference for living and holy images (ἀγάλματα) over abstract concepts (προτάσεις) has not endeared him to the majority of philosophers. It is perhaps no accident that the poets, painters and sculptors like Dante, Botticelli or Michelangelo have been the greatest inheritors of Plotinus rather than the philosophers or theologians.

Image and Imagination

The German word *Bild* means both image and picture. There is a deep ambivalence regarding the 'image' for the Romantics; and this is intimately connected to the Romantic view of the imagination and Lessing's magisterial essay *Laokoon, oder über die Grenzen der Malerei und Poesie* of 1766.[77] The statue of Laocoön was unearthed outside Rome on 14 January 1506. (In fact it was a Roman copy of a Greek original.) It seemed to embody what Winckelmann announced as the distinctive 'noble simplicity and quiet grandeur' (*edle Einfalt und stille Größe*) of the Classical model of beauty. In Virgil's *Aeneid*, Laocoön, priest of Apollo, objects to letting the wooden horse into Troy. Lessing attacks the painterly formality of French Classicism and defends a view of theatre deeply indebted to Shakespeare. Visual arts, for Lessing, constitute the inferior sibling of poetry. Poetry can inspire the imagination in a way that pictures cannot. The visual arts are '*einerlei art Sichtbar*', visible in a samey (i.e. monotonous) manner: '*Sichtbar und unsichtbar. Diesen Unterschied kann die Malerei nicht angeben: bei Ihr ist alles sichtbar; und auf einerlei art Sichtbar.*'[78] We render this as 'Visible and invisible. Painting cannot offer this distinction: all is visible and in a monotonous manner.' Prager convincingly argues that the great Romantic painters could be seen as unveiling the invisible through images. The point is not just that picture *per definitionem* represents what it is not, a point made graphically by the *Ceci n'est pas une pipe* of Magritte's '*la*

---

[77] Brad Prager, *Aesthetic Vision and German Romanticism: Writing Images* (Rochester, NY: Camden House, 2007), p. 26 gets the translation wrong by taking '*einerlei*' as 'in precisely the same way'. It is the limitation of the pictorial rather than its precision that is at stake in Lessing's discussion.
[78] Lessing, WB 5:2 102.

trahison des images'; but an unveiling of the invisible. This unveiling is the key to the visceral power of art: '*so wahr, so seiend*' (Goethe).

In his celebrated and deeply Kantian critique of the doctrine of the 'innocence of the eye', Ernst Gombrich insists that pictures are 'relational models of reality'.[79] Rather than perceiving what is 'given' to sight, perception is constructed such that 'making precedes matching'. What appears 'real' emerges out of the interrelation between schemata, practices and interests and the data of experience. The world of the beholder is forged and furnished by the productive constructions and technological developments such as the innovation of oil painting in fifteenth-century Flanders, perspective or photography. Art emerges from the human mind, not nature. Gombrich is reacting against the Romantic-Idealist tenet of transcendent power of sign qua symbol. Schelling employs this as the basis of his claim that art is the 'eternal organon and document of philosophy'. The artwork is a *Gegenbild* or Counter-Image of the Absolute, and as such is theophanic. The artist forges an image of the infinite. *Einbildungskraft* for Schelling is the *in-Eins-bilden* (or forming into one) of the infinite in the finite.[80] Unlike the pessimism of Hegel, with his death-of-art theory, Schelling offered a much more sanguine approach: beauty and art continue to disclose truths. When we look at some of the great painting of the nineteenth century, we see that there was an attempt to avoid the mimetic in any crudely realist sense. The Aristotelian principle that art imitates nature (*ars imitatur naturam*) is accepted with the modification that the *natura* at stake is *natura naturans* not *natura naturata*. The true artist is imaginatively imitating the intelligible dimension of nature rather than slavishly copying the appearances. This is paralleled in the seminal Romantic discussion of Raphael's Santa Caecilia in Wackenroder's renowned *Herzensergießungen eines kunstliebenden Klosterbruders* (*Outpourings of an Art-Loving Friar*, 1797): his soul was penetrated – '*sein Inneres war durchbohrt*'.[81] It is the power of the mind's eye that is at stake and the capacity of great art to serve the communication of the *logos* to the soul. *Logos* and

---

[79] Ernst Gombrich, *Art and Illusion* (New York: Phaidron, 1960), p. 253.
[80] Bernhard Barth, *Schellings Philosophie der Kunst Göttliche Imagination und aesthetische Einbildungskraft* (Freiburg: Alber, 1991). Cf. F. W. J. Schelling, *The Philosophy of Art* (Minneapolis: University of Minnesota, 1995).
[81] Prager, *Aesthetic Vision and German Romanticism*, p. 89.

Icon. Robert Rosenblum, in his rich and illuminating study *Modern Painting and the Northern Romantic Tradition* (1975), presents the sublime as a link between Caspar David Friedrich, Van Gogh, Kandinsky, and Mondrian up to Rothko and Barnett Newman.[82] The paradigm of both magical presence and consciously reflexive illusionism is sustained through Neoplatonic theory. Jung's view of the archetype as iconic rather than verbal is a further reflex of this Neoplatonic-Romantic legacy.

The attack upon the legacy of Panofsky and the employment of the Platonic tradition as a key to interpreting the great images, which is so widespread among art historians often relies anti-Platonic bias, often drawn from Heidegger or the French critics, of the privileging of transcendence in Platonism and the alleged denigration of the image qua image. This view often confuses the transparency of the image to transcendence with degradation of the image. The art historians who rail against the Hegelian ascendancy of the idea over the husk of the image in iconographers like Panofsky are directing their ire against a broader and (for them) generally baneful Platonic tendency to reduce or subordinate the image to intellect or ideal content. Such historians of art want to rescue the 'image' from Platonic transcendence and against the Platonic paradigm, they wish to assert the free standing integrity and autonomy of the image. It has to be conceded that such a critique has genuine force. We have argued, however, that one should not overlook a powerful strand of Platonism where the image itself is exalted as a bearer of non-propositional truth. In this tradition, Plotinus can develop on the basis of the demiurge of Plato's *Timaeus* and the doctrine of inspiration in the Platonic *Phaedrus* a version of creative demiurgy as both spontaneous and non–propositional, which is mirrored in the inspired activity of the true artist. Our exploration of the 'aesthetics' of Plotinus should underline the extent to which transcendence, for the Platonist, need not diminish the significance of the image. Indeed, it requires it. What the Platonist wishes to assert is that it is primarily, if not exclusively, the sense of transcendence that endows art

---

[82] Robert Rosenblum, *Modern Painting and the Northern Romantic Tradition* (London: Thames and Hudson, 1975).

with its unique and enduring power to captivate, console and galvanize the human spirit.

In order to address the misgivings of the secular critics of the Platonic commitment to transcendence, we have to turn from the history of aesthetics to fundamental questions of anthropology. What is the link, if any, between the artistic image and transcendence? In the next chapter we will turn to the question of anthropology. Why is the human being uniquely constituted to be absorbed by images?

2

Human Nature and the *Imago Dei*

Faciamus hominem ad imaginem et similitudinem nostrum
Let us make man in our image, after our likeness

                                                            Genesis 1.26b

Two of far nobler shape erect and tall,
Godlike erect, with native honour clad
In naked majesty seemed lords of all
And worthy seemed, for in their looks divine
The image of their glorious Maker shone,
Truth, Wisdom, Sanctitude severe and pure,
Severe, but in true filial freedom plac'd.
Milton, *Paradise Lost*[1]

Has the notion of the divine 'image' in humanity become unintelligible? This discourse on the image is not just the preserve of ancient and medieval theology. However much we may be inclined to view modern thought as based on the idea of human beings creating their own sphere and values, this runs counter to the facts. It is sufficient to consider John Locke's grounding of human rights in the idea of the *imago Dei* to recognize the momentous implications of the concept for modern thought.[2] Initially one might reasonably ask what the doctrine means. Edward Craig, the distinguished contemporary Cambridge philosopher, has written a powerful and often persuasive monograph in which he describes a shift from the 'Similarity Thesis' of the seventeenth and

---

[1] John Milton, *Paradise Lost*, ed. A. Fowler, (London: Longman, 1971), pp. 212–13.
[2] Jeremy Waldron, *God, Locke, and Equality: Christian Foundations in Locke's Political Thought* (Cambridge: Cambridge University Press, 2002); Samuel Moyn, 'Personalism, community and the origin of human rights', in *Human Rights in the Twentieth Century*, ed. Stephan Ludwig Hoffman, (Cambridge: Cambridge University Press, 2011), pp. 85–106.

eighteenth centuries, which is predicated upon the likeness of the human mind to God's intellect.[3] What Craig presents as the 'similarity thesis' in fact disguises significant disagreements. To illuminate these divisions of interpretation we shall look at the divergence between Aquinas and Eckhart. The Angelic Doctor and the Thuringian Master are taken as instances of the different ways that the doctrine could be construed. Yet, equally significant, how does the inherited and pivotal concept of the *imago Dei* relate to developments in our understanding of humanity in the wake of Darwin and evolutionary theory? We will consider two very unsatisfactory alternatives. The first is biological fatalism (the James Watson mantra that fate is not in your stars but your DNA) in which the psycho-cultural-physical composition of humanity is radically diminished.[4] The second is a theological positivism that blithely pays no heed to the 'cultured despisers of religion'.[5] In opposition to both of these extremes, I wish to present a case for human uniqueness based upon our capacity for introversion and contemplation and a version of the doctrine of the *imago Dei*. There are various models of *imago Dei*. Luther's anthropology was deeply pessimistic and Reformed theologians have tended to stress the impact of sin that has deformed the image. Modern philosophy has attacked the notion. Nietzsche's *Übermensch* or Heidegger's *Dasein* involve philosophical criticism of the doctrine of mankind as created in the *imago Dei*. It would be wrong to think of the doctrine as a pure theological legacy. The critique of the *imago Dei* and its anthropological/metaphysical implications has been a central aspect of Western philosophical thought. Indeed, we will draw upon one of the greatest pupils (and severest critics!) of Heidegger, Hans Jonas, and his attempt to rehabilitate the notion of the *imago Dei* through the idea of the freedom of image-making and the attendant notion of human dignity. We will also turn to the metaphysical-theological construal of the image in the medieval Neoplatonic tradition of Meister Eckhart.

---

[3] E. Craig, *The Mind of God and the Works of Man* (Oxford: Oxford University Press, 1987), pp. 13–14.
[4] James Watson: 'We used to think our fate was in our stars. Now we know, in large measure, our fate is in our genes.' Quoted in *Time*, 'The Gene Hunt', by Leon Jaroff, 20 March 1989.
[5] I am thinking of various forms of theological Neo-Orthodoxy or 'post-liberalism'.

Glabrous Apes?

Men at some time are masters of their fates:
The fault dear Brutus, is not in our stars,
But in ourselves, that we are underlings.[6]

C. S. Lewis declares, 'Man's conquest of Nature (one might say in this context, human nature) turns out, in the moment of its consummation, to be Nature's conquest of Man.' What is a human being? We are rational animals and, as such, exceptional: we seem a species apart, uniquely one not fixed by instinct.[7] At the same time we cannot 'carve nature at the joints' after Darwin.[8] Freud spoke of the three great humiliations of humanity: Copernicus, Darwin and himself. Let us leave aside Copernicus and Freud. After Darwin it seems clear that the only coherent definition of a member of *homo sapiens* is as a member of population group rather than a quasi Aristotelian essence. It therefore seems perfectly reasonable to speculate about the relation of our purported 'nature' to our own evolutionary history. Man bears, as Darwin claims, notwithstanding 'all his noble qualities' and 'godlike intellect' in his 'bodily frame the indelible stamp of his lowly origin'.[9] One can read an article in *Nature* announce that 'murder comes naturally to chimpanzees'.[10] The research was concerned with the question whether the violence had adaptive value or whether it resulted from extraneous factors such as human interference in, or threat to, the chimpanzee habitat. Since chimps and bonobos are our closest biological relatives (we are all great apes), the emergence of violence can be examined on the basis of such evidence. (Notwithstanding circumstances, bonobos, it would seem, do not kill.) Perhaps one can trace violence back to the common ancestor of chimps and humans, five to seven million years ago?

---

[6] Shakespeare, *Julius Caesar*, Act 1 Scene 2.
[7] It can be argued that chimps have culture, i.e. learned practices and patterns of behaviour. Thus it is often noted that one group will use a twig, another a leaf, to obtain honey from a tree. If this is 'culture', it is so minimal that it does not materially diminish our argument.
[8] Plato, *Phaedrus* 265e, 'to cut up each kind according to its species along its natural joints, and to try not to splinter any part, as a bad butcher might do' (trans. Nehamas & Woodruff, in *Plato. Complete Works*, ed. J. M. Cooper, London: Hackett, 1997).
[9] Darwin, *The Descent of Man* (Amherst, NY: Prometheus Books, 1998), p. 643.
[10] http://www.nature.com/nature/journal/v513/n7518/nature13727/metrics/news (accessed.

There are, however, two obvious problems. Firstly, does it make sense to speak of murder in relation to creatures that are following their instincts – however brutal those instincts might seem? Since a chimp does not possess a language, and certainly not a conceptual language, is not the talk of 'murder' an instance of egregious anthropomorphism? 'Murder' is a legal concept. Consider the problem in defining this concept in the legal realm. In most wrangles, it is the relation of the *actus reus* and the *mens rea* that is decisive. It is not the act alone, but the act with the intention that makes killing 'murder' rather than 'manslaughter'. Outside common law territories, there is the idea of *dolus eventualis*, literally 'the cunning of the event', to encompass the wilful exploitation of an unintended effect of a deed. Sometimes acts of intentional killings are deemed 'manslaughter' because of mitigating circumstances such as provocation. Yet if one thinks of cases of 'manslaughter', ranging from instances of crass driving offences to, say, assisted suicide, these presuppose considerations of responsibility that are startlingly absent in the case of the chimp. The seventeen-year-old driver may genuinely fail to grasp the devastating impact of high speed in an urban area and cause death. Responsibility may be mitigated by youth and inexperience but cannot be entirely exonerated. A carer may agonize over the suffering of a relative or patient and may reluctantly (even harbouring grave ethical anxieties) assist a suicide. How can such considerations even be possible, let alone have any force for the chimp?

Secondly, what does it mean to argue on the basis of analogies with our closest biological relatives? The fallacy is based upon imagining chimps, as Jonathan Marks observes, as walking ancestors. There are biological and genetic fallacies here. The biological lineage is not straightforward. Humans are descended from apes unlike chimps in distinct ways. And even if chimps represent the closest analogue to humans in most respects, in others they do not.[11] Chimps are intelligent animals, although their brains are much smaller than those of humans. With our comparatively large-headed babies, even the birth of humans is a social activity. Whereas chimps sometimes kill conspecifics approaching newly-born offspring, humans require immediate help with

---

[11] Jonathan Marks, *What It Means to Be 98% Chimpanzee: Apes, People, and Their Genes* (Berkeley: University of California, 2003).

neonates. The family seems to be the foundation of human social structures. As is often noted, kinship bonds such as aunts, husbands and grandmothers do not exist among apes. This fact may be linked to the social structures that humans require for the rearing of their babies, which are born in a comparatively helpless state and in need of years of support and inculturation.[12]

It is a trivial truth that we are animals. Is it more, however, than stating the obvious? Does the claim that humans are 'animals' occlude significant facts about human nature? Yet even if our ape ancestors were sufficiently close to modern *homo sapiens* to warrant such analogies, it is not clear what the philosophical import of this is. We are descended from apes but also descended from fish. We do not think of birds as theropod dinosaurs even if their descent through the Mesozoic era is fairly clear. If we are happy to go back six million years in order to explain human behaviour, why not even further?

The force of '*homo homini lupus est*' relies upon the striking metaphor of man as a wolf.[13] Since Darwin claims in *The Descent of Man* that 'there is no fundamental difference between man and the higher mammals in their mental faculties' and the differences are of degree, not of kind, should we be remotely surprised by acts of human savagery?[14] Indeed there has been burgeoning research on the evolutionary history of *homo sapiens*, especially in relation to the philosophical and empirical questions about 'human nature'. Is it an exploded anachronism or the crux of serious anthropology? The debate tends to be between the essentialist and the constructivist theories. We can avoid the Scylla and Charybdis of either an unbending genetic determinism of the kind that has become so popular since the Genome project at the end of the 1990s, or the relativisms of the social constructivists, relativisms which defy the striking kinship and commonality of human beings. We propose a theological-metaphysical alternative. We are forged of the same stuff as all other creatures and, as such, share the similitude of the created order with the author of all things. Here we can rely upon the role of the religious imagination. God is a transcendent spiritual being and humanity can have communion with him.

---

[12] Ibid.
[13] See Plautus, *Asinaria*, l. 495: '*lupus est homo homini, non homo, quom qualis sit non novi*'.
[14] Darwin, *The Descent of Man*, 1871, p. 67.

Steven Pinker's *The Blank Slate: The Modern Denial of Human Nature* (2002) and Jesse Prinz's *Beyond Human Nature: How Culture and Experience Shape the Human Mind* (2012) reveal the conflict between a universal theory of humanity based on psychology and biology, and the opposing claim that cultural diversity defies such universalism or essentialism.[15] Pinker represents a strong form of programmatic naturalism in his evolutionary psychology. The universal and innate 'nature' of human nature is constituted by the modular mechanisms which evolved during the Pleistocene. On this paradigm, the mind is a mechanism forged in the African Pleistocene and through a history of cultural effervescence within a hardwired biology. Human beings respond to features in culturally invariant ways involving qualia – smells, colours, aural tones, and other such 'feels'. These are the results of evolved psychological mechanisms. These mechanisms solve particular problems (the celebrated Swiss Army knife model of the mind). The mind is a machine, and its modular adaptations were forged in the African Pleistocene. Evolutionary biology is an extension of evolutionary neurobiology: the human mind responds to the environment in patterns determined by the modular adaptations that transcend time and culture.[16] Prinz counters such innatism with arguments about our bio-cultural nature. We have evidence of tools dating back 2.5 million years ago and it would seem that our thumbs co-evolved with tools. Hence, biological dexterity emerged along with technological developments. Another example of socio-cultural and biological co-evolution is menopause. Other apes remain fertile until death. It is puzzling that human females should have decades of life while being infertile. Examples of the bio-cultural can be seen through the grim examples of the Romanian orphanages. Children deprived of proper *cultural* input fail to develop properly *biologically*. The orphans of the Ceausescu-era were stunted in their brain development by the cruel destitution of the state orphanages in communist Romania.[17]

Our ancestors in East Africa 100,000 years ago were biologically almost indistinguishable from us, with chins and foreheads; though their jaws,

---

[15] I am very grateful to Aku Visala for his guidance with this literature.
[16] Anthony O'Hear, *Beyond Evolution, Human Nature and the Limits of Evolutionary Explanation* (Oxford: Oxford University Press, 1997).
[17] Charles A. Nelson. Nathan A. Fox and Charles H. Zeanah, *Romania's Abandoned Children, Brain Development, and the Struggle for Recovery* (Cambridge, MA: Harvard, 2014).

perhaps, were more powerful. We have barely changed physiologically in the intervening period. Since the cranium has not developed since then, it is plausible to assume that the brain has remained constant. Yet for tens of thousands of years nothing very much happened with humanity. Even though paleolothic anthropologists have been keen to stress the differences between *homo sapiens* and Neanderthals, the similarities are striking (e.g. brain size and physiognomy). The behaviour seems to have been similar with regard to the practice of hunting and the use of hearths. There is some debate about the colouring of bones, but generally there is a marked absence of symbolic activity. The egregious difference lies in the symbolic rather than the chin, say, or the general physique; the invisible, that is, rather than in the visible, the imagined rather than in that which must be the empirical that is perceived. The success of our ancestors, as Jonathan Marks has argued, was in the symbolic realm not the biological.[18]

Programmatic (as opposed to methodological) naturalism assumes continuity with nature, and this is ruptured by the cognitive revolution in 70,000 BC. Up until the emergence of human beings and their rise to pre-eminence in the animal world, changes were due to natural and sexual selection of genetic mutations under environmental pressures solely. From around 70,000 BC, human beings began to impress their collective images and beliefs upon the world. Religion, the holy and the aesthetic are central features of these 'imaginings'. The paintings of Chauvet are a striking testimony to prehistoric imaginings. In particular this development of the imagination occurred after the shift from the tribes of hunter-gatherers to a pastoral civilization, out of which cities and empires emerged. Amidst the technologies of agriculture, irrigation, and construction, nations, gods, demons come forth. Anthropologists such as Ian Tattershall note the ubiquity of religion in human society.[19] Indeed perhaps some inchoate *sensus divinitatis* precedes the emergence of technology.[20] This

---

[18] Jonathan Marks, *The Alternative Introduction to Biological Anthropology* (New York: Oxford University Press, 2012). The emphasis upon the uniquely symbolic capacities of human beings can be found in very different anthropologists like Steven Mithen, *The Prehistory of the Mind: A Search for the Origins of Art, Religion and Science* (London: Thames and Hudson, 1996).

[19] Ian Tattershall, *Becoming Human: Evolution and Human Uniqueness* (Oxford: Oxford University Press, 1998), pp. 200ff.

[20] I am not using the term in the specific manner of John Calvin or Alvin Plantinga.

precedence of religion over technology is perhaps illustrated by the greatest monument of the hunter-gatherer age: the pre-historic Gobekli Tepi, with its 40–60 to T shaped stones with theriomorphic carvings, a complex that has been interpreted as a pre-historic sacred shrine.

Imago Dei and the Similarity Thesis?

> Follow the ancient text and heed my coz the snake;
> With all your likeness to God you'll sometimes tremble and quake. Goethe, *Faust*

The natural history of evolution, as is well known, consists of a process of phylogenetic changes in populations over time. The pre-history of humanity makes the definitional question complex. There have been archaic humans (hominids) for two million years. For millions of years hominids were rather unspectacular animals. Our ancestors had large brains but relatively little brawn and were vulnerable to attack from many more powerful and dangerous animals. Perhaps 400,000 years ago hominids started hunting large animals. About 100,000 years ago it would seem that our ancestors changed from being prey to becoming the greatest predator on earth: in the emergence of *homo sapiens sapiens*. The initial signs of *homo sapiens* 300,000 to 200,000 years ago in East Africa did not seem initially to herald any greatly significant change. How should we think of the relation between *homo sapiens sapiens* and extinct hominids: Neanderthal, Denisovan, *homo erectus, homo floriensis, homo habilis*?[21] If *homo sapiens* mated with Neanderthals and Denisovans, how does this affect our view of the distinctively human? *Homo sapiens* burgeoned after 70,000 while other hominids died out: Java Soloenis became extinct 50,000 years ago, Denisovans 40,000, Neanderthaler 30,000 and Floris 12,000. *Homo sapiens* is the uniquely surviving hominid. Yet how far back in the African Pleistocene should one go back to find the distinctively human? What about the Australopithecus?

Notwithstanding the indistinctness of the biological category of the species, it is perplexing to deny the idea of humanity as an exclusive and unique species.

---
[21] Tattershall, *Becoming Human*, p?.

Quite apart from the ethical dimension, there does seem to be a trans-historical and cross-cultural humanity. This is not the citadel of fastidious humanists, those elevated principles of urbane bearers of reason and dignity but equally those rough-hewn and rude trans-cultural features that anthropologists dwell upon – habits of diet and sex, incest and cannibalism, and their correspondent taboos. In most cultures, to mention one of innumerable anthropological constants, females have longer and more elaborately worn hair.[22]

Up until the emergence of human beings and their rise to pre-eminence among the animal world, changes were due, to reiterate, to genetic mutation or environmental pressures. With the emergence of modern human beings this changes. Removed from the normal causal nexus involving all other animals, human beings are language users, free agents and able to contemplate ultimate ends as well as proximate means. We have a traditional language in the West for this – the 'image' of God.

Should this *imago* notion be dismissed as archaic mythic language? Or perhaps the relic of a dogmatic theological and philosophical world that is better off lost? The language of the 'Image and Likeness' is originally a Hebraism. However, this was transformed through the translation of Hebrew into the Hellenic milieu of the New Testament and preserved in the Imperial period into late antiquity. Irenaeus distinguishes between (εἰκών *eikōn*, Latin *imago*) and likeness (ὁμοίωσις *homóiōsis*, Latin *similitudo*). Mankind always has the image but individual humans have lost the likeness.[23] Clement and Origen take it over. Frequently, St Paul's 2 Corinthians 3.18 is employed in discussions of the image: 'But we all with unveiled face, beholding and reflecting like a mirror the glory of the Lord, are being transformed into the same image from glory to glory, *even* as by the Spirit of the Lord'. The occidental idea of the *imago et particeps Dei* was buttressed by the Delphic Oracle as interpreted by the philosophers: 'Know Thyself' means 'know the Divine element': i.e. reason.[24]

---

[22] One of the most striking objects of the Palaeolithic period, the Venus of Willendorf (or woman of Willendorf) – has braided hair. This reflects that fact head hair seems to have co-evolved with a certain cultural attentiveness.

[23] '*Image et ressemblance*' in *Dictionaire de spiritualité*, vol. 7 (1969), pp. 1410–71.

[24] Cf. Plato, *Timaeus* 41cd; Aristotle, *De anima* 408b 29; Cicero, *Tusc. Disput.* V, 13 §38; Augustine, *Enarrations* XLII, §6.

The ancient and medieval authors offer substantive accounts. For Origen sin is the sign of the soul that is no longer receptive to the 'seal of the Divine Image'.[25] In some metaphysical sense humanity mirrors the divine essence.[26] On this account there is an ontological reason why men and women are in the image of God, e.g. as bearers of a rational soul.

Thus Thomas Aquinas writes:

> *ut consideremus de eius imagine, idest de homine, secundum quod et ipse est suorum operum principium, quasi liberum arbitrium habens et potestatem.*[27]

Since the Reformation and the Enlightenment such metaphysical accounts have generally been replaced by more functional models. Van Huyssteen expresses a common sentiment when he writes that 'Substantive interpretations of the *imago Dei* have subsequently been replaced by so-called *functional interpretations*, precisely because substantive views were seen as too static, and too expressive of mind/body dualism.'[28] For some theologians the model of the 'image' is merely a fact about mankind's relation to God.[29] Humanity is related to God because of divine *fiat* or covenant. There may be no essential reason why man is in the image of God except the (possibly inscrutable) divine will or decision. Or the image may just be a function of human dominance over the rest of the created order.[30]

Some contemporary theologians opt for a Christocentric notion of human nature. On this view, we understand human nature purely through revelation rather than through intrinsic qualities of a human being, or what Alan Torrance, for example, calls a 'Christian epistemic base'.[31] An obvious problem with the theological definition is that it appears positivistic and stipulative. In a culture like modern Europe, where Christianity still exerts enormous influence but very little dogmatic weight, such a position seems somewhat

---

[25] Origen, *Commentary on Romans*, trans. Thomas P. Sheck, (Washington: Catholic University of America, 2001), p. 106.
[26] See Pierre Magnard, 'Imago Dei, Imago Mundi', *Miroirs et reflets, Cahier du Centre de recherche sur l'Image, le Symbole, le Mythe*, 4 (1989).
[27] Aquinas, *Summa Theologica, Prima Secundae, Prooemium.*
[28] J. W. van Huyssteen, *Alone in the World: Human Uniqueness in Science and Theology* (Grand Rapids, MI: William B. Eerdmans Publishing Co., 2006), p. 134.
[29] J. Richard Middleton, *The Liberating Image* (Grand Rapids: Baker, 2005).
[30] Ian A. McFarland, *The Divine Image: Envisioning the Invisible God* (Minneapolis: Fortress, 2005).
[31] A. Torrance, 'Is There a Distinctive Human Nature? Approaching the Question from a Christian Epistemic Base.' *Zygon*, 47 (2012): 903–17.

Quixotic. It is unsatisfactory because of the 'projectivism' challenge: the familiar objection of Xenophanes and Feuerbach that human beings are all too prone to project their longings on the universe. Since Xenophanes and Feuerbach, Marx and Freud have offered further reason why it may be more economical to view religious beliefs as projections and illusions rather than as deliverances of supernatural truth.

The Darwinian challenge suggests that functionalism is weakened, especially if evolutionary psychology is correct. Why do we think that humans are special? Why do we think that there is a universal human nature? One answer could lie in evolutionary prowess. We glabrous apes have changed from being relatively insignificant creatures to the most powerful animals in the world. Perhaps we are confusing our unique *power* with a purported universal and distinct human nature. The brain is the most obvious contender for generating human uniqueness but it is hard to understand its peculiar evolution. Its size requires a large skull and that makes childbirth in *homo sapiens* particularly precarious. Hence the potential benefits of the large brain were combined with some significant disadvantages. Yet there are considerable negative side effects of the upright posture. Childbirth is difficult and dangerous because of the limitation of the birth canal in obligate bipedals. Back pain is ubiquitous since posture is more difficult if not on all fours, and spinal problems constitute a common problem for humans (especially in the industrialized world). One can speculate that the centrality of posture in the yoga tradition is linked to this special difficulty posed by bipedalism. Mircea Eliade considered the emphasis upon posture in yoga as the attempt to overcome finitude and imitate eternal stillness: 'a sign of transcending the human condition'.[32]

Arnold Gehlen's concept of humanity as '*Mängelwesen*' or 'deficit creature' in *Der Mensch: seine Natur und seine Stellung in der Welt* (1940) pointed to this paradox. The lack of powerful teeth or claws to attack foes, the absence of proper body hair to protect from the weather, and even the relative lack of speed for flight from predators made prehistoric humans precarious creatures. Gehlen observes that we should have become extinct! Gehlen was arguing for the principle that the fiction of viewing humans as animals serves to

---

[32] Mircea Eliade, *Yoga, Immortality and Freedom* (Princeton: Bollingen, 2009), pp. 54f.; 67f.; 96f.

emphasize the relevance of the Promethean dimension of human life. Culture compensates for our weak instincts and feeble bodily powers.

Another distinguished twentieth-century German philosopher, Hans Jonas, presented three distinguishing elements of human culture: tools, images and graves.[33] The tool has existed for 2.5 million years.[34] Our thumbs seem to have co-evolved with tools. Other animals can skilfully manipulate the environment: an eagle, for example, can use winds to enhance its speed in flight but it cannot transform a landscape through fire as a hominid can. We can exploit and transform our habitat and environment through tools. The large skull and brain together with the upright posture (or more technically, obligate bipedalism) enables the intelligent use of the hands. Yet Jonas thinks that the image is more important than the tool. The human deployment of the image has its source in the 'hidden art in the depths of the human soul' to use Kant's language of imagination.[35] Through this hidden art and mysterious power of the imagination human beings are set loose from the constraints of the immediate environment and can represent entities and events through the mind's eye, not least the afterlife. Jonas notes that the most significant distinction is the awareness of death. Man knows death and reflects upon its significance and implications. Hans Jonas argued that the possession of tools, images and awareness of death distinguishes humans from other animals. Yet perhaps the sense of the image is primary.[36] Of course, Jonas wanted to claim, quite correctly, that we shape our environment through tools. We are the only animals that know that our lives are finite and can ask questions about whence and whither. As the Cambridge Platonist Benjamin Whichcote observed – 'It ill becomes us to make our intellectual faculties Gibeonites.'[37] It is reasonable for the philosophical pragmatist to claim that human needs may ignite much

---

[33] Hans Jonas, 'Tool, Image and Grave: On what is beyond the Animal in Man', in *Mortality and Morality, A Search for the Good After Auschwitz*, ed. Laurence Vogel (Evanston: Northwestern Press, 1996), pp. 75–86.

[34] Since the publication of Jonas' book there has been much research devoted to chimp tool use. This usage is, however, clearly very limited compared with humans.

[35] I. Kant, *Critique of Pure Reason*, trans. Norman Kemp Smith (London: Macmillan, 1933), A141–2/B180–1.

[36] Hans Jonas, 'Image Making and the Freedom of Man', *The Phenomenon of Life: Towards a Philosophical Biology* (Evanston: Northwestern, 2001), pp. 157–75.

[37] Benjamin Whichcote, *The Sermons of Benjamin Whichcote*, ed. William Wishart, 4 vols (Edinburgh: T. W. and T. Ruddimans, 1742), III, p. 186. The Gibeonites are a people condemned to menial tasks of woodcutting and carrying water. Cf. Joshua, 9.3–37.

speculation, but the *sense* of the eternal is one of the deepest human needs. Our encounter with goodness, truth and beauty as images of the eternal and felt as divine presence is that which the 'poet of Christian Neoplatonism' refers to as the human *prima voglia* and *desiderio supremo*.[38]

The Cartesian Theatre: An Outdated Intellectualism?

Kenneth Boulding observes: 'Human eyes and ears are not much better than those of other mammals, and the human nose is almost certainly much worse. It is the capacity or organizing information into large and complex images which is the chief glory of our species.'[39] It is not the biological equipment as much as the use to which a large brained creature can employ such tools. Perhaps Aristotle had this in mind when he defined the human being as a *rational* animal. Modern philosophers have toyed with the idea of reason as the slave to the passions. Yet Hume only awoke Kant. The thinker is not an addition to experience but its pre-condition. This is at the core of the transcendental unity of apperception: the unified consciousness that is more than a collection of images. It is a unified field of perception that requires a thinker. In this sense our perception of objects presupposes a thinking 'I' that can generate a unified field of vision. Is human consciousness an illusion like 'the setting of the sun' or an exploded error like the Renaissance theory of the humours? Daniel Dennett ridicules this with his characteristically rhetorical bluster as the 'Cartesian Theatre'; 'the illusion that there is a place in our brains where the show goes on, toward which all perceptual "input" streams and whence flow all "conscious intentions" to act and speak. I claim that other species – and human beings when they are newborn – simply aren't beset by the illusion of the Cartesian Theater.'[40] What might we ask, *pace* Dennett, is philosophically illuminating about the notion of the 'Cartesian Theatre'? In his chapter 'The Nobility of Sight', Hans Jonas presents a vindication of sight as

---

[38] P. Boyde, *Dante Philomythes and Philosopher: Man in the Cosmos* (Cambridge: Cambridge University Press, 1983), p. 287; p. 265.
[39] Kenneth Boulding, *The Image: Knowledge in Life and Society* (Ann Arbor, MI: University of Michigan Press, 1961), p. 25.
[40] D. Dennett, *The Intentional Stance* (London: MIT Press, 1989), p. 346.

'simultaneous unity' rather than a 'sequential unity'.[41] Within a field of vision the objects are given 'at once' rather than determined by a succession of items. Because of this, vision enables detachment. Through vision we encounter a simultaneous image and thus are capable of exploring the freedom of the contrast between Being and Becoming. The image of the world at a distance generated by the human imagination is a world that is subject to control. Consciousness can therefore function as an 'inner eye'. For humans, the mind does not depend upon the environment. One can think of dreams. The relationship between this inner world and the outer perceived environment constitutes the distinctively human. 'Seeing requires no perceptible activity on the part of the object or on that of the subject. Neither invades the sphere of the other.' Given that 'the object is not affected by our looking at it', Jonas observes that 'it is present to me without drawing me into its presence'. There is some recent neurophysiological experimentation that reinforces Jonas's claim that vision 'outdoes' the other senses.[42] An example from neuroscience can be used as an illustration of the priority of sight. The 'rubber-hand illusion' reveals the superiority of sight (or visual dominance) over other senses. In the experiment, the real hand is hidden from sight by a board and a rubber hand is placed in front of the subject as if it were his or her own. The tester strokes the rubber hand at the same time as the real hand is being stroked. Watching the rubber hand being stroked at the same time as the rubber hand is enough to convince the brain that the 'hand' in its visual field is its own. Thus, visual information can override proprocentric information from the muscles and tendons. The brain adopts the rubber hand. In the rubber-hand illusion, vision trumps proprioceptive information.[43]

Let us take Jonas's 'image' to mean not just paintings and art but the freedom to distance ourselves from the immediate environment, to go 'offline' if we may employ a metaphor from computers. There is a fundamental

---

[41] Jonas, 'The Nobility of Sight: A Study in the Phenomenology of the Senses', *The Phenomenon of Life: Towards a Philosophical Biology* (Evanston: Northwestern, 2001), pp. 135–56.
[42] I am very grateful to Carl Gillett for this reference. On the neurological data concerning variety of illusions of bodily 'ownership', see C. Lopez, P. Halje and O. Blanke, 'Body Ownership and Embodiment: Vestibular and Multisensory Mechanisms' in *Clinical Neurophysiology* 38, (2008): 149–61.
[43] Matthew Botvinick and Jonathan Cohen, *Nature* 391, (19 February 1998), p. 756.

ambivalence here. The nobility of sight according to Jonas is the foundation of the distinctively human capacity to establish a conception of objectivity. Yet as a (properly cantankerous) pupil of Heidegger, Jonas notes that this 'nobility of sight' can encourage us to forget the dimension of 'being-in-world', our biological being, our primordial relation to the world that obviously precedes any perception or vision of them.[44] According to Jonas, 'The complete neutralization of dynamic content in the visual object, the expurgation of all traces of causal activity from its presentation, is one of the major accomplishments of what we call the image-function of sight.' Humans are spectators that can contemplate reality in 'detachment from the actual presence of the original object'. This provides the possibility of those momentous distinctions between 'Being' and 'Becoming', time and eternity, essence and existence that lie at the core of Western philosophy. As Andrew Marvell writes memorably in 'The Garden':

> Meanwhile the mind, from pleasure less,
> Withdraws into its happiness;
> The mind, that ocean where each kind
> Does straight its own resemblance find,
> Yet it creates, transcending these,
> Far other worlds, and other seas;
> Annihilating all that's made
> To a green thought in a green shade.[45]

Coleridge asserts that the 'imagination at all events struggles to idealize and to unify'.[46] The decisive contribution of the imagination is in our consciousness of the world as a whole. It is the participation and imaginative engagement with the whole that generates the specifically religious aspect. This image of the world as a whole is closely linked to our emotional reactions, a sense of weal or woe. The mind can turn around upon itself. Man is self-consciously in the world and thus aware of the world as an arena of free agency: religion

---

[44] Peter Cheyne reminds me that being-in-the-world and biological being are utterly distinct, indeed contradictory notions for Heidegger, with the former an ontological category, and the latter an ontic one.

[45] Andrew Marvell, 'The Garden', in *Andrew Marvell*, eds F. Kermode and K. Walker (Oxford: Oxford University Press, 1990), p. 48.

[46] Coleridge, *Biographia Literaria*, eds J. Engell, W. Jackson Bate, (Princeton: Bollingen, 1983), 1.305.

and metaphysics are unavoidable. The representation through the image is a feature of the human capacity for choice.

The Similarity Thesis: The Indeterminate Image Model versus the Property View

'Nulla interposita creatura'
Augustine, *De Vera Religione*, ch.55, 113

We seem to have an impasse, caught between an inherited rationalism and revelatory positivism. The alternative would seem to be between an outmoded intellectualist 'substance' view of the *imago Dei* and a functionalist account which relies upon revelation trumping all other factors. The first gives a philosophical reason for the *imago Dei* but it is one that seems to clash with modern evolutionary biology. If we share 80–99 per cent of our genes with other great apes, or if we discover 4 per cent Neanderthal in Europeans, why should we think that *homo sapiens* is different in kind and not merely in degree from other animals? The appeal to a 'Christian epistemic base' avoids such problems but at the high price of ignoring the legitimate challenge of the 'cultured despisers'.

Let us indulge in some *Begriffsgeschichte*. The term 'reflection' has two obvious senses: the *reflectere* or 'bending back' of the mind upon itself. It also possesses the Platonic and Pauline sense of mirroring, and the connotation of participation.[47] In Neoplatonism, the two ideas are closely linked. It is because the finite mind participates in the infinite One that it can turn back and understand itself in terms of its transcendent Source.[48]

If God is spirit and we are in His image, then it is as spiritual beings. The most eloquent of the Cambridge Platonists, John Smith, writes:

> Reason in man being *Lumen de Lumine*, a Light flowing from the Fountain and Father of lights ... God only can so shine upon our glassy understandings, as to beget in them a picture of Himself, and turn the soul like wax or clay to the seal

---

[47] Pierre Hadot, "Conversion." *Encyclopaedia Universalis*, vol. 4, pp. 979–81. Paris: 1968.
[48] See the *Imago complicationis divinae* in Nicholas of Cusa, *Idiota De Mente* (Minneapolis: Banning, 1996), IV, 74. Here he is speaking of specific mirroring that is unique to the human. Whereas all other things are *explications* of God, only man is an image of the *complication*.

of His own light and love. He that made our souls in His own image and likeness can easily find a way into them. The Word that God speaks, having found a way into the soul imprints itself there as with the point of diamond ... It is God alone that acquaints the soul with the Truths of Revelation: and He also it is that does strengthen and raise the soul to better apprehensions even of Natural Truth: God being that in the *Intellectual* world which the sun is in the sensible, as some of the ancient Fathers love to speak, and the ancient Philosophers too, who meant God by their *Intellectus Agens*, whose proper work they supposed to be not so much to enlighten the Object, as the Faculty.[49]

From this passage it is clear how Smith employs the Platonic metaphysics of the image in order to justify a view of human nature as grounded in the divine archetype. When considering the doctrine of the 'image' of God in humanity, we need to appraise the status of the divine image in the rest of the created order. Bacon is quite adamant that the doctrine of the image applies only to humanity:

> For as all works do show forth the power and skill of the workman, and not his image; so it is of the works of God, which do show the omnipotency and wisdom of the maker, but not his image: and therefore therein the heathen opinion differeth from the sacred truth; for they supposed the world to be the image of God, and man to be an extract or compendious image of the world; but the Scriptures never vouchsafe to attribute to the world that honour, as to be the image of God, but only *the work of his hands; neither do they speak of any other image of God, but man*.[50]

Note that here the world is presented as an artifice. It reveals the 'omnipotency and wisdom' of the maker but not his image. There are, however, different – and incompatible – ways of construing the image. There is a difference between *similitudo* and *imago* in Dietrich of Freiburg and Meister Eckhart. *Similitudo* is just for created order. 'Imago' is solely applicable for intellect.[51] Rather than using the interpretation of Aquinas, we will consider

---

[49] Smith, *Select Discourses* (Cambridge: Flesher, 1660), pp. 382–84.
[50] Bacon, *Advancement of Learning*, book II, *Works*, eds Spedding, Ellis and Heath (London: Longman, 1857–74), III, p. 349.
[51] Kurt Flasch, 'Procedere ut imago: Das Hervorgehen des Intellekts aus seinem göttlichen Grund bei Meister Dietrich, Meister Eckhart und Berthold von Moosburg', *Abendländischen Mystik im Mittelalter*, ed. K. Ruh (Stuttgart: Metzler, 1986), pp. 125–34; 'Converti ut imago – Rückkehr als Bild. Eine Studie zur Theorie des Intellekts bei Dietrich von Freiburg und Meister Eckhart', *Freiburger Zeitschrift für Philosophie und Theologie*, 45 (1998): 130–50.

the position of Meister Eckhart, a position which relies upon the Augustinian doctrine that God is immediately present to the soul (*abditum mentis*). As the Bishop of Hippo insisted: God is nearer to the soul than it is to itself. Thus, there is nothing that intervenes between the soul and God (*nulla interposita est*).[52] Created things are caused by God according to a single idea; while intellect proceeds according to the likeness of God himself. For Dietrich and Eckhart, the *way* in which the intellect as *imago proceeds* (for Eckhart, 'boils') within/from God is different from how the rest of creation is *caused* by God.

Meister Eckhart (c. 1260-1328) draws upon the Neoplatonic idea of image as participating in its archetype.[53] *Bild* or 'image' is one of his favourite terms in the German works.[54] It can be translated into the Latin as *ratio, exempla, forma, imago, phantasma, species*.[55] Meister Eckhart presents the *imago* primarily in terms of *identity* rather than difference.[56] Dietrich refers to the consubstantiality of *imago* and the exemplar and Eckhart seems to be following Dietrich (or vice versa). The image is defined by its direct relation to its archetype: it originates in and only *is* in relation to its source. It is not a mere likeness, as two white eggs will resemble each other without one egg determining the other in any respect.[57]

Compare this with Aquinas:

> An image is so called because it is produced as an imitation of something else … But equality does not belong to the essence of an image; for as Augustine says (Octaginia Trium Quaest, Q74) 'Where there is an image there is not necessarily equality', as we see in a person's image reflected in a glass. Yet this is of the essence of a perfect image; for in a perfect image nothing is wanting

---

[52] Augustine, *De vera religione*, 55.113 – '*religet ergo nos religio uni omnipotenti deo, quia inter mentem nostrum, qua illum intelligimus patrem et veritatem, id est lucem interiorem per quam illum intelligimus, nulla interposita est*'.

[53] See Burkhard Mojsisch, *Meister Eckhart: Analogie, Univozität und Einheit* (Hamburg: Felix Meiner, 1983), esp. pp. 79ff. See also Olivier Boulnois, *Au-delà de l'image: Une archéologie du visuel au Moyen Âge Ve- XVIe siècle* (Paris: Seuil, 2008), pp. 301-30. See further Mauritius Wilde, *Das neue Bild vom Gottesbild: Bild und Theologie bei Meister Eckhart* (Freiburg: Universitätsverlag, 2000).

[54] Donald F. Duclow, '"Whose Image is this?" in Eckhart's Sermones' in *Masters of Learned Ignorance: Eriugena, Eckhart, Cusanus* (Ashgate: Aldershot, 2006), pp. 175-86.

[55] Alois M. Haas, 'Meister Eckharts mystische Bildlehre', *Der Begriff der Repraesentatio im Mittelalter*, ed. Albert Zimmermann (Berlin: Walter de Gruyter, 1971) pp. 113-38, p. 114.

[56] B. McGinn, *The Harvest of Mysticism in Medieval Germany: Volume IV in the Presence of God Series: 4 (Presence of God: A History of Western Christian Mysticism)*, (New York: The Crossroad Publishing Company, 2005), pp. 145-50.

[57] Eckhart, *Sermon 16b, Lectura Eckhardi*, eds G. Steer and L. Sturlese, (Stuttgart: Kohlhammer, 1998).

that is to be found in that of which it is a copy. Now it is manifest that in man there is some likeness to God, copied from God as from an exemplar; yet this likeness is not one of equality, for such an exemplar infinitely excels its copy. Therefore, there is in man a likeness to God; not indeed a perfect likeness, but imperfect.[58]

Aquinas stresses that the image is imperfect and consists of properties or powers of the mind.[59] One should note that Aquinas stresses the distance between the image and its paradigm. For Eckhart, the *Bild* is not to be characterized by specific *properties* which are distinctive of humanity – it is a '*non ens*'. The view of the soul as an image and thus *non ens* is part of a philosophical critique of the Thomist view of the soul as a substance equipped with specific powers and properties: intellect or will.[60] For Meister Dietrich and Meister Eckhart, the soul cannot be assimilated to the Aristotelian logic of the operations of the material realm. There is a distinct logic of the '*spiritualia*'. Every vessel has two characteristics: it takes in and it contains. There is a difference between spiritual vessels and material vessels. Wine is inside the vessel; the vessel is not in the wine, nor is the wine in the vessel in the sense that it is inside the bounds of the cup. If it were in the vessel in this sense, one could not drink it. It is different with a spiritual vessel. Everything that is taken into it is in the vessel and the vessel is in it and it is the vessel itself. Everything that the spiritual vessel takes in has the same nature [as the vessel]. It is God's nature that he gives himself to every good soul, and it is the nature of the soul that it takes God in. This can be said to be among the noblest things that the soul can do. Thus the soul wears the Divine image and is like God.[61]

One might consider the contrast between the physical container and the spiritual vessel. Whereas the bearer and the liquid in the cup are separated, the image and the exemplar coalesce. In another passage Eckhart says: 'In all spiritual matters we find that the one thing is in the other, one and

---

[58] Aquinas, *Summa Theologiae*, Ia.93, 1.
[59] Aquinas, *Summa Theologiae*, Ia.93, 7.
[60] Kurt Flasch, *Dietrich von Freiberg, Philosophie, Theologie, Naturforschung um 1300* (Frankfurt: Klostermann, 2007), esp. p. 209ff and pp. 301ff.
[61] Eckhart, *Sermon 16b. Lectura Eckhardi*, I, pp. 44f.

undivided.'[62] The error that Eckhart is warning against is that of modelling the unity of the spiritual upon that of material substances, although the temptation to imagine the spiritual in quasi-material terms is strong – each element as a *partes extra partes*. The liquid contained 'in' the other physical cup is still limited by the contours of the container. Hence the temptation to think of the soul as a 'homunculus', the object of justified scorn and *reductiones ad absurdum* for so many materialists. The human soul, however, as immaterial, can be 'in' the Divine just as the reflected image rests in its exemplar.[63]

The image points to that which is beyond itself: it has its *essence* in its exemplar or archetype (*Urbild*). It is not the relation of accidents to a substance. The specifically Neoplatonic dimension of this metaphysics of the image is particularly clear in Latin Sermon XLIX. In this passage the image is presented as having eight characteristics: it possesses likeness, and secondly is similar in its 'nature and species'. Thirdly, the perfect image is identical with its source. Fourthly, the image emanates from its source. Fifthly, it excludes any otherness. The image and its exemplar are not divided things or substances. It is characterized by reflection, by a *reditio completa* (perfect return) of the image to its exemplar. Finally, the image possesses the abundance of its source. In the following paragraph, Eckhart develops this theme of the image with his characteristic idea of the fecundity of the Divine goodness as '*bullitio*', boiling. This 'boiling-over' is an inferior and lower component of the intenal 'boiling' of the 'imago'.[64]

Eckhart, like his colleague and older contemporary Dietrich of Freiburg (1240–1320?), is insisting that Aristotelian categories do not apply to the realm of metaphysics of the image. The metaphysician, Eckhart contends, considers the image 'in abstraction from the efficient and final causes'.[65] That is, in abstraction from the properties of material objects and events in space and time. It is the *formal* causality that is Eckhart's concern, and that

---

[62] Eckhart, *Sermon Seventy*, Q 67, *The Complete Mystical Works of Meister Eckhart*, translated and edited by Maurice O'C. Walshe; revised with a foreword by Bernard McGinn (New York: Crossroads, 2001), p. 173.

[63] Werner Beierwaltes, *Platonismus und Idealismus* (Frankfurt: Klostermann, 1972), pp. 47–64, esp. 55ff.

[64] Eckhart, *Sermon XLIX*, *Lectura Eckhardi*, III, p. 237: '*Die Rolle der imago sowohl im Ausfliessen als auch im Zuruckfliessen aller Dinge in Gott ist ein zentrales Motiv in Eckharts Lehre.*'

[65] Eckhart, *Sermon XLIX*, *Lectura Eckhardi*, III, p. 214.

causality is the dynamic plenitude of the divine mind. The activity of the mind qua *imago* is a going-forth or procession rather than a causal making or mediation. The mind as *imago* is immediate or '*ane mittel*'. As such the mind qua *imago* is distinguished from the habitual matrix of animal *genus* and *species*. Kurt Flasch notes that it is far from clear that Eckhart, or his followers, were denying human creatureliness but it is explicated in a novel manner.[66] The participation of the human mind in its transcendent source and its procession as *imago* blurs the lines between finite and infinite because the intellect is not a specific material substance with definite boundaries.

The Thomist view of the *imago Dei* as residing in certain properties seems *prima vista* more plausible. The doctrine of the image stresses the difference rather than the identity between the human and Divine. But there are problems: what about the fact that we share so much genetically in common with chimps; do we include the Australopithecus? Within our own species some forms of illness – such as Alzheimer's, or severe forms of autism, might seem to bracket some persons off from inclusion within any common shared rationality. Yet such persons belong to the 'Kingdom of Ends'. Or what about hypothetical extra-terrestrials with a very different set of material properties and yet a capacity for belief and worship in a transcendent creator? The image/*non ens* model can more readily explain our capacity to be in the 'image of God'. There are no specific material properties or attributes linked to the substance or species of humanity by virtue of which we are in the image of God. The image is not a 'thing' with properties or a substance with attributes. It is not necessarily tied to species or genus. Human uniqueness is not defined by properties or by a percentage of genes.

Dignitas Hominis?

'Man is a giddy thing' says the philosophical poet.[67] It is a platitude of intellectual history to contrast the anthropological pessimism of the clerical Dark

---

[66] Flasch, Kurt, 'Procedere ut imago: Das Hervorgehen des Intellekts aus seinem göttlichen Grund bei Meister Dietrich, Meister Eckhart und Bertold von Moosburg', p. 133.
[67] Shakespeare, *Much Ado about Nothing* Act 5, Scene 4.

Ages with the optimism of the Renaissance. Generally the standard view of the *imago Dei* in the West, which emphasized its distance from its source, was not an obvious basis for a doctrine of human dignity. On the contrary, it could serve a dogma of the relative worthlessness of mankind. The Eckhartian view, shared by other German thinkers from 1250 to 1350, which stressed the identity of the image with its source, does provide a clear principle for a theory of human dignity.[68] The presence of God in the soul and the 'indeterminacy' of the image is pivotal. Awakening the soul to the *presence* of the divine is the key to the philosophical and spiritual life. This idea of the indeterminate image of the Divine, a model of creative plasticity of the human mind, found great resonance in the Renaissance. Pico della Mirandola set forth the paradigmatic expression of the ancient doctrine:

> At last, the Supreme Maker decreed that this creature, to whom He could give nothing wholly his own, should have a share in the particular endowment of every other creature. Taking man, therefore, this creature of indeterminate image, He set him in the middle of the world and thus spoke to him:

> We have given you, O Adam, no visage proper to yourself, nor endowment properly your own, in order that whatever place, whatever form, whatever gifts you may, with premeditation, select, these same you may have and possess through your own judgement and decision. The nature of all other creatures is defined and restricted within laws which We have laid down; you, by contrast, impeded by no such restrictions, may, by your own free will, to whose custody We have assigned you, trace for yourself the lineaments of your own nature. I have placed you at the very center of the world, so that from that vantage point you may with greater ease glance round about you on all that the world contains. We have made you a creature neither of heaven nor of earth, neither mortal nor immortal, in order that you may, as the free and proud shaper of your own being, fashion yourself in the form you may prefer. It will be in your power to descend to the lower, brutish forms of life; you will be able, through your own decision, to rise again to the superior orders whose life is divine.[69]

---

[68] Loris Sturlese, 'Von der Würde des unwürdigen Menschen', in Loris Sturlese, *Homo divinus. Philosophische Projekte in Deutschland zwischen Meister Eckhart und Heinrich Seuse* (Stuttgart: Kohlhammer, 2007), pp. 35–45.

[69] *Pico della Mirandola: Oration on the Dignity of Man: A New Translation and Commentary*, eds Francesco Borghesi, Michael Papio, and Massimo Riva (Cambridge: Cambridge University Press, 2012), 278pp. See Werner Beierwaltes, 'Subjektivitität, Schöpfertum, Freiheit. Die Philosophie der

For Pico our nature is not identical with our ancestry. We are creatures of 'indeterminate image', able to fall or rise, regardless of our brutish origins, to the Divine. In the seventeenth century, Anglican moderates like Edward Stillingfleet chastized those who, like Henry More, considered that the soul is 'the Image of God, as the Rays of light are of the Sun'. For such thinkers, the soul is 'a Particle not of *matter* but of the *Divine nature* itself, a little Deity in a Cottage, that stayes here awhile, and returns to that upper *Region* from whence it came'.[70] Stillingfleet was understandably concerned by the theological implications of this Eckhartian position among the Cambridge Platonists. The apparent arrogance or hubris of Eckhart's position dissolves upon realizing the ethical paradox that it is the humble person who becomes the place of divine presence, paradigmatically Christ, the man of sorrows. *Ecce homo* – behold the man in the suffering servant of the Passion.[71] Moreover, the birth of Christ in the soul is not an achievement of a few extraordinary and intrepid spiritual aristocrats but the very essence of humanity. Indeed, the insistence upon the theomorphic dimension of humanity is intimately linked to the theme of human dignity.[72] The dignity of the soul, for Eckhart, its *dignissima condicio et singularis dignitas*, lies in its indeterminacy and hence its openness to God. Eckhart tends to express this openness through paradoxes of negation. Since the soul is *not* a determinate entity – not a 'thing' – it alone can be the very house of a spiritual God.[73] It may seem paradoxical to stress the impact of the *imago Dei* for a doctrine of human dignity in a culture where the language of human rights is seen as the prerogative of the secular left.[74] It has been argued that *The Universal Declaration of Human Rights* of 1948 had deep roots in a theological view of humanity and was the product of 'Christianity's last golden age on the Continent'.[75]

Renaissance zwischen Tradition und neuzeitlichen Bewußtsein', *Der Übergang zur Neuzeit und die Wirkung der Tradition* (Göttingen: Vandenhoeck & Ruprecht, 1978), pp. 15–31.

[70] Edward Stillingfleet, *Origines Sacrae* (London, 1680), pp. 417–18.
[71] One might think of the Byzantine tradition in which humans are the image of the image. The image is given in the great Philippians hymn of St Paul.
[72] Moyn, 'Personalism, community and the origin of human rights', pp. 85–106.
[73] Loris Sturlese, *Homo divinus*, p. 43. John Smith writes of the perception of God, beholding Moses like the divine 'glory shining thus out upon us in the face of Christ', that Christians receive 'a copy of that Eternal beauty upon our own souls, and our thirstie and hungry spirits would be perpetually sucking up in true participation and image of his glory'. Smith, *Select Discourses*, p. 336.
[74] Helena Kennedy, *Justice and Human Rights* (London: The Athenaeum, 2014).
[75] Moyn, 'Personalism', p. 105.

Imago Dei and the Human Imagination

Since the scientific revolution, the transformation of the environment through human ingenuity and mastery has increased mightily. *Scientia potestas*! Lord Bacon's pithy adage points to the benefit of knowledge in evolutionary terms. If 'knowledge is power', it seems obvious why our ancestors wished to acquire it. Yet why is imagination so pronounced in *homo sapiens*? What, indeed, are the adaptive pay-offs? It has often been observed that the protracted period of play in human infants can furnish and develop sophisticated cognitive skills. Perhaps, for example, the logic of inferences in imaginative literature encourages fledgling intellects to contemplate myriad possibilities. Further, might not this imaginative activity foster recognition of the difference between a real cause and mere correlation? The child can thus select between random occurrences and genuine regularities. The recognition of a cause as a mere conjunction of events generates powers of prediction and the ability to think of invisible properties and counterfactuals based upon properties.

This theory, however, presents an outlandish and implausible view of children. Should we imagine three- and four-year-old infants as embryonic scientists exploring the causal world or inchoate philosophers trying to work out the logic of beliefs? The child's imagination is populated by many unlikely and improbable events and companions and its reasoning is heavily shaped by parents and social groups. It has even been suggested that children are more susceptible to errors of judgement because of their need for authority and guidance and their capacity to dwell in the past, present and future. Thus the experiments of Tetsuro Matsuzawa that show the superiority of chimps over children in some intellectual tests, especially of memory.[76]

'Art is the signature of man' said Chesterton.[77] The image is a primary and archaic medium of the human imagination. Jonas uses the example of cave paintings:

---

[76] Tetsuro Matsuzawa, *Primate Origins of Human Cognition and Behaviour* (Hong Kong: Springer, 2008).
[77] G. K. Chesterton, *The Collected Works of G. K Chesterton* (San Francisco: Ignatius Press, 1987), Rutler Azar and George Marlin (eds), p. 166.

Our explorers [hypothetically coming from another planet to ascertain the presence of men on earth] enter a cave, and on its walls they discern lines or other configurations that must have been produced artificially, that have no structural function, and that suggest a likeness to one another of the living forms encountered outside. The cry goes up: 'Here is evidence of man!' Why? The evidence does not require the perfection of the Altamira paintings. The crudest and most childish drawing would be just as conclusive as the frescoes of Michelangelo. Conclusive for what? For the more-than-animal nature of its creator; and for his being potentially a speaking, thinking, inventing, in short 'symbolical' being. And since it is not a matter of degree, as is technology, the evidence must reveal what it has to reveal by its formal quality alone.[78]

Through painting images such as those in the caves of Chauvet or Lascaux, our ancestors could visualize memories and represent imagined states, events and personae. Wentzel van Huyssteen in his Gifford Lectures *Alone in the World? Human Uniqueness in Science and Theology* interprets the *imago Dei* in terms of the imagination. He presents religion as a decisive part of the lives of our ancestors living in the Upper Palaeolithic. Van Huyssteen sees the paintings as the oldest significant products of human imagination and imbued as they are with religious and mythological meaning. 'They tell us about who our direct ancestors were, what they thought, and what they could do. They tell us about imagination, about creativity, about consciousness, about the Creator.'[79] Van Huyssteen writes: 'The most spectacular evidence of symbolic behaviour in humans – and some of the earliest – can be found in the Palaeolithic cave art in southwestern France and the Basque Country in northern Spain … As such, the Upper Palaeolithic holds an all-important and intriguing key to the naturalness of the evolution of religion, to the credibility of the earliest forms of religious faith, and to what it means for *Homo sapiens* to be spiritually embodied beings.'[80] Van Huyssteen's proposal has not gone unchallenged. The first problem relates to the interpretation of images tout court. How can one fix the nature of any interpretation of images – especially such ancient ones? Secondly, the shamanistic hypothesis of David Lewis-Williams, upon which

---

[78] Hans Jonas, *The Phenomenon of Life*. (Evanston, IL: Northwestern University Press, 2001), p. 158.
[79] J. Wentzel Van Huyssteen, *Alone in the World: Human Uniqueness in Science and Theology*. (Grand Rapids, MI: William B. Eerdmans Publishing Co., 2006), p. 15.
[80] Van Huyssteen, 2006, p. xvii.

Van Huyssteen builds some of his case, has been criticized. Van Huyssteen writes:

> More than simple, decorative pictures, these paintings were gateways to the spirit world, panoramas that, in their trance experience, shamans could enter and with which their own projected mental imagery could mingle in three animated dimensions ... the rock face was like a veil suspended between this world and the spirit world ... the potency filled paint created some sort of bond between the person, the rock veil, and the spirit world that seethed behind it.[81]

Whether or not Van Huyssteen is correct about the ancient denizens of Chauvet, the model of the cave has endured as a place of encounter with the sacred. Greece is a landscape with remarkable caves and its folklore and mythology is replete with the images of caves, into and including the Byzantine world. Orthodox chapels often feel like caves, sometimes are located within caves.[82] With his characteristic blend of conservatism and radicalism, Plato reverses the image of the cave as a place of encounter with the spirit-divine world into a model of the relation of appearance to reality, a place where human beings encounter images and traces of a fuller and richer world, and where the recognition of the world as 'images' stimulates the return and ascent to the Good, the True and the Beautiful.

Language provides an obvious difference between humans and other animals. The beliefs that we form about the world are conceptually grounded or suffused. What about the imagination? How useful are the images in the Palaeolithic cave? The evolutionary psychologist claims that psychological patterns or traits are modular adaptations. Yet the capacity to construct such images like those in Chauvet neither changes the agent nor the environment. It is barely conceivable that the cave images were produced for functional reasons, like a scarecrow, for example. The scarecrow is a natural likeness of a potential predator and hence its efficacy.[83] The Palaeolithic man entering into the cave will encounter a range of images that constitute a distinct realm of representations with intentional content. It is this intentional content that

---

[81] Van Huyssteen, op. cit., p. 209.
[82] Ernst Benz, *Die heilige Höhle in der alten Christenheit und in der östlich-orthodoxen Kirche* (Zurich: Rhein Verlag, 1954).
[83] Hans Jonas, The Phenomenon of Life (Evanston. IL: Northwestern University Press, 2001), p. 166.

makes the images so enigmatic since we do not share the specific beliefs and practices of our hunter-gatherer ancestors. Artistic activity is one of the earliest defining human characteristics. Is it art? This could be projecting false categories into prehistory – or is it? Perhaps we, however, can uniquely reflect upon our likeness and through our imaginings we can commune with ultimate reality and mirror its source. The paradoxical phrase of Meister Eckhart is apposite: 'The Eye with which I see God is the same Eye with which God sees me.'[84] Humanity has created images of the sacred since prehistoric times. These sublime images and imaginings of the transcendent become an instrument of revelation: the real presence of the eternal in human history and culture.

---

[84] Lectura Eckhardi, I, p. 30.

3

The Anagogic Image

Σεμνοὶ μὲν γὰρ πάντες θεοὶ καὶ καλοὶ καὶ τὸ κάλλος αὐτῶν ἀμήχανον· ἀλλὰ τί ἐστι δι' ὃ τοιοῦτοί εἰσιν; Ἡ νοῦς, καὶ ὅτι μᾶλλον νοῦς ἐνεργῶν ἐν αὐτοῖς, ὥστε ὁρᾶσθαι.

For all the gods are majestic and beautiful and their beauty is overwhelming: but what is it which makes them like this? It is Intellect, and it is because Intellect is more intensely active in them, so as to be visible.
Plotinus V8 3, 19ff. (A. H. Armstrong)

O Attic shape! fair attitude! with brede
Of marble men and maidens overwrought,
With forest branches and the trodden weed;
Thou, silent form, dost tease us out of thought
As doth eternity: Cold Pastoral! 45
When old age shall this generation waste,
Thou shalt remain, in midst of other woe
Than ours, a friend to man, to whom thou say'st,
"Beauty is truth, truth beauty", – that is all
      Ye know on earth, and all ye need to know.'
John Keats, Ode on a Grecian Urn, 41–50

Religion stands in need of the artistic imagination to illustrate or designate the experience of transcendent mystery with its sublime expression in the Pyramids, early Buddhas, Gothic cathedrals, the Alhambra or the Taj Mahal. The geometrical patterns in Islamic art which symbolize the ineffable perfection of the Godhead, the architecture that conveyed the infinite power of the Divine, constitute examples of this religious need to imagine the divine presence through art, even in a tradition where humans or animals are seldom represented. Art, however, withers without a residual sense of the sacred and of intimations of transcendence. Art requires the *inspiration* of the religious impulse. In this chapter we shall argue that the imagination has an *anagogic* dimension. To imagine is often for the mind to go beyond the sensory environment (e.g. daydreaming or conjecture). Such 'going beyond' usually relies upon a principle of analogy – a likeness between past and future, seen and unseen, etc. Our goal here, however, is *anagogy* rather than analogy: an imagination that not just connects the self to its wider environment but which raises or lifts up (*ana-gogein*) the soul to the Divine. We will look to the contribution of Roger Scruton to sustain our claim. Scruton, as we shall see, is a rather ambiguous ally in this.

The Dutch philosopher Gerardus van der Leeuw was fond of observing that the sacred dimension of art irritates the aesthetes while the purely aesthetic irks the pious.[1] Yet the profound link between the holy and the aesthetic is obvious to anyone remotely familiar with the history of art. Nor is a cosy Eurocentrism intellectually respectable. We can hardly ignore the world dimension. Voltaire rightly ridiculed Bossuet's *Discourse on Universal History* because it paid no heed to China and India. Yet giving due attention to the great cultures of the world generates real difficulties. Even within the subcontinent of India there are vast differences between rasa theory and Muslim aesthetics. It is little wonder that one has debates about the intelligibility of the category description 'Islamic Art', or whether some major figures in modern art are helpfully designated 'Jewish'. The interest here is not 'perennialist' but humanist in the sense of Erasmus or Samuel Johnson. Where we encounter

---

[1] Gerardus van der Leeuw, *Sacred and Profane Beauty: the Holy in Art* (Holt, Chicago: Rinehart and Winston, 1963), p. 3.

a continuity of esteem, that is itself a good reason for deeming it worthy of serious study. The commonalities of human experience through millennia must carry weight in the humanities.

Art, moreover, is a particularly puzzling category. Hegel defines art Platonically as the '*Scheinen der Idee*' or '*Idee in der Anschauung*'. The '*Idee*' here is the absolute or Divine Idea. Art, for Hegel, is thus adjacent to philosophy in providing the possibility of contemplative happiness in θεωρία. George Dickie defines art as 'any artifact ... which has had conferred upon it the status of candidate for appreciation by some person or persons acting on behalf of a certain social institution (the art world)'.[2] According to Dickie's definition, Duchamp's urinal is an art-work when displayed as such. It is singularly difficult to see any contemplative content in Duchamp's *soi-disant* 'Fountain'.

Let us consider the following passage from Proust on the imagination, which brings out a strong contemplative dimension to aesthetic activity.

> And is it not more beautiful we wonder, that the imagination, which neither the present nor the past could put into communication with life and so save from oblivion and the misinterpretation of thought and unhappy memories, the varied, individual essences of life-trains and hotel rooms, the fragrance of roses, the taste of stewed fruit, washrooms and roads from which we can look at the sea while, as it were, travelling elegantly in a carriage – is it not more beautiful that in the sudden leap which follows on the impact between an identical past and present, the imagination should thus be freed from time! For the pleasure of that experience is a sure sign of its superiority, and in it I have always put such trust that I write nothing of what I see, nothing at which I arrive by a process of reasoning, or of what I have remembered in the ordinary sense of remembering, but only of what the past brings suddenly to life in a smell, in a sight, in what has, as it were, exploded within me and set the imagination quivering, so that the accompanying joy stirs me to inspiration. This pleasure which seemed to me sufficient proof of the superiority of that state, is, perhaps, proof of the superiority of a state in which we have as object an eternal essence, and seems to indicate that only so sublime an experience can be captured by the imagination. And this deep-dwelling pleasure, by justifying us in giving to imagination the highest place, since we understand now that it is the organ which serves the eternal, does perhaps raise us too, and shows, because of the happiness we feel

---

[2] George Dickie, *Aesthetics, An Introduction* (Cambridge: Pegasus: 1971), p. 101.

when we are freed from the present, that our true nature lies outside of time, and is formed to feed on the eternal, never to be contented with the present nor ever to be saddened by the past. And that is why, living and knowing so many different times, and feeling melancholy in so many different rooms, we should not grieve overmuch at having spent our time in elegant carriages and fashionable salons. So often seeking beauty in a mountain or a sky we find it again in the sound of rubber-tyred wheels or the smell of a scrap of fabric, in the things which have hung about our lives, which chance has brought to hang there once again, though this time we may be better equipped to feel delight, separating their imagined past from their present reality, wrenching ourselves free from the slavery of the now, letting ourselves be flooded with the feeling of life everlasting.[3]

The power of imagination is a central theme for Proust. One might note that sense of being liberated from 'the slavery of the now' and 'letting ourselves be flooded with the feeling of life everlasting'. Imagination is 'the organ which serves the eternal', it shows that 'we are formed to feed on the eternal'. The strikingly Neoplatonic language employed by Proust is rather puzzling. It does not possess any authentically theological component. It is, however, clearly written in earnest. The contemplative activity of the human imagination is a feature of such preciousness, and a source of such deep felicity, that it demands philosophical articulation. The artist discovers truths that are otherwise hidden. The sentiment of Proust is most aptly explored in the aesthetic theory of Roger Scruton, a vigorous critic of a world in which 'we no longer make for ourselves images of the ideal and the transcendent, but in which we study human debris in place of the human soul'.[4] For, as Scruton claims, 'we aspire through art, and when aspiration ceases, so too does art'.[5] Indeed, he sees much contemporary art as an exercise in desecration, quite literally. The idea of the sacred is an indispensable component of Scruton's philosophy, and it is also linked to self-consciousness. To self-conscious creatures, art is an indispensable mirror of reality and it can serve to elevate us. It can, however, denigrate and inhibit the human capacity for transformation.

---

[3] Marcel Proust, *Jean Santeuil* trs. Gerard Hopkins (London: Weidenfeld and Nicholson, 1955), pp. 409–10.
[4] Scruton, quoted in Mark Dooley, *Roger Scruton: The Philosopher on Dover Beach* (London: Bloomsbury, 2009), p. 110.
[5] Scruton, loc. cit.

The task of culture is sacred and the intimations of the transcendental are key to Scruton's thought. Mark Dooley in his *Philosopher on Dover Beach* notes that 'it is through the aesthetic that human beings can fulfil their deepest longings – the longing to love and to belong'.[6] For Scruton, 'art has grown from the sacred view of life'.[7]

> It is of course nonsense to suggest that there are naiads in the trees and dryads in the groves. What is revealed to me in the experience of beauty is a fundamental truth about being – that being is a gift.[8]

To perceive the world in sacral terms is to view it in terms of subjectivity and freedom.[9] There is a special relationship between beauty and the sacred for Scruton. In this respect Scruton's thought seems close to the great tradition of Neoplatonic aesthetics from Plotinus to Ficino. Indeed, there is a *theo-iconological* facet to Scruton in this respect. When beauty is separated from the sacred, the face of God is masked and obscured.[10] Works of art are not sacred *per se* yet they serve to provide images and narratives of normative value. Klee remarked that, '*Kunst gibt nicht das Sichtbare wieder, sondern macht sichtbar*'.[11] To say that 'art does not represent the visible, it makes visible' is to contend that art can provide a means of seeing the inherent value and beauty of a world that is otherwise obscured by the habit, custom and 'film of familiarity'.[12]

Scruton is often viewed as an inheritor of Arnold and Leavis, but is best viewed as a member of a tradition of English thought concerning aesthetics which extends back from T. S. Eliot to Coleridge, Burke, and Sir Philip Sidney. In all of those writers the role of religion is prominent and clear. They may, as in the case of Eliot and Coleridge, have involved journeys from Unitarianism to Christian Orthodoxy. Yet, with the possible exception of Burke, none of those figures is an empiricist. As Scruton admits on the first page of his book

---

[6] Mark Dooley, *Roger Scruton: The Philosopher on Dover Beach* (London: Bloomsbury 2009), p. 110.
[7] Roger Scruton, *Modern Culture* (London: Continuum, 2005), p. 40.
[8] Scruton, *The Soul of the World*, (London: Bloomsbury, 2014), p. 151.
[9] Scruton, *Sexual Desire: A Philosophical Investigation* (London: Phoenix, 1994).
[10] Scruton, *The Face of God: The Gifford Lectures 2010* (London: Continuum, 2012).
[11] Klee, *Schöpferische Konfession*, in Paul Klee, *Schiften: Rezensionen und Aufsätze*, edited by Christian Geelhaar (Cologne: Du Mont, 1976), p. 118.
[12] Coleridge, *Biographia Literaria*, eds W. Jackson Bate and James Engell (Princeton, NJ: Princeton University Press, 1985), II, p. 7.

on Imagination, aesthetics tends to be the stronghold of Idealism, especially in its Platonic form. He, by contrast, is working within an empiricist mode. Yet aesthetics for Scruton is a relentless struggle against the reductionism of contemporary scientism and he is adamant that literature and culture nourish philosophy. Contemporary philosophy in many forms, however, has become the handmaiden of the hard sciences. The implications are dire: 'Language and science are abbreviations of reality; art is an intensification of reality.'[13] Without that intensification of reality which the arts bring with them, our humanity is diminished.

It has been shrewdly remarked that Scruton presents aesthetics as revealing the purpose and intelligibility of the world in the way that used to be catered for by natural theology. It is art and our sense of the beautiful that provides an awareness of the world that exhibits meaning and consolation, a world that we can feel at home in. In this respect, Scruton belongs to the Platonic strand, or even what Coleridge called 'Spiritual Platonic Old England'.[14] One of the great legacies of Platonism has been in the aesthetic domain. Plato's writings are imbued with the sacred dimension of beauty and Plotinus develops the theory of beauty that captivates the great poets, sculptors and painters of the Renaissance and the Romantic era.

Sartre on Imagination

In his first book, *Art and Imagination* (1974), Roger Scruton developed a precise theory of the imagination and puts it to the service of an aesthetic theory. While he uses the style and techniques of analytic philosophy, there is nevertheless the imprint of Sartre on this early work. Scruton uses the language of Wittgenstein ('seeing as') and Frege ('unasserted thought') but his theory resembles that of Sartre in various ways. Scruton admits to a deep but highly ambivalent attraction to Sartre, obviously one of his deepest influences.

---

[13] Ernst Cassirer, *An Essay on Man: An Introduction to a Philosophy of Human Culture* (New Haven: Yale, 1944), p. 143.
[14] Coleridge, *The Notebooks of Samuel Taylor Coleridge* vol. II, §2598.

We can draw a broad distinction between a generic or universal and a special theory of the imagination. Kant and Hume constitute typical examples of a generic theory of the imagination as pervading perception. Sartre and Wittgenstein represent instances of the special theory. On such a special theory, imagining constitutes a very special form of perceiving. Scruton supports such a special account. Sartre in his work *L'imaginaire: psychologie phenomenologique de l'imagination*[15] presents a critique of both:

1. Descartes's limited view: imagination as 'decayed sense'.
2. Husserl: the conflation of imagination and perception.

In opposition to these inadequate extremes, Sartre attempts to establish a *tertium quid*. Firstly, the imagination is not an extra component to consciousness and the image is not spatially 'within' the realm of consciousness. Imagination is rather a different kind of consciousness: indeed a mode of, or act of consciousness, rather than a container, as it were, of *quasi* objects (like Ryle). This is what he famously calls the 'illusion of Immanence'. Secondly, the object of imagination for Sartre is a quasi perception – it has perceptual characteristics but differs from perception. For example, we cannot be surprised by the imagination. There are no surprises and disappointments when we are imagining. Furthermore, the object of imagination is itself 'nothing'. This nothingness is the basis of freedom. As Mary Warnock observes, 'it is impossible to exaggerate the importance which Sartre attaches to the power of denial, of asserting not only what is but what is not the case'.[16] Mankind is the '*l'être par qui le Néant arrive dans le monde*'.[17]

Without the capacity to imagine, Sartre avers, life would be dictated by the real. It is because consciousness is able to posit the *irréel*, that it can escape the dictates of the world. Finally, we have the passivity of perception. We discover the object of perception. Imagination is spontaneity (but a pre-volitional kind). Imagined objects disappear as soon as we stop thinking of them. Sartre uses the example of Peter as imagined. If he actually comes into the field of vision, the

---

[15] Sartre, *L'imaginaire: psychologie phenomenologique de l'imagination* (Paris: Gallimard, 1940).
[16] Mary Warnock, 'Introduction' to Jean-Paul Sartre, *The Psychology of the Imagination* (London: Routledge, 1972), p. xvi.
[17] Sartre, *L'Être et le néant* (Paris: Gallimard, 1957), p. 59.

'image' of Peter in the imagination disappears. Sartre is concerned to posit a distinctive region of the imaginary and this provides a basis for his theory of art. His study of the imagination reveals an objective human activity grounded in our capacity to find consolation in the *irréel*. The work of art is an irreality (189/363); and beauty itself is a value that can only ever be applied to the imaginary (371).[18]

Sartre and Scruton

'Mystérieuse faculté que cette reine des facultés! ... L'imagination est la reine du vrai, et le possible est une des provinces du vrai. Elle est positivement apparentée avec l'infini.'[19]

When turning to Scruton's theory of imagination, let us remind ourselves that the arguments of *L'imaginaire* depend upon a contrast posited between imagination and perception. The radical distinction between imagination and the items of belief is key to Scruton's theory. He stresses the distinctively 'aesthetic attitude': the aesthetic response is characterized by the fact that we are not responding to a real object but an imaginary one. He writes: 'My experience of a work of art involves a distinctive order of intentionality, derived from imagination and divorced from belief and judgement.'[20]

1. Scruton identifies imagination as 'unasserted thought'. It should not be identified with what is 'given' to the senses but what we can summon.
2. Imagination is a rational endeavour and there are appropriate employments of it. Scruton takes the example of Marcus Aurelius. His admiration for the great Emperor infuses his attention to the bust.

'In aesthetic appreciation we might say that the perception of an object is brought into relation with a thought of the object ... this is one of the main

---

[18] Jens Bonnemann, *Der Spielraum des Imaginaren* (Hamburg: Meiner, 2007), esp. pp. 421ff.
[19] C. Baudelaire, *Curiosités esthétiques*, 'Salon de 1859', éd. Garnier, 1962, III, p. 321; Baudelaire *Selected Writings on Art and Artists*, trans. P. E. Charvet (Cambridge: Cambridge University Press, 1972), pp. 298ff: 'What a mysterious faculty is this queen of the faculties ... Imagination is the queen of truth, and the possible is one of the provinces of truth. Imagination is positively related to the infinite.'
[20] Scruton, *Art and Imagination: A Study in the Philosophy of Mind* (London: Methuen, 1974), p. 77.

activities of the imagination ... an aesthetic attitude towards a present object will lead to the thought and emotions characteristic of imagination ... the object serves as a focal point on which many different thoughts and feelings are brought to bear.'[21] However, the imagination is appreciating an aesthetic object 'for its own sake'. While the imaginative engagement is free, the appropriate experiencing is constrained.

Scruton's special theory of the imagination guarantees the unique status of human beings as opposed to the Hume/Kant theory.[22] If we have this capacity to posit unreal objects and to dwell upon aesthetic realms, then this is a capacity which distinguishes us from other animals. It is grounded in the *consciousness* of the irreality of its objects. However, if we conflate imagination and perception, this central defining aspect of human life, the ability to conjure the unreal and to contrast it with the real becomes lost. An animal can see but cannot imagine. Yet if we conflate imagination and perception, according to Scruton, we seem forced into the highly implausible position of denying perception to animals.

Scruton emphasizes the voluntary nature of imagination as giving a key to the creative imagination. He employs the example of Flaubert who:

> Set himself to imagine what it would be like for someone of a vain romantic disposition to be married to a country doctor in provincial France, he did not tell a story about the likely consequences of such a marriage. He chose the details of his story in the light of what he thought to be most revealing an expression of the provincial state of mind, whether or not such details were in any way likely to occur.[23]

The quality of the imaginative is that which goes beyond the facts. From this source, on Scruton's account, we have the capacity to have moral and aesthetic experience. This is fundamental for Scruton's contrast between Fantasy and Imagination. Imagination is a way of understanding reality through art whereas fantasy is a flight from reality. Fantasy is based upon feelings that are real and genuine though generated by non-objects. For the imagination there

---

[21] Scruton, *Art and Imagination*, pp. 154–5.
[22] Of course, Kant's theory of imagination is transcendental and in that sense very distinct from Hume's.
[23] Scruton, *Art and Imagination*, p. 99.

is a contrast. For in 'Imagination: neither feelings nor the Objects are real. The feeling is an imagined response to the imagined object which compels it. In fantasy there is a real feeling which, in being prohibited, compels an unreal object for its gratification.'[24]

In Roger Scruton's work we find both existential restlessness or disquiet and profound and illuminating explorations of sexuality and death. Very much in the Neoplatonic mode, Scruton suggests that Beauty and the sacred are inextricably entwined with the experience of transcendence: they point towards the spirit that hovers over our world. Perhaps there is a Scruton who is caught up in the world of Sartre between the *en-soi* and the *pour-soi* and haunted by the transcendent – like Baudelaire – in a universe in which there are real 'correspondences' between our yearnings and the ultimate structure of the universe. Sartre was a savage critic of Baudelaire's inauthenticity, his failure to develop a properly Promethean view of life. Yet Sartre was fascinated by Baudelaire's view of art as '*le spirituel*'. Christina Howells notes the deep affinity between the aesthetics and the metaphysics of both writers and Sartre's profound admiration for '*le fait poétique baudelairien*'.[25] She points to Baudelaire's sense of the agonistic relationship between mind and world. One might consider the proximity to Scruton's position to Baudelaire's 'Imagination is the queen of truth', or 'what is virtue without imagination?' The aesthetic object is determined by the imagination and the imagination can generate a healing of the rift between thought and being. Art can present a relationship *en-soi-pour-soi* (Being both subject and object) – the coalescence of being and existence.[26]

The Soul of the World

In his excellent recent work *The Soul of the World*, Scruton writes the following:

> For Sartre there is no God to provide the reason for my existence; hence it is I who must provide it, and in doing so I lean on the interpersonal intentionality

---

[24] Scruton, *The Aesthetic Understanding: Essays in the Philosophy of Art and Culture* (South Bend, IN: St. Augustine's Press, 1998), pp. 149ff.
[25] Christina Howells, *Sartre's Theory of Literature* (London: Modern Humanities Research Association, 1979), pp. 48ff.
[26] Howells, op. cit., pp. 52ff.

that points in a religious direction, but to which Sartre gives quite another and infinitely bleaker and more solitary slant. An alert reader of *Being and Nothingness*, which to my mind is a great work of post-Christian theology, will recognize that its true subject matter is the order of creation, in which annihilation and sacrifice confront us at every turn. In this work Sartre is also looking for a way of being that can be espoused completely, in the awareness that, if annihilation comes through 'commitment', it comes rightly and as a gift from the void.[27]

Scruton is surely correct to point to the theological dimension of this celebrated atheist. One obvious source is Augustine, who lies behind the great debates of the seventeenth century and Pascal, as well as behind Kierkegaard's theory of anxiety and Heidegger's *Being and Time*. The forlorn peregrine soul longing for the fullness of Being while wallowing in the mires of the *regio dissimilitudinis*: Augustine's Neoplatonic theology provided the inspiration and backdrop of the 'existentialism' of Pascal, Kierkegaard and Heidegger. In this case, the contrast is between the plenitude of true being and privation of being in the fallen world. Yet there is another, quite distinct sense of nothing, one which also emerges out of the Neoplatonic tradition. This is the emphatic nothing of the *nihil per excellentiam*: 'nothing' as paradoxical expression of the failure of finite language to capture the majesty and plenitude of true being. Yet Scruton compares Sartre's view of self-consciousness-as-nothing with the Neoplatonic view of the Deity in John Scot Eriugena (*nihil per excellentiam*). As Scruton claims: 'It is interesting to note that Scotus is saying of God just what Sartre says of the subject of consciousness. He is locating God in the realm of *le néant*.'[28] Sartre's contrast is between *en-soi* (that which is in itself) and *pour-soi* (that which is self-aware). *Le néant* is not an element in the realm of *en-soi* but *pour-soi*. It is only in the domain of *pour-soi* that *le néant* is significant because for self-conscious creatures, absence and deficiency is a part of lived experience.[29] It is the capacity to detach from the '*plein d'être*' realm of the *en-soi* and to find deficiency or lack in the world, that the desire to reform the world emerges. Sartre finds the justification for his humanism

---

[27] Scruton, *Soul of the World*, p. 188.
[28] Scruton, *Soul of the World*, p. 189.
[29] The *locus classicus* of Sartre's view is the café scene in *L'Être et Le néant*, pp. 44ff.

in such awareness of *le néant* that is determinative for self-conscious free agents. An immensely important part of Roger Scruton's philosophy is the idea of the sacred. Yet his cognitive dualism means that the sacred is consigned to a liminal realm. There is a sense of the sacred which emerges from a Durkheimian conception of the necessary bonds of society. There are occasions when Scruton seems to be upholding a Durkheimian stance:

> We know that we are animals, parts of the natural order, bound by laws which tie us to the material forces which govern everything. We believe that the gods are our invention, and that death is exactly what it seems. Our world has been disenchanted and our illusions destroyed. At the same time we cannot live as though that were the whole truth of our condition.[30]

Referring to the puzzlement felt by many contemporaries about the idea of God, Scruton points to Durkheim's *Elementary Forms of Religious Life* as providing an ingenious answer to this question. The loyalty and sacrifice required by membership of a community generates the sense of the sacred:

> One who is a member sees the world in a new light. All about him are events and demands whose meaning transcends their meaning for him. The destiny of something far greater – something, nevertheless, to which he is intimately bound – is at stake in the world. This thing is something that he loves, and that lives in him. But he is not alone in loving it. He has the support of his fellow members, and he shares with them the burden of a collective destiny. This, Durkheim suggests, is the core religious experience. And it translates at once into a conception of the sacred.[31]

Durkheim is an important presence in Scruton's thought. Membership or belonging is key. Much of Scruton's philosophical energy is expended trying to give an account of what it could mean to be at home in this alienating contemporary world dominated by machines and technology.

Religion, as Durkheim pointed out in his great study of its elementary forms, is a social fact. A religion is not something that occurs to you; nor does it emerge as the conclusion of an empirical investigation or an intellectual

---

[30] Scruton, *Modern Culture* (London: Duckworth, 1999), p. 73.
[31] Scruton, *Modern Philosophy: An Introduction and a Survey* (London: Sinclair-Stevenson, 1994), p. 122.

argument. It is something that you join, to which you are converted, or into which you are born. Losing the Christian faith is not merely a matter of doubting the existence of God, or the incarnation, or the redemption purchased on the Cross. It involves falling out of communion, ceasing to be 'members in Christ', losing a primary experience of home. All religions are alike in this, and it is why they are so harsh on heretics and unbelievers: for heretics and unbelievers pretend to the benefits of membership, while belonging to other communities in other ways.[32]

There is a tension between what we might call the Sartrean-Durkheim dimension of Scruton's thought and the Neoplatonic facet of his work. For Schelling, beauty is the infinite in the finite through images and signs. This view of art as the Counter-image or '*Gegenbild*' of the archetype or '*Urbild*' of the Absolute has its roots in the Neoplatonic aesthetics which we find in Scotus Eriugena. On such a metaphysical basis one can provide a reason for art providing images of transcendent ideals. Yet Scruton's cognitive dualism bars this option. As a result, his position hovers between the doctrine that art can provide a substitute for religion and the conviction that art necessarily points beyond itself to religion. The former works if Sartre and Durkheim can provide a substitute for one's alignment, the latter on the Neoplatonic model of art as an organ of contemplation.

Is Scotus saying of God what Sartre says of the subject of consciousness? This is implausible. Scotus develops the idea of the world as a *theophany*. The *nihil* of John Scot is a *nihil per excellentiam*, that is a God who is no-thing by virtue of his absolute and transcendent plenitude: 'God is the beginning, middle, and end of the created universe. God is that from which all things originate, that in which all things participate, and that to which all things eventually return.'[33] Thus John Scot's vision is the Neoplatonic overflowing of Divine goodness and the free return of the creature to transcendent Goodness through love.[34] How does this vision of great theophany relate to Scruton's cognitive dualism: the radical fact-value distinction that permeates *The Face of God* or *The Soul of the World*? The

---

[32] Scruton, *Gentle Regrets*, p. 221.
[33] Eriugena, *Periphyseon* III.621a–622a.
[34] Hilary Anne-Marie Mooney, *Theophany: The Appearing of God According to the Writings of Johannes Scottus Eriugena* (Tubingen: Mohr-Siebeck, 2009). See also Eric D. Perl, *Theophany: The Neoplatonic Philosophy of Dionysius the Areopagite* (Albany, NY: State University of New York, 2007).

Platonic Imagination (*sit venia verbo*) is an imagination of the *image*. The world is an enigmatic image or reflection of its source which cannot by definition be represented. God is no-thing and yet imprinted upon all creation. Thus, to imagine God is both to strip away all the properties of finite existence and to see God in the world that bears His image. Eriugena's theory of the world as theophany follows Plotinus in asserting that the world is an image of its source. That is to say that the cosmos participates in its transcendent source.[35] In the Neoplatonic account of participation, the effect bears the image of cause.

For Sartre *le néant* is the only respectable palliative to the brute realm of the *en-soi*. Scruton notes wistfully: 'there is an appealing idea about beauty which goes back to Plato and Plotinus, and which became incorporated by various routes into Christianity. According to this idea, beauty is an ultimate value – something that we pursue for its own sake, and for the pursuit of which no further reason need be given. Beauty should therefore be compared to truth and goodness, one member of a trio of ultimate values which justify our rational inclinations. Why believe p? Because it is true. Why want x? Because it is good. Why look at y. Because it is beautiful?'[36] Scruton is, of course, well aware of the assumption 'made explicit in the *Enneads* of Plotinus that truth, beauty and goodness are attributes of the deity'.[37]

Resemblance or Idealization?

It is sometimes claimed that the Platonic criticisms of art as servile copying generated the view of Plotinus shared by Ficino that art should more properly idealize. The process of idealization is linked to the identification of beauty with the intellect (*nous*) or the realm of the Ideas. This is the domain that Middle Platonism identified with the Divine Mind. For Plotinus the domain of ideas is subordinated to the supreme Unity; but for the sake of argument, the mind of God suffices as a description of the realm of the Ideas. They are not abstract universals but the creative energies and powers of the

---

[35] W. Norris Clarke, *The One and the Many: A Contemporary Thomistic Metaphysics* (South Bend, IN: University of Notre Dame, 2001), p. 318.
[36] Roger Scruton, *Gentle Regrets: Thoughts from a Life* (London: Bloomsbury, 2005), p. 2.
[37] Scruton, *Beauty*, p. 4.

transcendent source of Being. The true task of the artist is not to copy the stuff of the physical realm but to envisage their noetic archetypes.

> Thereof as every thing partakes,
> Or more or less by influence divine
> So it more fair accordingly it makes,
> And the gross matter of this earthly mine
> Which encloseth it, thereafter doth refine,
> Doing away the dross which dims the light
> Of that fair beam, which therein is empight.
> Edmund Spenser, *A Hymne in Honour of Beautie*, I, vv. 29–49

As we discussed in Chapter One, Plotinus thinks of the cosmos as a mirror-reflection of the divine rather than as a picture or artificer-image. Moreover, sensation and intellection are part of an ontological continuum:

> For all that meets the bodily sense I deem
> Symbolical, one mighty alphabet
> For infant minds; and we in this low world
> Placed with our backs to bright Reality
> That we may learn with young unwounded ken
> The substance from its shadow.
> Coleridge, *Destiny of Nations,* II, 18–23

Visible beauty and order point to their invisible creator.[38] This is also the basis of the Sufi tradition evinced in Ibn 'Arabi, Suhrawardi and Rumi and their religion of love based on a view of sensuous beauty pointing to a transcendent ineffable source. It is the same tradition as, mutatis mutandis, Dante's vision of Beatrice or the idealization of the female in Pasternak's *Dr Zhivago*.

Is it anachronistic to speak of Plotinus's aesthetics? His concern is beauty. One might think of Platonists as very dismissive of images. For Plato we should distinguish between the distinctively human *episteme* and animal *aisthesis*. The philosopher turns from sensation to contemplating the intelligible world, the 'region above the heaven' of Plato's *Phaedrus* 247. This realm is not material, and the 'eye of the mind', 'the pilot of the soul', should not be

---

[38] Henry Corbin, *Alone with the Alone: Creative Imagination in the Sufism of Ibn 'Arabi*, trans. R. Manheim (Princeton, NJ: Bollingen, 1969).

distracted by such lowly sensibles. Yet this is not the case. There is a surprisingly positive account of images in Plotinus.

In her essay 'Deux noms de l'image en grec ancient: idole et icône', Suzanne Saïd offers a neat explanation of the contrast between the good and the bad senses of image.[39] She has explored in some detail how the philological and philosophical development in ancient Greek thought from the Homeric period to Byzantine theology formed the contrast between icon and idol in their modern senses, sc. positive and pejorative respectively. The defenders of icons saw their enemies as iconoclasts while being accused of idolatry. From the *eidola* of Homer to Book X of Plato's *Republic* (516a) (as opposed to truth 527c) and the Sophist onwards, the *eidolon* is often a snare or bait – it appears to be something that it is not. The icon, by way of contrast, even in Homeric literature has the sense of representing the invisible through the visible. In a sense beauty is a bait – it lures the mind toward the intelligible. As Dante beautifully expresses the same thought many centuries later:

> *La mente innamorata, che donnea*
> *con la mia donna sempre, di ridure*
> *ad essa li occhi piu che mai ardea:*
> *e se natura o arte fe pasture*
> *da pigliare occhi, per aver la mente,*
> *in carne umana o nelle sue pitture,*
> *tutte adunate, parrebber niente*
> *ver lo piacer divin che mi refulse,*
> *quando mi volsi al suo viso ridente.*
> *E la virtu che lo sguardo m'indulse,*
> *del bel nido di Leda mi divelse,*
> *e nel ciel velocissimo m'impulse.*[40]

Dante is using the erotic imagery of Leda and the swan, and the reference to the 'eyes of my lady' is in the tradition of Petrarch and Laura, and Ibn

---

[39] Suzanne Saïd, Deux noms de l'image en grec ancient: idole et icône *Comptes rendus des séances de l'Academie des Inscriptions et Belles-Lettres*, v. 131, v. 2 (1987), 309–30.

[40] The enamoured mind that wooes my Lady continually burned more than ever to bring back my eyes to her; and if nature or art have made baits to take the eyes so as to possess the minds, in human flesh or in its portraiture, all these together would seem nothing beside the divine delight that shone on me when I turned to her smiling face. And the virtue that her look granted me drew me forth from the fair nest of Leda and thrust me into the swiftest of the heavens.

'Arabi. This theo-erotic theme is not deployed by Plotinus in this manner which required the courtly love tradition of medieval Europe. As evinced by Spenser's *Faierie Queen* and Shakespeare's 'From women's eyes this doctrine I derive: They sparkle still the right Promethean fire; They are the books, the arts, the academes, That show, contain and nourish all the world', are all in this tradition of the eternal feminine as *image* of eternal beauty.[41]

Plotinus likes to employ images as models for non-discursive intuition. He insists upon this point while maintaining the provisional nature of these images. The process described is one of meditating upon the image and purifying the image.

John Dillon has argued convincingly that there are two imaginations in Plotinus.[42] There is a legitimate imagination of the noetic as well as the imagining of the sensible. This higher imagination revolves around what Dillon calls 'dynamic images'; these require the active, creative use of the imagination for the clearer grasping of a truth which transcends all sense perception, though one must start from physical images in one's ascent to understanding. These are not propositional imaginings (like considering Othello's jealousy or a world without secondary qualities) but deliberate thinking with specific images. Some of these images are traditional mythological ones. The mythic image of the keen eyed Lynceus, 'who saw into the inside of the earth', for example (*Ennead* V8 4) is an important example of this.[43] In a discussion of the expression of the higher in the lower (*logos* in matter) Plotinus says:

> What image of it, then, could one take? For every image will be taken from something worse. But the image must be taken from Intellect, so that one is not really apprehending it through an image, but it is like taking a piece of gold as a sample of all gold, and if the piece taken is not pure, purifying it in act or word by showing that not all this sample is gold, but only this particular portion of the whole mass; here it is from the intellect in ourselves when it has been purified,

---

[41] See Charles Williams, *The Figure of Beatrice: A Study in Dante* (New York: Noonday, 1961).
[42] John Dillon, 'Plotinus and the Transcendental Imagination', in *Religious Imagination*, ed. James Mackey (Edinburgh: Edinburgh University Press, 1986), pp. 55–64.
[43] Paul Zanker, Björn Christian Ewald, *Mit Mythen Leben: Die Bilderwelt der roemischen Sarkophage* (Munich: Hirmer, 2004). Compare the image in Emerson of the 'transparent eyeball' as a model of the breaking down of subject and object in a state of contemplation in his 1836 essay 'Nature'. Ralph Waldo Emerson, *Works* (Cambridge: Harvard Press, 1980) 2: 10–11.

or if you like, from the gods, that we apprehend what the intellect in them is like. (*Ennead* V8[31].4, 13–22. (Armstrong))

The term is *eikon*. Saïd's contrast does not seem to work. The point is how one uses the icon rather than any fixed linguistic distinction between *eikon* and *eidolon*. Indeed, *eidolon* is frequently employed for the soul, which would be puzzling if it were generally a negative term for Plotinus:

> So much, then, for the beauties in the realm of sense, images (*eidola*) and shadows (*skiai*), which so to speak, sally out and come into matter and adorn it and excite us when they appear.[44]

Plotinus's terminology is quite fluid. It is the context and the metaphysical direction of the terms that is really significant. If pointing away from the transcendent and sacred source or *principium*, the image can generate delusion. As an instrument of anagogy, however, the ascent of the soul, it is a vehicle of genuine insight. Through Ficino and the meditation on this Platonic-Plotinian theme of theo-erotics, we find this theme in the English Romantics:[45]

> And lovely apparitions, dim at first,
> Then radiant, as the mind arising bright
> From the embrace of beauty (whence the forms
> Of which these are phantoms) casts on them
> The gathered rays which are reality –
> Shall visit us, the progeny immortal
> Of Painting, Sculpture, and rapt Poesy,
> And arts, though unimagined, yet to be.[46]

Coleridge defines imagination as the 'repetition in the finite mind of the eternal act of creation in the infinite I AM':[47] the human imagination as repetition is a reflection or *mirror* of the infinite, and it is often fired by the intimation of transcendence in the experience of beauty and the holy. To see with the eye of imagination is to grasp truth, even if its reality is obscure

---

[44] Plotinus, *Ennead*, I 6.
[45] I am grateful to Dr Leornard Lewissohn for this term.
[46] Shelley, *Prometheus Unbound*, III iii, 49–56.
[47] Coleridge, *Biographia Literaria* (Princeton, NJ: Bollingen, 1983), 1, p. 304.

or invisible to empirical perception. As a young man, Coleridge wandered the Quantocks and, amidst the verdant glory of the hills of Exmore and the cerulean splendour of the Bristol channel at Culbone, conjured a vision of Xanadu. Yet even the milk of paradise, or the laudanum!, was working upon a real landscape of 'forests ancient as the hills' and 'caverns measureless to man'. The 'deep romantic chasm' of the Somerset 'cedarn forests' overhanging a place 'as holy and enchanted' shows that Coleridge *sees* the eternal in or through the temporal. For Coleridge, as for any other Platonist, the sacred is neither the cement of social life nor the taboos that bond individuals into a community: the sacred is the beauty of holiness, that beauty which the poet has always considered his special privilege. If there is a legitimate sense of the holy, and Scruton is one of the eloquent advocates of its centrality in human experience, it must be grounded in a transcendent source. Otherwise, once reduced to a merely social or anthropological fact, it will wilt and wither. Hierophany, if it is not ultimately *theophany*, is an *ignis fatuus*.

Zwei Seelen wohnen, ach! in meiner Brust
'Two souls dwell, ah! In my breast'
(Goethe, *Faust*, 1808, Scene 2, prelude)

Scruton has been a fierce critic of theories of the imagination which conflate perception and imagination. That is the basis of his commitment to the Sartrean-Wittgensteinian special theory of the Imagination. The *imaginatio vera* of a Coleridge or Ficino is the intermediary between thinking and being. While the absolute source of all being remains inaccessible, or as Eriugena says, '*nihil*', it is manifested in the created order. The human imagination can have a noetic value insofar as it apprehends through symbols the veiled essence of the Divine. The mistake of design arguments for the existence of God is to claim too much. God is not revealed unambiguously from the world. God cannot be inferred from the world but must be imagined as its source and *telos*. And if the world is the product of a contemplating mind, it is art that recognizes this. Imagination, on this view, is a means of mediating between Being and Becoming. Rather than the either/or of reality and unreality in Scruton's empiricism, the Platonists offer a both/and of a world that bodies forth its divine archetype. Imagination, or in its highest sense – 'reason in her most exalted mood' as Wordsworth in *The Prelude* has it, is the capacity for seeing the archetype in the Image while recognizing the integrity of the image as an instantiation or particular. The particular privilege of art is to point beyond its material presence and thus to intimate the spiritual dimension, the awareness of the sacred which Scruton has done so much to rehabilitate. More than any other contemporary thinker, he has shown how Imagination is also important as a source of transformation: 'the possible's slow fuse is lit by the imagination' (Emily Dickinson).[48] The transformation of self is significant for Scruton's theory of art. He points out that Fafner the giant becomes Fafner the dragon. The metamorphosis is metaphysically impossible and yet is truthful on a moral or spiritual plane. But Poetry cannot redeem. If this engagement is more than a Sartrean palliative of existence, hierophany must be transformed into theophany.

Scruton's account can seem rather gloomy and pessimistic, like an elegy for lost culture. If you consider Christianity exclusively in its dogmatic or institutional expressions, one can obtain a deeply misleading view of European culture as one of radical disenchantment. When one recognizes, however, the power of certain images and symbols to permeate the culture, the overall 'picture' changes accordingly. The speeches of American presidents, the rituals and oaths of the British parliament, the architecture of Russian Orthodoxy mirror in myriad ways a rich and diverse Christian culture, even for and to those who do not enter a place of worship or entertain beliefs about God and the soul. The Munich theologian Jörg Lauster speaks of Christianity as the language of continuous enchantment of the world ('*Sprache einer kontinuierlichen Verzauberung der Welt*').[49] He argues forcefully that Christianity is more than dogma and institutions. Gregorian chants, the sculptures of Michelangelo, the novels of Dostoevsky, are all elements of deeply Christian imaginary that have profoundly influenced Modernity.

This legacy of the Christian imaginary can sometimes be evinced in foreboding and apparently saturnine art. The deep and enduring legacy

---

[48] R. W. Frankin, ed., *The Poems of Emily Dickinson* (Cambridge, MA: Belknap Press, 1999), p. 608.
[49] Jörg Lauster, *Die Verzauberung der Welt. Eine Kulturgeschichte des Christentums* (Munich: Beck, 2014), p. 13.

of the Christian Neoplatonic tradition can be seen in the contemporary Neo-expressionist painter Anselm Kiefer. His grand canvasses and massive installations, with scorched ruins and desolate landscapes with mere hints of human habitation, beget a sense of wonder and transcendence amidst the chaos and rage of human history. It has been remarked that his work has echoes of the great genre of historical painting of the eighteenth and nineteenth centuries with its ambitions of spiritual edification. In opposition to the radical rejection of narrative and symbolism in much twentieth-century avant-garde art, Neo-Expressionism employed and revitalized historical and mythological images: 'Kiefer's work can be read as a sustained reflection on how mythic images function in history, how myth can never escape history, and how history in turn has to rely on mythic images.'[50]

Kiefer, as Werner Beierwaltes has convincingly argued, constitutes a striking instance of this dimension of the Neoplatonic legacy in contemporary art.[51] Is this Neoplatonism or its evisceration?[52] There is a powerful mood of loss and melancholy in his paintings, but the presence of the heavenly or the transcendent haunts his scarred landscapes.

His canvas entitled 'Emanation' (1984–6) in the Walker Art Centre represents a dark sky above a brooding sea. A large central strip of molten lead refers, it seems, to the book of Exodus: 'By day in a pillar of cloud ... and by night in a pillar of fire' (Exod. 13.21). It is a vision of primordial creativity 'aching for form'.[53] It is a meditation upon creation. *Die Ordnung der Engel* (*The Hierarchy of Angels*) (1985–7) is a reference to the 'celestial hierarchy' of Pseudo-Dionysius the Areopagite. The title is engraved in this sombre dark grey-brown work in which nine rocks of lead are used to represent the heavenly ranks.

---

[50] Andreas Huyssen, 'Anselm Kiefer: The Terror of History, the Temptation of Myth', *October* 48 (Spring 1989): 27.
[51] W. Beierwaltes, 'Some Remarks about the Difficulties in Realizing Neoplatonic Thought in Contemporary Philosophy and Art', in *Neoplatonism and Contemporary Thought*, ed. R. Baine Harris, (Albany, NY: State University of New York), vol. II, pp. 269–84.
[52] I owe this point to Gretchen Reydam-Schils.
[53] I am grateful to Charles Taliaferro for this phrase. Jil and Charles Taliaferro were kind to accompany me to the basement of the Walker to show me the canvas.

The Enlightenment Legacy: Facts and Imagination

> The reason why the civilisation of 1600–1900, based on natural science, found bankruptcy staring it in the face was because, in its passion for ready-made rules, it had neglected to develop that kind of insight which alone could tell it what rules to apply, not in a situation of a specific type, but in the situation in which it actually found itself. It was precisely because history offered us something altogether different from rules, namely insight, that it could afford us the help we needed in diagnosing our moral and political problems.[54]

Reflection upon the nature of the aesthetic image of the world can have great theological pertinence.[55] One might compare Collingwood with Coleridge's cognate complaint about the 'barren fig tree of the mechanic philosophy'[56] and the 'OVERBALANCE OF THE COMMERCIAL SPIRIT' since 1688.[57] Such 'insight' required in historical judgement, morality or politics is essentially imaginative rather than deductive or inductive, though it must not be confused with make-believe or fantasy. Consider the following example. The proposition 'Rome is the capital of Italy' is true independent of any first person experience of the city on the Tiber. Imaginings or fantasies about that city seem prima facie remote from knowledge of the truth. Yet one can imagine witnessing certain events or facts from the first person. While in the 'mind's eye', one can travel in space and time, such a capacity to imagine events seems to conflict with the 'facts'. However, it is obvious that 'knowing' that Rome is the capital of Italy does not constitute much valuable knowledge. A child might learn in geography lessons that Rome is the capital of Italy and yet fail to link this true fact to any other aspects of the boot-shaped Mediterranean country or the rest of the world. Only when the child associates the name with the greatest empire of the ancient world, the forging of medieval Western Europe; or modern Italy, does the bare 'fact' start to constitute knowledge. The child who can make imaginative links between the ancient seven hills

---

[54] Robin Collingwood, *An Autobiography* (Oxford: Clarendon, 1999), p. 101.
[55] K. E. Boulding, *The Image: Knowledge in Life and Society* (Ann Arbor, MI: University of Michigan Press, 1961).
[56] Coleridge, *The Lay Sermons*, ed. R. T. White (Princeton, NJ: Princeton University Press, 1973), p. 109.
[57] Coleridge, *The Lay Sermons*, p. 171. I am grateful to James Vigus for this observation.

and the fratricide of Romulus and Remus, the assassination of Julius Caesar, the grandeur of Augustus and the madness of Nero, the aqueducts and roads, legionaries and the Pax Romana, gladiators and martyrs, will understand more about the dominant culture of antiquity and its formative legacy in modern life. Good teachers know this instinctively: the desire to know is awakened by imagination.

The example of the child learning the true proposition p, where p is simply the fact that Rome is the capital of Italy, reveals the importance of self-awareness. With human agents, what they sensed or experienced is at least as important as what occurred. Why Caesar crossed the Rubicon or why Hannibal did not attack Rome after victory at Cannae are impossible to address without considering the aims and interests of these generals. Even if, like Tolstoy, we wish to challenge naïve conceptions of historical agency, the profound and precious role of imagination in assessing history cannot be gainsaid.

The capacity to engage imaginatively with history presupposes the capacity to extricate the 'self' from its immediate environment and explore other realms. Theatre, the novel and cinema are intriguing instances of this capacity to inhabit another realm. We need to distinguish between signs and symbols. All animals are affected by signs. The dog sees her master returning home as a sign of likely feeding; the horse the riding crop as a message about an impending beating. Information is conveyed by such natural signs and the animal kingdom operates on the basis of such communication of signs. The symbolic realm opened by the forms of specifically human communication as engaged by the human imagination, not just the finite realm of the immediate environment, but the infinite space of the imagination with its capacity for lost, non-existent or potential domains. The specific vocal equipment necessary for the creation of a wide range of sounds (tongue, vocal chords, etc) are possessed only by human beings. Oddly, birds can imitate human sounds while our nearest kin in the primate world cannot produce the requisite sounds for physiological reasons.[58] The imagination is ubiquitous: 'Regarded as names for a certain kind or level of experience, the words consciousness

---

[58] Iain McGilchrist, *The Master and his Emissary* (New Haven: Yale, 2010), p. 101.

and imagination are synonymous.'[59] Perception of an object always involves more than sense data, but the imagining of properties which are not disclosed to the senses, or noticing what is seen. Hence there is a continuity between the imaginative component in habitual perceptual experience and artistic vision. R. G. Collingwood observes: 'Only a person who paints well can see well; and … conversely only a person who sees well can paint well.'[60] He suggests that 'one paints a thing in order to see it':

> This seeing refers not to sensation but to awareness. Awareness presupposes sensation but involves self-consciousness and the power of the mind itself. Rather than the power of the sensation on the mind (imagine here a raw pain), the mind is asserting itself upon the data of experience, not as a group of unrelated items but as 'a single indivisible unity'. [61]

This seems the opposite of Freud's theory of the artist finding compensation and escape from reality through inventive fantasy. The imagination is closely linked to the question of the inner and outer worlds. As self-conscious beings, we possess a distinctive perspective particular to the subject. The relationship between this inner world, known to introspection, and the external world of other agents and objects is mediated through imagination. I cannot 'know' that honey tastes just as sweet to my neighbour as it does to me; I cannot know that the passer-by will feel pain if I tread on his or her foot but I can imagine that they will. The work of the imagination in relation to the operations of intentional agents is often much more complex than that of objects in the world, and hence the particular pleasure and power of the dramatic imagination in theatre or the novel.

Art, Consolation and Metaphysics

Historically, art and religion have often been closely linked. Many of the objects which one observes in museums were originally in temples or churches. An integral element in this deep but ambivalent relationship between religion

---

[59] R. G. Collingwood, *The Principles of Art* (Oxford: Oxford University Press, 1938), p. 215.
[60] Collingwood, *The Principles of Art*, p. 304.
[61] Collingwood, *The Principles of Art*, p. 223.

and art is clearly the role of the imagination and its relation to metaphysical problems. Shakespeare's paean to the imagination in the speech of Theseus in *A Midsummer's Night Dream* extols the poet's prophetic eye glancing 'from heaven to earth, from earth to heaven' 'bodying forth' and giving shape to 'things unknown'. The imagination becomes, in the Renaissance and again in Romanticism, a vehicle of Divine Revelation. Is there any value left in such metaphysical-theological views of the imagination?

Consider Coleridge's much discussed distinction between Fancy as 'an aggregative and associative power' and Imagination as a 'shaping and modifying power': the Imagination is linked to the unconscious as well as to the will.[62] The imagination is more primordial and inscrutable than Fancy. Fancy is a 'mode of Memory emancipated from the order of time and space'.[63] This is the capacity of the mind to represent and combine remembered images. As such the term 'fancy' is not meant pejoratively; Fancy can have a perfectly respectable and indeed necessary function. It is hard to see how we could negotiate and adapt to the world without the capacity to use memory in this way. Empiricists from Aristotle to Hobbes are correct to emphasize the importance of memory employed to such ends, but wrong to identify this with the imagination in its most important meaning. The synthetic and magical power of imagination is both higher and, as it were, lower, or rather deeper, than Fancy. Imagination is more closely bound to the primordial unconscious power of the soul and to divine inspiration than the mundane Fancy. The activity of Fancy is more narrowly *instrumental*: it furnishes the means by which certain images, 'fixities and definites', are modified through choice for certain ends. The creative Imagination is no agency of expedience or contrivance but is rather the light and energy of soul as it relishes truth: knowledge 'wedded' to feeling. Coleridge's point, however, is that the relatively unproblematic mechanical mental capacity of fantasy (or Fancy as he calls it) should not be confused with the vastly more mysterious vital and creative Imagination, which endeavours to behold reality as a whole.

---

[62] Scruton uses a version of the distinction, in 'Fantasy, Imagination, and the Screen', *Grazer Philosophische Studien* 19' (1983), 35–46, and employs the distinction in his works thereafter.
[63] Coleridge, *Biographia Literaria*, eds James Engell and W. Jackson Bate (Princeton: Princeton University Press, 1983), I, p. 305.

We can draw a helpful parallel with Freud, who thinks of the discontent of civilization as linked to a lack of correlation between the inner and the outer realms of human experience. The inner world of the psyche – the ineluctably subjective point of view – is clearly structured by very early childhood experiences and forces and pressures which the agent can only partially grasp (some aspects of which are revealed enigmatically in dreams). If art can offer a partial reconciliation between the inner and the outer worlds, the artist – in giving outer expression to inner psychic energy – helps the observer gain a sense of understanding and control over his or her own interior turmoil and inchoate anxieties. The artistic imagination experiments with parts in order to create a new and beautiful whole, the attainment of which requires moral effort. The creation of a work of art as world *sui generis* cannot be intelligibly reduced to simple mechanisms of addition and comparison. The poet 'diffuses a tone, and spirit of unity, that blends, and (as it were) *fuses*, each into each, by that synthetic and magical power, to which we have exclusively appropriated the name of imagination.'[64] Parts are seen as a whole through the creative imagination: the 'poet, described in ideal perfection, brings the whole soul of man into activity.'[65] Here, the artistic imagination is not the unshackled expression of emotional forces or the mere receptivity of sensibility; it is a discipline and endeavour to realize one's being. Art for Coleridge is not a skill or craft which effects certain emotions, nor is it the production of certain artefacts, but is the imaginative communication with another rational soul, the 'compact between the poet and his reader,'[66] poetry making us poets. The great twentieth-century Oxford philosopher Collingwood writes in *The Principles of Art*: 'As Coleridge put it, we know a Man for a poet by the fact that he makes us poets. We know that he is expressing his emotions by the fact that he is enabling us to express ours.'[67] Collingwood and Coleridge are following Plotinus in insisting upon the essentially interior or spiritual dimension of art.

Collingwood distinguishes between crafts like the blacksmith's or the tailor's, whereby the craftsman knows what he is doing with the hammer (*pace*

---

[64] Coleridge, *Biographia Literaria*, I, p. 17.
[65] Coleridge, *Biographia*, II, p. 16.
[66] Coleridge, *Biographia*, II, p. 65.
[67] Collingwood, *The Principles of Art*, p. 118. He takes this from Coleridge, *Lit. Lects* I, 251 – my thanks to Peter Cheyne for pointing this out to me.

Heidegger!) and the anvil or the needle and the materials – imposing form upon a certain matter in order to achieve a specific end – with arts where the artist characteristically does not know what he is creating until it finds expression. The unconscious is made conscious of itself through the creative imagination. In the eighteenth century aesthetics became commentary upon Shakespeare among the English. When we come to that important aspect of Romantic criticism – its emphasis upon subjectivity – we often find the invocation of the borderland or recesses of conscious mentality. Shakespeare's imagined figures like Prospero and Hamlet help us to explore the unconscious, or the relation of mind to nature.

Contemporary culture is subtly suffused by images. If the artist is by temperament particularly finely-tuned to these images, that same artist bears a great responsibility.

> Art is not a luxury, and bad art is not a thing we can afford to tolerate. To know ourselves is the foundation of all life that develops beyond the mere psychical level of experience ... Every utterance and every gesture that each one of us makes is a work of art. It is important to each one of us that in making them, however much he deceives others, he should not deceive himself. If he deceives himself in this matter, he has sown in himself a seed which, unless he roots it up again, may grow into any kind of wickedness, any kind of mental disease, any kind of stupidity and folly and insanity. Bad art, the corrupt consciousness, is the true *radix malorum*.[68]

Are these often cruel and titillating worlds of images of much popular art the equivalent of the *panem et circenses* of the Romans? Is this not the reason why the relationship between art and religion has been conflictual, even violent? In Keat's celebrated couplet 'Beauty is truth, truth beauty, – that is all/ Ye know on earth, and all ye need to know' we find the expression of a view widespread in antiquity that beauty must be related to truth. Equally, beauty was thought to be intrinsically related to goodness. The phrase 'the beauty of holiness' in Psalm 29.2 captures this idea, contrasting it with the ugliness of sin. Of course, it is puzzling for many philosophers why or how beauty might be related to truth. Yet, creative fictions of great artistic beauty like the

---

[68] Collingwood, *The Principles of Art*, pp. 284–5.

works of Shakespeare aspire to a certain truthfulness. This is why some of the great Romantics popularized a distinction between imagination and fantasy or 'fancy'. If we wish to highlight the cognitive capacity of the imagination, it is important to distinguish it from those forms of imagination that can throw light upon the world and those fantasies that create a mawkish or cruel make-believe. Our emotions can be deepened or purified by a work of the imagination such that we can gain a clearer understanding of reality, whereas fantasy often indulges and gratifies the emotions without any real challenge or resultant benefit. The great artist is a seer: to contemplate nature fully is to see it as the manifestation of divine attributes. In this contemplation, art mirrors the divine order through the work of imagination. Michelangelo and Bach both produced their finest work under the inspiration of this idea. Anthony Blunt writes of Michelangelo:

> For Michaelangelo it is by means of the imagination that the artist attains to a beauty above that of nature, and in this he appears as a Neoplatonist compared with the rational Alberti. To him beauty is the reflection of the divine in the material world.[69]

One might conclude here with the Greek idea of *charis*. It can mean 'gift' or 'favour', divine 'grace' or 'beauty'. Are these linguistic connections random or meaningful? Though we are now accustomed to disassociate these meanings, they were held together in a unity by our ancestors.[70] 'Grace' is explored in all its senses within the Christian Platonic tradition. The greatest art is not dependent upon tools or mechanical procedures but is grounded in the exercise of humanity's spiritual nature in seeing. The 'seeing' is not to be construed in empiricist terms as the recording of verifiable data but as ineluctably imaginative. Furthermore, earthly beauty bears some analogy to divine glory and the creative activity of the artist reflects God's creation. The inner eye or the imagination can perceive the images of the sensible world as translucent signs of the intelligible domain.[71] Thus we can explain why the beauty of art is so consoling. Such art can reconcile the inner and the external worlds,

---

[69] Blunt, *Artistic Theory in Italy 1450–1600* (Oxford: Oxford University Press, 1962), p. 62.
[70] Martino Rossi Monti, *Il cielo in terra: La grazi fra teologia ed estetica* (Turin: Libreria, 2008).
[71] Plotinus, *Ennead*, I.6[1]1.

and point to a region where the contradictions of experience are resolved. If this consolation is to be genuine, if it is not mere wish fulfilment or temporary gratification of fantasy, it is because art can be a conduit, albeit through a glass darkly, to a supreme transcendent reality.

4

Freedom and the Narrative Image

Assem para et accipe auream fabulam[1]

Pliny

'Qu'est-ce que la vertu sans imagination'[2]

Baudelaire

In his *Areopagita* John Milton described Edmund Spenser as 'our sage and serious poet, whom I dare be known to think a better teacher than *Scotus* or *Aquinas*'.[3] Henry More agreed. Spenser was an epic poet and the claim is fictional narrative can teach. Fiction typically concerns non-existent characters and non-occurring events; it may involve non-existent times and places. Yet since Aristotle philosophers have noted that fiction can have cognitive components. In exploring a work of fiction, one can discover what it is to be like x, where x is an awkward and passionate adopted Russian count, or aboard a doomed whaling expedition from Nantucket for a great white whale. If living a moral life means developing more than a merely nominal assent to certain ethical principles but integrating those principles within one's dispositions and general attitudes, then fiction can quite possibly provide modes of imaginative engagement with the moral life that abstract discourses fail to furnish. Certain novels, says Martha Nussbaum, 'are, irreplaceably, works of moral philosophy'.[4] CS Lewis' novel *Till We Have Faces* is such a work.

Some philosophers are wary of such extravagant claims for the imagination through the instrument of literature: such literature does not provide, after

---

[1] Pliny, letter to Calvisius Epistles book II, 20: 'Prepare a penny and get a golden tale'.
[2] Baudelaire, 'Salon de 1859'. See P. E. Charvet, *Baudelaire, Selected Writings on Art and Artists*, (Cambridge: Cambridge University Press, 1972) p. 300.
[3] *Complete Prose Works of John Milton.* Ed. Don M. Wolfe et al. 8 vols. New Haven: Yale UP, 1953–82. 2:514–17.
[4] Nussbaum, *Love's Knowledge* (Oxford: Oxford University Press, 1990), p. 148.

all, propositional knowledge. Does all genuine knowledge, however, need to be propositional? Frank Jackson, in a classic thought experiment, imagines a young woman called Mary enclosed in a black and white domain and studying physics in this monochrome world.[5] Assuming Mary's detailed knowledge of the laws of physics, would it be fair to say that she knows what colours look like? If the answer to that is 'no', then it is reasonable to infer that even Mary, who knows all the laws of colour as described in physics, does not possess complete knowledge. This thought experiment provides a powerful argument to deny that all knowledge is propositional. One may acquire some propositional knowledge alongside the non-propositional, for example a knowledge of nineteenth-century Russian life and manners from reading Tolstoy's *War and Peace* or the world of the *American Transcendentalists* from Melville's Moby Dick'.

The Moral Imagination

We will also develop a contrast and comparison between C. S. Lewis (1898–1963) and Bernard Williams (1929–2003); this juxtaposition by analogy is not far-fetched, even if Lewis belonged to a previous generation. The first was a conservative Christian apologist and a literary scholar, the second a consciously secular philosopher and culturally a 'progressive' thinker.[6] Both studied *Literae Humaniores* or 'Greats' at Oxford, where they enjoyed a formidable training in both ancient philology and philosophy. The legacy of the Greeks is momentous for both, as is the intertwining of philosophy and literature – albeit in significantly different ways. Both writers stress the importance of imagination in serious thought and hostile to narrow rationalism. For both men, the great traditions of humanism and literature were living forces. Both writers could say of the Greeks, as did Williams forthrightly: 'They do not merely tell us about themselves. They tell us about us. They do that in every case in which they can be made to speak, because they tell us who we are.'[7]

---

[5] Frank Jackson, 'What Mary Didn't Know', *Journal of Philosophy* 83 (1986): 291–5.
[6] See my comparison in *Living Forms of the Imagination*, (London: T&T Clark, 2008), pp. 206ff.
[7] Bernard Williams, *Shame and Necessity*, 2nd edn (Berkeley: University of California, 2008),

The differences are, however, far-reaching and instructive. When the term 'imagination' is used of Lewis, we should recall the theological resonance of the word, as in Coleridge or Burke. In many respects Lewis is appealing to the 'moral imagination' that has been eroded by the scientific revolution, the Enlightenment and the French Revolution. He shares the sentiment expressed beautifully by Burke as the 'moral imagination' and its onslaught by Enlightenment rationalism:

> All the decent drapery of life is to be rudely torn off. All the superadded ideas, furnished from the wardrobe of a moral imagination, which the heart owns, and the understanding ratifies, as necessary to cover the defects of our naked shivering nature, and to raise it to dignity in our own estimation, are to be exploded as a ridiculous, absurd, and antiquated fashion.
>
> On this scheme of things, a king is but a man; a queen is but a woman; a woman is but an animal; and an animal not of the highest order. All homage paid to the sex in general as such, and without distinct views, is to be regarded as romance and folly ...
>
> On the scheme of this barbarous philosophy, which is the offspring of cold hearts and muddy understandings, and which is as void of solid wisdom as it is destitute of all taste and elegance, laws are to be supported only by their own terrors, and by the concern which each individual may find in them from his own private speculations, or can spate to them from his own private interests. In the groves of *their* academy, at the end of every vista, you see nothing but the gallows ...
>
> Nothing is more certain than that our manners, our civilization, and all the good things which are connected with manners, and with civilization, have, in this European world of ours, depended for ages upon two principles; I mean the spirit of a gentleman, and the spirit of religion.[8]

The vaunted realism of 'this barbarous philosophy, which is the offspring of cold hearts and muddy understandings', what Coleridge contemptuously referred to as the Anglo-Gallic philosophy of the Enlightenment, in fact leads to the evisceration of ethics. The problems of weal and woe, human passions, the development of character, the ends of the will, cannot be decided by considerations of a narrowly intellectual kind. It is through the

---

pp. 19–20.
[8] Edmund Burke, *Reflections on the Revolution in France*, ed. J. G. A. Pocock (Indianapolis: Hackett, 1987) pp. 66–7.

imagination that we try to apprehend reality as a whole in its concrete reality. Various recent philosophers have argued that questions of personal identity, purpose and value require a narrative structure. MacIntyre has noted that narrative is the key principle for explaining actions rather than events, and that narrative accounts are distinct from explanations in the natural sciences. The notorious problems faced by empiricist accounts of the self in terms of punctual psychological states – from Locke and Hume to Parfit – arise from this failure to grasp the centrality of narrative for the self: 'The unity of a human life is the unity of narrative quest.'[9] The point made by MacIntyre is not antirealist. It is not that the identity of the self is constituted by narrative, or even that narrative is more fundamental than personal identity. He says their relationship is one of 'mutual presupposition'.[10] A self-conscious person existing through *time* needs a way of representing episodes in a life in terms of the reasons, values, interests and obsessions of the self. Charles Taylor has also offered a view of ethics as requiring a narrative of value. In his *Sources of the Self* he claims the self requires an orientation through narrative. There is much to commend this view. Galen Strawson has been one of the most influential critics of the narrative theory of the self. Strawson distinguishes between the 'psychological narrativity thesis' and 'the ethical Narrativity thesis' and notes that the first could be interpreted as rendering the second otiose. If we naturally produce narratives of the self, what is there to be endorsed?[11] Strawson argued that both accounts are inadequate. There is no philosophical reason to accept the descriptive account of the self but also no reason to accept the normative claim. Strawson presents two kinds of personality. Firstly there is the *diachronic*, where persons are likely to view themselves as identified and fused with their past and future selves. There is however, also the *episodic* type. This is the sort of person who refuses to imagine the self '*hic et nunc*' as an element in a unitary sequence emerging from the past and extending into the future.

> I think that those who think in this way are motivated by a sense of their own importance or significance that is absent in other human beings. Many of them,

---

[9] MacIntyre, *After Virtue* (London: Duckworth, 1981), p. 203.
[10] MacIntyre, loc. cit.
[11] Strawson, *Ratio* 2004, 17, 4, pp. 428–52.

connectedly, have religious commitments. They are wrapped up in forms of religious belief that are – like almost all religious belief – really all about self.[12]

Strawson's position has a normative dimension. The 'narrativity camp' is occupied by fussy, selfish, controlling, diachronic types, whereas the episodic alternative has a more relaxed, bohemian and altruistic episodic population. We are, according to Strawson, potential self-fabulists, but this is not a prescription for the good life. One does not have to be committed to the view of the narrative as a straightjacket. The process of forging a unity will necessarily be often *extempore* and spontaneous.[13] Each agent is not simply an actor but an author and co-author with others.[14] In another memorable phrase, MacIntyre insists that 'stories are lived before they are told'.[15] What about the challenge of egoism? The need for an evaluative framework or what Charles Taylor calls a 'moral space' is linked to the need to identify and internalize values. Integrity has the etymology of wholeness or unity (*integer*). That does not require some spurious Archimedean Point, but it does require a capacity for relating proximate desires, challenges or pressures to higher order values. Frankfurt's famous designation of agents who cannot evaluate their desires in terms of higher order volitions as 'wantons' is appropriate for psychopathies like the borderline personality disorder. While neurosis is the inability to adapt to the environment and modify one's behaviour in a positive way, and psychosis is failure to grasp reality, the borderline is characterized through a lack of a core self exhibited through signs of emotional instability, feelings of emptiness, and erratic and unpredictable behaviour. A typical characteristic of the borderline personality disorder is the incapacity to hold together the negative and positive aspects of persons. Friends or acquaintances are typically either idolized or demonized. Indeed, this black and white perception of other and the self is linked to a terror of abandonment, self-loathing and manipulative behavior.[16] There is perhaps a failure to imagine shades of character in oneself or others. The typically disturbed patterns of

---

[12] Strawson, *Ratio* 2004, 17, pp. 428–52.
[13] Anthony Rudd, 'In Defence of Narrative', *European Journal of Philosophy* 17, 1 (2009), 60–75.
[14] Strawson, p. 199.
[15] MacIntyre, p. 211.
[16] Jonathan Sklar, *Landscapes of the Dark* (London: Karnac Books, 2011).

attachment of the borderline seem to be linked to failure of narrative: their lives seem like fragmented episodes.[17]

It can also be argued that not just our selves but our world is structured by story. Contemporary culture has been shaped by counter-narratives that have emerged out of the Renaissance and Enlightenment. Often an abstract principle is conveyed with more force through a story. Lewis's philosophy is based upon a particular view of the continuity of esteem and the value of a received tradition: his is a Christian humanism committed to an objective moral order that can be seen in his philosophy of the Tao – committed to enduring standards, or what Cudworth called 'Eternal and Immutable Morality'.[18] It is the imagination alone which can combine the sensuous with the super-sensuous domain of the ethical. Only through the imagination can the antagonisms and tensions of immediate, lived, experience of weal and woe and the 'higher law' of universal and persisting ideals of justice and goodness be reconciled and atoned.

Bernard Williams's critique of the Morality System constitutes one the most eloquent and elegant attempts in recent philosophy to reconsider the relevance of ancient Greek tragedy for contemporary ethics. Autonomy and guilt are in this way exposed as radically deficient and systematically misleading terms for a world only 'partially intelligible' to human agency.[19] Admittedly, this is not because, as in Greek tragedy, we are subject to the inscrutable whims of the gods, but as a result of the intricate opacity and intractability of human circumstances. We are 'beyond Christianity' and its 'Kantian and Hegelian legacies', and so:

> We know that the world was not made for us, or we for the world, that our history tells no purposive story, and that there is no position outside the world or outside history from which we might hope to authenticate our activities.[20]

Williams is unambiguous: ethics has no need of a tyrannical overseer. 'Nietzsche's saying, God is dead, can be taken to mean that we should now treat God as a dead person: we should allocate his legacies and try to write an

---

[17] See T. Fuchs, 'Fragmented Selves: Temporality and Identity in Borderline Personality Disorder', *Psychopathology* 40 (2007), 379–87.
[18] C. S. Lewis, *The Abolition of Man* (Oxford: Oxford University Press, 1943), pp. 15ff.
[19] B. Williams, *Shame and Necessity*, p. 164.
[20] B. Williams, *Shame and Necessity*, p. 166.

honest biography of him.'[21] Williams develops the Nietzschean genealogical critique of the inherited institution of the 'morality system' as the contingent upshot of profound philosophical distortions:

> Many philosophical mistakes are woven into morality. It misunderstands obligations, not seeing how they form just one type of ethical consideration. It misunderstands practical necessity, thinking it peculiar to the ethical. It misunderstands ethical practical necessity, thinking it peculiar to obligations. Beyond all this, morality makes people think that, without its very special obligation, there is only inclination; without its utter voluntariness, there is only force; without its ultimately pure justice, there is no justice. Its philosophical errors are only the most abstract expressions of a deeply rooted and powerful misconception of life.[22]

Thus, for Williams, the morality system is distorted by its monolithic nature: the exclusive concentration upon ethical obligations, the failure to account for other types of necessity, the false alternative between overriding obligation and ethical anarchy.

It is clear how deeply opposed the respective positions of Lewis and Williams are. Nietzsche considers the self as a grammatical and ethical fiction. Williams does not present such a radical position as Nietzsche on the metaphysics of the self, but Williams views a fairly similar diagnosis of the metaphysical alienation of physical reality and the substitution of a bogus 'ultimate reality' (e.g. the Forms, or the noumenal world) as a core defect in Western thought.[23] Williams opposes a Whiggish view of inevitable progress that blithely assumes that 'the Greeks had primitive ideas of action, responsibility, ethical motivation, and justice, which in the course of history have been replace by a more complex and refined set of conceptions that define a more mature form of ethical experience.'[24] At the centre of this problematic legacy is the misconception of ethics as 'morality system', the legacy of Plato, Christianity and Kant, with its obsession with obligation, free will and responsibility. Like Nietzsche, Williams believes that free will is an illusion and he is doubtful about responsibility,[25] proposing maturity in the

---

[21] B. Williams, *Ethics and the Limits of Philosophy* (London: Fontana, 1993), p. 33.
[22] B. Williams, *Ethics and the Limits of Philosophy*, p. 196.
[23] Maudemarie Clark, 'On the Rejection of Morality: Bernard Williams's Debt to Nietzsche', in *Nietzsche's Postmoralism: Essays on Nietzsche's Prelude to Philosophy's Future*, ed. Richard Schacht (Cambridge: Cambridge University Press, 2011), p. 2.
[24] Williams, *Making Sense of Humanity*. (Cambridge: Cambridge University Press, 1995), p. 5.
[25] Williams, 2003, pp. 56f.

stead of responsibility. Williams sees himself renewing the Greek concern with how to live rather than Plato's moralized psychology or the Kantian obedience to a moral law. Whereas Plato possessed an ethicized psychology, this was absent in Homer and the tragedians. In one of the most famous tales of ancient philosophy, Glaucon and Adeimantus contemplate the ring of Gyges, a magical ring by which Gyges can become invisible at will and thus immune to shame and punishment. Socrates insists that the soul is affected by evil deeds, even if the body is indiscernible.[26] Lying behind the story is the question whether morality is more than the fear of punishment and disapprobation.

C. S. Lewis, in stark contrast, considers that the erosion of a Christian humanist legacy embodied by Edmund Spenser has left the contemporary at the mercy of a bogus humanism and a narrow rationalism that lacks the spiritual resources of the old Graeco-Roman-Christian conglomerate. Lewis wrote to Barfield in August 1942 that it was the great nineteenth century heresy that love could be 'pure' without undergoing crucifixion and re-birth.[27] The sacrifice must be wrought in the self. There are varieties of love and the mature agent needs to grow to understand in love in order to appreciate the proper demands of conscience.

Till We Have Faces

'for the human being the invisible needs to be represented through something visible'.[28]

C. S. Lewis's *Till We Have Faces* is a retelling of the Cupid and Psyche myth as contained in the novel of Apuleius, *The Golden Ass*. It is 'A myth retold'. There is also the myth within the myth – the story of Venus and Anchises recounted.[29] Lewis deliberately includes various mythological elements in the narrative, such as the avoidance of looking directly at the divine, and the

---

[26] Plato, *Republic*, 2.359a–2.360d.
[27] Hooper, Walter, ed. *The Collected Letters of C. S. Lewis*, Volume II: *Books, Broadcasts, and the War 1931–1949* (HarperOne, 2004), p. 530.
[28] *Kant: Religion within the Boundaries of Mere Reason And Other Writings*, trs. Allen Wood and George di Giovanni (Cambridge: CUP, 2004), §6:192, p. 184.
[29] C. S. Lewis, *Till We Have Faces* (Orlando: Harcourt, 1984), p. 8.

jealousy of the gods. Venus, for example, is jealous in the tale, yet perhaps Lewis is also alluding to the jealous YWHW? Mark Edwards notes that this is a 'literary fable' for Lewis, though it contains powerful mythic elements which Lewis discusses in his *An Experiment in Criticism*, defining myth as a story with the power to move us even if poorly worded.[30] All that essential and indescribable part of man that is called imagination dwells in the realm of symbolism and still lives upon archaic myths and theologies.[31] Some literary stories have a 'mythical quality': *Dr Jekyll and Mr Hyde* or *Lord of the Rings* are examples which Lewis notes. *Till We Have Faces* is a fiction with a deliberate proximity to the mythic.

Orual is the narrator of the novel. Certain images dominate her narrative, such as the Grey Mountain or the statues of the gods. One is reminded of Coleridge, who uses the Aeolian Harp as a model of how the mind can be attuned to nature. It was a piece of fashionable garden furniture, or was placed on open window-sills, and produced sound though the wind. It can serve as a model of how symbols and metaphors can strike the mind before they are understood – as in Gaston Bachelard's acute phrase – 'But the image has touched the depths before it stirs the surface'.[32] For Lewis, thinking in such images is also a way of countering the rationalism of the Greek-Stoic slave in the novel, the Fox. The style of *Till We Have Faces* is one wherein images are meant to exert a primordial power. With reference to the mythic in relation to MacDonald's fiction: 'It gets under our skin, hits us at a level deeper than thoughts or even our passions, troubles oldest certainties till all the questions are re-opened, and in general shocks us more fully awake than we are for most of our lives.'[33] Lewis is using the thought of his day, especially *The Golden Bough*.[34] Freud and Jung are all important for him. Yet his use of myth 'involves the belief that Myth in general is not merely misunderstood history (as Euhemerus thought) nor diabolical illusion (as some of the

---

[30] C. S. Lewis, *Experiment in Criticism* (Cambridge: Cambridge University Press, 1961), pp. 40–2.
[31] Eliade, 1961, p. 19.
[32] Gaston Bachelard, *Poetics of Space*, trs. Maria Jolas (Boston: Beacon, 1994), xxiii.
[33] Mircea Eliade, *Images and Symbols: Studies in Religious Symbolism* (Princeton: New Jersey, Princeton University Press, 1961), p. 19.
[34] See John B. Vickery, *The Literary Impact of The Golden Bough* (Princeton, NJ: Princeton University Press, 1973).

Fathers thought) nor priestly lying (as the philosophers of the Enlightenment thought) but, at its best, a real though unfocussed gleam of divine truth falling on human imagination'.[35] Lewis applies in his novel the principle of the *Interpretatio Graeca*: the idea that various ancient peoples and nations shared the same gods with different names.[36]

Notwithstanding his criticism of the original, Lewis may well have been inspired by the model of Apuleius in this. In *The Golden Ass* of Apuleius, Psyche is the worldly counterpart of the heavenly Venus but is so comely that she is confused for the latter. Venus is jealous of the beautiful mortal Psyche and sends her son Cupid-Love to take revenge on her but he falls in love with her and becomes her lover, while hiding his face and hence identity as a god. Through the guile of her jealous sisters, she is persuaded to look at him and thus loses him. Psyche is then subject to various punishments and various trials of Venus until Cupid rediscovers her. Finally, she is married to Cupid and their child is *voluptas* (pleasure). Why is this story so enthralling for Lewis? I suspect that the philosophical element provides the answer and the key to the theological reworking.

Let us first consider the dimension of image and archetype as explored by Apuleius. Mark Edwards sees Venus as representing 'the inexorability of natural law, to which the soul is subject during periods of embodiment'. He sees Cupid as the beauty of Plato's super-celestial realm depicted in the Phaedrus 'from which erring souls descend and to which they are not allowed to return until they have suffered the appointed term of exile. To grasp prematurely at beauty is to incur a second fall, after which the soul will experience discipline as bondage, nature as fate. On this account, the soul saves herself; in Lewis's revision it is Orual, the ugly sister of Psyche, who expiates her crime.'[37] We have a version of the Neoplatonic view of the soul in a state of exile of its true home. We also have the key theme of beauty from Plato's *Symposium* and *Phaedrus*.[38] In this Platonic tradition the myth portrays 'the soul's capitulation

---

[35] C. S. Lewis, *Miracles, A Preliminary Study* (New York: Macmillan, 1968), p. 134.
[36] See below Chapter Seven.
[37] Mark Edwards, 'The Tale of Cupid and Psyche', *Zeitschrift für Papyrologie und Epigraphik* 94 (1992): 77–94.
[38] Edwards, 'The Tale of Cupid and Psyche'.

to inferior desires'.³⁹ If we find Platonic themes adumbrated in *The Amor and Psyche* of Apuleius, it is also in Ficino and in Spenser that the soul is an *eidolon* – an image of the Divine mind both at a distance from its archetype and longing for its return. The epistemology of longing and the ontology of the image is beautifully expressed by Spenser:

> Fair is the heaven where happy souls have place,
> In full enjoyment of felicity,
> Whence they do still behold the glorious face
> Of the divine eternal Majesty;
> More fair is that, where those Ideas on high
> Enranged be, which Plato so admired,
> And pure Intelligences from God inspired.⁴⁰

There is also the folktale dimension of the tale which Lewis omits. The parallel with *Cinderella* and *Beauty and the Beast* (i.e. elements such as the wicked stepmother or the beast lover). Here the point of the folktale seems quasi erotic – the themes are those of fear and sexuality. In Lewis, such elements are barely developed: we find a very significant reworking and re-imagining. He admits, in particular, to making the palace invisible and shifts the emphasis to the sister.

In the different versions of the myth, Psyche has deep failings, but through love she is redeemed. Psyche is frivolous and Aphrodite takes pity on her. For example, Psyche has boasted that she is more beautiful than Aphrodite, and this arrogant vanity offends the gods. Or she obtains the casket from Underworld – and because of her curiosity opens the casket – then goes to sleep. In Lewis, there is no element of such weakness. There is a marked difference of interpretation of the myth where the god does not want her to see him because of an error on his part. In the ancient myth the god is guilty of transgression, in the Lewis version the mortal woman is unworthy of seeing him. In Lewis's version, the wanderings of Psyche are substituted by the tasks and sufferings of Orual as Queen of a barbaric world. In this imagined ancient realm Lewis writes with a farmyard realism: it is a world where the children

---

³⁹ Edwards, 'The Tale of Cupid and Psyche', p. 92.
⁴⁰ Lilian Winstanley, *Edmund Spenser's The Fowre Hymns* (Cambridge: CUP, 1930), pp. 32–41.

play in snow with the 'stale', or urine of beasts, or there is savage castration of the unfortunate amorous suitor Tarin.

Lewis saw the particular veiled imaginations of Christianity in the archaic pagan myths and the 'Lies of poets'.[41] Bernard Williams derided the gusto and power of Lewis' Christian prose as 'jarringly hearty' and portrayed Lewis as a generally anachronistic and occasionally alarming thinker.[42] The intellectual world of Lewis is the inheritance of a Christian Platonism, with its sources in Coleridge's and Butler's theory of conscience in a 'superior principle of reflection'.[43] Eminent professionally as a scholar of the late medieval and Renaissance period, Lewis is deeply shaped by the English Romantics. There is truth to R. J. Reilly's characterization of Lewis's thought as 'Romantic Religion'.[44] Here we should consider the role of images in thinking.

The Romance Form

Till We Have Faces is a *Bildungsroman* with a mythic dimension. It has elements of popular novels such as those by Rider Haggard and Robert Louis Stevenson. Love, with its different forms, was a theme that Lewis had explored in his scholarly works throughout his career.[45] Edmund Spenser (1552–1599) provides a distinctly and powerfully Platonic precedent in his *Fowre Hymnes, Mutabilitie Cantos, Fairie Queene*.[46] In these works, the themes of the soul, eros and ascent are developed.[47] Like Shakespeare's romances, there is a mixture of realism and fairy tale; one might compare here how the prison in *The Winter's Tale* or the ship in *Pericles* can function as the equivalent of the

---

[41] Lewis, *Till We Have Faces*, p. 8.
[42] Williams, *Essays and Reviews: 1959–2002* (Princeton, NJ: Princeton University Press, 2014), p. 25.
[43] On *The Discarded Image: 1959–2002*, p. 20 we find a reference to Coleridge's *Aids to Reflection* and to Coleridge's terminology: pp. 88, 157, 162 and 165. Butler's conscience (e.g. Sermon II §8) is ubiquitous in Lewis.
[44] R. J. Reilly, *Romantic Religion: A Study of Barfield, Lewis, Williams and Tolkien* (Athens: University of Georgia, 1971).
[45] C. S. Lewis, *The Four Loves* (London: Geoffrey Bles, 1960).
[46] Thomas Hyde, *The Poetic Theology of Love: Cupid in Renaissance Literature* (Newark: University of Delaware Press, 1986).
[47] Thomas Bulger, 'Platonism in Spenser's Mutabilitie Cantos', in *Platonism and the English Imagination*, eds Anna Baldwin and Sarah Hutton, pp. 126–38.

Platonic cave.[48] Chesterton noted that children prefer justice to mercy since they have not lived long enough to need mercy. 'For children are innocent and love justice; while most of us are wicked and naturally prefer mercy.'[49] The theme of mercy and forgiveness is certainly a key element in Shakespeare's late romances.

C. S. Lewis was a celebrated authority on the nature of romance, and there are distinct elements of the romance tradition in *Till We Have Faces* from the sense of the numinous to the idea of the veil. Whereas the philosophical poem has pedigree, e.g. Lucretius, it may seem bizarre to view a romance in philosophical terms. What is romance?[50] There is no conceptual equivalent in Classical Greek or Latin. The themes of romance (or the 'roumant' in its Middle English form) are characteristically love, travel and adventure and there are works in antiquity that fit this description: *The Golden Ass*, *The Alexander Romance*, or *Apollonius of Tyre* could all be considered as ancient forms of romance. What we now think of as the 'novel' may not then have been thought of as a coherent genre.

The *Hymnus Eucharisticus* is a traditional hymn sung by the choir of Oxford Magdalen boy choristers and lay clerks. There is a scene depicting this in Richard Attenborough's film about the life of C. S. Lewis, 'Shadowlands'. The presumed author of the text of the *Hymnus* is Nathaniel Ingelo (1621–83), who published *Bentivolio and Urania* (1660 and 1664), in which the soul's ascent to deiformity and the return to her divine home are presented in a romance. This work stands in the tradition of More's *Platonick Song of the Soul*: 'Bentivolio denotes God's will, from the Italian Bentivoglio. It is us'd by them for a proper name and so it is here for the Brother of Urania, ie. Heavenly Light. By celestial wisdom and Divine Love the Soul passes happily through all states of this World to Immortal perfections and Glories.'[51] Samuel Hartlib (1600–1662, a friend of John Worthington who described the work as 'that excellent scheme of divine morality'), tried to scrounge a copy directly off

---

[48] P. Munoz Simonds, *Myth, Emblem, and Music in Shakespeare's Cymbeline: An Iconographic Reconstruction* (Newark: University of Delaware Press, 1992).
[49] Chesterton, *On Household Gods and Goblins*, in *On Lying in Bed and Other Essays*, selected by Alberto Manguel (Calgary: Bayeux Arts, 2000), pp. 437–41.
[50] Elizabeth Archibald, 'Ancient Romance', in *A Companion to Romance from Classical to Contemporary*, ed. C. Saunders (Oxford: Blackwell, 2004), pp. 1–25.
[51] Nathaniel Ingelo, Preface, *Bentivolio and Urania*.

the author. We know that Henry More and Lady Anne Conway read it. It was attacked by the notorious rake and libertine Rochester in his poem *A Satyr against Reason and Mankind.*

> Hold, mighty man, I cry, all this we know
> From the pathetic pen of Ingelo;
> From Patrick's *Pilgrim*, Sibbes' soliloquies,
> And 'tis this very reason I despise:
> This supernatural gift, that makes a mite
> Think he's an image of the infinite.

Ingelo was a Cambridge Platonist.[52] Joseph Glanvill (1636–78), in his *Essays* of 1676, describes the fictional Bensalem as a university and church (i.e. Cambridge) rescued by the 'Cupri-cosmites' (from *cuprum* – copper?) from dogmatism and fanaticism, and in this he mentions Nathaniel Ingelo, who is referred to as 'Ilegon' among the 'Cupri-Cosmits'.[53] Ingelo was a close friend of John Worthington, the Vice Chancellor of the university and Master of Jesus College, Cambridge.[54] Ingelo, a graduate of Edinburgh, was Fellow at Queens' from 1644 to 1646. He became pastor of a congregation in Bristol, and was later Fellow of Eton. Ingelo accompanied Sir Bulstrode Whitelocke in a delegation to Christina of Sweden between November 1653 and June 1654. He obtained his Doctor of Divinity in 1658. Ingelo writes enthusiastically about Plotinus: 'Plotin, the chief of the Platonists pronounces roundly that the Denial of an Allwise Creator is … so irrational that it can be approv'd by none but those who have neither Understanding nor Sense' (Preface). He is also approving of Cicero and hostile to Epicureanism. Ingelo's paradigm seems to be Henry More.

Henry More's (1614–87) allegorical poem *Psychozoia* takes Mnemon (the Mindful One – remembering), a name taken from *The Faerie Queene* III 9,

---

[52] Jon Parker, *Taming the Leviathan* (Cambridge: Cambridge University Press, 2007), pp. 202ff. and p. 304.
[53] See R. Crocker, 'The Cupri-cosmits and the Latitude-Men', in *Henry More: 1614–1687*, ed. Sarah Hutton (Dortrecht: Springer, 1989), pp. 79–92, esp. 81.
[54] Nathaniel Ingelo, *Bentivolio and Urania, in Four Books* (London: Printed by J. Grismond for Richard Marriot, 1660); idem, *Bentivolio and Urania, the Second Part* (London: Printed by J. Grismond for Richard Marriot, 1664), both reprinted many times; Ian William McLellan, 'Ingelo, Nathaniel' Dictionary of National Biography (Oxford, 2004). Cornelia Wilde, Nathaniel Ingelos Bentivogllio und Urania als philosophischer Romance. Aspekte Antique Philosophien in christlich-neuplatonischer Erbauungsliteratur, in Ernst Osterkamp, ed. *Wissensästhetik: Wissen über die Antike in ästhetischer Vermittlung* (Berlin: de Gruyter, 2008), pp. 171–97.

representing the genuine pilgrim soul escaping from the lowest realm, that of brutishness: Adamah or Beiron or Beirah (brute). This is distinguished from Dizoia (double-life) the higher region of Autaesthesia – (self-awareness). Finally, he reaches salvation in Theoprepia (Divine-fitting). Mnemon encounters a variety of intellectual positions on his journey. Don Psittaco Parrot (a comic representation of Presbyterianism) is the guide. Don Corvino (the crow) is a resolute defender of church and tradition and Don Graculo, a stout cathedral dean and a strict rationalist. There is a further character, Glaucis the owl, who stands for the spiritualist or Quaker position of inner illumination. Mnemon, having gone through the gate of humility to Dixoia 'double-livednesse', meets two forms of temptation: Pantheothen (more accurately called Pandaemoniothen) and Pteroessa, 'land of winged souls'. These represent the alternative temptations of self-righteous cruelty (that is, in fact, self-will) and a smug and self-seeking intellectualism, especially as represented by three maidens: Pythagorissa, Platonissa, and Stoicissa. Mnemon is so impressed by the latter that he thinks he has arrived in Theoprepia, but is corrected by Simon. Mnemon eventually recognizes Simon as a part of his own being, and then is able to enter the realm of Theoprepia and attain deification. More's allegory may seem tiresome but it is part of his theory of Psyche's veil: the enigmatic dimension of the cosmos: part hidden, partly revealed to this soul. More has the sense of a higher imagination (which he calls Semele), one that can employ those 'raging raptures' of the chastened and philosophical soul that constitute experiences of the divine:

> Prophets and poets have their life from hence
> Like fire into their marrow it searcheth deep,
> This flaming fiery lake doth choak all sense
> And binds the lower man with brazed sleep.[55]

Nathaniel Ingelo's *Bentivolio and Urania* is a romance about the pursuit of deiformity, a prose allegory of the soul's journey to salvation which draws deeply upon Henry More's *Platonick Song of the Soul*. The major theme is conversion: the necessary turn from material things and false images and

---

[55] Robert Crocker, *Henry More, 1614–1687: A Biography of the Cambridge Platonist* (Dortrecht: Springer, 2003), p. 34.

the ascent to contemplation of the ideas. The main figures Bentivolio, Urania and Panaretus wend their way through the countries of Argentora, Piacenza Vansembla and reach the land of Theoprepia: the god-pleasing. Before they can rise to the higher Theoprepia they fall into Theriagene, the land of degenerate beasts. The last book is called *Elenchus* (refutation). It concerns questions about the existence of God and the life of Christ, and consists of a battle against Antitheus and the atheist denizens of Theriagne. The opponent of *Antitheus* is *Alethion* – a 'prince of philosophers and an Ideal ruler':

> The peace of my soul shines clear within, and is no more clouded with this Disaster, then a light which is guarded with thick Lantern upon the stern of a Ship is in danger of being put out with those blustering winds which make a noise about it.[56]

There is also a conversation between Aristander and Synthnescon about the immortality of the soul. This debate concludes with the move to higher *Theoprepia* – heaven (as in H. More). Platonists like Henry More or Nathaniel Ingelo were denying the Calvinist doctrine of the 'invincible infirmity of the soul' and imputed righteousness. Henry More insists that the sacrifice of Christ must be wrought in the self and uses the language of 'self denial' to reinforce the principle that self-love can be set aside and deification is a renewal of the self – the divine seed in the soul. Hence the conviction that true love culminates in love of God. On the title page of *The Four Loves* are words from John Donne: 'that our affections kill us not, nor dye'. The love of God builds upon, and does not destroy, other loves.

Lewis shares the view of the great Western mystics that selfishness is hell and spirituality is the journey from the God with us to God in us. The line of Coverdale's rendering of Psalm 27: 'When thou saidst, Seek ye my face; my heart said unto thee, Thy face, Lord, will I seek', must lie behind the title of the novel. Union with the Divine is the goal.

> The Fox and I were alone again.
> 'Did you really do these things to her?' I asked.
> 'Yes. All here's true.'
> And we said we loved her.

---

[56] Ingelo, *Bentivolio*, II 51.

'And we did. She had no more dangerous enemies than us. And in that far distant day when the gods become wholly beautiful, or we at last are shown how beautiful they always were, this will happen more and more. For mortals, as you said, will become more and more jealous. And mother and wife and child and friend will all be in league to keep a soul united with the Divine Nature.'[57]

This unity with the Divine nature is the central theme of the novel. In another striking passage we read of:

Two figures, reflections, their feet to Psyche's feet and mine, stood head downward in the water. But whose were they? Two Psyches, the one clothed, the other naked? Yes, both Psyches, both beautiful (if that mattered now) beyond all imagining, yet not exactly the same.[58]

This is the old Platonic doctrine: that the soul is an *eidolon* or image expressed by Apuleius and developed by Lewis in a specifically Christian direction. The ancient Platonic *amor Dei intellectualis* is supplemented by the doctrine of the *sacrificium*. The true self is the image of its archetype in the great I AM of Exodus 3.14 and the Johannine 'I am' sayings of Christ:

How then can mortal tongue hope to express
The image of such endless perfectness?[59]

Idea of the Veil

The eternal Truth of God cloath'd in Flesh goes wandering up and down in this strange country of the World as a Stranger and Pilgrim, neglected and despised of all, a man of Sorrow and weariness ... (the world) is a 'large sign or symbol of some Spiritual Truths that nearly concern' the soul.[60]

Vertue; which, though by reason of its innate beauty it least needs any adventitious ornament, yet doth not scorn the light vail of Romance.[61]

Regarding the notion of the veil: as Dionysius says, the divine ray cannot

---

[57] Lewis, *Till We Have Faces*, p. 304.
[58] Lewis, *Till We Have Faces*, p. 308.
[59] Lilian Winstanley, *Edmund Spenser's The Fowre Hymns* (Cambridge: CUP, 1930), pp. 32–41.
[60] Henry More, *Discourses on Several Texts of Scripture*. (London: IR, 1692), p. 123.
[61] Ingelo, *Bentivolio*, Preface.

reach us unless it is covered with poetic veils.[62] The erotic and the religious dimension of the veil cannot be discounted: the imagination is required to apprehend truths.[63] In *Till We Have Faces*, Orual is a writer. It is noteworthy that Lewis is writing a novel from the perspective of a woman.[64] And in the traditional tale, the wicked sister interrupts the joy of the couple. Here, Lewis is exploring the relation of woman and the perspective of a highly intelligent and reflective woman whose destiny has been cruelly determined by her outward appearance. The problem of injustice is central: we encounter the beauty of Psyche and the ugliness of Orual. There is also Orual's anger towards the god of the Grey Mountain. The theme of visibility and confession pervades. Orual is un-recognizable: for a long while she is only known by her veil. Psyche knows her husband but cannot see him. Orual cannot see the palace of the god because she does not believe in the supernatural realm and Lewis thinks that these are truths that can only be perceived spiritually. The Vision of God is linked to experiences of the sublime. When Orual meets the god – she knows why there is no answer. Encounter with God is better than formulation in words. This is the *mysterium tremendum et fascinans*: 'My terror was the salute that mortal flesh gives to immortal things.'[65] Here Lewis articulates a component of aggression and resistance in the apprehension of spiritual beauty. The word 'Face' has the sense of the spiritual integrity of the agent, as in the Church of England Book of Common Prayer (1559) when the words before communion ask: 'With what face then … shall ye hear these words?'

Suffering and Trial

Lewis presents a relationship between the ancient pagan world and Greek rationalism. The Fox represents stoicism with his fatalistic pantheism – rationalistic and materialistic.[66] The moral emotions of fear and jealousy are

---

[62] Edgar Wind, *Pagan Mysteries of the Renaissance* (London: W. W. Norton, 1968), p. 25.
[63] Patricia Oster, *Der Schleier im Text. Funktionsgeschichte eines Bildes für die neuzeitliche Erfahrung des Imaginären* (Munich: Fink, 2002), esp. pp. 9–24.
[64] Lewis's fellow Platonist Henry Corbin referred to the Islamic tradition of the woman as a mirror of the soul: *Alone with the Alone: Creative Imagination in the Sufism of Ibn Arabi*, p. 161.
[65] p. 171.
[66] Schakel, *Reason and Imagination* in C. S. Lewis, (Grand Rapids, MI: W. B. Eerdmans Publishing Co., 1984), p. 39.

prominent and the Lucretian view of religion as rising from fear is clear at the onset of the novel. Orual exclaims:

> I am old now and have not much to fear from the anger of the gods ...
> I will accuse the gods, especially the god who lives on the grey mountain.[67]

Lewis has often been criticized for his naïve view of suffering and pain. Yet he was of the same First World War generation as Rupert Brooke, Siegfried Sassoon and Wilfrid Owen: it is easy forget that – as much as they – Lewis was steeped in the crisis of Modernism and the problem of suffering. After his first experience of the war, Brooke wrote:

> I marched through Antwerp, deserted, shelled, and burning, one night, and saw ruined houses, dead men and horses: and railway-trains with their lines taken up and twisted and flung down as if a child had been playing with a toy. And the whole heaven and earth was lit up by the glare from the great lakes and rivers of burning petrol, hills and spires of flame. That was like Hell, a Dantesque Hell, terrible. But there – and later – I saw what was a truer Hell. Hundreds of thousands of refugees ... to unending lines of them, the old men mostly weeping, the women with hard drawn faces, the children playing or crying or sleeping. That is what Belgium is now: the country where three civilians have been killed to every one soldier ... It's queer to think one has been a witness of one of the greatest crimes of history. Has ever a nation been treated like that? And how can such a stain be wiped out?[68]

Yet unlike the tragic Brooke, Lewis fought in the Somme.[69] Lewis knew that Man is not just *homo ludens* but *homo necans*. When we read in the novel 'For suffering, it seems, is infinite, and our capacity without limit,'[70] this is a man who experienced the apocalyptic hideousness of 'the horribly smashed men still moving like half-crushed beetles, the sitting or standing corpses, the landscape of sheer earth without a blade of grass.'[71]

Lewis creates a barbaric land on the edge of civilization to depict what Burke calls our 'naked shivering nature'. One might draw a parallel between the Kingdom of Glome (the proximity to gloom, twilight and darkness seems

---

[67] Lewis, *Till We Have Faces*, p. 171.
[68] *The Letters of Rupert Brooke*, ed. by G. Keynes (London: Faber and Faber, 1968), p. 632.
[69] I am grateful to Clemens Hedley for discussion about this.
[70] Lewis, *Till We Have Faces*, p. 277.
[71] *The Cambridge Companion to C. S. Lewis*, p. 203.

deliberate) and Dante's Hell.[72] One of the problems that emerges from Dante's Inferno is the interpretation of the place. Is this an objectively ordained structure of divine retribution or the state of the souls of those who are themselves engaged in wickedness? The punishments of the Inferno mirror the deeds of the perpetrators. Of course, the larger process of the *Commedia* is a process of self-discovery. Moreover, Hell is a realm of the torment of guilt as opposed to mere (external) shame. The Fox functions rather like Virgil in Dante's *Commedia*. He is a good guide for Orual, but can only guide her so far. The Fox, like Virgil, has his limitations.

Sacrifice

In 'The Parable of the Old Man and the Young', Wilfred Owen claims 'half the seed of Europe' had been cruelly sacrificed because the leaders of the European nations, symbolized as old men through the biblical image of Abraham, did not want to 'offer the Ram of Pride instead of [his son]'. And it is Owen who rejects the image of military sacrifice in the Horatian dictum as the old lie – *'dulce et decorum est pro patria mori'*. Yet the idea of sacrifice, notwithstanding its perversion in propaganda and apparently obsolete ideas of religion, plays an important role in Lewis's thought. Of his celebrated conversion with J. R. R. Tolkien and Hugo Dyson along Addison's Walk in Magdalen College, Oxford, Lewis tells us that this conversation was about the mysterious core of Christianity: the sacrifice of the god-man, the *agnus Dei*. He reports that he was happy with such ideas in Balder, Adonis or Bacchus, but rejected similar notions in Christianity. Through Tolkien and Dyson, Lewis was persuaded to see Christianity as true myth. Lewis distinguishes between thin and thick religion in his lecture 'Christian Apologetics' and here we find the conflict between the priest and the fox in the novel. There is a conflict between the rationalism of the Fox and the Priest and blatant irony in the words: 'We are hearing much Greek wisdom this morning.' This rationalism however, 'brings no rain and grows no corn; sacrifice does both'.

---

[72] He was deeply familiar with Dante and Lewis's good friend Charles Williams was a great enthusiast for and admirer of Dante.

> Holy places are dark places. It is life and strength, not knowledge and words, that we get in them.[73]

In the conflict between priestcraft and rationalism, the wily Greek Fox comes to realize the limits of his rationalism when he says of Orual:

> I never told her why the old Priest got something from the dark House that I never got from my trim sentences … Of course I didn't know; but I never told her that I didn't know. I don't know now. Only that the way to the true gods is more like the house of Ungit … The Priest knew at least that there must be sacrifices. They will have sacrifice – will have man.[74]

Any true religion, according to Lewis, must address the lower and the higher dimensions of humanity, the dark depths of the human soul as well as the nobler aspirations. The terrors of the human psyche, the holiness of heart's affection and the truth of imagination; all must be redeemed and integrated alongside reason.

Nietzsche saw Christianity and its morality as a construct of the imagination: 'this entire fictional world has its roots in *hatred* of the natural (–actuality!–)'.[75] Bernard Williams drew upon this aspect of Nietzsche's diagnosis of the malaise of Western thought in his critique of the 'peculiar institution of Morality' and shared a similar preference for a Hellenic non-Christian domain. This is the key to Williams' 'anti-progressivism'.

> It has, and needs, no God … It takes as central and primary questions of character, and of how moral considerations are grounded in human nature: it asks what manner of life it is rational for the individual to live. It makes no use of a categorical imperative. In fact – though we have used the word 'moral' quite often for the sake of convenience – this system of ideas basically lacks the concept of *morality* altogether, in the sense of class of reasons or demands that are vitally different from other kinds of reason or demand.[76]

The naturalism of Williams opposes the tenet that morality is *sui generis* and irreducible to non-moral features of agents or the world. Like Nietzsche,

---

[73] Lewis, *Till We Have Faces*, p. 50.
[74] Lewis, *Till We Have Faces*, p. 295.
[75] Nietzsche, *The Anti-Christ*, §15. It is worth noting that the obvious reading of the German title of Nietzsche's work is *The Anti-Christian*.
[76] Williams, *Moral Luck* (Cambridge: Cambridge University Press, 1981), p. 251.

Williams considers tragedy to be a rich reservoir of reflection upon the ethical. Whereas Greek philosophy, 'in its sustained pursuit of rational self sufficiency' seeks to insulate the good life from chance, Greek literature, and above all tragedy, provides the awareness 'that what is great is fragile and that which is necessary may be destructive'.[77] Both are concerned with tragedy. Lewis sees sacrifice as central for tragedy, Williams associates its core significance with luck. Williams asserts: 'the idea of a value that lies beyond all luck is an illusion'.[78] Furthermore, Shame is akin to moral luck in revealing the limits of an ethical model based upon the notion of guilt.

Shame, Guilt and Sacrifice

Shame is conventionally understood as the trespassing of social or cultural values whereas guilt is the transgression of inward principles. Shame tends to be the unveiling of weaknesses or faults to other agents; guilt emerges out of the self or self-image. It is intelligible to imagine being ashamed of secrets or to feel guilty about actions that are applauded. Guilt is tied to interiority whereas shame is linked to the interaction with and perception of an outward world. The distinction was popularized by E. R. Dodds in his *The Greeks and the Irrational* (1951).[79] The immediate target of Williams would seem to be Adkins' *Merit and Responsibility: A Study in Greek Values* (Oxford: Oxford University Press, 1960) in which the dominance of merit or success over responsibility in the great Hellenic authors is the key theme. Shame, in early Greek literature, is narrowly about losing face. Williams offers a good critique of that position.[80] The Greeks had no equivalent of moral guilt but they had *aitios* and *anaitios*.[81] In *Shame and Necessity* Williams is deeply critical of

---

[77] Williams, *Moral Luck*, p. 248.
[78] Williams, *Ethics and the Limits of Philosophy*, 1985, p. 196.
[79] E. R. Dodds, 'From Shame Culture to Guilt-Culture', in *The Greeks and the Irrational* (Berkeley: University of California, 1951), pp. 28–63. Peter Cheyne notes that the distinction was made earlier than that, in Ruth Benedict, *The Chrysanthemum and the Sword*, (Boston, Houghton Mifflin Company, 1946).
[80] 'Williams on Greek Literature and Philosophy' in *Bernard Williams*, ed. Alan Williams (Cambridge: Cambridge University Press, 2007), pp. 155–80.
[81] Op cit. p. 174.

Plato: 'Shame can understand guilt but guilt cannot understand shame.'[82] The narrative of *Till We Have Faces* is a narrative about the awakening of the protagonist to her true self. Orual wears a veil (shame about her ugliness) teased by her father.[83] She has to understand her guilt and remorse. The process of unveiling for Orual is a journey of self-discovery. Williams uses anger felt by others as a way of distinguishing between shame and guilt. In the novel, Orual only learns later of the frustration that her behaviour has caused. Edgar Wind observes that the torture of the mortal by the god who inspires him was a central theme in the revival of the ancient mysteries.[84] Amor and Psyche is a model of conversion. Metamorphosis can be mere physical change but conversion requires inner transformation. Orual needs to be released from guilt that is covered and concealed by the veil. The love of Orual is inadequate: she finally comes to see herself and can recognize herself through conscience. The epigraph of the novel is the first line of Shakespeare's Sonnet 151: 'Love is too young to know what conscience is.' The second line is: 'Yet who knows not conscience is born of love.'

In Act 3, Scene 2 of *Hamlet*, the prince stages a play that images his theory of the death of his father, with the intent of provoking the conscience of his uncle and stepfather Claudius. It cannot be the attempt to shame his uncle by staging the murder of Gonzago; there is no public humiliation. Hamlet wishes to trigger the workings of conscience *within* Claudius. The problem of conscience is expounded with particular power in Cymbeline. The full force of remorse and the intangible power of the moral law is imagined vividly:

> My conscience, thou art fetter'd
> More than my shanks and wrists: you good gods, give me
> The penitent instrument to pick that bolt,
> Then, free for ever! Is't enough I am sorry?
> So children temporal fathers do appease;
> Gods are more full of mercy. Must I repent?
> I cannot do it better than in gyves,
> Desired more than constrain'd: to satisfy,

---

[82] Williams, *Shame and Necessity*, p. 93.
[83] Lewis, *Till We Have Faces*, p. 11.
[84] Wind, *Pagan Mysteries of the Renaissance*, p. 175.

> If of my freedom 'tis the main part, take
> No stricter render of me than my all.
> I know you are more clement than vile men,
> Who of their broken debtors take a third,
> A sixth, a tenth, letting them thrive again
> On their abatement: that's not my desire:
> For Imogen's dear life take mine; and though
> 'Tis not so dear, yet 'tis a life; you coin'd it:
> 'Tween man and man they weigh not every stamp;
> Though light, take pieces for the figure's sake:
> You rather mine, being yours: and so, great powers,
> If you will take this audit, take this life,
> And cancel these cold bonds. O Imogen!
> I'll speak to thee in silence. (*Cymbeline* 5.5. 102–22)

The Divine stamp of the soul is a pervasive model of the self in Shakespeare's plays. Crimes of conscience ensuing in breaches of the natural order, and supernatural apparitions such as the appearance of the ghost of Caesar to Brutus or Richard III, abound in Shakespeare.

> Conscience is but a word that cowards use,
> Devis'd at first to keep the strong in awe:
> Our strong arms be our conscience, swords our law.
> March on, join bravely, let us to't pell-mell;
> If not to heaven, then hand in hand to hell. (*Richard III*, 5, 3)

The same monarch can say:

> My conscience hath a thousand several tongues, And every tongue brings in a several tale, And every tale condemns me for a villain.
> Perjury, perjury, in the high'st degree;
> Murder, stern murder in the dir'st degree,
> Throng to the bar, crying all, 'Guilty!, Guilty!' (*Richard III*, 5, 4, 172)

Macbeth or Richard III can supress conscience but it returns to torment them. The king is the embodiment of power and prestige. The startling imaginative presentation of conscience, however, as the 'thousand several tongues', vision of a throng of witnesses to his myriad crimes, is a graphic image of his inward horrors and vulnerability. In twelfth book of the *Iliad*, Achilles is moved by the fact that the king of the Trojans will throw himself at the knees of the man who had slain so many of his own sons, and especially after the brutal humiliation of Hector. How else can a bad person affirm goodness whilst performing wicked deeds? The famous lines of Medea: *video meliora proboque, deteriora sequor*[85] express the divided self that has the capacity to recognize the better and approve it as such, yet to follow the worse.

Let us now turn to the idea of conscience and guilt as an image of transcendence. Consider the case of the brilliant modern composer Carl Orff (1895–1982), who was partly of Jewish descent and seems to have been outwardly accommodating to National Socialism, while inwardly cynical and probably contemptuous. He achieved great success with *Carmina Burana*, perhaps the most celebrated and successful musical compositions of the Nazi era. As a result of this success, he was asked to write an 'Aryan' replacement for proscribed 'Jewish' Mendelssohn's *Midsummer Night's Dream*. Orff was a friend of Kurt Huber, a Munich philosopher and musicologist who had helped him with the Carmina Burana libretto, as well as being an active member of the German resistance to the Nazis and a founder of the White Rose (*Die Weisse Rose*). It would seem that his work *Antigonae* is a tribute to the remarkable courage of a 21-year-old girl, Sophie Scholl (1921–43), a student of philosophy and biology. Scholl joined a cell of resistance, largely a group of students in Munich, through her brother Hans Scholl. Motivated by a profound awareness of the ethical and political catastrophe, this group of Christian students of different denominations between June 1942 and February 1943, distributed leaflets among major German cities encouraging opposition to the National Socialist dictatorship. The Scholl siblings, Sophie and her brother Hans, a medical student, 24, brought a suitcase of anti-Nazi flyers to the University of Munich on 18 February 1943 and left them outside lecture halls for students to discover. Sophie flung the last of the leaflets in the atrium of the main university building. This act was seen by the custodian, who alerted the police. Hans and Sophie were detained by the Gestapo, tried and executed on 22 February; yet their startling defiance and heroic pluck at the trial earned them great admiration. Professor Huber was arrested by the Gestapo in February 1943. He was tortured, received a show trial. Orff visited Huber's house the day after the arrest. Ignorant of the events, he

---

[85] Seneca, *Medea* 7.20–1.

was told by Mrs Clara Huber about her husband's fate. Orff's first reaction was concern about the perilous consequences of his own connection with Huber: 'I am ruined' he is reported to have exclaimed. Huber's wife implored Orff to help her husband but Orff refused. She never met the composer again.[86]

After the war Orff was subjected to the denazification process. He was deemed to be sufficiently uncompromised by his past to be cleared and he worked as a successful composer until 1982. He was, it seems, haunted by the events of the failed efforts of the White Rose. His *Antigonae* looks like a memento for the remarkable and heroic Sophie Scholl, who like Antigone, defied the cruel power of the state. Orff was a man whose public life and work life was a success, both before and after the Second World War, and through the great turmoil and tumult of central European history. *Carmina Burana* is one of the most popular works of twentieth century music, regularly performed throughout the world, and ubiquitous as advertising or theme music. Orff was not *shamed* or openly compromised by his dealings with the Nazi state. His failure to help Huber is not obviously reprehensible and Orff might have legitimately feared that any such action on his part would have been fruitless and punished in the most draconian manner. It does not seem fair to accuse him of failing to live up to the heroic standards of Huber or the Scholl siblings. He seems, however, to have suffered deep feelings of *guilt*. Should one consider the distinction between guilt and shame coherent?

At the end of *Till We Have Faces*, there is a great judgement scene. Orual reads her complaint to the judge; however:

> The complaint was the answer. To have heard myself making it was to be answered. Lightly men talk of saying what they mean ... When the time comes to you at which you will be forced at last to utter the speech that has lain at the centre of your soul for years, which you have all that time, idiot-like, been saying over and over, you'll not talk about the joy of words. I saw well why the gods do not speak to us openly, nor let us answer. Till that word can be dug out of us, why should they hear the babble that we think we mean? How can they meet us face to face till we have faces?[87]

---

[86] Tony Palmer's 2008 documentary film *O, Fortuna, Carl Orff and Carmina Burana* is a powerful and arresting depiction of the complex life of Orff, especially the guilt.
[87] Lewis, *Till We Have Faces*, pp. 294ff.

This is the doubling. The tasks that Venus gives Psyche are mirrored by the task undertaken by Orual, whose journey is a reflection of the odyssey of the soul (*psyche*). Orual is the narrator of the tale and the process of narration mirrors her own gradual recognition of her previous misapprehensions. Thus, when Orual hears the Cupid and Psyche story from the Essurian priest, she is appalled by the inaccuracies.[88] She is angered by the idea, explicit in the narration of the Pyche and Cupid tale by the Essurian priest that she might be jealous of Psyche:

> Jealousy! I jealous of Psyche? I was sickened not only at the vileness of the lie but its flatness. It seemed as if the gods had minds just like the lowest of the people.[89]

The theme of the jealousy of the gods recurs throughout the novel. Ansit, the long-suffering wife of Bardia, says: 'Oh Queen Orual, I begin to think you know nothing of love. Or no; I'll not say that. Yours is Queen's love, not commoners'. Perhaps you who spring from the gods love like the gods'.[90] For Ansit there is clearly no love in Orual, just a grasping and destructive selfishness. As Henry More avers:

> For, seeing that the most rich and precious Excellencies of the *Divine nature* cannot be discovered by the soul as they ought to be but by becoming *Divine* ... If thou beest it, thou seest it, as Plotinus speaks.[91]

Or another Irish Platonist (Yeats):

> I'm looking for the face I had
> Before the world was made.[92]

Both God and the soul are perceived indirectly and mutually linked. We have no direct access to God/the gods – we need to be shielded from that – and we only have real self-vision and vision of God through moral struggle.

The language of the mirror points to dimensions of the self which are initially puzzling or obscure. The doubling of Orual-Psyche as both an actual relationship and internal to the mind is an intriguing aspect of the novel. The

---

[88] Lewis, *Till We Have Faces*, pp. 243ff.
[89] Lewis, *Till We Have Faces*, p. 245.
[90] Lewis, *Till We Have Faces*, pp. 262f.
[91] Henry More, *Divine Dialogues* (London: James Flesher, 1668), p. 287.
[92] W. B. Yeats, 'A Woman Young and Old', *The Collected Poems of WB Yeats* (London: Vintage Books, 1992), p. 280.

god speaks to Orual: 'Now Psyche goes out into exile. Now she must hunger and thirst and tread hard roads. Those against whom I cannot fight must do their will upon her. You, woman, shall know yourself and your work. You also shall be Psyche.'[93]

The relationship between Orual and Psyche is not merely shame and recognition. As Jonathan Lear observes: 'A person is, by his nature, out of touch with his own subjectivity.'[94] Such is Orual's state. She must become Psyche. Lewis's critique of possessive love or affection should be seen alongside his critique of the narcissism and materialism of modern culture. Orual's loss of her sister is great pain, although not an evil. Wordsworth speaks in 'Peel Abbey' (after the death of his brother) of the deep distress that humanizes. Orual is told by the Goddess: 'Die before you die'. There is no chance after.[95] She must practice renunciation.

Depth psychology shows the nature of our estrangement in making the unconscious conscious. Schelling's twentieth-century pupil Paul Tillich explored the demonic dimension of human alienation from the Divine. He associated demons with those archetypal and trans-personal forces explored by depth psychology (and the literature of Dostoyevsky). When the troubled psyche splits unbearable instincts and drives from consciousness awareness, these impulses can nevertheless wrest control of the agent in a demonic fashion. This is not limited to a few perverse individuals: it is the fate of a neurotic-psychotic society.[96]

Alongside the idea of 'acceptance' in the psychoanalytic mode, Tillich also draws upon the ancient Platonic doctrine of the eros, the longing of the soul for God. Depth psychology attributes healing powers to insight, which means not a detached knowledge of psychoanalytic theory or of one's own past in the light of this theory but a repetition of one's actual experiences with all the pains and terrors of such a return. Insight in this sense is a reunion with one's own past and especially with those moments in it which influence the present destructively. Such a cognitive union produces a transformation just as radical

---

[93] Lewis, *Till We Have Faces*, pp. 173–4.
[94] Jonathan Lear, *Love and Its Place in Nature: A Philosophical Interpretation of Freudian Psychoanalysis* (New Haven: Yale University Press, 1998), p. 4.
[95] Lewis, *Till We Have Faces*, p. 279.
[96] See *Sacrifice Imagined*, p. 192.

as that presupposed and demanded by Socrates and Paul.[97] (One might think of the *daimonion* of Socrates and his ecstatic state at the beginning of the *Symposium*, esp. 175b and the report of Alcibiades of his astonishing motionlessness at Potidaea in 220d).[98]

When Tillich claims that 'Persons can grow only in the communion of personal encounter', he may well be showing his debt to Schelling.[99] Schelling insists, in *On Human Freedom*, that 'only the personal can heal the personal, and God must become man, so that man can come again to God'.[100] Paul Tillich claims that when asked to sum up the Christian faith, he says that it is the message of a 'New Creation'. His account of the relationship between suffering and the awareness of truth is urgent and expressed with eloquence:

> There is no excuse permitting us to avoid the depth of truth, the only way to which lies through the depth of suffering … Religion and Christianity have often been accused of an irrational and paradoxical character. Certainly much stupidity, superstition, and fanaticism have been connected with them. The command to sacrifice one's intellect is more daemonic than divine. For man ceases to be man if he ceases to be an intellect. But the depth of sacrifice, of suffering, and of the Cross is demanded of our thinking mind, and not only of our body. Every step into the depth of thought is a breaking away from the surface of former thoughts. When this breaking away occurred in men like Paul, Augustine, and Luther, such extreme suffering was involved that it was experienced as death and hell. But they accepted such sufferings as the road to the deep things of God, as the spiritual way, as the way to truth. They expressed the truth they envisioned in spiritual words – that is, in words contrary to all surface reasoning, but harmonious with the depth of reason, which is divine. The paradoxical language of religion reveals the way to truth as a way to the depth, and therefore as a way of suffering and sacrifice. He alone who is willing to go that way is able to understand the paradoxes of religion.[101]

---

[97] Paul Tillich, *Systematic Theology* (Chicago, University of Chicago Press: 1951), vol. 1, p. 96.
[98] I am grateful to John Bussanich for this point. See his 'Socrates' Religious Experience', in *The Bloomsbury Companion to Socrates*, ed. J. Bussanich and N. Smith, (London: Bloomsbury, 2012), pp. 276–300.
[99] Tillich, *Systematic Theology*, vol. 1, p. 177.
[100] F. W. J. Schelling, 'Denn nur Persönliches kann Persönliches heilen, und Gott muss Mensch werden, damit der Mensch wieder zu Gott komme'. *Über das Wesen der menschlichen Freiheit* (Stuttgart: Reclam, 1964), p. 96 (379/380).
[101] Paul Tillich, *Shaking the Foundations* (Harmondsworth: Penguin, 1969), p. 69.

Tillich insists, however, that the end is joy, which is deeper than suffering. And this joy is 'ultimate' – but it cannot be reached by 'living on the surface'.[102] Orual, in Lewis's novel *Till We Have Faces* has to discover her own beauty through her suffering: 'Perhaps, thought I, this is what the god meant when he said *You also shall be Psyche*. I also might be an offering.'[103] Hence the claim we can only see God when we have faces.

Till We Have Faces explores in an imaginative form philosophical and theological questions. Like Coleridge's *Rime of the Ancient Mariner*, it is about conversion. 'If a man say, I love God, and hateth his brother, he is a liar: for he that loveth not his brother whom he hath seen, how can he love God whom he hath not seen?' (1 John 4.20).

The Face of God is an image of the Divine presence. Consider Psalm 27:

> O Lord, when I cry with my voice: have mercy also upon me, and answer me.
> When thou saidst, Seek ye my face; my heart said unto thee, Thy face, Lord, will I seek.
> Hide not thy face far from me; put not thy servant away in anger: thou hast been my help; leave me not, neither forsake me, O God of my salvation.

St Paul in 1 Corinthians 13.12 writes of seeing through a glass *darkly* but then 'face to face'. The 'glass' is the murky mirror of the ancient world, made out of polished metal. The vision of the Divine is imperfect. It is not, for Lewis, that the phenomena of the world point unambiguously to God but that the religious imagination provides a richer interpretative framework of the phenomena than the secular alternatives. In the ancient Christian tradition there is a theme of progression in images through which the faithful 'with open face beholding as in a glass the glory of the Lord, are changed into the same image from glory to glory' (2 Cor. 3.18). The believer legitimately starts with accessible images like the shepherd or the teacher and gradually evolves towards more spiritual likeness of the transcendent Godhead. What does freedom consist in? It is the seeing, interpreting, and pressing into service of images.

---

[102] Tillich, *Shaking the Foundations*, p. 69.
[103] Lewis, *Till We Have Faces*, p. 216.

5

Symbol, Participation and Divine Ideas

Lo, make all things in accordance with the pattern that was shown thee upon the mount.

Exodus 25.40

Yea, gazing round
On the wide landscape, gaze till all doth seem
Less gross than bodily, and of such hues
As veil the Almighty Spirit, when he makes
Spirits perceive his presence

Coleridge, *This Lime-Tree Bower my Prison*

C. S. Lewis once wrote to Charles Williams:

> A book sometimes crosses one's path which is so much like the sound of one's native language in a strange country that it feels almost uncivil not to wave some kind of flag in answer, I have just read your *Place of the Lion* and it is to me one of the major literary events of my life.[1]

The novel *The Place of the Lion* is conceived of as both a 'thriller' and as disclosing theological truths in an imaginative mode.[2] The plot of *The Place of the Lion* concerns a celestial invasion, in what appears to be a theological-metaphysical version of H. G. Wells' *The War of the Worlds*. The domain of archetypal ideas or elemental/celestial energies is unleashed upon the physical

---

[1] C. S. Lewis, *Letters*, ii, p. 184.
[2] Dennis L. Weeks, *Steps Toward Salvation: An Examination of Coinherence and Substitution in the Seven Novels of Charles Williams* (New York: Peter Lang, 1991), pp. 51–76 and George P. Winship, 'The Novels of Charles Williams', in Mark Hillegas, *Shadows of Imagination*, (Carbondale: Southern Illinois, 1969), pp. 111–24.

world, when in the fictional Hertfordshire town of Smetham they begin to appear. The Neoplatonic lineage of the link between angels and ideas is made very clear by Williams.[3] There is a book within the book entitled *De Angelis* by the fictional Marcellus Victorinus, one who has translated a Greek text about the angels.[4] L. S. B. McCoull has written a very helpful article upon this fictional work.[5] It would seem that Williams is drawing upon Pseudo Denys' *Celestial Hierarchy* and Dante's *Paradiso*. A central character, Damaris Tighe, is working on her doctoral thesis on 'Pythagorean Influences on Abelard' and her bookshelves contain Neoplatonic writers like Proclus, Iamblichus, St Anselm and presumably the Islamic Neoplatonists ('the Moorish culture in Spain').[6] She gives a lecture to a study circle led by a certain Mr Berringer on 'The Eidola and the Angeli'. She quotes in passing Meister Eckhart's famous reference to Plato as the great priest (*'der grosse Pfaffe'*).[7] Damaris is exploring the process by which Platonic forms became Christian angels: Proclus turned the 'ideas' of Plotinus into 'gods' or '*henads*' and his Christian Syrian pupil Dionysus placed them as angels in the Celestial Hierarchy. What she fails to realize, in her sterile scholarly desiccation, is that she is studying primal and terrifying realities of the *hic et nunc*! Damaris's talk is interrupted by the invasion of an archetypal serpent into the lecture room.[8]

> 'Even if it's what you say, how do you know you were *meant* to see it? We're only men – how should we be meant to look – at these things?'
>
> 'The face of God ...' Anthony murmured.[9]

The novel is the attempt to expound glimpses of the beholding of the 'holy imagination'.[10] In one passage we read: 'He knew them in the spiritual intellect,

---

[3] Sarah Klitenic Wear and John Dillon, *Dionysius the Areopagite and the Neoplatonist Tradition: Despoiling the Hellenes* (Aldershot: Ashgate, 2007), pp. 72–3; Glenn Peers, *Subtle Bodies: Representing Angels in Byzantium* (Berkeley: University of California Press, 2001), pp. 4–5.
[4] Williams, *The Place of the Lion*, p. 134.
[5] L. S. B. McCoull, '"A Woman Named Damaris": Pseudo-Dionysius' Celestial Hierarchy in The Place of the Lion', in *Charles Williams and his Contemporaries*, eds Suzanne Bray and Richard Sturch (Newcastle: Cambridge Scholars, 2009), pp. 118–29.
[6] Williams, *The Place of the Lion*, p. 25.
[7] Williams, *The Place of the Lion*, p. 31.
[8] Williams, *The Place of the Lion*, pp. 31ff. See Raymond Barfield, *The Ancient Quarrel between Philosophy and Poetry* (Cambridge: Cambridge University Press, 2011), p. 97.
[9] Williams, *The Place of the Lion*, p. 64.
[10] Valery Rees, *From Gabriel to Lucifer: A Cultural History of Angels* (London: I B Tauris, 2013). p. 186.

and beheld by their fashioned material bodies the mercy which hid the else overwhelming ardours; man was not yet capable of naked vision.'[11] The narrative frequently has a Dantean quality, with its bizarre and burlesque transformations. At one point there is a discussion about 'comedy' which is redolent of Dante's great poem.

The narrative begins with an apparently normal lion, which seems to have escaped from the zoo, but the beast waxes greater until it becomes clear that this is no merely zoological specimen but that the 'lion' is a supernatural being: the archetype of particular lions. These powers display themselves as monumental animal-like figures: Strength is the lion; Subtlety bodies forth as a snake; Beauty as a butterfly. The manifestations constitute power separated from intellect and in the imaginative narrative of Williams the archetypes draw created being back into themselves. Hence these are powerful and dangerous energies that consume or destroy the human agents in the course of the novel. A figure called Dora Wilmot, full of guile and deceit, is transformed into a snake.

The majority of the protagonists are oblivious to the real nature of the appearance of Divine ideas in the world. The chief character in the novel, Anthony Durrant, the sub-editor of an academic journal, struggles against these unleashed energies and finally, aided by divine grace in the form of the archetype of the Eagle (the standard symbol or representation of St John the Evangelist), he is courting the scholarly and rather prim Damaris Tighe. She is an ambitious young scholar exploring the Platonic legacy in medieval philosophy. The question that she is working on as a scholar, the debate between nominalists and realists in the Middle Ages, erupts as the very theme of the drama as a Lion, an Eagle, Serpent, and other great celestial powers. It is only through the love of Anthony and a conversion experience, that Damaris herself is able to see the ideas as realities: 'Now this world in which they exist is truly a real world.'[12] Her father, however, dies. Anthony's friend, Quentin Sabot, is initially daunted by the intrusion of the powers, but he eventually overcomes his initial terror. Many of the key events in the narrative occur in

---

[11] Williams, *The Place of the Lion*, p. 90.
[12] Williams, *The Place of the Lion*, p. 53.

the house of an occultist named Mr Berringer. He is savaged by the Lioness/Lion in his garden, which results in a coma. His house is called the 'Joinings', with the implication that this place is a connection between two realms, material and spiritual.[13]

If Quentin is horrified by the forms, the narcissistic Damaris denies them. It is she who ironically takes a merely abstract and notional interest in these forms and their transformation in the Christian West.[14] 'Theories which were interesting in Plato became silly when regarded as having anything to do with actual occurrences.'[15] Damaris has a dream in which Quentin sings the Latin tag from Abelard that

> *Est in re veritas*
> *Jam non in schemate*
>
> Truth is always in the thing;
> Never in the reasoning[16]

Damaris asks herself: 'What was the phrase in the Phaedrus? – the soul of the philosopher alone has wings.'[17]

The winged philosopher is one of the most familiar images of the Western tradition. That customary image is fused with the wings of an eagle in the plot of the novel. Anthony is on the landing in Berringer's house when the landing merges into terrifying precipice:

> He was standing above a vast pit, the walls of which swept away from him on either side till they closed again opposite him.[18]

Anthony seems to have been lured towards an abyss of self-destruction but encounters 'a winged form', a 'giant of the eagle kind', on whose wings he is

---

[13] Robert Louis Abrahamson, 'Models for Sacramental Reading in the Place of the Lion', *Charles Williams and his Contemporaries*, p. 132.
[14] The Christian name Damaris links her with the Areopagus of Paul's preaching in Acts 17.34, and by association with the great mystical Neoplatonic writer, Denys the Areopagite. The name Tighe may have links with an editor of the Christian Neoplatonic divine of the eighteenth century: William Law. Richard Tighe produced *A Short Account of the Life and Writings of the Late Rev. William Law* 1813 (London: Harvey and Darton, 1828). Charles Williams was an admirer of William Law.
[15] Williams, p. 60.
[16] Williams, *The Place of the Lion*, p. 103.
[17] Williams, *The Place of the Lion*, p. 104.
[18] Williams, *The Place of the Lion*, p. 113.

raised.[19] In the midst of this he is confronted with a vision of his failings, and 'his whole being grew one fiery shame'. Yet he also has a profound vision of reality:

> he grew into his proper office, and felt the flickers of prophecy pass through him, of the things of knowledge that were to be. Borne now between the rush of gigantic wings he went upward and again swept down ... he saw the forms – the strength of lion and the subtlety of the crowned serpent, and the loveliness of the butterfly and the swiftness of the horse – and other shapes whose meaning he did not understand. They were there only as he passed, hints and expressions of lasting things, but not by such mortal types did the Divine Ones exist in their own blessedness. He knew, and submitted; this world was not yet open to him, nor was his service on earth completed. And as he adored these beautiful, serene, and terrible manifestations, they vanished from around him. He was no more in movement; he was standing again on his ledge; a rush of mighty wings went outward from him.[20]

Symbolic images both reveal and conceal: 'not by such mortal types did the Divine Ones exist in their own blessedness'. 'The image is taken up into the reality it represents'[21] on the principle of 'As above, so below'. Yet renewed by this vision, by this contact with the transcendent source of Being, Anthony moves 'with a new simplicity'.[22] Anthony has had wings like the soul of Plato's philosopher in the *Phaedrus* and the visionary power of great prophets like Ezekiel. After this episode of the transformation of Anthony, we encounter 'The conversion of Damaris Tighe'. She encounters a terrifying apparition: 'There she stood on the edge of a swampy pool, with a pterodactyl wheeling round in the sky, and one remote companion.'[23] She calls to Anthony for help. He arrives and 'another flying thing sailed into sight and floated slowly down to his shoulder'.[24] Some have speculated that the pterodactyl is a fossilised prehistoric version of the Eagle and

---

[19] Williams, *The Place of the Lion*, p. 115.
[20] Williams, *The Place of the Lion*, p. 116.
[21] Stephen Medcalf, 'The Athanasian Principle in Williams's use of Images' in *The Rhetoric of Vision: Essays on Charles Williams*, eds Charles A. Huttar and Peter J. Schakel (Bucknell: Lewisburg, 1996), pp. 27–43.
[22] Williams, *The Place of the Lion*, p. 120.
[23] Williams, *The Place of the Lion*, p. 132.
[24] Williams, *The Place of the Lion*, p. 134

thus represents Damaris's own desiccated and sterile approach to life and scholarship.[25]

We are shown 'The thing she had rejected and yet used gathered and expanded round him as if a glory attended him.'[26] Damaris admits her previous pettiness and cruelty: she has been treating Anthony as a means rather than an end, and she failed to grasp the real meaning of her studies. Anthony seems changed and yet senses his newly acquired 'power and intelligence'.

The occultist Berringer has two pupils named Foster and Wilmot. They represent the dangers of magic and are transformed into, and in a sense destroyed by, the celestial powers they wish to control. Proper and sacred control is presented in a visionary manner at the end of the novel. There Anthony is transformed into an Adamic figure, one who gives names to the animals and drives the primordial forces from the terrestrial world and restores them to their proper place. Damaris is an onlooker and seems like Eve observing Adam:[27]

> He called and he commanded; nature lay expectant about him. She was aware then that the forest all around was in movement; living creatures showed themselves on its edge, or hurried through the grass. At each word that he cried, new life gathered, and still the litany of invocation and command went on. By the names that were the Ideas he called them, and the Ideas who were the Principles of everlasting creation heard him, the Principles of everlasting creation who are the Cherubim and the Seraphim of the Eternal. In their animal manifestations, duly obedient to the single animal who was lord of the animals, they came.[28]

Terrors of malice and envy and jealousy faded; disordered beauty everywhere recognized again the sacred laws that governed it. Man dreamed of himself in the place of his creation.

'The vision passed from them' and 'the exalted moment' has gone.[29] Now the distance that separates the celestial and the earthly has been restored: 'The

---

[25] Abrahamson, 'Models for Sacramental Reading in the Place of the Lion', p. 136.
[26] Williams, *The Lion*, p. 134.
[27] Williams, *The Lion*, p. 204.
[28] Williams, *The Lion*, p. 202.
[29] Wordsworth?

Symbol, Participation and Divine Ideas 125

guard that protected earth was set again; the interposition of the Mercy veiled the destroying energies from the weakness of men.'[30]

In Charles Williams, the doctrine of the Platonic Ideas and the Nature of God as co-inherence are central tenets of his thinking that 'He is us and we in him'. The 'affirmation of images' is of paramount significance for Williams.[31] The way of affirmation starts with a feeling of 'stupor' and 'an astonishment of the mind'. The proximate cause of such a 'romantic' mood must possess the following three qualities:

> '(I) it must exist in itself, (II) it must derive from something greater than itself, (III) it must represent in itself that greatness from which it derives'.[32]

Williams has a profound sense of the numinous and the uncanny in experience. This sensibility is allied to his avowedly basic metaphysical principal of 'Coinherence', which he perhaps derived from Coleridge,[33] and the theological principle of the sacramental.[34] The universe is a vibrant system of interconnection and mutual dependence. Even God as *esse ipsum* is related to the world in creation and incarnation. The 'feeling intellect', however, is requisite to appreciate the presence of the Divine. In his *The English Poetic Mind* Williams views great poetry as enabling readers to acknowledge the 'hiding-places of the power and of the glory'.[35] Great art, for Williams, allows us to see transcendent reality in the world.

Coleridge reckoned the highest question of philosophy to be whether the ideas are regulative or constitutive.[36] He is speaking of Divine ideas. Why should we still use the language of the Divine ideas? Is this not an egregious instance of the Hellenization of Christian thought captured in Gibbon's taunt

---

[30] Williams, *The Place of the Lion*, pp. 204–5.
[31] Mary Carman Rose, 'The Christian Platonism of C. S. Lewis, J. R. R. Tolkien, and Charles Williams', *Neoplatonism and Christian Thought*, ed. D. J. O'Meara (Norfolk, VA: International Society for Neoplatonic Studies, 1982), pp. 203–22.
[32] Williams, *The Figure of Beatrice: A Study in Dante* (New York: Noonday Press, 1961), p. 7.
[33] Coleridge, 'The Statesman's Manual', in *Lay Sermons*, ed. R. J. White. (Routledge and Kegan Paul, 1972), p. 114. See also *Aids to Reflection*, ed. John Beer (Princeton, NJ: Princeton University Press, 1994), pp. 216ff.
[34] Glen Cavaliero, *Charles Williams, Poet of Theology* (London: Macmillan, 1983).
[35] Williams, *The English Poetic Mind* (Oxford: Clarendon Press, 1932), p. 199 and *Figure of Beatrice*, p. 10.
[36] Coleridge, 'The Statesman's Manual', in Coleridge, *Lay Sermons*, ed. by R. J. White, vol. 6 of *The Collected Works of Samuel Taylor Coleridge* (Princeton, N. J. Princeton University Press, 1972).

that Plato taught the doctrine of the Logos before St John revealed it? Does it not beget theological chimeras?

The doctrine of Divine ideas is a significant element of Christian theology as we find it in writers such as Augustine or Aquinas. Augustine in *On Eighty-Three Different Questions*, qu. 46.2, notes that in Latin the Platonic Ideas are called '*formae*' or '*species*'. These, he tells us, are *logoi* and explicitly identifies them with immutable forms within the Divine mind. These are the archetypes of the created order (cf. *Free Choice of the Will*, book 2.) The brilliant early medieval thinker John Scot Eriugena developed a theory of the ideas as creative energies rather than abstractions, i.e. '*causae primordiales*' (cf. Augustine, *The Literal Meaning of Genesis*, VI,10,17). Thomas Aquinas has a developed theory of Divine ideas – although Gilson and Sertillanges thought it was an unfortunate relic of Augustinianism that sat ill with the doctrine of Divine simplicity. The ancient Greek noun ἰδέα (*idea*, 'form, pattern'), from the root of ἰδεῖν (*idein*, 'to see'), denotes the appearance or impression (derived from the aorist ὁρᾶν). The term εἶδος is older and in the *Iliad* denotes visual impressions. In the Latin tradition the terminology employed includes *forma, figura, exemplar, exemplum* or *species*: Seneca speaks explicitly of *ideae Platonicae*.

In a letter to Philipp van Limborch in 1668 Cudworth explained his own personal development from strict predestinarian Calvinism to his Platonism:

> As for me personally, I admit that I had sucked different (i.e. Calvinistic) doctrines downright with my mother's milk and imbibed them thoroughly in the first years of my youth. Nevertheless, the power of truth prevailed and tore down the confines of these prejudices. One of my main motives was that I came to realize that all of the ancient philosophers, not only the Peripatetics, but also the Platonists, whom I enjoyed reading now and then, kept asserting ... But when I considered ethics more attentively and saw clearly, both that there are wholly immutable natures of moral good and bad and that in reality they do not depend upon God's will, this difference between honest and disgraceful rather being necessarily derived from God's immutable nature, I could not ascribe to God those horrible decrees by which he, just as he pleases, condemns innocent people to guilt and sin inevitably punished by eternal tortures. Moreover, it seemed absolutely certain to me that the proponents of these decrees did away with the nature of sin itself entirely. Hence, when, fifteen years later, I set about to gain my doctorate, I put all my trust in the truth and decided to defend

the following thesis in the public assembly: 'There are eternal and immutable reasons of good and bad.'[37]

That thesis was entitled '*Dantur boni et mali rationes aeternae et indispensabiles*' and delivered 1664. For Cudworth belief in the ideas is based upon the conviction that divine commands are not the setting forth of an inscrutable sovereign will, one that could order x at t1 and forbid x at t2. Moral obligation, rather, is grounded in the eternal and immutable wisdom of God himself.

Why is the problem one of Divine ideas? With the death of logical positivism, a great openness to considering some questions about abstract objects emerged. Perhaps most importantly, there is the indispensability argument. We cannot do science without numbers, and Platonism about numbers is an attractive position. Furthermore the revival of Perfect Being Theology added to the revisiting of the question.

Are there necessary truths about God? Some may opine ruefully that this idea limits the sovereignty of God. Some of these ancient worries about Divine sovereignty and necessary truths have been revisited by analytic philosophers since the publication of Alvin Plantinga's seminal and profound *Does God Have a Nature?* Plantinga has been designated a Platonist since he defends the view that God has a nature which is compatible with his absolute sovereignty and that this is compatible with the necessary existence of abstract objects. He recognizes that some theists might be troubled by both the thought of a nature that God cannot alter and eternal abstract entities. Plantinga eventually proposes a version of Platonic realism in which abstract objects are dependent upon the Divine mind: 'Augustine saw in Plato a *vir sapientissimus et eruditissimus* (*Contra Academicos* III, 17); yet he felt obliged to transform Plato's theory of ideas in such a way that these abstract objects become ... part of God, perhaps identical with his intellect. It is easy to see why Augustine took such a course, and easy to see why most later medieval thinkers adopted similar views. For the alternative seems to limit God in an important way; the existence and necessity of these things distinct from him seems incompatible

---

[37] Georg Hertling, *John Locke und die Schule von Cambridge* (Freiburg im Breisgau: Herder, 1882), p. 164, n.2. The English translation is that of Christian Hengstermann.

with his sovereignty.'[38] Plantinga concludes his discussion (pp. 145–6) with a position that looks very close to Augustine.

Plantinga's stunning revival of the doctrine of ideas re-awakened a complex array of puzzles. What is the relation between traditional universals and Divine ideas, between predication and ontology? What is the status of certain properties? Anselm was convinced of the importance of this link for theology. 'He who does not understand that several men are specifically one man how would he understand that, in the mist mysterious of all natures, several persons, each of whom is a perfect God, are one God?'[39] Although we agree with Anselm's claim that the bond between universals and the Divine nature is important, the relation of realism and nominalism about universals and theology is rather murkier than often assumed.

Caught between Plato's Beard and Ockham's Razor?

Let us consider the relationship between the mind and the structure of the physical world: knowledge and being. We do predicate sameness of discrete items. *Prima facie*, it is plausible that the world consists of more than brute discrete facts. We can re-identify particulars but that implies that we can refer to genuine identities across time and space: the same tiger or the same kind of tiger or from the Morning Star to the Evening Star. There must be ontological facts about the world that enable us to posit sameness and not just difference.

To think, it would seem, is just to spawn abstract entities and various diligent disciples of Ockham have thought of ways of trimming Plato's beard. A predicate nominalist considers the employment of certain predicates in terms of unanalysable facts about the world. Resemblance nominalism tries to replace universal predicates with primitive resemblances which do not require invoking a higher order universal. Trope nominalism proposes numerically distinct properties but which evince identical qualities. Common to all three forms of nominalism is the attempt to deny the instantiation of a non-spatial abstraction. It is clear how a Humean or Russellian ontology of atomic facts

---

[38] A. Plantinga, *Does God Have a Nature?* (Milwaukee: Marquette, 1980), p. 5.
[39] Anselm, *De incarnatione Verbi*, ch.2 *Patrologia latina*, v.158,265B.

generates such a model. Further, we have the problem of necessarily existing abstract objects. Not only do we seem committed to patterns in the world or underlying unities without which experience would be incoherent but we also are confronted with the need for abstract objects: numbers, sets, etc.

We have a contrast between a Quinean desert landscape of concrete particulars and a more cluttered ontology (indeed, a jungle perhaps). The latter claims to be 'saving the appearances', the former is rejecting ontological extravagance. The real conflict is between nominalist and materialists on the one hand, and on the other, those inheritors of Plato or Aristotle who think that the predication of universals presupposes more than the mere assemblage of brute facts in the world.

Aristotle's Critique of Plato and the Legacy of the Schoolmen

Aristotle has some scathing criticisms of Plato's 'theory' of the forms, especially the vicious regress argument (the Third Man) and the alleged confusion of the particular and the universal in Plato's reified universals. Let us leave aside the question of the validity or otherwise of Aristotle's criticisms. However, they have left the impression that Plato and Aristotle were squabbling about the existence of universal properties and their relation to particulars. Yet that is not the only way of considering the dispute. The judicious Cornford wrote:

> It must once more be stated that no satisfactory account of the relations of Platonic Forms can be given in terms of Aristotelian logic. We have seen that Plato was not concerned with propositional forms; his Dialectic studies realities, and his conception of these realities was radically different from Aristotle's ... the goal of Dialectic is not to establish propositions ascribing a predicate to all the individuals in a class.[40]

Perhaps we are still Freudians and thus it is natural for us to think in terms of deep conflicts between fathers and sons – even metaphorically. Plato's brightest student wrote at some length on the ideas and replaced Plato's

---

[40] F. M. Cornford, *Plato's Theory of Knowledge: The Theaetetus and the Sophist of Plato translated with a running commentary* (London, New York: Harcourt, Brace and Company, 1935), pp. 268ff.

with his own theory of universals. This seemingly obvious fact was not so obvious for at least two millennia of reflection on the doctrine of the ideas. For example, Thomas Aquinas seems quite happy to combine an Aristotelian theory of substances with a Platonic theory of participation, the latter theory of which seems to assume dependence of those substances on transcendent ideas. For many centuries before Thomas, Aristotle was seen as a critically-minded Platonist.[41]

Another reason why Platonic ideas are often confused with universals lies with the medieval disputes. The medieval university was much occupied with debates about genera and species. Those famous medieval controversies concerning universals being *ante* or *post rem* have perhaps muddied the waters. In the formative medieval discussions, derived from the explorations by Porphyry and Boethius of Aristotle's categories, the issue was the nature genera and species – questions of logic and epistemology – rather than the Divine ideas.

The Platonic Ideas should not be straightforwardly identified with universal properties. Lloyd Gerson has argued very convincingly that the theory of universals in Aristotle is not a replacement for a theory of the forms.[42] Moreover, Plato's theory of the forms should not be understood as a theory of hypostasized universals, as if Plato were offering *ante rem* universals as opposed to the Aristotelian *post rem* universals.[43] Many Platonists have seen the doctrine of ideas as primarily an ontological rather than a logical or epistemological claim. One solution is to distinguish between the eternal and immutable Idea and the capacity to make universal judgements. Moreover, a theory of the forms does not have to withstand scrutiny as a theory of universals per se. The theory of the forms provides an account of the ontological *preconditions* of universal predication. We can, on this theory, give an account of why there are patterns of sameness in difference. Thus universal predication can be seen not as an alternative to a theory of forms but as presupposing it. The Platonic Idea is the ontological basis for the application of predicate terms. I am bracketing the problems that Plato himself raises about the Forms, such as the relation

---

[41] L. P. Gerson, *Aristotle and Other Platonists* (Ithaca, NY: Cornell University Press, 2005).
[42] http://individual.utoronto.ca/lpgerson/Platonism_And_The_Invention_Of_The_Problem_Of_Universals.pdf
[43] E.g. Nicholas Wolterstorff, *On Universals: An Essay in Ontology* (Chicago, University of Chicago Press, 1970), pp. 263ff.

between simple properties and normative ideals. I am also assuming that Plato and Aristotle were correct that we cannot derive our concepts on strictly empiricist principles. Aristotle clearly holds for the priority of the intelligible form over the sensible.

It was this ontological dimension of the Platonic Form that explained its theological development within Middle Platonism. Philosophers came to sense that there was something unsatisfactory with positing Forms per se. Some encompassing causal principle of the ideas was required, and this is exactly what emerged in Middle Platonists like Philo.[44] God became the dynamic bearer of the eternal ideas. With God as the thinker of the ideas, one can have a vertical hierarchy of forms and universals: ideas and universals belong to different levels of reality. The first belong to the transcendent and ineffable Divine mind and the second to empirical reality. This has various advantages. With this framework we can combine both realism and scepticism. With regard to the Divine mind, it is clear that we do not have ready access to its 'contents'! With regard to universals in the physical world, we can adjudicate the relevant scientific considerations. A good example is provided by the problems in biology with the definition of a species. After Darwin, we think of this in rather nominalistic terms as belonging to a population with quite blurred edges. If we find that it is difficult to find clear cut boundaries for the species *Homo sapiens*, we can still accept this while upholding the view that the distinctiveness of humanity is grounded in an archetypal quality, however dimly perceived. We can think of the patterns that we encounter in the world as a dark mirror or glass (sometimes more like a palimpsest) of patterns which ultimately reflect the eternal archetypes in the Divine mind – however obscurely. I would rather think of these patterns as images *(eikones)* of archetypes rather than universals *in rebus*.

This also enables us to address the characteristic postmodern worry. If no essences are available to us, then 'metaphysics' is an obsolete exercise. That does not follow. We can identify items and patterns in the world, the schism between fact and values, the puzzles of time, etc. without being able to peer into, as it were, Aristotelian essences. In fact, the Platonic view sketched above

---

[44] J. M. Dillon, *The Middle Platonists* (Ithaca, NY: Cornell University Press, 1977), p. 95.

suggests, like Hamlet to Horatio, that some truths are unattainable and there may be many facts beyond the grasp of the finite mind.

The desert landscape of nominalism is distinctly uninviting. It is manifestly implausible to consider the identities instantiated in the order, beauty and simplicity of the physical cosmos to be *merely* verbal. A materialist will find the rejection of abstract objects as congenial as the rejection of ethical or aesthetic facts, but a theist is more readily open to a domain beyond the purview of the hard sciences. An Aristotelian world of substances is equally hostile to materialism and nominalism as the Platonic doctrine of a world that participates in transcendent forms.

Abstract Objects and Aseity

The genius of Plato, informed by his own meditation or by the traditional knowledge of the priests of Egypt, had ventured to explore the mysterious nature of the Deity. When he had elevated his mind to the sublime contemplation of the first self-existent, necessary cause of the universe, the Athenian sage was incapable of conceiving *how* the simple unity of his essence could admit the infinite variety of distinct and successive ideas which compose the model of the intellectual world; *how* a Being purely incorporeal could execute that perfect model, and mould with a plastic hand the rude and independent chaos. The vain hope of extricating himself from these difficulties, which must ever oppress the feeble powers of the human mind, might induce Plato to consider the divine nature under the threefold modification – of the first cause, the reason, or *The Logos*, and the soul or spirit of the universe. His poetical imagination sometimes fixed and animated these metaphysical abstractions; the three *archical* or original principles were represented in the Platonic system as three Gods, united with each other by a mysterious and ineffable generation; and the Logos was particularly considered under the more accessible character of the Son of an Eternal Father, and the Creator and Governor of the world. Such appear to have been the secret doctrines which were cautiously whispered in the gardens of the Academy; and which, according to the more recent disciples of Plato, could not be perfectly understood, till after an assiduous study of thirty years.[45]

---

[45] Edward Gibbon, *The History of the Decline and Fall of the Roman Empire*. 3 vols, ed. David Wormersley (London and New York: Penguin, 1994), vol I, p. 771.

This wonderfully and characteristically eloquent passage by Gibbon is replete with his wit and irony. He studied the Christian Fathers and he was familiar with the profound links between pagan Hellenic metaphysical questions and Christian theology. For all its irony, we have a limpid account of the link between the one and the many and the Christian Trinity in the first centuries after Christ. The status of abstract entities was a motor of speculation in the Academy and the status of mathematical objects in particular was a characteristically Platonic interest in the ancient world.[46]

To what extent is the debate about abstract objects in contemporary thought related to problems concerning the ideas? It is often observed that modern nominalists are more concerned with denying abstract objects than universals or forms. This often-contested distinction between abstract and concrete objects is a modern one, with roots in Frege's claim in *The Foundations of Arithmetic* of 1884 that numbers are objective and *a priori*. Possible worlds, sets, relations and properties are frequently viewed by contemporary philosophers as abstract objects in this sense. There have been both distinguished proponents of the existence of abstract objects like Hilary Putnam and opponents of the theory such as Harty Field.

The problem for theology emerges from the avowal of necessarily existent abstract objects and doctrine of divine aseity. The theist is usually committed to the doctrine that God is *a se*

1. Independent of any other existent
2. The source of the existence of all other beings.

This aseity doctrine is referred to in the literature as AD. If AD is correct, then we face a problem if the theist wants to accept abstract objects.

1. Abstract objects exist necessarily
2. Abstract objects depend upon God
3. As necessary, abstract objects are uncreated and independent.

If one rejects 1 we are faced with the inhospitable Quinean landscape of nominalism. Many theists turn to nominalism explicitly because of the

---

[46] Dillon, *The Middle Platonists*; J. N. Findlay, *Plato: The Written and Unwritten Doctrines* (London: Routledge & Kegan Paul, 1974), pp. 57ff.

abstract objects. William Lane Craig calls it 'the most powerful anti-theistic argument ... the vaunted problem of evil could not compare with its force and rigour. For if abstract objects cannot be created by God and such things do exist ... then theism at its very heart is logically incoherent.'[47]

The denial of 2 raises the problem of ultimacy: God seems to be denied his role as ultimate principle of reality. The denial of 3 raises the problem of dependency. How can eternal abstract objects be said to depend on anything?[48] There are parallels with aesthetic and ethical considerations, most famously the Euthyphro dilemma. If God is goodness, then does this limit his sovereignty? The theological nominalist is wary of a slippery slope from an initial Platonism into a loss of Divine sovereignty: culminating, perhaps, in some sinister and flat Spinozism: *Deus sive natura*.

The Platonic Menagerie and Sancta Simplicitas

One of the key problems that emerges out the multiplicity of the Ideas is the tenet of the unity of the self-sufficient *arche* or *principium* of all reality.[49] Neoplatonism has a solution to this problem by distinguishing between levels of divinity. But this was not available to Christians working in the Platonic tradition, and they tended to telescope what is distinguished by the pagan Platonists. The 'ideas' are often rather confusingly thought of as 'objects'. But this is an unfortunate instance of what the Heideggerians call 'Verdinglichung' or reification. The ideas as objects of intellection in the Divine mind became fused with Aristotle's model of the Divine mind as thought thinking itself, particularly in Plotinus's extraordinary vision of the transcendent plenitude, the Divine Intellect as the creative self-awareness and interpenetrating totality of the world of Forms. Plotinus is the source of the doctrine of holenmerism,

---

[47] W. Lane Craig, 'A Nominalist Perspective on God and Abstract Objects', *Philosophia Christi*, 13, 2, (2011), 305–18.
[48] Paul Gould, 'The Problem of God and abstract objects', *Philosophia Christi*, 13, 2 (2011), 255–74.
[49] W. Norris Clarke, 'The Problem of the Reality and Multiplicity of Divine Ideas in Christian Neoplatonism', in *Neoplatonism and Christian Thought*, ed. D. J. O'Meara (Albany, NY: State University of New York Press, 1982), pp. 109–27.

i.e. that in the spiritual world the whole is present *as whole* in each part.[50] This theory emerged out of the attempt to think of the Divine mind as unitary in so far as having internal aspects, relations or differentiations without thereby being sundered into parts.[51]

This noetic cosmos is neither subject nor object in any obvious sense but the active and illuminating principle of all thought in finite agents. We can find instances of this in the intelligible world of the Cappodocians or Augustine – from the uncreated Logos to the created world of ideas and angels. We can remain agnostic about the contents and structure of the Divine mind and the noetic realm in general; unlike Dante who boldly exposes Gregory's self-correction in the *Paradiso* XXVII, an episode in which the post-mortem Gregory realizes that it was Dionysius who correctly depicted the details of the celestial realm! We can also bracket speculation about the Divine essence and the energies. But it is clear that the question of properties is very mysterious at this level.

While Plantinga seems close to holding a theory like that of Augustine at the end of *Does God have a Nature?*, he is severely critical of the doctrine of simplicity (DDS) 'If God is identical with each of his properties, then each of his properties is identical with each of his properties, so that God has but one property.' But this contradicts the obvious fact that God has several properties; 'he has power and mercifulness, say, neither of which is identical with the other'. Secondly, and more seriously, 'if God is identical with each of his properties, then, since each of his properties is a property, he is property – a self-exemplifying property'. But God is a person and not a property. Plantinga goes on to assert vigorously: 'No property could have created the world; no property could be omniscient, or, indeed, know anything at all. If God is a property, then he isn't a person but a mere abstract object; he has no knowledge, awareness, power, love or life. So taken, the simplicity doctrine seems an utter mistake.'[52]

The simplicity of God, however, is not a specific property which might be identified with other related properties like beauty or goodness. Just as the

---

[50] On this doctrine, see R. Pasnau, *Metaphysical Themes 1274–1671*, V.8[31] (Oxford: Oxford University Press, 2011), pp. 339ff.
[51] The *locus classicus* is Plotinus, *Ennead* V 8.
[52] Plantinga, *Does God Have a Nature?* p. 47.

absolute One should not be confused with numerical one, the simplicity of the Divine One is not a unique attribute nor the phenomenon that several Divine properties may regarded as (however puzzlingly) identical, but rather the One is prior to any attribution of properties.[53]

It will not do, as is the wont of many staunch defenders of DDS, to deny the personality of God. That makes a nonsense of the first lines of the Lord's prayer, among other problems. But to say that God is a 'person' is at least as problematic as saying that he is 'simple'. The very idea of an infinite person, as Spinoza observed, is not immediately intelligible. And orthodox doctrine won't help us since Chalcedon says that he is one substance and three persons!

Plantinga admits that Aquinas on Divine simplicity is puzzling, but that is hardly surprising given the latter's negative theology. The ascription of properties that we habitually employ in relation to composite material items in relation to a transcendent simple Being requires analogy. It cannot mean that Aquinas identifies God with a property or attribute. Simplicity is not another attribute of the Divine but the key principle of Thomas's apophaticism.

Brian Davies says of the doctrine of divine simplicity: 'It is an agnostic conception of divinity.'[54] However, negation is a relative term. One might strip away the fussy and ornate Victorian additions to a sublimely beautiful eighteenth-century chapel and discover thereby an even more powerful place of worship. But that is unlike the complete demolition of the edifice and creating a void. The theist wants to 'strip away' the barriers to contemplating the Divine plenitude rather than dissolution in Nirvana. The Thomist doctrine of simplicity is the motor of negative theology but it is not just that. It is also the preparation for the contemplation of the transcendent perfection of the Divine nature. It is simplicity – the One *in* the many – that forms the precondition of any form of explanation. How can a world that is merely a receptacle of numerically separate and unrelated individuals be an object of scientific inquiry? It is through the employment of theories of elegance and simplicity that the turbid, eerie and menacing environment of our hunter-gather ancestors became the intelligible and predictable domain of modern science.

---

[53] Plotinus, *Ennead* V.3[49]. 12.51-2. The One is '*pro tou ti*'.
[54] Brian Davies, *Philosophy of Religion* (Oxford: Oxford University Press, 2000), p. 560.

Indeed, Davies's critique of Plantinga leaves out the theory of Divine ideas in Thomas – his account of the *rationes rerum* in the Divine Word (*Verbum*) and it is through these ideas that *ad quas facta sunt omnia*, according to which ideas all things are made (excepting of course the *imago Dei* itself, the spontaneity of which, for Dietrich, Eckhart and Cusanus, requires something more profound. Eckhart's exposition of the classic passage of the 'I am that I am' Exodus 3.14 'Ego sum qui sum' is pertinent, where he meditates upon the overflowing fecundity, the 'boiling over' of the self sufficient great I am,[55] through whom, as the Creed puts it, all is made in made in heaven and on earth).[56] Aquinas quotes the Neoplatonic philosopher Proclus:

> 'Every divine thing is simple in the first and greatest degree, and because of this it is self sufficient in the greatest degree (*maxime per se sufficiens*).'[57]

Aquinas writes approvingly about the Neoplatonic text known in the Middle Ages as the *Liber de causis*:

> But, the author of (the *Liber de causis*) passes over the first part of Proclus's proposition, which concerns simplicity, presupposing it as it were, and speaks only self sufficiency, which he signifies by the word 'riches'. And where Proclus says in his proposition that God is 'self sufficient', the author says 'the first is rich owing to itself' (*Primum est dives propter seipsum*).[58]

Aquinas is recommending this vision of the transcendent unity-simplicity of the First Principle (i.e. God) that is a self-sufficient plenitude or abundance out of which the plurality of items in the physical cosmos emerges. It is clearly a powerful and productive source and cause rather than a vacuum or a sterile abyss. The paradigmatic biblical passage of Exodus 3.14 was traditionally interpreted in the light of the doctrine of simplicity. The self-utterance of the Divine to Moses was taken as the identity thesis: whatever God has, he is.

We could, of course, say that our ancestors were labouring under hermeneutical illusions. Yet in terms of Christian theology, I do not see why this

---

[55] See Beiewaltes, *Platonismus und Idealismus*, 2nd ed. (Frankfurt; Klostermann: 2004) 37–67.
[56] Vivian Boland, *Ideas in God According to Saint Thomas Aquinas: Sources and Syntheses* (Leiden: Brill, 1996).
[57] Peter Weigel, *Aquinas on Simplicity: An Investigation into the Foundations of his Philosophical Theology* (Bern: Peter Lang, 2008), p. 115.
[58] Ibid.

interpretation of Exodus is less legitimate than, say, the Christian appropriation of the Psalms.

The problem of simplicity and the Ideas bears analogy with the problem of the coherence of the Trinity. The Christian theologian has often claimed that simplicity is not compromised by the mutual interpenetration of persons existing in relation within the Triune Godhead: the περιχώρησις or co-inherence (circumincession) of *personae* does not constitute a complex assemblage of material or quasi material items. The unity of the Godhead is not composite. We may distinguish between the persons of the Trinity on the basis of Scripture and tradition but remain conscious that these distinctions do not correspond to ontological divisions within the Divine unity.

> The office of philosophical *disquisition* consists in just *distinction*; while it is the privilege of the philosopher to preserve himself constantly aware, that distinction is not division. In order to obtain adequate notions of any truth, we must intellectually separate its distinguishable parts; and this is the technical process of philosophy. But having so done, we must then restore them in our conceptions to the unity, in which they actually co-exist; and this is the *result* of philosophy.[59]

In the case of the Trinity, we need to distinguish while not attributing division. If we do that to safeguard the unity of Trinity, I do not see why we cannot apply distinctions to the unity of the Divine intellect without thereby attributing any diremption of the same into *parts*.

The conflict is between the 'mystical theism' that has been nourished by Neoplatonism and what one could deem 'monarchical theism', in which the contrast or gulf between God and creation is stressed. The former is hostile to positing 'otherness' in the Divine as a virtually idolatrous confusion of Divine transcendence with remoteness. The truly transcendent Divine is not 'other' in the manner of different material objects. In fact, this 'non-otherness' of the Divine is precisely a characteristic of His difference from all finite beings. For the Monarchical theism, mystical theism appears to collapse pantheism or a denial of the fully personal nature of God.

---

[59] Coleridge, *Biographia Literaria*, eds J. Engell and W. Jackson Bate (Princeton, NJ: Princeton University Press, 1983), II, p. 11.

Why Persist in Using the Language of Divine Ideas?

Empson writes:

> The western half of the Eurasian land mass, unlike the eastern, has long regarded its supreme God or ultimate reality as a person; but it has also realized that this is a tricky belief which requires a subtle qualification. His Godhead must be mysteriously one with Goodness itself, so that he neither imposes moral law by (fiat) nor is himself bound by it as external to him. As regards his Godhead, he is the impersonal Absolute of Hinduism; he is built into the moral structure of the universe so as to be quite unlike other persons, and his other unique powers (Omnipotence, omniscience and absolute foreknowledge) are merely a result.[60]

Empson, hardly a very sympathetic critic of Western theism, is making a telling observation. There is a tension in the Western intellectual tradition between the monarchical and mystical models of the deity; the one stresses the strangeness and even terror of the Godhead, the other the presence; the one underlines the personal dimension, the other the radical perfection of the transcendent source.

Coleridge avers that 'to suppose God without Ideas … would destroy the very conception of God'.[61] The place of the Divine ideas implies a connection, however mysterious, between God's essence and creature, the necessary and the contingent.[62] The physical cosmos is the mirror of the Divine: a theophany. This world is a luminous array of images reflecting (although often enigmatically) the perfect being of the Divine. I want to stress the idea of the *continuity* between the transcendent cause of all reality, potential and actual, and particular effects of that cause. For the sake of clarity, we are not speaking of any pantheistic continuity. The ultimate transcendence of the source is maintained. I wish to suggest the continuing pertinence of the language of 'participation'.

Plato momentously presents the physical cosmos as 'participating' in the ideas (*Phaedo* 99c6ff.). In the *Timaeus*, the world of becoming is a 'likeness'

---

[60] W. Empson, *Milton's God* (New York: New Directions, 1961), p. 94.
[61] Coleridge, *Opus Maximum*, ed. Thomas MacFarland (Princeton, NJ: Princeton University Press, 2002), p. 223.
[62] For some of these issues in medieval debates see G. Leff, *Medieval Thought: St Augustine to Ockham* (London: Merlin Press, 1958), p. 268.

of its intelligible archtetype. In the *Republic* V 480a or the *Symposium* 211c we find the celebrated ascent to 'absolute beauty'. The various terms in Greek for participation are not much clearer than their English counterparts but the term has since been taken (especially through the enormous influence of the *Timaeus*) as expressing the connection between the sensible and intelligible world – the visible '*kosmos aisthetos*' as the '*eikon*' of the '*kosmos noetos*'. Aristotle, in rejecting the language of participation, dismissed this as merely a poetic manner of speaking, *Metaphysics* (987b7-14; 991a20-22; 1079b24-26). Unlike Plato's relatively inchoate and suggestive theology, Aristotle has a clear conception of the Divine mind. The God of Aristotle is a final cause and not an efficient cause of the physical cosmos. Moreover, Aristotle's deity is not the basis for any exemplarism. It is with the Neoplatonists, however, that we find a clearly *causal* view of participation, whereby the imperfect domain is dependent upon a perfect transcendent source for its being. The idea of 'participation', through the influence of Neoplatonism, was a pivotal aspect of late antique and medieval thought, e.g. Avicenna, Maimonides and Aquinas. The distinguished American Thomist W. Norris Clarke, S. J. (1917–2008) offered the following definition:

> Participation (in the order of real being) = a structure or order of relationship between beings such that they all share in various degrees of fullness in some positive property or perfection common to them all, as received from the same one source: all finite beings participate in existence from God. A Neoplatonic (not Aristotelian) doctrine adapted by Aquinas to express his own essence/existence metaphysics.[63]

Creatio Ex Nihilo, Emanation and Other Red Herrings?

It is often claimed that the distinctive Judaeo-Christian doctrine of *creatio ex nihilo* is a necessary bulwark against the theory of emanation. It is the contrast between the freely chosen gift of creation and the necessary manifestation of an impersonal absolute. Many theists opine that if we accept eternal abstract

---

[63] W. Norris Clarke, *The One and the Many: A Contemporary Thomistic Metaphysics* (South Bend: Notre Dame, 2001), p. 318.

objects, the doctrine of *creatio ex nihilo* is threatened.[64] How do we understand '*creatio ex nihilo*', and how do we understand emanation? Much has been written about this. I restrict myself to couple of polemical remarks.

The theist wishes to maintain the asymmetry of the relation between God and world *against* the pantheist, and this asymmetry is well protected by DDS. If we take *creatio ex nihilo* to mean the lack of pre-existing materials, then any serious Platonist can accept that. If it means made 'out of thin air', concocted randomly, i.e. the arbitrary or wilful appearance of the world, then the Platonist will object. What about emanation? If 'emanation' means a series composed of a succession of stages in which each level proceeds from the former stage, then the Christian theist cannot tolerate this. However, if the term is used in a looser sense (as by Denys the Areopagite or Thomas Aquinas), it is not clear why the Christian theist cannot make use of such models of 'flowing'.[65] If God's nature is love and it is God's nature to communicate that love, this is a form of necessity. It is a necessity grounded in the divine essence – it is intrinsic to God. Insofar as it is not *extrinsic* to God, we can say that this manifestation of love is an act of self-determination. It reflects God's nature and not any arbitrary will.[66]

John Smith writes:

> God is the *First Truth and Primitive Goodness*; true *Religion Efflux and Emanation of Both* upon the Spirits of men and therefore is called *a participation of the Divine nature.*[67]

Jonathan Edwards insists in full Platonic vein:

> as there is an infinite fullness of possible good in God, a fullness of every perfection, of all excellency and beauty ... And as this fullness is capable of communication or emanation *ad extra*; so it seems a thing amiable and valuable

---

[64] See Brian Leftow, 'Is God an Abstract Object?', *Nous* 24 (1990), 581–98.
[65] I am grateful to Joshua Robinson for sharing his unpublished paper: Emanation, Creation *ex nihilo*, or *tertium quid?*: Proclus, Nicholas of Methone, and Dionysius the Areopagite. See also T. Bonin, *Creation as Emanation: The Origin of Diversity in Albert the Great's On the Causes and the Procession of the Universe* (South Bend: Notre Dame Press, 2001). See my own article: 'Pantheism, Trinitarian Theism and the Idea of Unity: Reflections on the Christian Concept of God', *Religious Studies*, 32 1 (1996), 61–77.
[66] Schelling denied creation out of nothing: *Werke*, 21.288-89; 2.2.32-33. 'All finite beings have been created out of relative nonbeing yet not out of nothing', *Werke*, 1.7.436.
[67] John Smith, *Select Discourses* (Royston: Flesher, 1660), p. 380.

in itself that it should be communicated or flow forth, that this infinite fountain of good should send forth abundant streams, that this fountain of light should, diffusing its excellent fullness, pour forth light all around. And as this is in itself excellent, so a disposition to this in the Divine Being must be looked upon as a perfection or an excellent disposition; such an emanation of good is, in some sense, a multiplication of it.[68]

The language of the communication or emanation of the Divine diffusing its 'excellent fullness' is unmistakably the language of participation. Sixty-two years later, S. T. Coleridge (1774–1832) writes of the symbol as: 'the translucence of the eternal through and in the temporal. It always partakes of the reality which it renders intelligible; and while it enunciates the whole, abides itself as a living part in that unity of which it is the representative.'[69] Coleridge clearly builds on a conviction that the symbol has an ontological foundation.

The Divine Nature or Voluntarism?

The place of the Divine ideas, we have argued, implies a real connection, however mysterious, between God's essence and the created world, the necessary and the contingent. This, in turn, is tied to the rejection of the idea of an arbitrary deity. This, I aver, is a very important consequence of the doctrine of Divine ideas. Many critics of Christian theism assume that the Divine command theory is the default account. And one has to admit that there are manifold reasons for this: Why did God choose Jacob over Esau? What should we think of Kierkegaard's odd relish of Abraham's near sacrifice of Isaac on Mount Moria? How should we view Joshua's laying waste to Canaan or the later Augustine's dark and troubling theory of predestination? The tenet of Divine ideas forms a way of insisting upon God as goodness itself, the culmination of being, rather than a continent and wilful being.

Plantinga brusquely dismisses liberal Protestantism in his *Does God have a Nature?* I have sympathy for that out-of-fashion Liberal Protestant claim that we can know something of the 'Jesus of History'. There is nothing remarkable

---

[68] J. Edwards, 'Dissertation', *Works* 8:433.
[69] Coleridge, 'Statesman's Manual', p. 30.

about Jesus's insistence on Divine sovereignty. It is that Jesus was preaching a doctrine of Divine love that is hard to parallel in the eschatological asperities of John the Baptist or the legalism of the Pharisees. (This, after all, was the teaching that struck Tolstoy, Gandhi and Martin Luther King with such inspirational force.) If that doctrine and life is a mirror into the Divine nature, which Christians wish to maintain with the *homoousion*, then perhaps the teaching and life of the Galilean Rabbi reveals the Divine essence and not the arbitrary will of a cosmic demiurge.

It is part of the warp and woof of Platonic metaphysics to envisage physical cosmos as exhibiting *patterns* which are exemplified in individuals. Such patterns are repeatable and form the basis of laws and thus predictions.[70] These law-like regularities are so deeply entrenched that it is implausible to view them in the nominalist mode as conventions. 'To explain is to strip the reality of the appearances covering it like a veil, in order to see the bare reality itself.'[71] To pass a drink widdershins, or to drive on the right in Great Britain, are breaches of convention. These are matters of etiquette, superstition, road safety or law. If a brown rabbit turns purple, or a cat flies, this is an abrogation of a far deeper law: one of nature. It is very difficult for Empiricism, with its wariness of attributing 'occult powers' to objects and relations, to generate properly the required distinction between law-like generalizations and accidental regularities. Science requires counterfactual resilience and robust inductive strength for a satisfactory account of a scientific law. This raises the spectre of the ontological extravagance of Platonism.

The Platonist views individuals and nomic events of 'nature' as part of a rule-based hierarchical system of relations at the apex of which is a transcendent *prius*: the Good, the One or the Absolute.

---

[70] Simon Conway Morris's concept of 'convergence' as expressed in *Life's Solution: Inevitable Humans in a Lonely Universe* (Cambridge: Cambridge University Press, 2003) seems to me the application of a Platonic intuition to biology. He uses the instances where animals that are biologically remote produce similar evolutionary features in response to similar pressures of selection. There are many examples of this phenomenon – often cited are species of Australian marsupial mammals and completely distinct placental mammals outside Australia. Conway Morris emphasises that the existence of existence of laws implies predictability and that evolution must have developed in a particular direction, and that human evolution in particular was 'inevitable'. See S. Conway Morris, *The Runes of Evolution* (West Conshohocken: Templeton, 2015).

[71] Pierre Duhem, *The Aim and Structure of Physical Theory* (Princeton, NJ: Princeton University Press, 1954).

If one accepts the idea of the physical world as a complex set of intelligible law-like relations, i.e. a *cosmos* in the etymological sense of its beauty and order, but denies the cognate idea of the transcendent ground of that intelligibility, the prerequisite for science – the very intelligibility of the world – becomes bewildering. As Coleridge observes: 'There is in Form something which is not elementary but divine. The contemplation of Form is astonishing to Man and has a kind of Trouble or Impulse accompanying it, which exalts the soul to God.'[72]

This supreme principle is Being *itself* rather than an instance thereof, however exalted. It must exist necessarily. This *ens necessarium* must also be unique since there cannot be a multitude of absolute beings! It must be simple and cannot be sundered into parts. This simple and necessary Being must have the capacity to generate contingent and dependent beings and to encompass all that derivative reality, actual or potential. The supreme principle must possess some form of mind, however remote to the human, and constitute ultimate value. In traditional Platonism, the supreme principle begets a sphere of ideal intelligences or ideas (in more metaphysical forms of early Christian theology this is Logos). From this domain of perfect intellect the subordinate realm of mutable, derivative, contingent and imperfect instantiations emerges. Yet equally if the supreme *prius* is conceived of as a highly elevated, remote or supreme individual, there is a tendency to imagine dependents in the created order as mere minions. Similarly, the First cause can be viewed as essentially arbitrary.

Coleridge's notion of the symbol as an exemplification or participant of the idea (unlike metaphor) is closely related to a metaphysics of instantiation.

> a Symbol (*ho estin aei tautêgorikon*) is characterized by a translucence of the Special in the Individual or of the General in the Especial or of the Universal in the General. Above all by the translucence of the Eternal through and in the Temporal. It always partakes of the Reality it renders intelligible; and while it enunciates the whole, abides itself as a living part in that Unity, of which it is the representative. The other are but empty echoes which the fancy arbitrarily associates with apparitions of matter, less beautiful but not less shadowy than the sloping orchard or hill-side pasture-field seen in the transparent lake below.[73]

---

[72] *The Notebooks of Samuel Taylor Coleridge*, II, 22.
[73] Coleridge, 'The Statesman's Manual', p. 30. See *Symbol and Intuition: Comparative Studies in Kantian and Romantic-Period Aesthetics*, eds Helmut Kühn and James Vigus (Leeds: Maney, 2013).

The symbol presupposes the metaphysics of participation. The symbol 'partakes' in the reality it conveys. The positivists who have shaped Western society so deeply, from Voltaire, Darwin, Freud, or Watson, see changes in terms of society, biology, psychology or genetics. For these, the crudity and superstitions of theology and myth are gradually and properly replaced by a rigorously scientific approach. Perhaps history, however, is the result of participation, constituted by encounter with and responses to the transcendent. Such a history becomes a 'drama of theophany'.[74] Eric Voegelin (1901–1985) was a philosopher who wrote much about participation and 'metaxy' in the context of political thought. He was absorbed by what he viewed as a 'process of transfiguration' in periods of intellectual and social upheaval.[75] Unconvinced by the efforts of the positivists to reduce the explanation of culture and politics to biology or economics, Voegelin saw human agents as quite naturally seeing themselves in a larger drama of seeking 'attunement' with the transcendent.[76]

God's *eternal being* becomes real presence through the imagination – there is an imaginative kinship. Religious imagination functions still without revelation, while revelation stands in need of imagination. Scripture is based upon the claim that finite imagination and the Divine word coincide. One might consider the notion of the prophet. We are confronting individual personalities, quite possibly autobiographical information: Hosea's marriage, Isaiah in Jerusalem and Ezekiel on the bank of the Chebar. Yet his life and particular perspective is by no means eradicated or diminished by his becoming a vehicle of the divine. The prophet is both himself and yet the instrument of Divine communication.

Baudelaire seems to assume something quite close in a beautiful sonnet when he writes:

La Nature est un temple où de vivants piliers
Laissant parfois sortir de confuses paroles;
L'homme y passé a travers des forêts de symbols
Qui l'observent avec des regards familiers[77] (*Correspondances* 1-4)

---

[74] Eric Voegelin, *The Ecumenic Age*, (Baton Rouge: Louisiana State University Press,1974), p. 290.
[75] He was influenced by Schelling's difficult doctrine of the 'Potenzen', a theory which has its roots in Plato's Ideas. These potencies are known primarily in history. See Schelling, *Weltalter: Werke*, 1.8.289-90.
[76] Glenn Hughes, *Mystery and Myth in the Philosophy of Eric Voegelin* (Columbia: University of Missouri Press, 1993), p. 81.
[77] The Christian Platonic elements in Baudelaire have an evident source in Joseph de Maistre. See *Sacrifice Imagined*, pp. 8-12.

The poet is sensitive to the mystery of existence with all the wonder of the child and the intellectual force and critical awareness of the adult.

It is reasonable to appreciate the grasping of ideas as intuitive (although most analytic philosophers deny this). If one views the grasping of ideas as intuitive, then the symbol provides a medium of intuitive vision. The prophet can perceive unity and order where others see only confusion and a world at odds, a whole world rather than a radically disparate composite. The symbol is not a 'concrete' image for an abstract idea but the 'manifestation in a lower mode of the higher reality it symbolizes'.[78]

If the model of the prophet seems unduly 'elitist', it should be noted that there is a distinctly democratic side of the symbol. If ideas can indeed be conveyed through images, there is immediacy to this knowledge and these ideas can be grasped by those who lack the wherewithal, leisure or education to pursue the principles in an abstract manner. Certain truths about morality or society or nature can be conveyed through such images.

This might be described as a middle position between the 'absolute knowledge' of Hegelianism and its fantasy of rational insight into the whole and a reductive positivism. The proper alternative to the Scylla of the Hegelian god's-eye view of reality or the Charybdis of an empiricist positivism lies in the idea of participation. Moreover, the symbol – properly understood – provides a middle way between a debilitating scepticism and an idolatrous and credulous superstition. Human self-consciousness is a 'participation in reality'.[79] This means a subjectivity that is constitutive of human existence and an encounter with objective reality. The ensuing vision is not a fanciful construction but an imaginative response to a transcendent mystery. This vision is intertwined with theophany.

Paul Tillich (1886–1965) would be another writer who explicitly employs the terminology of participation in his theological writings. Thus when we look more carefully, the apparent erosion of the language of 'participation' looks more like a transposition or transformation. Tillich remarks: 'A symbol participates in the reality it symbolizes.' Symbols are figurative expressions of

---

[78] Martin Lings, *Symbol and Archetype, A Study of the Meaning of Existence* (Louisville, KY: Fons Vitae, 2006), p. 67.
[79] Hughes, *Mystery and Myth in the Philosophy of Eric Voegelin*, p. 4.

a non-figurative reality.⁸⁰ The most important distinction between sign and symbol rests in the fact that symbols bear the power of the Unconditional. Hence the *via eminentiae* and *via negativa* are dialectically related in *via symbolica*. There is identity between the divine and human and there is difference; there is a dialectic of negation and affirmation in the symbolic. We see this in the transparency or translucency of the symbol, e.g. water for baptism cleanses physically while representing a spiritual fact. Wine or bread bridge in a similar manner the physical with the spiritual. Yet note that such a concept of the symbol is not merely figurative: its very power presupposes participation in another realm.

There is another order to which we, as human beings, belong, an order which makes man *always* dissatisfied with what is given to him. Man transcends everything in the historical order, all the heights and depths of his own existence. He passes, as no other being is able to pass, beyond the limits of his given world. He participates in something infinite, in an order which is not transitory, not self-destructive, not tragic, but eternal, holy, and blessed.⁸¹

In the *Systematic Theology* Tillich notes that 'philosophers like Cusanus and Leibniz have asserted that the whole universe is present in every individual, although limited by its individual limitations. There are microcosmic qualities in every being, but man alone is microcosmos. In him the world is present not only indirectly and unconsciously but directly and in a conscious encounter. Man participates in the universe through the rational structure of mind and reality.'⁸² One recalls that in Leibniz's *Monadology* there is the famous theory of limited participation of each monad in the Divine perfections (*chaque substance simple ... est ... un miroir vivant perpétual de l'univers*). Once the *imago Dei* doctrine is joined with the *microcosmos*, one has a bridge between the Platonic view – the world as a mirror of divinity – and the scriptural.

The image, as the symbol of a higher reality, is a channel of discernment of the transcendent unity of man and nature in God as the creative source of all being. The poet's vision of the interrelatedness of all contrasts with the

---

[80] Tillich, *The Courage to Be* (London: Fontana, 1962), p. 169.
[81] Tillich, *Shaking the Foundations* (Harmondsworth: Penguin, 1969), p. 31.
[82] Tillich, *Systematic Theology*, Vol. 1, p. 176.

ubiquitous mood of humanity confronting a fractured, 'fallen' and insubstantial world. In his seminal work *From Religion to Philosophy*, F. M. Cornford lays stress upon the ritual and 'mystical' sources of Plato's doctrine of the Forms in the mystery cults, with the emphasis upon the active presence of the deity in the believers.[83] The Neoplatonists sustained this 'religious' dimension of Plato's thought and developed it systematically. Without wishing the embrace the whole of Cornford's account of Plato's doctrine of participation, this observation remains perspicacious. The doctrine of participation is more than an abstract theory: it is a summons to conversion.

---

[83] F. M. Cornford, *From Religion to Philosophy* (New York: Longmans, Green and Co., 1912).

6

Idolatry and Iconoclasm

'The true Neoplatonist is at once an idoloclast and an iconodule.'[1]

Idols and Icons

The distinguished French phenomenologist and philosopher of religion Jean-Luc Marion brought the theme of idolatry to the forefront of the phenomenological tradition in philosophy. From his earliest writings, Marion wishes to emancipate God from the bogus restrictions of ontology. The idol limits God and serves as a mirror of the human gaze. The icon, by contrast, opens up the vision of the invisible – the irreducible transcendent God of love. Whereas the idol is the product of the gaze, the icon admits the transcendent invisible. While the idol, for Marion, serves to abolish the proper distance between God and creation, the icon points to the infinite. Through the icon, human concepts are overwhelmed.

Through the influence of Heidegger, the opposition of idol and icon is linked to a bypassing of the tradition of metaphysics. Deeply influenced by both the 'Death of God' in Nietzsche and by Karl Barth and von Balthasar, Marion fuses an emphasis upon primacy of Divine self-revelation with the insistence upon freeing that self-revelation from the bounds set by metaphysics or modern subjectivity (which according to Heidegger are cognate phenomena).[2] Marion

---

[1] A. H. Armstrong, *Downside Review* 95 (1977), 176–89 [reprinted in *Plotinian and Christian Studies*, XXIV].
[2] On the question of Heidegger and the Greek metaphysical tradition see Beierwaltes, 'Heideggers Rückgang zu den Griechen' in *Fussnoten zu Platon* (Frankfurt: Klostermann, 2010), pp. 345–69 and 'EPEKEINA. Anmerkung zu Heideggers Platon-Rezeption', *Fussnoten zu Platon*, pp. 371–88. See also Narbonne, *Hénologie, Ontologie et Ereignis (Plotin- Proclus-Heidegger)* (Paris: Les Belles Lettres, 2001).

stresses the denial of presence.³ Not that even the young Marion was held entirely spellbound by the *'Meister aus Deutschland'.*⁴ Heidegger himself comes under fire for his residual philosophy of subjectivity qua *Dasein* and the exclusion or prescription of God through the overarching concept of Being. Marion's critique of the 'idol' relies upon this theological critique of the domestication of God, i.e. the restriction of divinity itself to the pale of human subjectivity.⁵ Rather than the gaze of the human subject, the icon is constituted by the reversal: Christ the paradigmatic icon is God looking at the human subject.⁶

I cannot do justice to Marion's rich phenomenology of the saturated phenomenon and his critique of Kant, nor to his complex relationship with Levinas. The strong aesthetic and contemplative, indeed liturgical, dimension of Marion's work is a powerful corrective. The relentless polemic against epistemology, however, means that Marion is reluctant to discuss the experience or the imagination of God apart from invoking the familiar Neoplatonic paradoxes, derived in the main from Pseudo-Denys, and Marion's theological mentor, von Balthasar.

Marion's insistence is that God's revelation is incomprehensible. Is this compatible with the tenets of Christian theology, with St Paul in Romans 1.20. Indeed for revelation to be understood as revelation, it requires some point of contact with the recipient. If the icon is supposed to supplant the activity of the imagination, then this will collapse into a theological positivism. The problem can be seen in relation to the self. His recent book on Augustine is entitled *Au lieu de soi*.⁷ Much hangs upon the interpretation

---

³ Gary Gutting, *Thinking the Impossible* (Oxford: Oxford University Press, 2011), pp. 149ff.
⁴ Rüdiger Safranski, *Heidegger. Ein Meister aus Deutschland: Heidegger und seine Zeit* (Munich: Hanser, 1997). The word play in the title is lost in the English translation: Heidegger: *Between Good and Evil. Ein Meister aus Deutschland* resonates with Paul Celan's 'Der Tod ist ein Meister aus Deutschland' in his beautiful and terrifying poetic meditation on the Holocaust, *Todesfüge*, as well as Meister Eckhart.
⁵ Marion, *The Idol and the Distance: Five Studies* (New York: Fordham University Press, 2001), pp. 6ff. Pavel Florensky's *Iconostasis* (Crestwood, NY: St Vladimir's Seminary Press, US, 1996) is the modern classic on icons. See Tsakiridou, *Icons in Time, Persons in Eternity: Orthodox Theology and the Aesthetics of the Christian Image* (Aldershot: Ashgate, 2013).
⁶ One might note that not all icons are starkly formal and static. Cretan icons emerged out of a more realistic and less stylized tradition of icon painting influenced by Venetian art. Hence El Greco could rapidly become a 'Western artist'.
⁷ Marion, *Au lieu de soi: L'approche de St Augustin* (Paris: Presses Universitaire de France, 2008). Translated as *In the Self's Place: The Approach of St Augustine*, trans. J. Kosky (Stanford: Stanford University Press, 2012).

of the self. John Smith insists that 'Self-Will is the greatest Idol in the world: it is an Anti-Christ; it is an anti God.'[8] Such self-will is the striving of a false self, the bloated ego. Yet for Augustine the interior ascent of the soul to God in contemplation is the *transformation* rather the *obliteration* or brute *substitution* of the self. The spiritual life is one of participation in a reality greater than the self; however it can only be interpreted and appreciated through self-consciousness. The self that rises to the Divine is the product of conversion not replacement.[9] A good and simple example of subjectivity which is not 'shut off' from the world is reading. It is by definition a private affair – the decoding by an individual of symbols on a page. Yet this private and necessarily subjective practice is the path to a much wider world: *tolle lege*!

Although neither Plotinus nor Augustine employs the language of imagination to express this conversion of the self, it is the wholly appropriate language of 'learned ignorance'.[10] However scandalous or troubling, for revelation to have meaning, it has to address some basic human needs and desires. If God's goodness and purposes, however remote and surpassing, do not provide some basis for *imaginative* engagement, it is hard to appreciate what the meaning and force of the Christian message could be.

By way of analogy, I think it is misleading to set up a strict either/or of *icon* or *idol*. Christianity transformed the pagan idols rather than obliterated them. Before the fourth century, there is not much evidence of specifically Christian icons. Especially after Constantine, Christianity seems to have integrated the common pagan use of images. Thus the icon not only has Hebraic antecedents, but is, moreover, the product of a syncretistic development – a harrowing *and* hallowing of heathen practice. One might see a parallel with sacrifice. When Paul frequently speaks of the Christian life as an 'offering and fragrant sacrifice' (e.g. Ephesians 5.2) this is the transformation of the pagan sacrifice rather than its complete rejection. Like René Girard, Marion is drawn into an overwrought and uncompromising antithesis between the Christian

---

[8] Benjamin Whichcote, *The Sermons of Benjamin Whichcote* 1–4, ed. William Wishart (Edinburgh: TW and T Ruddimans, 1742), p. 75.
[9] This is not to deny the complexity surrounding the concept of selfhood in antiquity.
[10] See Beierwaltes, *Das Wahre Selbst: Studien zu Plotins Begriff des Geistes und des Einen* (Frankfurt: Klostermann, 2001).

and pagan, which is belied by the actual language and argument of Paul, Augustine or Origen.

The relation between Christian and pagan antique culture was often deeply conflictual and the fear of idolatry a central aspect of Christian teaching and practice; not least because of persecution and martyrdom. In the early years of the emergence of Christianity as a mass religion in the Mediterranean and Asia Minor, some Emperors like Domitian (AD 81–96) fiercely persecuted Christians. In AD 111 Pliny, the governor of the Roman province of Pontus and Bithynia, wrote to the Emperor Trajan about the problem he faced with the Christians. The Christians refused to worship the emperor and offer sacrifices to the Roman gods. Although he could not take seriously the rumours about cannibalism and though they seemed otherwise law-abiding citizens, Pliny wanted advice about how to deal with this puzzling phenomenon. The judicious emperor Trajan replied that Pliny had acted correctly in attempting to enforce the Roman cult, with its sacrifice. He did, however, warn against anonymous accusations as at odds with the 'spirit of the age' and unworthy of Roman culture. Clearly this monotheistic sect, with its roots in Judaism, was a powerful irritant in the early Roman Empire, provoking both cruel repression and puzzled and strained forbearance. The throng of ancient gods is identified with demons in later Christian writers like Milton:

> Nor had they yet among the Sons of Eve
> Got them new Names …
>
> Men took
>
> Devils to adore for Deities:
> Then were they known to men by various Names,
> And various Idols through the Heathen World
>
> Th' Ionian Gods, of Javans Issue held
> Gods, yet confest later then Heav'n and Earth
> Their boasted parents; Titan Heavn's first born
> With his enormous brood, and birthright seis'd
> By younger Saturn, he from mightier Jove
> His own and Rhea's Son like measure found;

> So Jove usurping reign'd these first in Creet
> And Ida known, thence on the Snowy top
> Of cold Olympus ruled the middle Air
> Their highest Heav'n; or on the Delphian Cliff,
> Or in Dodona, and through all the bounds of
> Doric land[11]

Here the humanist Milton articulates the widespread theory that the Greek gods were demons, which goes back to Augustine.

Sacrifice is often a key element in the critique of 'idols'. The Sanskrit 'puja', which in the Classical tradition means worship in the broadest sense, may well refer to the daubing of the stone of icon with sacrificial blood.[12] Lucretius caustically observes '*tantum religio potuit suadere malorum*' while discussing the sacrifice of Iphigenia by her father Agamemnon.[13] Monotheistic religion has had a complex relation to the idea of sacrifice, but it has often been associated with cruel and superstitious polytheism. Smith refers to the moving account of sacrifice of Iphigenia in Lucretius.[14] There is a long Neoplatonic tradition of the critique of anthropomorphism and credulity. Superstition, the Cambridge Platonist John Smith claims, is 'an overtimorous and dreadfull apprehension of the deity'.[15] The Sufi tradition in Islam shares this fear of anthropomorphism and credulousness. Ibn Arabi writes:

> In general, most men have, perforce, an individual concept of their Lord, which they ascribe to Him and in which they seek Him. So long as the reality is presented to them according to it they recognise Him and affirm Him, whereas if presented in any other form, they deny Him, flee from Him, and treat Him improperly, while at the same time imagining that they are acting towards him fittingly. One who believes (in the ordinary way) believes only in the deity he has created himself, since a deity in 'beliefs' is a mental construction.[16]

Indeed, superstition for John Smith leads to a sense of religion as bribery. Pharasaick Righteousness comes from the 'bare External appearance of

---

[11] John Milton, *Paradise Lost* 1: 364ff.
[12] Diana Eck, *Darsán, Seeing the Divine Image in India* (Chambersburg, PA: Anima Books, 1985), p. 61.
[13] De rerum Natura, trans. W. H. D. Rouse. Rev. Martin Ferguson Smith. (London: Heinemann, 1975). I.101: Also III, 51–4; IV 1236–9; V 1198-1203 for a critique of sacrifice.
[14] De rerum Natura, 1.80-101
[15] John Smith, *Select Discourses*, p. 26.
[16] Ibn 'Arabi, *The Bezels of Wisdom*, trans. R. W. J. Austin (Mahwah, NJ: Paulist Press, 1980), p. 137.

Religion'. Criticizing Plutarch, Smith considers polytheism (which he associates with demons) just a branch of superstition.

The pantheon of exotic Hindu deities may seem to resemble their Indo-European kin in the Graeco-Roman gods. Hinduism is a religion that has been perennially associated with idolatry and polytheism. The Vedic period seems aniconic; the iconic image in Hinduism seems to be about 2,000 years old.[17] In the Jabala Upanishad it seems that the image is a mere instrument: 'Yogins see Siva in the soul and not in images. Images are meant for the imagination of the ignorant.'[18] In Hinduism Shiva and Vishnu frequently have iconic and aniconic forms, yet it is widely agreed that the supreme deity is beyond form. Partha Mitter, in *Much Maligned Monsters* discusses in great detail European perceptions of Indian art as idolatrous, especially depictions of the Indian gods as 'monsters'[19], a view which lasted throughout the Middle Ages until it diminished in the seventeenth century.[20] Alexander Duff described Hinduism as 'a stupendous system of error.'[21] Alfred Lyall refers to

> looking down upon a tangled jungle of disorderly superstitions, upon ghosts and demons, demigods, and deified saints; upon household gods, tribal gods, local gods, with their countless shrines and temples, and the din of their discordant chaos...looking down upon such a religious chaos.[22]

Mitter, as a pupil of Ernst Gombrich, insists that 'whenever we try to understand something unfamiliar, we proceed from the known to the unknown.'[23] Mitter proposes that the 'known' was the Graeco-Roman world of mythological creatures inherited from classical Antiquity. These monsters of India were initially considered by the Europeans to be generally harmless.[24] They were increasingly identified, however, with Christian devils and demons, and assumed a more sinister and malevolent dimension. On Mitter's account, the Classical tradition of 'monstrous races' and the Christian theme of 'demons'

---

[17] Eck, *Darsán*, p. 34. Aniconic in the sense of natural elements like fire or stones.
[18] Heather Elgood, *Hinduism and the Religious Arts* (London: Cassell, 1999), p. 36.
[19] Partha Mitter, *Much Maligned Monsters: A History of European Reactions to Indian Art* (Chicago IL: University of Chicago Press, 1992), p. 2.
[20] Mitter, *Much Maligned Monsters*, p. 27.
[21] Ankur Barua, *Debating Conversion in Hinduism and Christianity* (London: Routledge, 2015), p. 65.
[22] Barua, *Debating Conversion in Hinduism and* Christianity, p. 65.
[23] Mitter, *Much Maligned Monsters*, p. 4.
[24] Mitter, *Much Maligned Monsters*, p. 9.

fused.²⁵ Mitter uses Ludovico di Varthema of Bologna, travelling in South India between 1503 and 1508, as an instance of monsters of the Western Imagination. Varthema, remarked that even though the King of Calicut seemed to be a monotheist who recognised a supreme god, he also paid homage to the devil.²⁶ Varthema's depiction of this devil, however, reveals European rather than Indian roots. Imagery drawn from the book of Revelation, especially imagery of the Anti-Christ, seems to have played a considerable role.

Such perceptions persisted well into the 19th century and 'the essence of evil idolatry begins only in the idea or belief of a real presence of any kind, in a thing in which there is no presence…Nearly all Indian architecture and Chinese design arise out of such a state.'²⁷ John Ruskin saw art as the expression of moral principle and saw the savagery of the 1857 uprising against the British rule as indicative of it. Mitter notes that Ruskin maintained that the beauty expressed by Indian art, with its dazzling colour and ornamentation, was the product of an immoral society.²⁸

There is also the question of power. The cult of the Roman emperors like Augustus was linked to the power associated with images. In the twentieth century the power of images has been evinced in both sophisticated liberal capitalist and totalitarian states. Monotheism has often viewed itself as presenting a powerful antidote to the natural human tendency to invest a superstitious credulity in base and cruel images.

The great monotheistic religions, Judaism, Christianity, and Islam, all insist upon the necessity of adherence to their mutually exclusive and specific beliefs for salvation. The conflicts in many regions of the world are explicitly fuelled by ideological disagreement: especially about the validity of their scriptures. Christians see their scriptures as fulfilling the Jewish scriptures. Muslims see the Koran as the culmination of the provisional revelations to the Jews and Christians. Deutero-Isaiah constitutes the first expression of resolute monotheism in the Old Testament: 'I am the first and I am the last; besides me

---

[25] Ean Seznec, *The Survival of the Pagan Gods: The Mythological Tradition and its Place in Renaissance Humanism and Art*, translated from the French by Barbara F. Sessions (Princeton: Princeton University Press, 1953).
[26] Mitter, *Much Maligned Monsters*, p. 16.
[27] Mitter, *Much Maligned Monsters*, p. 243.
[28] Mitter, *Much Maligned Monsters*, p. 243ff.

there is no god.' In Isaiah 44.9-20 we find a trenchant critique of idol worship, and the doltishness of the carpenter worshipping carved pieces of wood. This postexilic Jewish monotheism was normative for Christianity and later Islam.

The Advantages of Polytheism and Idolatry

David Hume observed pithily: 'The errors in religion are dangerous; those in philosophy only ridiculous.'[29] Hume's *Natural History of Religion* was the inheritor of a long-lasting wrangle about monotheism and polytheism which had its roots in Pierre Bayle and the early French Enlightenment and went beyond these sources to the Cambridge Platonists. Cudworth regarded the history of religions as a process of gradual decline from a primordial monotheistic revelation. Hume sees rather a process of 'to and fro' between crass and more refined ideas of deity, continuing in Christianity itself. He writes of the oscillation of humanity between monotheism and polytheism fuelled by febrile fantasy: 'The feeble apprehensions of men cannot be satisfied with conceiving their deity as a pure spirit and perfect intelligence; and yet their natural terrors keep them from imputing to him the least shadow of limitation and imperfection. They fluctuate between these opposite sentiments.'[30] Fear, not reason, is the motor of religious belief. Hume diagnoses in the superstitious core of religion a strong tendency towards idolatry:

> And thus, however strong men's propensity to believe invisible, intelligent power in nature, their propensity is equally strong to rest their attention on sensible, visible objects; and in order to reconcile these opposite inclinations, they are led to unite the invisible power with some visible object.[31]

In his view, the shift from polytheism to monotheism was a regression to violence and intolerance.[32] Hume's view of Christianity was shared by Gibbon.

---

[29] Hume, *Treatise of Human Nature* book 1, part iv, § vii (Oxford: OUP, 1981) 2nd ed. Nidditch, p. 272.
[30] Hume, *Natural History of Religion*, 5.2. See M. Andreas Weber, *David Hume und Edward Gibbon: Religionssoziologie in der Aufklärung* (Frankfurt a.m.: Anton Hain, 1990).
[31] Hume, *The Natural History of Religion*, in David Hume, *Principal Writings on Religion*, ed. J. C. A Gaskin (Oxford: OUP, 19993), V p. 150.
[32] Hume, *The Natural History of Religion*, in David Hume, *Principal Writings on Religion*, ed. J. C. A Gaskin (Oxford: OUP, 1993), VIII p. 160.

Historians like Gibbon have often compared the intolerance of the Christians with the latitude of the antique world. A polytheistic imaginary is more inclusive than its monotheistic rivals. One might consider the witty scorn of Gibbon's words: 'The various modes of worship, which prevailed in the Roman world, were all considered by the people, as equally true; by the philosopher, as equally false; and by the magistrate, as equally useful.'[33] This was a 'religious concord' breached only by the dogmatism of the Israelites and their Christian offspring, according to Gibbon. Gibbon viewed a disdainful indifference to religious truth among the Roman elite as engendering a 'prudent liberality'. After the extinction of paganism, the Christians were 'more solicitous to explore the nature, than to practise the laws of their founder.'[34]

Hume and Gibbon exerted a deep influence upon German eighteenth-century thought.[35] This Hume-Gibbon thesis that polytheism, claiming no single truth about a unique god, is more tolerant than monotheism, was revived in 1997 by the distinguished German Egyptologist Jan Assmann in his innovative work *Moses the Egyptian: The Memory of Egypt in Western Monotheism*.[36] In this book he develops the 'Mosaic distinction'. This is the distinction between true and false religion. Assmann starts from the adverse imaginary of Egypt in the Hebrew Bible, in particular in the story of Exodus. Egypt represents idolatry: 'Israel embodies truth, Egypt symbolizes darkness and error.'[37] The contrast is between the sole true God and the false deities of the idolators. For Assmann, 'cultural or intellectual distinctions such as these construct a universe that is not only full of meaning, identity and orientation, but also full of conflict, intolerance, and violence.'[38] Before the Mosaic distinction, we encounter in the ancient world polytheistic or cosmotheistic systems of thought. The gods of the ancient world were often seen as part of a broader interpretative grid: 'nobody contested the reality of foreign gods and

---

[33] Edward Gibbon, *The History of the Decline and Fall of the Roman Empire*. 3 vols. (London and New York: Penguin, 1994), vol 1, p. 56.
[34] Gibbon, *Decline and Fall*, vol. II, p. 932.
[35] Christoph Bultmann, *Die biblische Urgeschichte in der Auklärung* (Tübingen: Mohr-Siebeck, 1999), pp. 113–30.
[36] I am very grateful to John Yusko for his advice on Assmann's work.
[37] Assmann, *Moses the Egyptian: The Memory of Egypt in Western Monotheism* (Cambridge, MA: Harvard University Press, 1997), p. 7.
[38] Assmann, *Moses the Egyptian*, p. 1.

the legitimacy of foreign forms of worship.'[39] The Mosaic distinction constitutes a new form of religious life, the development of 'counter-religion', in contrast to paganism. Paganism encompasses all the other (and hence 'false') religions. Instead of the interpretation and translation of other religions, we find an ideology of conscious estrangement. Whosoever is without the 'true' religion, must be *resisted* as an alien.

Exodus 20.5:

> Thou shalt not bow down thyself to them, nor serve them: for I the Lord thy God am a jealous God, visiting the iniquity of the fathers upon the children unto the third and fourth generation of them that hate me.

Or Exodus 34.14:

> For thou shalt worship no other god: for the LORD, whose name *is* Jealous, *is* a jealous God.

Prohibitions of the creation of images appear six times in the Pentateuch; they are aimed at idolatry. The most detailed injunction is Deuteronomy 4.15-18:

> For your own sake, therefore, be most careful – since you saw no shape when the Lord your God spoke to you at Horeb out of the fire – not to act wickedly and make for yourselves a sculptured image in any likeness whatever: the form of a man or a woman, the form of any beast on earth, the form of any winged bird that flies in the sky, the form of anything that creeps on the ground, the form of any fish that is in the waters below the earth.

For Assmann, Holy Israel castigates Egypt as idolatrous pagans and Egypt's 'most conspicuous practice, the worship of images, came to be regarded as the greatest sin'.[40] Idolatry and polytheism are fused as the cardinal religious mistake; Egypt and Israel represent the battle between idolatry and true religion. Yet perhaps one can over stress the iconoclasm of the Hebrews. We can see in the description of the Tabernacle and the Jerusalem Temple a deep concern for beautiful objects and spaces. The iconoclasm of the Second Commandment stands in stark contrast with the praise of Betzalel and the

---

[39] Assmann, *Moses the Egyptian*, p. 3.
[40] Assmann, *Moses the Egyptian*, p. 4.

other craftsmen later on in Exodus who are described as being filled with 'divine spirit of skill, ability and knowledge'.[41]

Assmann is an Egyptologist and his argument depends upon the testimony of the third-century BC Egyptian priest Manetho (from the Ptolemaic period) as recorded by Josephus who presented Moses as a 'rebellious Egyptian priest who made himself the leader of a colony of lepers',[42] a narrative which Assmann claims is, in fact, the story of Akhenaten, who in the fourteenth century BC attempted to introduce monotheism. The painful memory of Akhenaten was repressed by the Egyptians and the theological revolution he inaugurated became associated with Moses, together with the momentous distinction between true and false religion. After his death, Egyptian monotheism was abolished. The name of Akhenaten was forgotten and the 'traumatic memories of his revolution encrypted and dislocated' were fixed on the Jews.[43]

Assmann is clearly standing in the tradition of Freud's *Moses and Monotheism*, in its speculation about Moses, for whom there is no historical evidence outside the biblical account. The images of Moses have exerted a momentous influence upon Western culture. Reflecting upon this power of the imagination of Moses, Assmann presents a new intellectual discipline, 'mnemohistory'.

Unlike history, mnemohistory is concerned not with reconstructing the facts of the past as such, but with the influence of the past as remembered. Mnemohistory is thus not the opposite of history, but a subdiscipline. For Assmann (following Warburg's idea of *Nachleben*) mnemohistory is reception theory applied to history. It is not a narrow or mechanical reception of data but rather how we imagine the past and how we are 'haunted by it' – how the past continues to shape and mould the present.

Assmann was variously criticized for misrepresenting monotheism. Others agreed with his diagnosis but rejected the implication that Western civilization was built on such inherently violent foundations. Some saw anti-Semitism in his book, others a return to polytheism. In *The Price of Monotheism*, Assmann came to answer his critics. In this work Assmann develops his ideas about

[41] See Exodus 31.3.
[42] Assmann, *Moses the Egyptian*, p. 59.
[43] Assmann, *Moses the Egyptian*, p. 5.

Jewish monotheism: 'not one religion but two stand behind the books of the Old Testament'.[44] He develops the idea of two kinds of monotheism: 'evolutionary' and 'revolutionary'. In the first case we have the gradual evolution of a religion towards monotheism. Here there is a gradual elevation of a high god to a superior status without implying strict exclusivity or the falsity of other religions.

Assmann sees in the 'Mosaic distinction', however, a rupture. Whereas the 'priestly' writings emerging out of the temple cult in Jerusalem recognize other religions, it is the radicalism of the Deuteronomist that marks a distinctive shift. In Deuteronomy we have the emergence of a strict legalism with a radical monotheism. No other God should be worshipped and obedience to the Divine word rather than ritual orthopraxy is foremost. Images are idols and sacrifices and rituals are critiqued:

> one religion requires its people to turn towards the world in rituals of cult and sacrifice, giving their rapt assent to the divine order of creation; the other demands, above all, that they turn away from the world by assiduously studying the writings in which god's will and truth have been deposited.[45]

Assmann develops an analogy with science:

> Just as monotheistic religion rests on the Mosaic distinction, so science rests on the 'Parmenidean' distinction. One distinguishes between true and false religion, the other between true and false cognition.[46]

Science is 'counterknowledge' just as the monotheism created by the Mosaic distinction is 'counterreligion'; each has a regulatory code that establishes what is compatible with its propositions, and rejects what is not compatible. Assmann's analogy with the intolerance of scientific knowledge is meant to demonstrate that he does not *simply* identify radical monotheism of the Mosaic distinction with bigotry. Indeed, the very term 'counterreligion' should not suggest a perverted spiritual force or evil form of religion; merely that one system of beliefs is upheld in direct opposition to other false beliefs. Secondary religion must be intolerant, 'that is, they must have

---

[44] Assmann, *The Price of Monotheism* (Stanford, CA: Stanford University Press, 2010), p. 10.
[45] Assmann, *The Price of Monotheism*, p. 9.
[46] Assmann, *The Price of Monotheism*, p. 12.

a clear conception of what they feel to be incompatible with their truths if these truths are to exert the life-shaping authority, normativity, and binding force that they claim for themselves.'[47] Assmann also considers the criticism that his idea of the Mosaic distinction is hostile to religion because it means that monotheism bred hatred, intolerance, and violence. Assmann does not subscribe to the naïve belief in an idyllic world of primary religion. Assmann claims that the Mosiac distinction was a new form of intolerance, one directed towards idolaters, pagans, heretics: those without the new religious system. Such exclusion is not dangerous *per se*. Violence emerges when the intolerance becomes hatred.

Assmann is claiming that the dark side of monotheism – its violent potential – needs to be remembered and thought through. He notes how Christianity and Islam have been guilty of attempting to subjugate the entire world in the name of the one and only true religion from the Mosaic distinction to the present. Violence is not a necessary upshot of the Mosaic distinction but the propensity to violence becomes clear – indeed, the Hebrew Bible has hundreds passages describing deadly violence. From his mnemohistorical perspective, Assmann asks why biblical monotheism represents itself in violent terms. The price of monotheism is this violence. The ferocity and brutality depicted is frequently violence within the nation rather than without; the rooting out of paganism in order to demonstrate the supremacy of the One True God. Assmann explores the discussion of Moses in the seventeenth and eighteenth centuries because it dismantles the Mosaic distinction, by viewing the Egyptian mysteries as part of an ancient theology. The aspiration of the narrative is Freud's *Moses and Monotheism*: 'In making Moses an Egyptian and in tracing monotheism back to ancient Egypt, Freud attempted to deconstruct the murderous distinction.'[48]

Assmann's *Moses the Egyptian* is a brilliant book but radically teleological and the target is the Freudian exposure of the true nature of 'religion' and especially monotheism.[49] Such a 'history' can be extremely illuminating,

---

[47] Assmann, *The Price of Monotheism*, p. 14.
[48] Assmann, *Moses the Egyptian: The Memory of Egypt in Western Monotheism* (Cambridge, MA: Harvard University Press, 1997), p. 6.
[49] I am grateful to John Robertson for a conversation about this.

although one is reminded of Schlegel's remark that history is retrospective prophecy.[50] It is history that culminates in Freud. Such teleological histories are often enlightening and intellectually captivating but they clearly ought to be consumed *cum grano salis*! There are three major problems in Assmann's account. Firstly, there is the Deuteronomic, secondly the Neoplatonic, and thirdly there is his perception of the early modern deconstruction of the mosaic distinction. On the first count, the Deuteronomic is one (powerful) position within the Old Testament but it conflicts with other positions in the canon. Other strands of the Hebrew Bible, like the Priestly, have quite different, sometimes contradictory interests. Moreover, there are archaic elements that cannot be reconciled with the Deuteronomic position.[51] After God forbids his people from making graven images, he institutes images of cherubim representing the Divine presence above the Ark and such images were placed in Solomon's Temple. Byzantine iconogaphy can be seen quite reasonably in a tradition of rendering heavenly beings that goes back to the ancient Hebrews.

Secondly, the philosophical-pagan monotheism that Christian theology inherited had an inclusivist aspect. John Kenney notes that for pagan monotheism (or as he designates it 'mystical monotheism') was based upon the principle of ultimacy rather than singularity.[52] Indeed, that is why those early Christians like Justin Martyr should have developed strategies of integrating pagan wisdom, especially pagan monotheism but also the poets, into Christian theology.[53] Thirdly, Cudworth's monotheism is not a staging post to Deism but a sincere and learned retrieval of late antique Platonism. It is hardly surprising that a seventeenth-century Cambridge Platonist, a man of latitude should have been opposed to the more narrow and intolerant forms of Christian theism. It is true that he wanted to distinguish between an arcane monotheism and a popular polytheism. Yet that was part of a broader strategy of defending the claims of (Platonic) theism against Hobbesian or Spinozistic

---

[50] Ernst Cassirer, *Essay on Man: An Introduction to a History of Human Culture* (New Haven: Yale, 1944), p. 178.
[51] Margaret Barker, *The Older Testament* (London: SPCK, 1987).
[52] John Kenney, *Mystical Monotheism* (Wipf & Stock, 2010), p. 40.
[53] See Noel Pretila, *Re-appropriating 'Marvellous Fables': Justin Martyr's Strategic Retrieval Myth in I Apology* (Eugene: Pickwick, 2014).

'atheism' rather than developing an immanentist monism. The inclusivism of Cudworth's position was based upon his monotheism, rather than in tension with it.

The Case of Judaism and Islam: Myths of Iconoclasm

Austin Farrer with apt force notes that: 'The rejection of idolatry meant not the destruction but the liberation of images. Nowhere are the images in more vigour than in the Old Testament, where they speak of God but are not he.'[54] The ubiquitous representations of divinity in the ancient world probably stifled the imagination of an invisible transcendent Divine Being. The imagining of the transcendent was not based on haphazard fancy. The striking visions of God that one finds in the second Temple period in what is known as Apocalyptic literature seem to have been based upon imaginings of the lost First Temple.[55] These 'mystical visions' became the foundation of Christian and rabbinic imaginings of God. They survived the destruction of the Jerusalem.

Judaism has played a considerable role in the twentieth-century world of fine art. Successful and famous artists like Marc Chagall worked on Jewish subjects. Barnett Newman and Mark Rothko were dominating figures in the development of abstract expressionism. It has even been argued that abstraction was a distinctively Jewish aesthetic ideal. Yet many have argued on the basis of the Second Commandment that Judaism prohibited images and is an aniconic religion of the word. Given such prohibition of the visual, Jewish art is an anomaly.[56] The facts, however, are rather different. The greatest Jewish thinker, Moses Maimonides, for example, argued that the 'prohibition against fashioning images for beauty applies only to the human form and, therefore, we do not fashion a human form in wood or plaster or in stone ... However, if

---

[54] Austin Farrer, *The Rebirth of Images* (Westminster: Dacre, 1949), p. 14.
[55] Margaret Barker, *The Gate of Heaven: The History and Symbolism of the Temple in Jerusalem* (London: SPCK, 1991).
[56] Asher Biemann, 'Art and Aesthetics' in Martin Kavka, Zachary Braiterman, and David Novak, eds. *The Cambridge History of Jewish Philosophy: The Modern Era* (Cambridge: Cambridge University Press, 2012). p. 761.

the form is sunken, or of a medium like that of images on panels or tablets or those woven in fabrics, it is permitted.'[57] Maimonides admitted the legitimacy of representations of or images of non-human creatures.[58] Richard Cohen in his book *Jewish Icons* shows how images were ubiquitous in Judaism – decorated Ashkenazi synagogues in Europe or illuminated medieval manuscripts and has convincingly demonstrated the existence of a 'vibrant Jewish visual culture'.[59] Melissa Raphael claims plausibly that the view of Judaism as an aniconic religion has been refuted in recent scholarship, especially by Kalman Bland and Zachary Braiterman. Indeed the great tradition of Jewish art extends back to the Greco-Roman period. Yet Jewish art is not mere decoration. Focusing mainly on paintings in the modern era, Raphael claims that Jewish art is more than ornament and adornment. It has a sacred meaning. Raphael points to depictions of Jewish men in the nineteenth and twentieth centuries such as Isidor Kaufmann's *Man with Fur Hat*, which she regards as 'like icons in the Christian Orthodox tradition ... not depictions of God but ... translucent to the image of God in the human'.[60] At a somewhat more marginal level, the rabbinic acceptance of magic and the tradition of rabbinic portraiture ensured a long-standing tradition of Jewish religious art.[61]

Islam has a similarly complex relationship to iconoclasm. It is often just assumed that Islam possesses no representations.[62] The art of Islam resides in calligraphy or architecture. Persis Berlekamp's *Wonder, Image and Cosmos in Medieval Islam* is the interpretation of early illustrated wonders-of-creation manuscripts from the late thirteenth through the fourteenth century. Persis Berlekamp considers the earliest-known copies of Zakariya ibn Muhammad al-Mahmud al-Qazwini's *'Aja'ib al-makhluqat wa ghara'ib almawjudat* ('The Wonders of Creation and the Oddities of Existing Things') and Ahmad al-Tusi's 'The World-Showing Glass'. These were cosmographical works produced

---

[57] Maimonides as quoted in Vivian B. Mann, *Jewish Texts on the Visual Arts* (Cambridge: Cambridge University Press, 2000), p. 24.
[58] Ibid.
[59] Richard I. Cohen, *Jewish Icons: Art and Society in Modern Europe*. By (Berkeley, University of California Press, 1998), p. 259.
[60] Melissa Raphael, *Judaism and the Visual Image: A Jewish Theology of Art* (London and New York: Continuum, 2009), p. 81.
[61] I am grateful to Ranana Dine for pointing this out to me.
[62] Thomas Arnold, *Painting in Islam: A Study of the Place of Pictorial Art in Muslim Culture* (Oxford: Clarendon, 1928).

during the Ilkhanid (Mongol) period in Iran. Their purpose was the generation of wonder about God's creation after the shock of the savage Mongol conquest. Berlekamp claims that these illustrated manuscripts stress the Neoplatonic 'divinely arranged order of the cosmos'.[63] She has one chapter entitled 'Iconic Images: Platonic Forms and the Awe-Inspiring Cosmos'.[64] In this she discusses the influence of the Neoplatonic doctrine of ideas upon the Muslim art of the period: that 'the "form" of the bee … is both the visible image on the page and its invisible essential "Form" … in the philosophical sense of a Platonic Form'.[65] Given the Neoplatonic theory of the production of all things by God, the 'wonder' corresponds to the order of emanation. There is thus a visual movement towards an increase of understanding and the sense of wonder at the Divine mystery. Of course these manuscripts were the preserve of a tiny minority in medieval Islamic culture. The influence of the Neoplatonic themes of the visible, the invisible and the mirror, especially the image of the polishing of the heart is quite clear.[66] Phenomena in the visible world point back to their invisible source.[67] Consider the following observation about the Mosque:

> There is no more perfect symbol of the Divine Unity than Light. For this reason the Muslim artist seeks to transform the very stuff he is fashioning into vibration of light. It is to this end that he covers the interior surfaces of a mosque or a palace – and occasionally outer ones – with mosaics in ceramic tiles. This lining is often confined to the lower part of the walls, as if to dispel their heaviness … the muquarnas also serves to trap light and diffuse it with the most subtle gradations.[68]

Assmann writes: 'Among the precepts of the Moses religion there is one that is of greater importance than appears to begin with. This is the prohibition against making an image of god – the compulsion to worship a god whom one

---

[63] Berlekamp, *Wonder, Image, and Cosmos in Medieval Islam* (New Haven, CT: Yale University Press, 2011), pp. 16–17.
[64] Berlekamp, *Wonder, Image, and Cosmos in Medieval Islam*, pp. 37–57.
[65] Berlekamp, *Wonder, Image, and Cosmos in Medieval Islam*, p. 43.
[66] Roxburgh, *Prefacing the Image: The Writing of Art History in Sixteenth-Century Iran* (Leiden: Brill, 2001), pp. 181ff.
[67] Sayyed Hossein Nasr, 'The World of Imagination' and the Concept of Space in the Persian Miniature', *Islamic Quarterly* 13, 3 (July–Sept. 1969), 129–34, esp. 133–4.
[68] Titus Burckhardt, *Art of Islam: Language and Meaning* (Bloomington, IN: World Wisdom, 2009), p. 77. See Henry Corbin, *Alone with the Alone: Creative Imagination in the Sūfism of Ibn 'Arabi*. Trans. Ralph Manheim (Princeton: Princeton University Press, 1998).

cannot see. In this, I suspect, Moses was outdoing the strictness of the Aten religion. Perhaps he merely wanted to be consistent: his god would in that case have neither a name nor a countenance. Perhaps it was a fresh measure against magical abuses. But if this prohibition were accepted, it must have a profound effect. For it meant that a sensory impression was given a second place to what may be called an abstract idea – a triumph of intellectuality over sensuality or, strictly speaking, an instinctual renunciation, with all its necessary psychological consequences.'[69]

Immanuel Kant's remark that 'perhaps the most sublime passage in the Jewish law is the commandment: Thou shalt not make unto thee any graven image …' would be one of the most influential examples of this emphasis on the Second Commandment.[70] In Kant's estimation, it was Judaism's wariness towards images that 'alone can explain the enthusiasm that the Jewish people in its civilized era felt for its religion when it compared itself with other people.'[71]

Hegel took a different position. While he also emphasized the Second Commandment while discussing Judaism, he thought that the iconoclasm of the second commandment generated far too abstract a God. Asher Biemann, in his chapter on art and aesthetics, explains that for Hegel 'it was the very absence of the visual and the "dead abstraction" [*tote Abstraktion*] of their God that barred the Jews from all concrete content of reality and, above all, reason.'[72] Freud was writing in the tradition of German reflection upon Mosaic iconoclasm.

Idolatry: Schopenhauer and Spinoza

> Even the understanding of the true Metaphysical and Contemplative Man must still contend with the Imaginative Powers that will be breathing a grosse dew upon the pure Glasse of our Understandings.[73]

---

[69] Assmann, *Moses and Monotheism*, pp. 359–60.
[70] Kant as quoted in Kalman P. Bland, *The Artless Jew: Medieval and Modern Affirmations and Denials of the Visual* (Princeton: Princeton University Press, 2001), p. 15. Cf. Alain Besançon, *The Forbidden Image* (Chicago, IL: Chicago University Press, 2009), pp. 193ff.
[71] Ibid.
[72] *The Cambridge History of Jewish Philosophy: The Modern Era*, vol. 2, eds. Martin Kavka, Zachery Braiterman, David Novak, vol. 2 Aesthetics and Art 759–79
[73] John Smith, *Select Discourses*, pp. 20, 21.

John Smith's critique of the 'grosse dew upon the Glasse of our Understandings' can seem rather severe. Psychoanalysis insists that real human lives are shot through with fantasies, many harmless, others less so. Don Quixote and Emma Bovary, in this sense, are realistic creations of imagination. Yet not only are some human imaginings dark and cruel, but they can be harnessed to unkind and dishonest ends. The role of deception in human society, for example, is closely linked to the imagination. The capacity for deceit is evident among our relatives among primates – although this raises questions about levels of consciousness and the asymmetry between the human and the non-human. The much-employed example is that of covert copulation between non-alpha males and females within range of the dominant male.[74] The idea is that even primates have a capacity to deceive and be deceived.

Deception is precisely how many thinkers in the Modern period perceive religion. Developing Lucretius's lament '*tantum religio potuit suadere malorum*', Spinoza, Schopenhauer and Nietzsche offer a critique of religion as deception and delusion. Such critics of religion detect a brutal and self-serving desire to impose a destructive phantasy upon others. 'What is the idea of God other than the perfect rejection of humanity, the sacrifice of humanity, the negation of humanity?'[75]

This critique had its roots in the seventeenth-century wars of religion and the horrors that they occasioned. The rejection of good and evil, freedom of choice, teleology and a personal deity in Spinoza's metaphysics is the repudiation of the errors of the imagination and deception. These errors are aligned to Spinozas's rejection of prophetic authority, miracles and the inspiration of the Pentateuch – in turn part of a critique of state-sanctioned religious power grounded upon superstition.[76] Spinoza's defence of republicanism and freedom of worship and intellectual inquiry exerted a considerable influence upon Enlightenment Europe.

Schopenhauer's great work is called *Die Welt als Wille und Vorstellung*. One of the great atheistic philosophers of the Western tradition, his *Hauptwerk*

---

[74] *Primate Societies*, Smuts, Cheney, Seyfarth, Wrangham, (Chicago, 2008), pp. 438ff.
[75] Bruno Bauer, *Christianity Exposed*, ed. Paul Trejo, (Lewiston: Mellen, 2002), p. 70.
[76] See Sue James, *Spinoza on Philosophy, Religion, and Politics: The Theologico-Political Treatise* (Oxford: Oxford University Press, 2012).

could be translated as *The World as Will and Imagination*.[77] It is a theory of imagination as delusion. For Schopenhauer, as for Kant, we need to construct a world of appearances.[78] Whereas for Kant the transcendental necessity of constructing the realm of appearances leads to the doctrine of the regulative ideas in the *Critique of Pure Reason* and teleology remains on the Kantian horizon, for Schopenhauer this can only be a ludicrous fantasy. For Kant, it is transcendentally necessary to construct the phenomenal world and the demands of science and ethics drive us to assume a harmonious and structured reality without the activity of a transcendental ego; Schopenhauer derives a much bleaker dualism between the concept-soaked world of phenomenal experience (*Vorstellung*) and the realm beyond its application (*Wille*). He rejects Kant's schematism and doctrine of the transcendental imagination for an essentially empiricist theory of concept formation and an insistence upon the somatic component of knowledge.[79] The world of representations is a practically necessary compression of perceptual data which suffices to negotiate the immediate environment, but which offers no intimation or evidences of a transcendent 'beyond'. On this, Schopenhauer entirely agrees with Kant's rejection of natural theology.

Yet the recognition of ultimate reality as inexorable will generates an immense vacuum in the wake of the destruction of Western theism. Schopenhauer is aware that much of occidental thought relies upon the buttress of theism. His attempt to find a substitute for theism in his own eclectic version of Hinduism and Buddhism is part of an attempt to find a spiritual replacement for the failure of theism.

Schopenhauer's contempt for German Idealism can be seen in his rejection of the idea of the Absolute of Hegel or Schelling, or the supposed instruments of knowledge by which the finite mind can reach such an Absolute – Schelling's intellectual intuition or Hegel's dialectic. This further makes clear that Schopenhauer's *Wille* is not supposed to be a quasi Deity or hidden causal principle lying beyond the phenomenal realm. This, for Schopenhauer,

---

[77] James Vigus notes that it would be an odd translation. Yet it conveys an aspect of the word lost in the usual English translation.
[78] C. Janaway, *Self and World in Schopenhauer's Philosophy* (Oxford: Oxford University Press, 1999).
[79] Janaway, *Self and World in Schopenhauer's Philosophy*, pp. 159, 172–87 on Schopenhauer's materialistic construal of Kant.

is precisely the mistake of the German Idealists, to develop a crypto-deity of the kind that had been comprehensively refuted by Kant.

The first line of Schopenauer's *opus magnum* reads: 'Die Welt ist meine Vorstellung': this could well be translated as 'the world is my imagination'.[80] 'The world' is usually translated as 'Representation' but the term in German has a broader connotation.[81] This claim is immediately associated with both Kant and Indian thought – that the world that the mind confronts is never unmediated.

Schopenhauer's deep pessimism has been described as Gnostic.[82] The term 'Gnostic' is highly problematic. As long as we do not try to pin down too definite a meaning upon the term, there is some justice in the claim. For Schopenhauer, the world *ought* not to exist: reality is inherently bad.[83] And unlike Spinoza, for whom in the third book of the *Ethics* passions divide human beings from each other whereas reason, properly employed, can help unite, Schopenhauer thoroughly disapproves of even this rather niggardly optimism of Spinoza. Schopenhauer sympathizes with Spinoza's critique of theism as fancy and he wholeheartedly agrees with Spinoza's determinism, his doctrine of resignation, negation of the will and solace in the arts is far removed from Spinoza's optimism that the intellectual love of God or nature can overcome the passions and misery created by disturbing emotions. Schopenhauer's influence upon artists was considerable. The artist can penetrate the illusion of the realm of appearances, the domain of *maya*.[84]

The value of Christianity lies in its implicit repudiation of the banal optimism of Semitic monotheism. Christianity shares the deep pessimism of

---

[80] See Eva Brann, *The World of the Imagination: Sum and Substance* (Lanham, MD: Rowman & Littlefield, 1991), p. 103.

[81] 'dies ist die Wahrheit, welche in Beziehung auf jedes lebende und erkennende Wesen gilt; wiewohl der Mensch allein sie in das reflektierte, abstrakte Bewußtsein bringen kann: und tut er dies wirklich, so ist die philosophische Besonnenheit bei ihm eingetreten. Es wird ihm dabei deutlich und gewiß, daß er keine Sonne kennt und keine Erde; sondern immer nur ein Auge, das eine Sonne sieht, eine Hand, die eine Erde fühlt; daß die Welt, welche ihn umgibt, nur als Vorstellung da ist, d.h. durchweg nur in Beziehung auf ein anderes, das Vorstellende, welches er selbst ist. Arthur Schopenhauer, *Die Welt als Wille und Vorstellung* (Zurich: Diogenes), vol. 1, p. 5.

[82] Besançon, *The Forbidden Image*, p. 302.

[83] '... ist Denen, in welchen der Wille sich gewendet und verneint hat, diese unsere so sehr reale Welt mit allen ihren Sonnen und Milchstraßen – Nichts'. Arthur Schopenhauer, *Die Welt als Wille und Vorstellung* (Zurich: Diogenes, 1977), vol. 2, p. 508.

[84] Besançon, *The Forbidden Image*, pp. 296ff.

Indian thought: the 'inmost kernel and spirit of Christianity is identical with that of Brahmanism and Buddhism; they all teach 'a great guilt of the human race through its existence itself'.[85] Christianity itself is the fragile compromise between Semitic optimism and the pessimism of Indic thought.[86]

One can see the influence of Schopenhauer's gloomy atheism and his gospel of renunciation upon a contemporary British philosopher like John Gray.[87] Gray considers myths as instruments employed to evade facts: humans are driven by fanciful and yet immensely powerful dreams. Indeed, he views myth as integral to all human thought – and not as the refuge of superstition and piety.

'Modern politics is a chapter in the history of religion.'[88] Barry Cooper presents terrorism as emerging out of a spiritual disease.[89] Explanations of violent and irrational behaviour may, of course, have powerful socio-economic components, such as poverty and alienation. Yet many of the young people from the Western cultural milieu feel not merely anger towards their 'homes' but hatred. What is fuelling the hatred? What substitute and fantastical existence is provided by radical Islam? There is an evident gulf between reality and the rhetoric in radical Islam of the late twentieth and early twenty-first century. The appeal to the restoration of a caliphate betokens a radical Muslim conservatism critiquing Western decadence. Yet the use of modern media to advertise draconian savagery and shamefully abusing minority religions of the Middle East, like the Yazidis, shows the evident hypocrisy.

Radical Islamist movements often appeal to violence as a means to create a new society. They frequently attack traditionalist Islamic societies and practices (like kite flying) that such societies engaged in for centuries, or harmless pastimes like soccer, while clearly[90] and deeply influenced by Western ideas and technologies like mobile phones. They use the internet to exploit the romantic phantasies of young Muslim teenage girls, as the

---

[85] Schopenhauer, *Die Welt als Wille und Vorstellung* (Zurich: Diogenes, 1977), vol. 4, p. 707.
[86] Christopher Ryan, *Schopenhauer's Philosophy of Religion: The Death of God and the Oriental Renaissance* (Leuven: Peeters, 2010).
[87] John Gray, *Straw Dogs: Thoughts on Humans and Other Animals* (London: Granta, 2003).
[88] John Gray, *Black Mass: Apocalyptic Religion and the Death of Utopia* (London: Allen Lane, 2007), p. 1.
[89] See his work *New Political Religions, or an Analysis of Modern Terrorism* (Columbia: University of Missouri, 2004).
[90] See Abderrahmane Sissako's film *Timbuktu*, 2014 about the control of the city by violent extremists.

phenomenon of jihadi brides shows. Gray's view that such radical Islamic groups follow the specifically Christian model of the 'pursuit of salvation in history' is doubtless too extreme.[91] Yet he is correct to highlight the paradoxically 'Western' dimension of radical Islam.

Yet perhaps such radical religious ideologies provide a reassuring narrative – a bogus security. For young and vulnerable people, on the threshold of becoming adults, such extreme groups motivate an 'imaginaire', an either/or between the cruel, decadent and infidel West and radical Islam that has potent appeal.

Religion, Magic, Ritual

The magic of art has led to the comparison of the artist with the magician. Indeed, it is common to confuse religion with magic. One might think of Freud's observation that art as we know it from the French cave painting was originally magic and his *obiter dicta* that art is a realm of modern life that remains close to magic.[92] The parallels between religion and magic are numerous and palpable. Both religion and magic employ rituals and special language. Rappaport finds that 'the performance of more or less invariant sequences of formal acts and utterances not encoded by the performers', establishes the basis for the emergence of religion. Rappaport's definition is helpful but uncontentious. There is a tradition stemming from Durkheim that sees rituals as serving a pragmatic purpose. An example of such view is Michael Suk-Young Chwe: '[R]ituals are ubiquitous features of social life because they provide the common focal points and common cultural knowledge that provide actors with information about how others will act. This makes mutual assurance possible and helps actors solve the coordination problems that usually bedevil and obstruct effective collective action.'[93]

The rituals of magic are instruments of control and manipulation. One striking aspect of religious rituals is their apparent pointlessness. The wafers

---

[91] John Gray, *Black Mass*, p. 72.
[92] Freud, 'Animism, Magic and the Omnipotence of Thought', in *Totem and Taboo*, translated and edited by James Strachey (London: Routledge, 1961), p. 90.
[93] *Rational Ritual: Culture, Coordination, and Common Knowledge* (Princeton, NJ: Princeton University Press, year), p. 34.

and wine of the communion are not sustaining. The water of the baptism will not clean the infant, but only make it cry! Magical rituals are goal orientated. Yet the very pointlessness of the religious ritual is its meaning! They point to a dimension of reality that is significant per se, that transcends any calculation of benefit or disadvantage.[94]

Harold Bloom praises Shakespeare above all others for his creation of a world populated by such realistic characters that he 'seems to have usurped reality ... sustaining the illusion that his men and women walk among us'.[95] The eighteenth-century view of Shakespeare was dominated by a sense of the uncanny. Shakespeare was the Prospero controlling a supernatural-spirit world and conjuring the transcendent. Images of the imaginative worlds of Shakespeare were often created by the efforts of John Boydell, who set up a gallery in London as part of a project to make an illustrated edition of the plays of Shakespeare.[96] It is clear from these depictions that the image of the great bard in that epoch was that of the poet of the imagination of the unseen world. He is the poet of the supernatural 'summoning spirits from the vasty deep' (like Glendower in *Henry V*). Shakespeare is a Prospero figure who can produce the 'weird sisters' of Macbeth, with their prophetic powers, or the Hamlet who 'waxes desperate with imagination' when he encounters the ghost of his father (Act 1, Scene 4):

> The spirit that I have seen
> May be the devil, and the devil hath power
> T' assume a pleasing shape. Yea, and perhaps
> Out of my weakness and my melancholy,
> As he is very potent with such spirits,
> Abuses me to damn me. (Act 2, Scene 2)

Shakespeare's genius exploits the ambiguity of such apparitions. Are they mental or concrete realities? The literature of the period offers an array of differing opinions. Shakespeare may well have been affected by the contemporary sceptic, the English MP Reginald Scott and his influential work *The Discoverie of Witchcraft, wherein the Lewde dealing of Witches and*

---

[94] I am very grateful to W. Dupre for this observation.
[95] Harold Bloom, *The Anatomy of Influence* (Garden City: Doubleday, 1982), p. 31.
[96] I am grateful to Peter Holland for the reference to Boydell.

Witchmongers is notablie detected, in sixteen books ... whereunto is added a Treatise upon the Nature and Substance of Spirits and Devils, 1584, which argued for the irrationality and impiety of belief in witchcraft, which he rejected as the work of imposters and buttressed by popish superstition.[97] The majority of Protestant clergy upheld belief in the existence of witches.

The eminent early modern historian Stuart Clark in his work *Vanities of the Eye: Vision in Early Modern European Culture*, argues eloquently that the question of the verisimilitude of vision becomes particularly acute in the early modern period.[98] Rather than an overweening confidence in the capacity of the eye to map and control the world, we have a period of intense debate about the reliability of vision. This debate about the validity of vision was provoked by various factors – the Renaissance development of techniques of perspective by artists, disruption of Aristotelianism by the New Science, i.e. the distinction between primary and secondary qualities and controversies surrounding the Reformation about the status of images. Clark also sees demonology as playing an important role in these debates. Since it was assumed that demons could interfere and disrupt the natural world, this had profound implications for the question of perception. This uncertainty about perception was the context of the Macbeth's 'dagger before me' or Banquo's ghost.

Doderer and the Perversion of Imagination

Notwithstanding the frequency of the charge that religion can generate violence, it has been often noted that many of the overtly secular regimes of the twentieth century were frenzied and callous in their cruelty. The German/American philosopher and political theorist Eric Voegelin spent a career obsessed with what he perceived as the central malaise of the twentieth century: the eclipse of the divine as the foundation of order and its replacement with a purely human source of order. Voegelin diagnoses many of the mass movements of the twentieth century (fascism, communism, etc.) as Gnostic

---

[97] Keith Thomas, *Religion and the Decline of Magic* (New York: Charles Scribner, 1973), pp. 684–5.
[98] Stuart Clark, *Vanities of the Eye: Vision in Early Modern European Culture* (Oxford: Oxford University Press, 2007).

Ersatzreligionen.[99] We can bracket the very reasonable worries about the applicability of a term like 'Gnosticism' in the twentieth century context. Voegelin viewed these versions of 'anthropolatry' as rebellion against the divine order. They are forms of spiritual sickness or 'Pneumopathological', a term he seems to have taken from Schelling's notion of *Geisteskrankheit* or *Gemüthskrankheit*. Voegelin borrowed the term 'second reality' from the novel of Heimito von Doderer, *Die Dämonen*. This is Voegelin's favoured term for the wilful and narcissistic blindness of those ideologues who substitute their bizarre fantasies, for example of a race or class, in the stead of authentic perceptions of reality: 'For Doderer, the demonic world of illusion is what appears when we do not apperceive, when we fail to take into account the whole of God's created and historical world.'[100] The 'second reality' is characterized by 'the rigid pattern'.[101] Indeed ideology is a form of escapism: 'The revolutionary flees from what is hardest for him to bear, the aimless variety of life; he seeks perfection, which in the world of his trivialities can at best mean completeness.'[102]

The persecution of religion in the Soviet Union, the expropriation of religious property, destruction of the vast majority of the churches, public derision of religion, persecuted and murdered millions of believers, and promulgation of atheism in schools, is an intriguing instance of a fantastical endeavour to obliterate the idea of the sacred. This persecution in the Soviet period was fanatical and fuelled from outset by Lenin's and Trotsky's implacable hatred of religion. The moderate metropolitan Tikhon (1865–1925) could not limit the ruthless persecution of Orthodox Christianity in the Soviet Union. Later Stalin and Khrushchev continued draconian campaigns to eradicate churches, monasteries and seminaries and almost obliterated the Orthodox Church, and a thousand years of Russian culture.[103] Conscious of the loss, Russians would attend state atheist museums to read parts of scripture:

---

[99] Jerry Day, *Voegelin, Schelling and the Philosophy of Historical Existence* (Columbia: University of Missouri Press, 2003), p. 36.
[100] David Luft, *Eros and Inwardness* (Chicago: University of Chicago Press, 2003), p. 178.
[101] Charles Embry, *The Philosopher and the Storyteller: Eric Voegelin and Twentieth Century Literature* (Columbia: University of Missouri, 2008), p. 95.
[102] Embry, *The Philosopher and the Storyteller*, p. 97. Compare this with Jung's thesis that neurosis is a substitute for authentic suffering.
[103] Scott Kenworthy, *The Heart of Russia: Trinity-Sergius, Monasticism and Society After 1825* (New York: Oxford University Press, 2010) is an informative case study. I am grateful to Scott for discussions about such questions in Notre Dame.

preserved in order to ridicule. Literary works such as *Dr Zhivago* and *The Master and Margarita* emerged out of this milieu of intense persecution.

The theistic conviction here is that any proper political order requires the recognition of moral truths grounded in the transcendent, and in the proper relations of nature, man and God. Such truths can be apprehended but are often oblique and obscure. When this transcendent reality is rejected, however, whether by an individual or even a society, the result is a substitute domain of secondary reality in which morality is understood as a purely human affair. Doderer refers to such encounters with transcendent reality as *'jenseits in diesseits'* or 'transcendence in immanence'.[104]

The imagination enables an agent to respond and engage fully with the world in a way that a purely cognitive reaction could not. 'When the first reality, which is the expression of spiritual substance, cannot be developed because of the absence of such a substance, in its place there will develop an artificial reality – that is, a reality that has the external form of reality but which is not substantially supported by the spirit. We enter here upon a realm of spirit-like non-spirit or anti-spirit, which finds its representation on the plane of politics in the ideological mass movements. Doderer in particular, in his book *The Demons*, has been concerned with the second reality as a phenomenon of social and political disorder.'[105] The key to this 'spiritual disease' is a refusal to recognize the nature of the *metaxy*. He distinguished between 'thing reality' and 'It reality'. These two dimensions correspond to 'intentionality' and 'luminosity'. The goal of novel writing is *'eigentliche Wissenschaft von Leben'* – 'authentic knowledge of life'.[106] The long and involved narrative of *Die Dämonen nach der Chronik des Sektionsrates Geyrenhoff* (*The Demons*) is somewhat akin to the Paris of Proust's *À La Recherche du Temps Perdu* or the London of Anthony Powell's *Dance to the Music of Time* and contains various sub-plots.[107] The main story concerns Georg von Geyrenhoff, who is in the process of composing a chronicle about a group of upper-class Viennese of the

---

[104] Doderer, *Die Dämonen*, pp. 1010, 1120, 1135 and 1146.
[105] Voegelin, 'The German University' in Charles Embry, *The Philosopher and the Storyteller*, p. 81.
[106] Elizabeth Hesson, *Twentieth Century Odyssey: A Study of Heimito von Doderer's Die Dämonen* (Columbia: Camden House, 1982), p. 92.
[107] On the influence of Proust on Doderer, see F. Schroeder, *Apperception und Vorurteil: Untersuchungen zur Reflexion Heimito von Doderers* (Heidelberg: Winter Verlag) 1976), pp. 162–8.

Ringstrasse era, '*die Unsrigen*' ('our own kind'). The events take place between the autumn of 1926 and the summer of 1927 burning of the Ministry of Justice on 15 July 1927 the riot in the Palace of Justice which Doderer regarded as a devastating blow for Austria – as the '*Cannae der Osterreichischen Freiheit*' the Cannae of Austrian freedom. Weakening the fragile Austrian state, it prepared the way for the *Anschluß* with Nazi Germany.

The life denying, neurotic and demonic 'second reality' exhibited by some of the characters is starkly contrasted with the vitality of the brilliant young man Leonhard Kakabsa, in many respects the hero of the narrative.[108] Coming from a working-class culture, he scorns the anti-intellectualism of his own milieu and provides the model of a Christian humanism as a bulwark again totalitarian fantasies and pathologies. Leonhard Kakabsa embodies the relish of reality and life in freedom envisaged by Doderer. His epiphanic insight emerges through his study of Latin, culminating in his encounter with the Christian Platonism of Pico della Mirandola's *De hominis dignitate*. The boy teaches himself Latin, inspired by the encounter with a gifted and cultivated girl who is studying Latin and Greek at school. The culminating point is Kakabsa's confrontation with the Christian Neoplatonism of *De hominis dignitate* of Pico.[109] Kakabsa provides a stark contrast to the rather decadent and dissolute fantasies and distractions of 'die unsrigen'.[110]

The figure of Georg von Geyrenhoff also provides a meditation upon the theme of first and second reality. The chronicle is itself a diversionary tactic, an immersion in a 'second reality'. Geyrenhoff, however, by chance, roots out an attempted fraud. Charlotte von Schlaggenberg (usually called 'Quapp' in the novel) was almost disinherited by the financial dishonesty of a financial advisor called Levielle. Geyrenhoff restore the inheritance to Quapp. Geyrenhoff also develops an attachment with the widow of Quapp's genuine father, Captain Georg Ruthmayr, whose name is Frederike Ruthmayer.

There is a substantial subplot involving René von Stangeler, an unsuccessful academic historian who is hired by the merchant Jan Herzka, who has inherited

---

[108] Dietrich Weber, *Heimito von Doderer* (Beck: Munich, 1987) pp. 77ff. See also Ingrid Werkgartner Ryan, *Zufall und Freiheit in Heimito von Doderers 'Dämonen'* (Vienna: Hermann Böhlhaus, 1986), pp. 82–127.
[109] Doderer, *Dämonen*, p. 659ff. See also pp. 989, 994.
[110] On Pico, see Beierwaltes, *Fußnoten zu Plato*, pp. 280ff.

a castle, Schloss Neudegg, through his mother's family in Carinthia, to catalogue and order the library. There is also a manuscript on witchcraft and Stangeler is employed to interpret it.[111] The demonic in Doderer's narrative is characterized by its emptiness. Hesson notes: 'For Doderer the key concept in the teachings of St Thomas is that of the *analogia entis*, the belief that creation is the manifestation of the Divine Being. It is thus *ipso facto* good; outside this divinely-ordained pattern lies nothingness. Man's refusal to perceive this goodness and search for what lies outside creation is the source of all his ills.' This metaphysical doctrine obviously strikes a chord with Doderer and links with his theory of '*Apperzeptions-Verweigerung*', the refusal of the individual to perceive in all its connotations, reality in the world as it is.[112] Doderer views a sign of the demonic in the creation of tremendous agitation without real substance.

The tale of the Baron Achaz von Neudegg is a 'ridiculous farce of the passions' but it is a narrative of cruelty, sexual humiliation and control.[113] The perverted baron, 'a very modern person', is like a medieval de Sade.[114] The fifteenth century Lord is a paradigm of the neurotic behaviour that Doderer sees as life in second reality. His relation to those in his power is entirely artificial. 'Satan has always regarded man's sexuality as his most vulnerable point and is ready to provide an infernal mistress'.[115] One might here note C. S. Lewis's observation on Eros and Idolatry in *The Four Loves:* 'Eros, honoured without reservation and obeyed unconditionally, becomes a demon.'[116]

Norman Cohn's work on witchcraft presents arguments for the fantastical nature of the trials.[117] Indeed, Cohn also sees the persecution of the Jews as grounded in demonization in the medieval period. 'As intemperance and sensuality make us Beasts; so Pride and Malice make us Devils.'[118] Hell is rather a nature then a place.[119] 'The Devil is not only the name of one

---

[111] See Weber, *Heimito von Doderer*, pp. 206ff.
[112] Hesson, *Twentieth Century Odyssey*, p. 80.
[113] Hesson, *Twentieth Century Odyssey*, p. 744.
[114] Doderer, *Dämonen*, p. 1021.
[115] George P. Winship, Jr, 'The Novels of Charles Williams', in Mark Hillegas, *Shadows of Imagination* (Carbondale: Southern Illinois University Press, 1969), p. 117.
[116] Lewis, *The Four Loves* (London: Geoffrey Bles, 1960), pp. 135–40.
[117] Norman Cohn, *Europe's Inner Demons: An Enquiry Inspired by the Great Witch-Hunt* (London: Sussex University Press, 1975).
[118] Whichcote, *Moral and Religious Aphorisms* (Edinburgh: Printed by T. W. and T. Ruddimans, 1742).
[119] Smith, *Select Discourses*, pp. 446–7.

particular thing but a nature' and 'it is the difference of a name rather than any proper difference of natures that is between the Devil and Wicked men. Wheresoever we see Malice, Revenge, Pride, Envy, Hatred, Self will, and Self love, we may say Here and There is that Evil Spirit.'[120] The Elizabethan Age was a period of witch hunts. Pope Innocent VIII issued his '*summis desiderantes affectibus*', a papal bull in 1484, which endorsed the persecution of witches. Within the Germanophone context, the theme of Faust and the lure of magic was thematized paradigmatically by Goethe.

Charles Williams has written most lucidly about witchcraft. The primary concern that Williams shows in the topic is psychological.[121] Witchcraft is an 'aberration of the spirit'. And the persecution of witches showed the reality of the devil in the *persecutions*: 'Most children and most youths take pleasure in fancies; the secret of those fancies is sometimes a part of them ... But if a religious heart and mind were, for some reason, oppressed and antagonized by the order of religion in the world, or if greed or curiosity sprang high, there might be every kind of opportunity to welcome and enjoy some other fancy, however preposterous – what fancies are not? – of a powerful, satisfying, and secret justification of oneself.'[122]

Magic is a perverted mirror image of the Christian sacramental vision. The great eighteenth-century Anglican Divine William Law writes 'that the darkness of hell is but the Divine Nature falsely invoked by the self and that the only dissipator of it' is the Spirit of Love 'in his own blessed nature ... it restored again the light of Redemption, which the bigots of redemption have done so much to obscure'.[123] For William Law, hell is primarily a spiritual state, but no less real for that.

'Thought Infused Seeing'

Mark Wynn has argued that we can contemplate religious truths in our sensory experience of the world. He wishes to explain how our perceptual and bodily encounter with the world can be legitimately suffused by spiritual

---

[120] Smith, *Select Discourses*, thanks to Justin Hedley for his thoughts on these issues, p. 463.
[121] Glen Cavaliero, *Charles Williams, Poet of Theology* (London: Macmillan, 1983), p. 142.
[122] Charles Williams, *Witchcraft* (London: Faber, 1941), p. 154.
[123] Charles Williams, *Witchcraft* (London: Faber, 1941), p. 302.

concerns and commitments. He does this through developing the idea of 'thought infused seeing' in his work *Renewing the Senses*. Wynn develops a complex argument about the emotions, in which he resists overly sharp divisions between 'feelings' and 'thoughts', 'emotional values' and 'physical facts' – whereby the former are construed as 'subjective' and the latter as 'objective' and how thoughts can usher in particular perceptions. Indeed, in religious contexts, perceptions and concepts should be viewed as infused by feeling.[124] These can be real shifts in the emotional state of a person and the phenomenological dimension of experience, the experience of the physical cosmos, 'patterns of salience' as Wynn calls them. He uses the example of a dog approaching rapidly: the fear of the beast, or the delight, is an emotion that generates salience in the perception.[125] A place may, for example, take on a new hue if you are told that it was the place of historical acts of savagery. The location assumes a new significance with the additional knowledge. Thus the grasp of *reality* can be genuinely enhanced by such 'patterns of salience'.

Wynn uses the example of melancholy as an example of how an emotional state of dejection (the example is that of Tolstoy in mid-life) affects the perception of the world. Such melancholics refer to the world as devoid of significance and reality. In this way, imagination is – in the terms of Wynn – thought infused seeing. It can be a mode of thinking that is indispensable for an intense and rich engagement with the realm of the sacred:

> O the mind, mind has mountains; cliffs of fall
> Frightful, sheer, no-man-fathomed. Hold them cheap
> May who ne'er hung there.[126]

Or in another terrifying exploration of depression:

> Not, I'll not, carrion comfort, Despair, not feast on thee;
> Not untwist – slack they may be – these last strands of man
> In me or, most weary, cry *I can no more*.[127]

---

[124] Wynn, *Emotional Experience and Religious Understanding: Integrating Perception, Conception and Feeling* (Cambridge: Cambridge University Press, 2005).
[125] Wynn, *Renewing the Senses* (Oxford: Oxford University Press, 2013), p. 34.
[126] G. M. Hopkins, 'No worst, there is none. Pitched past pitch of grief' in *The Poems of Gerard Manley Hopkins* (London: Oxford University Press, 1967).
[127] Hopkins, 'Carrion Comfort' in *Poems*.

Wynn uses the argument about a world of the melancholic, a realm devoid of significance and salience in relation to the theistic world view. I would like to link Wynn's observation about thought infused seeing to the formidable and powerful work of psychiatrist and literary scholar Iain McGilchrist. McGilchrist's work concerns the relation between the right and left brain hemispheres. His great work *The Master and his Emissary: The Divided Brain and the Making of the Western World* (2010) starts from a very simple observation. The brain, the isthmus of mind and matter, is both divided and asymmetrical. The two hemispheres are different in size, shape, and weight. Why should this be so? He dispatches the crude idea that the two hemispheres represent the logical and imaginative sides of the mind and replaces it with the position that the right is holistic and concrete and the left is focused on detail and abstract. Moreover, the right is significant for bodily awareness. In the second half of the book McGilchrist presents a powerful critique of an Occidental culture that has been progressively ruled by the left brain. Hence the title of his book. The left hemisphere is properly the *emissary* of its master, the right. McGilchrist is a practising psychiatrist. He links many characteristic disorders of modern society to an imbalance of the hemispheres. From these psychiatric observations, McGilchrist moves to observations about our culture. The mechanistic, abstract, technocratic and secular world of the industrialized West mirrors the undue dominance of the right hemisphere. The Cartesian division of *res cogitans* and *res extensa* seems to express drastically the right hemisphere deficiency bemoaned by McGilchrist. Our society is a culture that has a diminished sense of participation. This is deeply irritating for those who want clear-cut and simplistic answers. The ability to tolerate and live with ambiguity, risk and doubt is associated with the right hemisphere and the proper balance of the right and left hemispheres.[128]

For Wynn, it is precisely in the human confrontation with the sensory and empirical world the religious dimension emerges. The change in the emotional condition of the religious convert and 'a change in the phenomenology of their experience of the world' and the attendant sense of renewal is not

---

[128] McGilchrist, *The Master and his Emissary* (New Haven, CT: Yale University Press, 2010), pp. 82, 187.

typically experienced as an escape from the world.[129] Indeed, in the accounts of William James, from whom Wynn draws much, the characteristic feature of the religious convert is often the 'iron of melancholy'. The reduced sense of engagement or participation that is characteristic of right hemisphere deficit and an overly 'rational' and instrumental (i.e. left hemisphere) approach to the world is actually a diminishing of the experience of reality. McGilchrist notes how the anorexic patient is caught in a distorted relationship to his or her body, where the body becomes an object of control rather than the vehicle of life. The narcissist or the borderline patient is similarly refusing to recognize a domain impinging upon them beyond their own whims or anxieties, and so failing to accept certain realities, the state of things as they exist, beyond any agent's wishes or society's conventions.

McGilchrist's diagnosis of a culture that is incapable of living with ambiguity can be fruitfully compared with Eric Voegelin's critique of totalitarianism. For Voegelin, totalitarian political regimes are the product of phantasy and a failure to recognize reality. They are what Voegelin calls 'imaginative oblivion'. The failure to negotiate reality produces a substitute world. The ideological straightjacket is put into contrast with the flexibility and openness of a genuine engagement with reality: 'Living in openness to reality offers the prospect of love and community.'[130] Voegelin's preoccupation with order was shaped by his experience of chaos in central Europe in the 1930s. Central to his own vision of order is the principle of 'Community of Being'. Mankind dwells in a state of *metaxy* or participation. There is a proper recognition of human limits within this order of God, man, world, society that the neo-Gnostics occlude or refuse.

---

[129] Wynn, *The Renewal of the Senses*, p. 40.
[130] Embry, *The Philosopher and the Storyteller*, p. 113.

7

Mythology and Theogony

Monotheism of reason and the heart, polytheism of the imagination and art, that is what we need!

Schelling[1]

Russell's Teapot

Bertrand Russell waggishly offered an imaginative burden of proof argument against theism. If someone were to offer a theory that there is a china teapot orbiting the earth, there would be no need for the sceptic to refute such a theory. Similarly, why should the atheist feel any need to engage in the throes of theological combat? There is, however, no genuine analogy with theism. Why should 'God' be any more puzzling than, say, 'causality' or 'freedom'? Perhaps all of these concepts are rooted in deep (perhaps innate) cognitive dispositions. Unlike Russell's whimsical cosmic teapot postulate, however, theism is a theory with a venerable heritage. The concept of 'God' or 'arche' or 'principium' has a long philosophical history from the Pre-Socratics in the West through Cicero into medieval Europe, and most of the greatest philosophers in the West up to the late nineteenth century have held the theory in some form. It enjoys continuity of esteem and it has found adherents in both Eastern and Western philosophy. And 'theism' is not merely a 'theory' but usually linked to a way of

---

[1] Or Hegel or Hölderlin. Known as the 'Oldest System Programme of German Idealism'. *Das älteste Systemprogramm des deutschen Idealismus*. Monotheismus der Vernunft und des Herzens, Polytheismus der Einbildungskraft und der Kunst, dies ist's, was wir bedürfen! In Georg W. F. Hegel, *Mythologie der Vernunft. Hegels älteste Systemprogramm des deutschen Idealismus*, eds Christoph Jamme und Helmut Schneider (Frankfurt a.M.: Surkamp, 1988), p. 1.

life in the rituals and images of specific communities. If true, the metaphysical and ethical implications are enormous. If false, it raises the question why this false belief should exert such a grip upon the imagination of so many that it still generates an array of perplexing issues about belief, self-deception and the nature of society that could not emerge with the cosmic teapot. Russell's apparent argument dissolves into the merely rhetorical.

The German-American philosopher-theologian Paul Tillich insisted upon the identity of the God of the philosophers and the God of Abraham, Isaac and Jacob as Being itself. Far from being an oddity of Western culture, and especially the poisoned chalice of Plato, speculative philosophy emerged in Greece and India at about the same time (sixth century BC) with abstract concepts like Being or questions like 'what is the primary element in reality' and how can we know it?

> Come now, I will tell you – and bring away my story safely when you have heard it – the only ways of inquiry there are for thinking: the one, that it is and that it is not possible for it not to be, is the path of Persuasion (for it attends upon Truth), the other, that it is not and that it is necessary for it not to be, this I point out to you to be a path completely unlearnable, for neither may you know that which is not (for it is not to be accomplished) nor may you declare it. [2]

In the *Upanishads* we find the same 'ultimate concern' as in the Hellenic tradition stretching back to Parmenides and Plato.

> In the beginning, my dear, this [universe] was Being (Sat) alone, one only without a second. Some say that in the beginning this was non-being (*asat*) alone, one only without a second; and from that non-being, being was born.[3]

Whereas Heidegger tries to readdress the ancient question of Being through an attack on Platonism and his often curious and sometimes tendentious readings of pre-Socratic philosophers and of Eckhart and Hölderlin, Tillich attempts to reinvest the Platonic tradition with contemporary intelligibility. In his essay 'Participation and Knowledge' of 1955, Tillich writes:

> Without accepting the basic assumption of Husserl's phenomenology, viz. the bracketing of existence, I believe that the Platonic Tradition in all its variations

---

[2] Fragment 2, translation in Cohen, Curd, and Reeves' *Readings in Ancient Greek Philosophy*, 2nd edn (Indianapolis: Hackett Publishing, 2000), p. 37.
[3] *Chandogya Upanishad*, 6.2.1

is right in asking a question which empiricism never can answer, namely, the question of the structural presuppositions of experience.[4]

Why did philosophy, as we understand it, start in Greece and India at about the same time? One possible answer is the development of money. Perhaps the emergence of abstract value as currency stimulated inquiry into other forms of abstract value.[5] Answers to such a question are, of course, highly speculative. The fact remains that very abstract questions like why the existence of the universe per se, or why the existence of a universe with the properties of this universe, developed in these two cultures at about the same time, a kind of philosophical 'axial age'.

Consensus Gentium

Another, deeper, argument has troubled philosophers: the argument from hiddenness and the problem of non-culpable disbelief. If God exists and is good and loving, all reasonable people ought to believe. Since some reasonable people do not believe, God does not exist.

There is, however, a counter argument commonly known as the *consensus gentium*. This is an argument based upon the widespread 'agreement of the peoples'. If belief in God is found in various and distinct cultures, this seems to provide some justification, at least, for the belief. There is, of course, no *necessary* link between the widespread nature of a belief and the truth of that belief. It suffices to defuse the Russell argument if theism is deeply entrenched in both Western and Eastern culture. This raises the question of imagination. Plotinus speaks of the spiritual sense that all possess but only a few employ. Is there an inchoate or incipient *sensus divinitatis* or *semen religionis* in the human mind?

Why is it that we find such a remarkable convergence of philosophical views of the deity in radically different traditions? Why do Plotinus, Ibn Arabi,

---

[4] P. Tillich, *Philosophical Writings* (Berlin, New York: De Gruyter, 1989), p. 384.
[5] Richard Seaford, *Money and the Early Greek Mind: Homer, Philosophy, Tragedy* (Cambridge: Cambridge University Press, 2004).

Meister Eckhart or Ramanuja share so much in common in their metaphysics, across Europe and Asia, from Hellenic paganism, Sufi mysticism, Christian metaphysics or speculative-vedantic Indian theology?[6] Why has the absolute been imagined as supreme being in such similar terms? Is it merely a striking coincidence or a fact about elaborate trading routes and channels of influence? At the very least it means that Russell's cosmic teapot is *legerdemain*. The contemplation of a transcendent *prius* of all being potential and actual has been the driving force of much philosophy throughout the great epochs of philosophy rather than some credulous will o' the wisp.

Aelian produced an encomium to the piety of the heathens, which he contrasted with the sceptical impiety of the Greeks.[7] Philostratus in *Life of Apollonius of Tyana* has his protagonist go on a philosophical pilgrimage to India and presents the Indians as the wisest of humanity and a people living in the presence of God. Indeed, they are foremost proponents of the view of 'God as the creator of the universe in its origin and in its essence, and his goodness as the motive that gave him the idea of this plan'.[8] John Walbridge observes that while the Greeks referred to foreigners as barbarians, they were fascinated by the 'barbarians'. In particular, since the Platonists were committed to a philosophy that placed a particular emphasis upon intuition and symbols, they turned in particular to the myths and symbols of the East. Walbridge describes this phenomenon as the 'persistent Pythagorean/Platonic/Neoplatonic fascination with a romanticized Orient'.[9] The tenet that Pythagoras and Plato had visited the Brahmins in Sir William Temple's *Essay upon the Ancient and Modern Learning* (1690) and Creuzer's vision of India as the cradle of mankind have their forebears in antiquity.[10] Yet long before Christian missionaries went to Africa or the Far East, Nicholas of Cusa wrote:

---

[6] This is the presupposition of David Bentley Hart's, *The Experience of God: Being, Consciousness, Bliss* (New Haven, CT: Yale University Press, 2013) as an elaborate construal and interpretation of the venerable Sanskrit triad *Sat-cit-ananda*.
[7] Aelian, *Varia Historia, or Historical Miscellany*, ed. and trans. N. G. Wilson (Cambridge: Loeb, 1997), 2.30.
[8] Philostratus, *Apollonius of Tyana*, VIII, 22, 5ff, trans. Christopher Jones (Cambridge: Loeb, 2006), p. 349.
[9] John Walbridge, *The Wisdom of the Mystic East* (Albany, State University of New York, 1981), p. 13.
[10] Partha Mitter, *Much Maligned Monsters*, p. 207

Now, to various nations. You sent various prophets and teachers—some at one time, others at another.[11]

This is the author of *De Deo abscondito*. The hidden God is an explicit theme of Cusa, as is '*Religio una in rituum varietate*'. We do have astonishing similarities as John Hick has recently eloquently and forcefully argued.[12] These similarities have been noted by many non-Christians. The great Persian scholar Al Biruni (973–1048) noted theistic aspects of Hinduism among the elite and he developed a sophisticated 'comparative mythology'.[13] The parallels between the Hindu, Christian and Sufi saints is striking.[14]

In more recent years, John Hick (1922–2012) trail-blazed his comparative philosophy of religion, which he presents as the shift from a 'Ptolemaic' Christ-centred view of religion to a 'Copernican' multifaith view of religious truths.[15] In his Gifford lectures entitled 'An Interpretation of Religion: Human Responses to the Transcendent', Hick developed a theory of the *Personae* and the *Impersonae* of the real.[16]

One of the central weaknesses of Hick's account is that he tries to force too much recalcitrant material into his neo-Kantian model of the interpretative grid of religious experience and the noumenal (and unknowable) ultimate reality. This has the tendency of downplaying genuine differences between, say, Buddhists and Advaitans. Our claim is more modest than Hick's. Rather than see all religions as sharing a basic structure, we are only committed to noticing the surprising currency and universality of theism among different cultures. Far from being a specifically Hellenic-Abrahamic phenomenon, theism has a powerful role in Indic thought. In order to make this claim, we

---

[11] De Pace Fidei 1§4, p. 634 in Nicholas of *Cusa's De Pace Fidei and Cribatio Alkorani: Translation and Analysis* (Second Edition) by Jasper Hopkins (Minneapolis: Arthur J Banning, 1994).

[12] An easily accessible expression of Hick's thought is to be found in *The Fifth Dimension: An exploration of the Spiritual Realm* (London: One World Publications, 1999).

[13] John Walbridge, *The Wisdom of the Mystic East* (Albany: State University of New York, 1981), p. 27ff.

[14] S. Radhakrishnan, *East and West and the End of their Separation* (New York: Harper and Brothers, 1956). See also David Bentley Hart, *The Experience of God: Being, Consciousness and Bliss* (New Haven, CT: Yale University Press, 2013).

[15] John Hick, 'The Copernican Revolution in Theology' in *God and the Universe of Faiths* (London: Collins, 1977) pp. 120–32.

[16] Hick, *An Interpretation of Religion: Human Responses to the Transcendent* (London: Macmillan, 1989), pp. 252–96.

need to disabuse ourselves of some common misapprehensions about the rich tradition of historical Indian metaphysics.

In order to understand this phenomenon, we might reflect upon the German Idealist dictum: 'Monotheism of reason and the heart, polytheism of the imagination and art, that is what we need!'[17] The monotheism of India differs from the biblical paradigm because it supports a plurality of epiphanies of the absolute, in many respects paralleling the developments in late antique culture.[18] A. H. Armstrong refers to this a 'Hellenic monotheism' and John Kenney calls it 'mystical monotheism', to distinguish it from Abrahamic forms. Such a monotheism posits an ultimate transcendent source of all being – the principle of all but which is different from all (and hence distinct from any monism of strict identity). While emphasizing difference or separation like the Abrahamic theist, the Indian theist nevertheless flinches from making the division into rupture.

The Case of Hinduism

> They call it Indra, varuna and Agni
> And also heavenly, beautiful Garutman:
> The Real is one, though sages name it variously.
> *Rig Veda* I 164:46[19]

John Stuart Mill viewed Indian culture as arrested in its infancy.[20] The Romantics were more positive. Coleridge writes: 'In Egypt, Palestine, Greece and India, the analysis of the mind had reached its noon and manhood while experimental research was still in its dawn and infancy.'[21] The great nineteenth-century Cambridge Divine Brooke Foss Westcott was an enthusiast for India. Edward Bickersteth (1850–1897) founded the Delhi Mission and yet Brooke Foss Westcott (1825–1901) was the *spiritus rector*. Westcott

---

[17] Christoph Jamme, Helmut Schneider eds., *Mythologie der Vernunft. Hegels ältestes Systemprogramm des deutschen Idealismus* (Frankfurt am Main: Suhrkamp, 1988).
[18] Garth Fowden, *Empire to Commonwealth: Consequences of Monotheism in Late Antiquity* (Princeton, NJ: Princeton University Press, 1993), esp. p. 5 and pp. 40f.
[19] Hick, p. 253.
[20] Ankur Barua, *Debating Conversion in Hinduism and Christianity* (London: Routledge, 2015), p. 47.
[21] I mention this in *Living Forms of the Imagination* (London T&T Clark, 2008). On Coleridge, see Antonella Riem Natale, *The One Life: Coleridge and Hinduism*. (Jaipur: Rawat, 2005).

'saw the Mission as an opportunity to reassert the principles of Alexandrian Christianity, searching for traces of the Logos in distant faiths'.[22] He observes: 'The West has much to learn from the East, and the lesson will not be taught till we hear the truth as it is apprehended by Eastern minds.'[23]

There was a particular relationship between Romanticism and India. Whereas the Enlightenment often looked to China for inspiration, the Romantics often felt a deep affinity with the luxuriant metaphysics and exotic imagination of Indian speculation. It began with the translation of classical Indian texts by British and French scholars that generated the 'oriental renaissance' of the Romantic period.[24] Herder in *Ideen zur Philosophie der Geschichte der Menschheit* (1784–91) and Schelling asserted the kinship of the spiritual religion of India with the Pauline strand of Christianity and the superiority of both to merely legal religions of the book. Schlegel published his influential *On the Tongue and Wisdom of the Indians* in 1808.[25] Schlegel sees Indian religion, however, as declining from an original revelation. The Indian model of Cosmogony is presented as emanationist rather than *creatio ex nihilo*. In the wake of emanationism,[26] Indian religion degenerates from such sublime heights into 'Astrology and Wild worship of nature', whereby the Dionysian-Shiva-Durga cult drives a cruel and immoral religion of human and animal sacrifices. In opposition to Herder, Schlegel saw pantheism as a corruption of the original doctrine of India, and generating an enervating fatalism (which he linked to the famous *Spinozastreit* about pantheism). Hegel, too, is rather ambivalent about Indian thought and yet he also bears the clear mark of the Oriental Renaissance. 'Over against the thoroughly prosaic mind of the Chinese, we find set the dreaming unregulated fancy of the Hindus; the unimaginative realism of the former is confronted by the fantastic idealism of the latter.'[27]

---

[22] Millington, Constance, *Whether We be Many or Few: a history of the Cambridge/Delhi Brotherhood* (Bangalore: Asian Trading Corporation, 1999) p. 11.
[23] B. F. Westcott, *Essays in the History of Religious Thought in the West* (London: Macmillan, 1891). For a very different view see Alain Daniélou, *Gods of Love and Ecstasy: The Traditions of Shiva and Dionysus* (Rochester: Inner Traditions, 1984).
[24] Chris Ryan, *Schopenhauer: The Death of God and the Oriental Renaissance* (Leuven: Peeters, 2010).
[25] *Uber die Sprache und Weisheit der Inder*.
[26] Bradley L. Herling, *The German Gita: Hermeutics and Discipline in the German Reception of Indian Thought* (London: Routledge, 2006).
[27] Mitter, *Much Maligned Monsters*, p. 210.

If the great period of Indian philosophy is eclipsed during the seventeenth century, there was a remarkable re-emergence or revival of Vedantic thought during the Bengal Renaissance. Raja Ram Mohan Roy (1772–1833), one of the greatest Indians of the modern period, was partly shaped by the syncretism that emerged out of the opposition to, and influence of, British educational projects in Calcutta, and the Western ideas that they conveyed. The revival of thought and culture that emerged generated figures as eminent as the Nobel laureate Rabindranath Tagore (1861–1941). Raja Ram Mohan Roy, initially the leading figure of the Bengal Renaissance, developed the monotheistic potential of Hinduism which emerged as a potent force in the reform movement and this exerted a great influence upon later figures like Vivekananda.[28] Roy's own Hindu 'Church', The Brahmo Samaj, defined the worship of God as 'the contemplation of the attributes of the Supreme Being'.[29] Vivekananda is an intriguing instance of the meeting of East and West. William Hastie, the Scottish principal of Vivekananda's college in Calcutta, the Scottish Church College, while teaching Wordsworth's *Excursion*, suggested that the students went to visit the illiterate sage Ramakrishna.[30] Thus was born the great Ramakrishna movement associated with the charisma and energy of Swami Vivekananda. Here Vivekananda found his guru and was able to communicate the vision throughout the world while also encouraging a revival of Vedanta in India.

Ancient Theology Revived!

It is customary to view the Enlightenment as bringing the demise and end of the ancient theology and yet this in some way is deeply misleading.[31] The syncretism of late antiquity was further developed in the seventeenth and

---

[28] Partha Mitter, 'Rammohun Roy et le nouveau language du monotheisme' in *L'impensable Polytheisme: Etudes d'historiographie religieuse*, ed. Francis Schmidt (Chippenham: Anthony Rowe, 1988), pp. 257–97.
[29] E. C. Dewick, *The Indwelling God* (Mysore: Oxford University Press, 1938), p. 58.
[30] Narasingha Prosad Sil, *Swami Vivekananda, A Reassessment* (London: Associated Universities Presses, 1997), p. 36.
[31] Anthony Grafton, *Defenders of the Text: The Traditions of Scholarship in an Age of Science, 1450–1800* (Cambridge, MA: Harvard University Press, 1994), pp. 162–77. D. P. Walker, *Ancient Theology* (Ithaca: Cornell, 1972), esp. 18–19. John Marenbon, *Pagans and Philosophers. The Problem of Paganism from Augustine to Leibniz* (Princeton, NJ: Princeton University Press, 2015).

eighteenth centuries by figures like the Cambridge Platonists, Jacob Bryant and Sir William Jones. Friedrich Creuzer developed his own highly influential and idiosyncratic version of the *Prisca Theologia*.[32] There were, moreover, distinguished exponents of this Romantic-revival of ancient theology in the twentieth century among Platonists like Coomaraswamy (1877–1947) and Eliade (1907–86). Coomaraswamy was shaped by the romantically inspired vision of India as a path to deeper and older spiritual values occluded by the materialism and rationalism of modernity. His acquaintance Mircea Eliade writes: 'All that essential and indescribable part of man that is called imagination dwells in realms of symbolism and still lives upon archaic myths and theologies.'[33] Eliade's own work on the imagination was grounded in formative indological researches.[34]

Coomaraswamy was a passionate advocate of the view that Indian thought, with its inheritance of Brahmanic understanding, involves a 'constant effort to understand the meaning and purpose of life'.[35] For him, the Brahmanical creed was one of a unity of all life, and their regard of its realization as the highest goodness and truth.[36] Coomaraswamy insisted upon the significant role that art plays in conveying real truths. Within the Indian perspective Coomaraswamy emphasized his belief, 'subjective and objective are not irreconcilable categories, one of which must be regarded as real to the exclusion of the other. Reality (*satya*) subsists there where the intelligible and sensible meet in the common unity of being.'[37] For Coomaraswamy such truth can be attained by the artist through the yogic practice. Yoga, demanding rigorous mental concentration, is a route to achieve the unity of the absolute truth by bringing the yogic to an overcoming of alienation between himself and the object of contemplation. Such contemplation is a 'means of achieving harmony or unity of consciousness'.[38] Coomaraswamy maintains that, in Indian thought, it is well known that, to the mind able to truly direct and

---

[32] Mitter, p. 210.
[33] Mircea Eliade, *Yoga, Immortality and Freedom* (Princeton, NJ: Princeton University Press, 1961), p. 19.
[34] See Morny Joy,
[35] Coomaraswamy, *The Dance of Shiva*, p. 22.
[36] Coomaraswamy, *The Dance of Shiva*, p. 27.
[37] Coomaraswamy, *The Transformation of Nature in Art* (Cambridge, Mass.: Harvard University Press, 1934), p. 11.
[38] Coomawaswamy, *The Dance of Shiva*, p. 43.

concentrate itself, all knowledge is available without the use of the senses.[39] One might think of the great theophany in Chapter 11 of the Gita, or consider other symbols like the *sankha* (conch), *chakra* (wheel), and *padma* (lotus).

Coomaraswamy was a stalwart advocate of the healing power of imagination, as a means to recover the vitality through seeing the sacred. Partha Mitter, a sharp critic of Coomaraswamy, also insists on the profound link between art and religion in India.

Indian architecture is uncommonly impressive, particularly in its temples, for example the rock-cut Kailasa temple in Ellore, which dates from around AD 750, and is dedicated to Shiva, and The Elephanta caves in Mumbai harbour exhibit particularly beautiful sculptures wrought in the rock. Some Europeans thought that the beauty and stateliness of the temples showed their classical origins in Alexander the Great.

Bronze statues were often depictions of the gods and their actions such as Shiva's dance. Ananda Coomaraswamy describes the image of Shiva as 'the manifestation of primal rhythmic energy',[40] and 'the clearest image of the activity of God which any art or religion can boast of'.[41] Shiva is generally represented in his dance as having four arms, with the left leg raised. Standing within an arch of flames, symbolizing the manifest universe as *samsara*, Shiva's dance is both an image of creation and destruction. Characteristically holding a drum in his upper right hand – symbolizing the creation of noise, and in his upper left, fire to symbolize destruction. The second right hand of Shiva makes the sign of *abhaya mudra*, the symbol of fearlessness that drives away fear. The second left hand points to his raised left leg, the position of which represents the emancipation from ignorance. Shiva is usually depicted standing over a conquered demon. This demon is ignorance. But there is a palm raised while the other points to the foot of the deity as a source of refuge.[42]

Leslie Willson refers to the 'mythic image of India'. Diana Eck notes that Hinduism is an imaginative, an 'image-making', religious tradition in which the sacred is seen as present in the visible world – the world we see in multiple

---

[39] Coomawaswamy, *The Dance of Shiva*, 46.
[40] Coomaraswamy, *The Dance of Shiva*, p. 83.
[41] Coomaraswamy, *The Dance of Shiva*, p. 84.
[42] Diana Eck, *Darśán, Seeing the Divine Image in India* (Chambersburg, PA: Anima Books, 1985), p. 30.

images and deities, in sacred places, and in people.'[43] One of the problems with such accounts of 'Hinduism' is the very idea of Hinduism as a unitary religion. Some scholars deny the usefulness of such a term as a Western imposition. Julius Lipner takes a more moderate view. Whilst recognizing the difficulties, he describes the pluralism of Hinduism through an image – that of the Banyan tree.

> From widespread branches (a banyan) sends down aerial roots, many of which grow thick and strong to resemble individual trunks, so that an ancient banyan tree looks like an interconnected collection of trees and branches in which the same life sap flows ... Like the tree, Hinduism is an ancient collection of roots and branches, many indistinguishable one from another, microcosmically polycentric, macrocosmically one, sharing the same regenerative life sap, with a temporal foliage which covers most of recorded human history.[44]

Indian philosophy is an immensely rich and fertile field. Husserl's view that only Greek philosophy counts as being authentically philosophical can be summarily dismissed as absurd.[45] Given the widespread cliché of pervasive and stultifying monism, however, it should be noted that many of the key themes of Indian philosophy can be discussed with little or no reference to theology or 'mystical' enlightenment.[46] There is a great range of positions from abstract monism to theism, deism, strict materialism and hedonism.[47] Indian philosophy has inherited through Hinduism, however, a powerful theistic component implicit in the *Rig Veda* (especially the creation Hymn of the *Rig Veda* X, 129) and the Upanishads and explicitly from the *Gita* onwards. If Shankara represents a strict, some might say rigid, monism, there have been notable critiques of his position that tend towards theism.

The *Gita* places an emphasis upon devotion *(bhakti)* and the identification of ultimate Brahman with Krishna. Since Krishna is immanent and transcendent, the sustainer of all, though not identical with all beings, Krishna is even a spectator of the natural world (XIII, 21). The word *'bhakti'* from the

---

[43] Eck, *Darsán, Seeing the Divine Image in India*, p. 7.
[44] Lipner, *Hinduism*, p. 5.
[45] Edmund Husserl, 'Philosophy and the Crisis of European Man', in *Phenomenology and the Crisis of Philosophy*, trs by Quentin Lauer (New York: Harper Torchbooks, 1965), p. 159.
[46] S. Radhakrishnan and C. A. Moore, *Sourcebook in Indian Philosophy*. Princeton, NJ: Princeton University Press, 1967).
[47] See Jonardon Ganeri, *Philosophy in Classical India: The Proper Work of Reason* (London: Routledge, 2001).

Sanskrit verb *bhaj*, which originally meant 'to divide, share, or distribute', and had derivative meanings of 'enjoy, participate, to eat and to make love'.[48] It appears in the *Svetasvatara Upanisad* (500 BC?) and the *Bhagavad-Gita*. The tradition of the spiritual practice of *bhakti* went back to the seventh century AD and worship of God in this tradition assumes an idea of grace.[49]

A powerfully emotional form of Krishna *bhakti* emerged in the Tamil country in the hymns of the Alvars (c. AD 800). The devotion centres upon Krishna, the lord of the universe. This highly emotional Krishna *bhakti* can be distinguished from what F. Hardy has called the 'intellectual *bhakti*' found in the *Bhagavad-Gita*. Whilst *intellectual bhakti* purges in order to refine the empirical perceptions of the self, this *emotional bhakti* has a distinctly aesthetic, erotic psychology – fired by both myth and poetry, of the ecstatic encounter of the devotee with Krishna.[50] Andal, the ninth-century AD female Alvar poet, composed two poems: 'Tiruppavai' and 'Nacciyar Tirumoli', in which she develops the myths of Krsna and the *gopis* as images of his desire for union with Krsna. The works of the female poet Mirabai (c. AD 1500), hailing from northwest India, show that *viraha-bhakti* was not limited to the Tamil literature of the South. The existence of this strong tradition of *bhakti*, 'devotional renaissance', shows that it is quite inadequate to view Hinduism either in terms of impersonal abstraction or crude polytheism.[51] Indeed, it has been claimed that 'Mirabai is the one who has most fired the imagination of India over the centuries.'[52]

Ramanuja (1056–1137) is a philosopher of the Absolute Brahman but his theology has a theistic shape, and he was able to give the more emotional effusions of the Alvars a philosophical rigour and power.[53] Ramanuja, the founder of the Visista-Advaita school (literally, 'non-duality of qualified being/s'),[54] rejected the Advaitic understanding of the dissolution of the individual in Brahman. Instead, Ramanuja presents the philosophical goal as loving communion of the *atman*

---

[48] A. Schelling, *The Oxford Anthology of Bhakti Literature*, (Oxford: Clarendon, 2011), p. xvi.
[49] See R. Otto, *Gnadenreligion: Indiens und das Christentum* (Gotha: Klotz, 1930).
[50] F. Hardy, *Viraha-bhakti: The Early History of Krsna Devotion in South India* (New Delhi: Oxford University Press, 2001) p. 9.
[51] A. J. Alston, *The Devotional Poems of Mirabai* (Delhi: Motilal Banarsidass, 1980), p. 9.
[52] Schelling, *The Oxford Anthology of Bhakti Literature*, p. 137. See also Michelle Voss Roberts, *Tastes of the Divine: Hindu and Christian Theologies of Emotion* (New York: Fordham, 2014), pp. 57ff.
[53] J. Lipner, *The Face of Truth: A Study of Meaning and Metaphysics in the Vedantic Theology of Ramanuja* (Albany: State University of New York, 1976).
[54] Lipner, *The Face of Truth*, p. 47.

with God through *bhakti*. For Ramanuja, Brahman is personal, the creator and animating soul of the world.[55] Just like Shankara, Ramanuja holds to the celebrated principle of the *Tat Twam Asi*. He interprets it in a different manner. The 'is' or '*asi*' is not an 'is' of *identity* but one of *predication*. The human self possesses its own identity, which is not simply negated by the Absolute. Rather, it must realize its true kinship with the Absolute which is realized through the indwelling of the Divine. Max Mueller noted: 'Translated into the language of the early Christian philosophers of Alexandria, this lifting up of the Tvam into the Tat might prove the equivalent of the idea of Divine sonship. If properly understood, these Vedanta teachings may, under a strange form, bring us very near to the earliest Christian philosophy, and help us understand it, as it was understood by the great thinkers of Alexandria'.[56] In the twentieth century Simone Weil sees Krishna and Dionysus as 'images of Christ'.[57]

Ramanuja's insistence upon a method of 'identity-in-difference' aimed to preserve both the transcendent sovereignty of the eternal Ground of all existence, 'causal Brahman', over the manifold forms of *atman*, and the immanent presence of God in the physical cosmos, which is Brahman's 'body'.[58] On his account, such a creator who manifests himself through the generation of the cosmos is a greater one than the unknowable absolute of Shakara. Even more radical is the dvaitic (dualistic) system of Madhva (1238–1317), which rejects both Sankara's monism and Ramanuja's modified monism.[59]

The Indian concept of *Lila*, of cosmic play, has an important role in Indian theology. Sometimes translated as 'sport' or 'play', the word also has sexual connotations, evinced in erotic temple sculptures or the Shiva Linga as a symbol of Divine energy.[60] It has been used by Indian metaphysicians to explain why the One becomes Many, i.e. why God creates. If God is inherently self-sufficient perfection, (the *saccidananda*) why create another domain?[61]

---

[55] Ankur Barua 'God's Body at Work: Ramanuja and Panentheism', *International Journal of Hindu Studies* 14, 1 (2010): 1–30.
[56] Max Mueller, *The Six Systems of Indian Philosophy* (London: Longmans, Green & Co., 1919), p. 124.
[57] Simone Weil, *First and Last Notebooks* (Oxford: Oxford University Press, 1970), pp. 321ff.
[58] Lipner, *The Face of Truth*, p. 44.
[59] B. N. K. Sharma, *Philosophy of Sri Madhvacarya* (Delhi: Motilal Banarsidass, 1991).
[60] Eliade, *Yoga, Immortality and Freedom*, p. 265.
[61] John F. Butler, 'Creation, Art and Lila', *Philosophy East and West*, vol. 10, No. 1/2 (April–July 1960), pp. 3–12. See also Frederic F. Fost, 'Playful Illusion: The Making of Worlds in Advaita Vedanta', *Philosophy East and West*, no. 3, (July 1998), pp. 387–405.

How can it desire something else without possessing some lack? This is a problem in both Eastern and Western thought.

One may see this concept as attempting to bridge two extremes which also occur in Western theology – extreme voluntarism and necessitarianism: is the world the product of arbitrary and brute will or the mechanical and inexorable emanation of the absolute? Neither alternative is theologically attractive. In the first, the Divine becomes wilful and anthropomorphic and in the second a sub-personal or impersonal being. The notion of 'play' may be viewed as a median position between these two options. God is not 'constrained' or needful in his activity but neither is this work wanton or groundless. The Sanskritic *lila* can be seen in parallel to the problem of the 'causal joint' problem of divine action which has been discussed by philosophers and theologians in the West in recent decades. How and 'where' does God 'touch' the world? If God 'touches' the world too much, we head towards pantheism, and if God does not 'touch' the world sufficiently, we veer towards Manichaeism. The Vedantic response to the Hindu version of this problem is elaborated in terms of *lila*.

The concept of *Lila* forms a link between the 'aesthetic' concepts of play employed in relation to dance and architecture, and the abstract metaphysics and complex theories of God and world, of the *Brahma Sutras*. How does the One hold together and forge a unity out of the Many? How should the sustaining dynamism of divine action be viewed? The sustaining and cohesive power of the One in the Many is cosmic play.

Lila is thus linked to Shakti and the image of the Divine spouse.[62] This 'consort is his *shakti*, his outpouring energy, touched with the emotion of love. As *maya-shakti*, this is in great tracts of Indian thought, regularly conceived of as the agent in creation'. There are obvious parallels with the wisdom motif in Western thought, especially the personification of wisdom in Proverbs 8.22–30, where she becomes a principle of creation itself, or in the book of Revelation where the woman in the holy of holies, clad with the sun, gives birth to the Messiah.[63]

---

[62] Butler, 'Creation, Art and Lila', p. 6.
[63] Stephen Barton, *Where Shall Wisdom be Found?: Wisdom in the Bible, the Church and the Contemporary World* (Edinburgh: T&T Clark, 1999). See Louis Bouyer, *Le trône de la sagesse* (Paris, Éditions du Cerf René Guénon, *Études sur le hinduisme*: 1987).

The idea of *Lila* has been applied to aesthetics.[64] Again, there are profound occidental parallels since imagining God as an artist lies deep in the Western tradition. Indeed, it has been claimed by Guénon that *maya* should be interpreted in aesthetic terms.

> He who produces the manifestation through the means of his 'art' is the Divine Architect, and the world is his 'work of art'; thus thought, the world is no less 'real' than our works of art, which, due to their relative impermanence, are also 'unreal' if compared to the art 'abiding' in the artist. Indeed, the main danger one runs into when using the word 'illusion' is that we can too easily use it as a synonym for 'unreality' in an absolute sense, that is considering things as illusory, as if they were absolutely nothing, while they are only different gradations of reality.[65]

The world is a manifestation (*abhasa*) of Shiva, which emerges from his consort Shakti. 'Shakti' is a mirror in which Shiva can contemplate himself. Ramanuja presents the world as a 'playground in which the jivanmukta has the same power as Isvara to create worlds out of his own imagination and to move through such worlds according to its desires – either in a dreaming manner or by taking on bodily presence in a form equivalent to a divine avatara.'[66]

The jivanmukta is the liberated sage and Isvara is God and the *avatara* is the Sanskrit form of the moral familiar 'avatar' or manifestation of the deity. Guénon's reflections upon the language of *maya* are supported by the paradigmatic rope-snake example of Shankara. The man treading on what he thinks is a snake will be in a state of real terror, even if the 'snake' turns out to be a length of rope. The experience is sufficiently 'real', even if the agent is mistaken about the object of his fear.

The image of *Lila* in Hindu thought is profoundly instructive. There are facets of the idea that belong to the specific Hindu tradition. There are other dimensions of this view of creation that furnish clear and compelling parallels with the Western metaphysical tradition. The term is also used to express the thought that God as supreme being cannot be constrained. It is not clear

---

[64] Hilde Heine, 'Play as an Aesthetic Concept', *The Journal of Aesthetics and Art Criticism*, vol. 27, no. 1, (1968), pp. 67–71.
[65] Guenon, *etudes sur le hinduisme*, quoted in Natale, p. 9.
[66] Fost, 'Playful illusion', p. 396.

that the image provides a solution. It also provides a structure of *exitus* and *reditus*.

Plotinus strikingly uses certain images to express the freedom of the supreme principle, whose 'activity was always and a something like being awake, when the wakener was not someone else, a wakefulness and a thought transcending thought which exists always, then he is as he woke himself to be'.[67] The Plotinian wakefulness is not quite the playfulness of *Lila*. Plotinus does, however, use the language of love: 'And he, that same self, is lovable and love and love of himself and in himself, in that he is beautiful only from himself and in himself.'[68] And Plotinus employs the language of radiant light: 'borne to his own interior, as it were well pleased with himself, the "pure radiance", being himself this with which he is well pleased'.[69]

It is Plotinus that we find shaping the thought of figures as diverse as Aquinas and Meister Eckhart. Bede Griffiths notes that for Eckhart creation was the expression of the eternal Verbum and that Thomas claims that the created order exists in the eternal Divine ideas:

> When creation comes into being in time, then each of us assumes his own particular created form, his separate identity, but the divine archetype is present still in each one of us. In this sense the world can be said to be a 'manifestation' of God. The created world is a 'reflection' of the uncreated archetypal world. Like an image in a mirror, it has only a relative existence. Its existence is constituted by this relation to God. It is in this sense that we can say with the Hindu school of Advaita, that God and the world are 'not two' (advaita). The created world adds nothing to God and takes nothing from him. Creation makes no change in him; change is in the creature.[70]

Myth in Modernity

Thomas Traherne writes:

> The Lord God of Israel, the living and true God, was from all eternity, and from all eternity wanted like a God. He wanted the communication of His divine essence,

---

[67] Plotinus, *Ennead* VI.8[39].16, 32ff.
[68] Plotinus, *Treatise*, VI 8, 15, 1ff.
[69] Plotinus, *Treatise*, VI 8, 16, 14ff.
[70] Bede Griffiths, *The Marriage of East and West* (London: Harper Collins, 1982), p. 85.

and persons to enjoy it. He wanted world, He wanted spectators, He wanted joys, He wanted treasures. He wanted, yet he wanted not, for He had them.[71]

In this passage we have hints of not merely the theophanic but the theogonic deity. This passage is rather puzzling in its insistence upon the 'wanting' of God. Yet it is clear that Traherne views God as self-communicative. If one combines such a sense of the self-communicative goodness of the deity with the ancient Alexandrian thesis of the spermatic logos, then perhaps these mythic images can be seen as revealing something of the Godhead. Are we encountering randomly assorted 'images' of the Divine or can the Indic and the Semitic deities be related to a common historical process? Even in pagan antiquity there was a concerted effort to harmonize the gods of the differing cultures in the so called *Interpretatio Graeca*.[72] The English week days are themselves an instance of the ancient desire to harmonize the deities of different mythological systems, e.g. 'Thursday' or Thor's day is the West Germanic equivalent to the Romance *giovedi* in Italian or *jeudi* in French, i.e. *Iovis dies*.

Yet would it be quite another step to conceive of correspondences as theogonic?[73] I will turn to the model of Schelling, who proposes that mythology needs to be integrated into a theory of revelation. *Extra ecclesiam nulla salus*: 'Without the Church there is no salvation' is a much discussed, debated and contested principle of Catholic teaching. The obvious reading is that salvation is denied to those visibly outside the confines of the Church. Yet there have always been the doubters. '*Das Christenthum ist so alt wie die Welt.*'[74] Justin Martyr thought that there were Christians before Christ and Nicholas of Cusa pursued this more liberal view of salvation, whereby it is the quality of life rather than the content of belief that fixes salvation. It is the tenet expressed in the *Rime of the Ancient Mariner*: 'He prayeth best who loveth best'.

Schelling's significance cannot be appreciated apart from a serious consideration of his radically metaphysical estimate of mythology. Mythology in

---

[71] Thomas Traherne, *Centuries of Mediations* (London: P. J. and A. E. Dobell, 1927), p. 41.
[72] Jan Assmann, *Moses the Egyptian: The Memory of Egypt in Western Monotheism* (Cambridge, MA: Harvard University Press, 1997), pp. 44–54.
[73] Cf. Eric Voegelin, *Order and History*, vol. 4, *The Ecumenic Age* (Columbia: University of Missouri Press, 2000), p. 251.
[74] Ernst Benz, *Theogony*, p. 226. Benz, *Augustins Lehre der Kirche* (Wiebaden: Steiner, 1954), p. 61. Benz cites *Retractationes* I XIII, 3.

Schelling's later thought becomes part of a weapon against Hegel's hyperbolic rationalism. If art is the *einbilden* or 'informing' of the infinite in the finite, art requires mythology: the gods. For Hegel, the link between art and the gods (or mythology) is a feature of the Greek world and thus one contested, however ambiguously, by Christianity, which in turns inaugurates a post-mythological and secular world. Schelling is forced to uphold the persisting relevance of the mythical within the modern world. Whereas for the majority of modern thinkers, myths are primarily psychic images or cultural phenomena, Schelling views them as part of an *historia sacra*: they are revelations of transcendence through myth and symbol that constitute human society. The distinctive contribution of Schelling consists in his exploration of such images in his vision of myth as history.[75]

A neo-Schellingian attempt to combine myth with revelation might seem jejune in the modern age. And yet modernity itself is deeply mythical.[76] From the idealist 'System Programme of German Idealism' to Wagner and Freud and the structuralists, modernity has been deeply shaped by the question of myth.[77] Myth in that sense is 'modern'. Moreover, if language is deeply and necessarily metaphorical, we are always confronting the mythic. The Age of Romanticism was an epoch of intensive reflection upon pre-Christian and non-Christian religion and myths. It is no accident that myths have played a great role in twentieth-century psychology. Freud regards the unconscious as the source of myths, and he explicitly links myths with dreams. Freud takes this as psychological factum but he does not inquire further, and has no interest in the metaphysical dimension on account of his 'scientific' straightjacket, especially the pansexual interpretation. For Freud myths are useful as tools to understand dreams.[78]

Jung endeavours to answer the questions about myths that Freud shunned.

---

[75] Hadi Fakhoury has pointed out to me the decisive influence of Schelling upon Henry Corbin, especially upon the latter's idea of hierohistory and the visionary recital.
[76] John B. Vickery, *The Literary Impact of The Golden Bough* (Princeton: Princeton University Press, 1973).
[77] Angus Nichol, *Myth and the Human Sciences: Hans Blumenberg's Theory of Myth* (London and New York: Routledge, 2015).
[78] In fact, his theories about human sexuality rather limit his perspective on myth. See Richard Buxton, *Imaginary Greece: The Contexts of Mythology* (Cambridge: Cambridge University Press, 1994), p. 131.

For Jung, myth is like an arsenal or storehouse of images. Only by reflecting imaginatively upon such images can the soul come to terms with its vocation. The answer of Jung is that the great images constitute a repository of mysterious and numinous archetypes.[79] Yet, as we noted, Jung is coy about the metaphysical implications of his archetypal images.

There is, however, a complex historical-political critique of the recourse to mythology as a camouflage for reactionary politics or as a covert route to fascism. One might consider observations such as that of Bruce Lincoln concerning the radical reduction of myth to ideology:

> A taxonomy is encoded in mythic form, the narrative packages a specific, contingent system of discrimination in a particularly attractive and memorable form. What is more, it naturalizes and legitimizes it. Myth, then, is not just taxonomy, but *ideology* in narrative form.[80]

The problem with Lincoln's account is its widespread tendency (especially prevalent in the North American Academy via the pervasive influence of Foucault) to substitute the classic concerns of European humanism with covert political interests and strategies. If Lincoln is correct, 'postmodernity' is just as mythical as modernity. Anything goes, and anything can be legitimized as myth.[81]

Schelling's late *Philosophy of Mythology* and his *Philosophy of Revelation* is one of the most documented public 'failures' in European intellectual history. His much-vaunted appointment to the chair of philosophy in Berlin to vanquish and purge the supposed Dragon's seed of Hegelian pantheism (*die Drachensaat des Hegelianismus ausreuthen*) ended in disappointment. Schelling does nevertheless offer an intriguing and powerful response to Hume, and one that is little appreciated in the Anglo-Saxon world. Schelling possessed enormous erudition with his philological genius and was deeply

---

[79] See *Living Forms of the Imagination*, p. 116ff.
[80] Bruce Lincoln, *Theorising Myth: Narrative, Ideology and Scholarship* (Chicago, IL: Chicago University Press, 1999) p. 147. For a more philosophical perspective see myth arises from self-awareness – we cannot just think of ourselves as a part of nature but need to look beyond nature, Kolakowski, *The Presence of Myth*, translated by Adam Czerniawski (Chicago, IL: The University of Chicago Press, 1989), p. 116.
[81] For a concise demolition of Foucault's position see Roger Scruton, *Modern Philosophy: An Introduction and Survey* (New York: Penguin Press, 1995), pp. 5–6.

impressed by the emergence of Christianity as a genuine world religion in the nineteenth and twentieth centuries.[82] Schelling and Hegel both thought that world Christianity was one of the pre-eminent historical developments of the modern period.[83] Schelling was also keenly aware that human historical self-consciousness has been traditionally rooted in religious myths.

Hume's *Natural History of Religion* (1757) is a pivotal text in the European history of religions and develops a critique of religion indebted to Lucretius, Hobbes and Spinoza, especially the view that religion is grounded in fear and ignorance rather than any *sensus divinitatis* or *semen religionis*. The unstable relationship between monotheism and polytheism was one of the key themes of the book: 'a kind of flux and reflux in the human mind ... men have a natural tendency to rise from idolatry to theism, and to sink again from theism into idolatry'.[84] This oscillation or flux and reflux is linked to the key difficulty of theism in Hume's *Dialogues*, which identifies the tendency either to succumb to an anthropomorphized deity or an unsustainable 'mystical' transcendence.

For Schelling, myths reveal a manifest pattern in history. This pattern is a history of human development and a divine history: a theogony.[85] History, for Schelling, is a process of changes in human consciousness, and philosophy is the narration of this process or protocol of Divine revelation in and through history: '*in urkundliche Folge*'.[86] The means by which human consciousness is transformed by, includes and reveals the Divine mind is through the imagination. The theogonic poem is an organon of revelation: 'Monotheism was only the content of the mysteries in as far as within them the history of the gods became God's history. Instead of turning them into, or explaining them away as fables, the history of the gods becomes truth.'[87]

---

[82] For an excellent account of Schelling in English see: Joris Geldhof, *Revelation, Reason and Reality: Theological Encounters with Jaspers, Schelling and Baader* (Leuven: Peeters, 2007).
[83] P. 8 Offenbarung, Schelling XIV 77, 78.
[84] Hume, *The Natural History of Religion*, in David Hume, *Principal Writings on Religion*, ed. J. C. A Gaskin (Oxford: OUP, 19993), p. 158
[85] Angus Nicholls, *Myth and the Human Sciences: Hans Blumenberg* (London: Routledge, 2015).
[86] 'die positive Philosophie sei in Ansehung der Welt Wissenschaft a priori, *ganz von vorn anfangende, alles gleichsam in urkundlicher Folge, vom prius herleitend*, in Ansehung des vollkommenen Geistes aber Wissenschaft a posteriori'. Philosophy of Mythology 12th lecture. In '*urkundliche Folge*' is difficult to translate – in 'documentary sequence', which is what I construe as the idea of a protocol of Divine revelation.
[87] *Monotheismus war also nur insofern Inhalt der Mysterien, als ihnen die Gottergeschichte zur Geschichte*

The drama of the late Schelling is a theory, not just a doctrine of 'the gods', but a *history* of the gods and a metaphysical theology. God is viewed by Schelling as a process and the myths and heathen religions constitute different levels of this theogonic transformation: 'Christianity is not one-sidedly derived from Judaism. It has this and heathendom as its presupposition: only in this way was the great world historical appearance, for which it was always valid. The mysteries 'taught the history of God. There are Expressions in Plato that are the intimations (*Ahndungen*) of Christianity.'[88]

In his audacious move from myth to history, Schelling's theogony was, in part, an attempt to improve on Creuzer. The theogonic protocol meant that he could dispense with Creuzer's theory of mediating, wandering priests transmitting myths from one domain to another.[89] Creuzer was significant because of his emphasis upon the symbol. He was able to shift this idea that was so important for German aesthetics in the eighteenth century into a theory of religion.[90] In his *Idee und Probe alter Symbolik* (Idea and Sample of Ancient Symbolism, 1806) Creuzer refers explicitly to Plotinus's claim that the hieroglyphic symbol-language of the Egyptians is to be considered the most felicitous expression of all philosophy. He directly quotes Plotinus's seminal treatise on the beauty of the divine intellect (Ennead V8[31].5-6).[91]

In Chapter Three of *Symbolik und Mythologie: Ideen zu einer Physik des Symbols und des Mythus*, Creuzer writes: 'In the symbol our soul is seized and the necessity of nature rules over us.'[92] And he thinks that these symbols were conveyed by priests 'From India, through Persia and Palestine, through Asia Minor to Greece and Italy and beyond.'[93] Of the symbol, he writes:

Gottes wurde, wodurch, anstatt zur Fabel oder als Fabel erklart zu warden, die Göttergeschichte vielmehr zur Wahrheit wurde. Offenbarung I 503.

[88] Schelling, *Werke* 2.1.460-61.
[89] George Williamson, *The Longing for Myth in Germany: Religion and Aesthetic Culture from Romanticism to Nietzsche* (Chicago, IL: University of Chicago Press, 2004), p. 172.
[90] Leslie Willson, *A Mythical Image*, (Durham, NC: Duke, 1964), pp. 106-8; Williamson, *The Longing for Myth in Germany*, pp. 78-81.
[91] Benedetto Bravo, 'F. Creuzer et F. G. Welcker' in *L'impensable polytheisme: Études d'historiographie religieuse*, Paris 1988, Schelling, Friedrich Wilhelm Joseph, *Philosophie der Offenbarung, Ausgewälte Werke*, vol XIII & XIV (Darmstadt: Wissenschaftliche Gesellschaft, 1974).
[92] *In Symbol fulhlt sich unsere Seele ergriffen, und die Notwendigkeit der Natur waltet uber uns.*
[93] F. Creuzer, *Symbolik und Mythologie der alten Völker* (Leipzig and Darmstadt: 1843) vol. IV, p. 5478. *Von Indien her, uber Persien und Palestina, durch Kleinasien hin, bis nach Griechenland und Italien hinuber*, p. 548.

> In the symbol a general concept assumes an earthly garment and presents itself as a meaningful image to our spirit. In myth the brimming soul expresses its intuition or knowledge in a living word. It is also an image, although one that goes in another direction, through the ear, to reach the interior meaning.[94]

Schelling employs Creuzer's syncretism and theory of the symbol and places it within a speculative process, whereby 'The Pheonician Melkart, Egyptian Osiris, Indian Shiva, Greek Dionysus are representations of Christ.' Mythological religion, and the Revealed religion of the Jews and the Incarnation are all parts of a process of theogony. Schelling interpreted the Mysteries, in close proximity to Creuzer, as the Greek religion of mankind. The Greek Mysteries shape the philosophy of Plato and they find their fulfilment and historical realization in Christianity.[95] The gods are ultimately the expression of a monotheistic order.

Schelling is adamant that the meaning of Christianity is to be found with the process of world religions and history. And his perspective is that of a metaphysician:

> The content of all true religion is eternal, i.e. does not preclude any period absolutely. A religion which is not from the world and through all times, cannot be the true religion. Christianity had to be in heathendom, which had the same substantial content. It would be impossible for human nature to live for thousands of years on the basis of pure error. A human consciousness full of vain nonsense could not endure. It is unthinkable that humanity could go through centuries without a relation to that principle in which salvation alone can be found. Whosoever considers the condescension of the Divine in the Old Testament and the divine appearances for more than pure fables, will not deny the truth of heathen theophanies.[96]

---

[94] F. Creuzer, *Symbolik und Mythologie der alten Völker* (Leipzig and Darmstadt: 1843) vol. IV, p. 559. *Im Symbol nimmt ein allgemeiner Begriff das Irdische und tritt als Bild bedeutsam vor das Auge unseres Geistes. Im Mythus äussert die erfüllte Seele ihr Ahnen oder Wissen in einem lebendigen Worte. Es ist auch ein Bild, aber ein solches, das auf einem andern Wege, durch das Ohr, zum inneren Sinne gelangt.*

[95] George Williamson, *The Longing for Myth in Germany* (Chicago: Chicago University Press, 2004), p. 172f.

[96] *Schellings Werke*, XIV, 77f. *Der Inhalt aller wahren Religion ist ein ewiger, also von keiner Zeit absolute auszuschliießender Inhalt. Eine Religion, die nicht von der Welt her, die nicht durch alle Zeiten ist, kann nicht die wahre seyn. Das Christenthum muß also auch im Heidenthum gewesen seyn, dieses hatte denselben substantiellen Inhalt ... Es wäre der menschlichen Natur unmöglich gewesen, Jahrtausende lang bloß vom Irrtum zu Lebe: ein mit Nichtigkeiten erfülltes menschliches Bewußtseyn konnte nicht dauern. Es ist undenkbar, daß die Menschheit Jahrtausende hindurch ohne allen Bezug*

If Schelling's theogonic protocol of myth and revelation appears arcane and preposterous, one might note a successor in the thought of a subsequent Munich philosopher, Erich Voegelin, especially his philosophy of history.[97] For Voegelin, history is not 'mere unfolding of events ... but the pattern of the meaning of human existence'.[98] As for Schelling, history for Voegelin has a powerfully and ineluctably theological dimension. Voegelin's opening lines of his *Order and History* read: 'God and man, world and society form a primordial community of being.' The starting point of human experience is not the deracinated epistemic encounter of the subject with an array of objects real and possible but dwelling in society and the natural world and the confrontation with and participation in the sacred that both involve.[99] It has been claimed that Voegelin attempts to rework Schelling's historiography.[100] In Voegelin's own theory of history, there are 'Spiritual outbursts' or leaps of Being in the history of Israel or Greece.[101] The prologue of the Johannine Gospel is a decisive historical document for Voegelin, with its identification with the Divine presence in Jesus.[102] History, for Voegelin, is ineluctably linked to a seeking for meaning and the longing for the transcendent principle that forms the world and furnishes ultimate meaning. Human beings are historical and social beings. There are different levels of 'attunement of man with the order of being': the paradigms of Moses leading the Israelites from bondage, the Platonic eros and contemplation of the Good, or the Christian celebration of the new life of the Spirit, all constitute instances of encounters with the

---

zu demjenigen Princip gestanden hätte, in dem allein das Heil ist ... Wer die Herablassung Gottes im Alten Testament bedenkt und die göttliche Erscheinungen in demselben nicht auch für bloße Fabel halt, wird auch den Theophanien des Heidenthums nicht alle Realität abspreche. Die Heiden waren vom Angesicht des Vaters gleichsam verwiesen, aber eben ihnen gab er Christhum zum Herrn, wenn dieser gleich unter ihnen nur als naturliche Potenz wirkte. Das Heidenthum- eben darum weil das Christenthum nicht seine absolute Negation sondern seine Wahrheit ist – hat auch in sich selbe relative Wahrheit ... Das Christenthum ist nicht einseitig aus dem Judenthum hervorgegangen, es hat ebensowohl als dieses das Heidenthum zu seiner Voraussetzung: nur dadurch ist sein Enstehung die große weltgeschichtliche Erscheinung, wofür sie von jeher gegolten.

[97] For a very helpful account of Voegelin's relationship to Schelling, see Jerry Day, *Voegelin, Schelling and the Philosophy of Historical Existence* (Columbia: University of Missouri, 2003).
[98] Glenn Hughes, *Mystery and Myth in the Philosophy of Eric Voegelin* (Columbia: University of Missouri Press, 1993), p. 69.
[99] Voegelin, *Order and History, Israel and Revelation* (Baton Rouge: Louisiana State University Press, 1974), p. 1.
[100] Day, *Voegelin, Schelling and the Philosophy of Historical Existence*, p. 183.
[101] Hughes, *Mystery and Myth in the Philosophy of Eric Voegelin*, p. 72.
[102] Voegelin, *Order and History, IV, The Eucumenic Age* (Baton Rouge: Louisiana State, 1974), pp. 11ff.

transforming Divine presence that have decisively shaped human history. On this view, history is an 'ongoing drama of theophany'.[103] History is a 'process of transfiguration, whether in the Tao sages, the Upanishads, or the life of the Buddha, a series of momentous responses to transcendence'.[104] All of the great visionary outbursts in human history are fired by a sense of participation or 'metaxy' in a greater or sacred dimension and a subsequent transformation on the basis of this encounter.

Two key notions are that of attunement and the ancient image of the stage. Human life can be more or less 'attuned' to the transcendent. Such 'attunement to being' is more than adaptation to environment and contingency but participation in reality through recognition and response to theophany.[105] There is also, however, a requirement for human agents down to participate actively in their roles.[106]

There are obvious parallels here between the historical and the mythic in Schelling's model development of human consciousness and Voegelin's.[107] Voegelin sees Plato in relation to Christianity on the model of the Church Fathers. It is a model of philosophy culminating in Christ. Paul's 'pneumatic' experience, or vision, of the risen Christ is viewed as the culmination of a process from Deutero-Isaiah, Daniel, Plato and Aristotle and a pivotal moment in his idea of historical metaxy.[108] The noetic revelations of the Greeks are correlated with the pneumatic experience of St Paul.[109]

---

[103] Voegelin, op. cit. p. 226.
[104] Voegelin, *The Ecumenic Age*, p. 285, Glenn Hughes, *Mystery and Myth in the Philosophy of Eric Voegelin*, (University of Missouri Press, Columbia, Missouri, 1993), p. 78f
[105] See *Living Forms of the Imagination*, p. 112ff.
[106] Glenn Hughes, *Mystery and Myth in the Philosophy of Eric Voegelin*, p. 55ff.
[107] Ernst Benz, 'Theogonie und Wandlung des Menschen bei Friedrich Wilhelm Joseph Schelling', in *Urbild und Abbild: Der Mensch und die mythische Welt*. (Gesmmelte Eranos-Beiträge), (Leiden: Brill, 1974), pp. 69–130 English translation: 'Theogony and Transformation in Friedrich Wilhelm Schelling, in *Man and Transformation: Papers from the Eranos Yearbooks*, ed. Joseph Campbell (1964), pp. 203–49.
[108] Day, *Voegelin, Schelling and the Philosophy of Historical Existence*, p. 252.
[109] Schelling, Derselbe Gott, der in unerschütterlicher Selbstgleichheit die Einheit erhielt, mußte, sich selbst ungleich und wandelbar geworden, nun ebenso selbst das Menschengeschlecht zerstreuen, wie er es woher zusammenhielt, und wie er in seiner Identität die Ursache seiner Einheit war, so in seiner Vielfältigkeit die Ursache der Zertrennung werden. Schelling, *Werke*, XI, 105.

Chariot

> If the spectator could enter into these Images in his Imagination approaching them on the fiery chariot of his Contemplative Thought ... then would he arise from his Grave then would he meet the Lord in Air & and then he would be happy.[110]

There is a recurring image of the soul's *ascent* to the Divine or the *Descent* or revelation of the Divine which crosses various cultures: the chariot. Constructed by King Narasimhadeva I in the thirteenth century AD, the ruined and sublime Konarak Great Temple dedicated to the sun-god Surya at Orissa is shaped like a huge and magnificently embellished chariot on twenty-four intricately carved stone wheels each of which is about ten feet in diameter, and drawn by seven horses, walls and pillars. Rabindranath Tagore said of this temple, 'here the language of stone surpasses the language of man'.[111] It is a work created to inspire awe. There is a written tradition: in *Rig Veda* X.135 in the *Mahaitereya Upanishad*, the *Chagaleya Upanishad*, *Katha Upanishad*, and the *Miatrayani Upanishad* we find the use of this central image. The general image is that of the human mind as like a charioteer following a path of knowledge. The horses represent unruly desires and energy in need of harnessing in order to attain the goal of knowledge: true being. In Parmenides, Plato and the *Katha Upanishad* the intellect or (*Buddhi*) is the charioteer. In the *Maitareya Upanishad*, it is the mind (*manas*). In the *Katha Upanishad* the goal is Vishnu's highest place or footprint-step (*parama pada*). In Parmenides it is the abode of the Goddess; in Plato the realm above heaven or the 'plain of truth'.

In the *Proem* of Parmenides one finds an *anabasis* or 'apocalyptic' ascent of the mind to Being which is also a revelation.[112] The Parmenidean charioteer is accompanied by sun maidens. On the journey they come to the threshold of the gates of day and night. The maidens persuade *Dike* or Justice to release the bolts of the gates and the chariot can pass through to the realm of day.

---

[110] Blake, *A Vision of the Last Judgement* (Garden City: Anchor Books, 1982), p. 550.
[111] Manish Telikicherla Chary, *India: Nation on the Move: An Overview of India's People, Culture, History, Economy, IT and more* (Bloomington: Indiana, 2009), p. 389.
[112] 'Apocalyptic' here in the sense of Orphic accounts of the afterlife.

The charioteer is greeted by the Goddess, who explains the radical distinction between Divine truth and human opinion. In Parmenides it is a journey to the Goddess and strongly conveys the role of inspiration and conversion. Through the encounter with the Goddess the charioteer encounters truth. In Plato's use of the same image, the soul-charioteer ascends to the *hyperouranian* domain and sees what truly 'is' (*Phaedrus* 249c).[113]

Coomaraswamy writes of the Indian symbol of the chariot:

> The horses are the sensitive powers of the soul. The body of the chariot our bodily vehicle, the rider the spirit. The symbol can therefore be regarded from two points of view; if the untamed horses are allowed to go where they will, no one can say where this will be; but if they are curbed by the driver, his intended destination will be reached. Thus, just as there are two 'minds', divine and human, so there is a fiery chariot of the gods and a human vehicle, one bound for heaven, the other for the attainment of human ends, 'whatever these may be' (TS v.4.10.1). In other words, from one point of view, embodiment is a humiliation, and from another a royal procession.[114]

One might note that even in the Indian tradition that the chariot, just like the vision of Ezekiel 1, can represent both an ascent to the Divine and the Divine descending in revelation. In one of the classic scriptural moments of revelation in the Indian tradition, the classic tale of Arjuna and Krishna in the Kurukshetra War depicted in the *Bhagavad Gita*, it is in the chariot, and as the charioteer that Krishna reminds Arjuna of his eternal vocation.[115] The chariot comes to symbolize the journey of detachment, contending with suffering and loss, while maintaining the goal of ultimate encounter with the Divine.

The image of the chariot conflicts with any strict monism, i.e. a philosophy which upholds the re-absorption of the self into ultimate Unity. The image of the chariot tends to emphasize the dynamic activity of the self qua self as the soul comes to encounter ultimate transcendent reality. Just as in Plotinus – the spiritual self approaches this 'other' through 'sight' or 'touch'.[116] The mystery

---

[113] There is an ancient debate about the meaning and legacy of Parmenides. See J. Palmer, *Plato's Reception of Parmenides* (Oxford: Oxford University Press, 1999), pp. 18ff.

[114] Coomaraswamy, *Door in the Sky* (Princeton, NJ: Princeton University Press, 1998), p. 187.

[115] Indian chariots were built for a charioteer and warrior. Krishna, paradoxically, has the humbler role of the charioteer.

[116] E.g. Plotinus θιγεῖν, VI.9[9].4, 27 or θέαν VI.9.4.13.

of the soul's individuation is preserved by the chariot paradigm in a manner akin to the 'dualistic' imagery of sight or touch. The image of the chariot poses the problem of a characteristic and distinctive identity of the self in relation to, but not dissolved into, a higher unity. This may explain why philosophers in the Buddhist tradition employed the image of the chariot to dismantle or subvert the idea of the self. Such an argument, however, was probably playing upon the familiar associations of the chariot as the paradigmatic image of the vehicle of selfhood.

In the Old Testament we have various encounters with the Divine – theophanies. The Psalms speak of the Darkness of God (e.g. Psalm 18.11). But we also have visions like those of Ezekiel. Henry More sees Pythagoras as a pupil of Ezekiel: 'That Pythagoras was acquainted with the Mosaical or Jewish Philosophy, there is ample testimony of it in writers; ... Clemens calls him the Hebrew Philosopher ... Clemens again, who writes that it was a common fame that Pythagoras was a disciple of the Prophet Ezekiel.'[117]

The author of the book of Revelation seems to be (like the author of John's Gospel) Jewish and possibly of priestly stock. The book of Revelation is a vision of the heavenly liturgy and worship around the Divine throne, and one which is very close to Ezekiel's fiery chariot vision 700 years earlier. The Throne of God is clearly linked to the Ezekiel Theophany or the strand of the Divine throne speculation that is to be found in the book of Enoch. As in Enoch, John of Patmos is taken into the heavens, where he sees a throne.[118] In Revelation 4 we read that 'on each side of the throne are four living creatures; full of eyes in front and behind; the first living creature like a lion, the second living creature like an ox, the third living creature, the face of a man, and the fourth living creature like a flying eagle'.

Farrer notes the clear link between the Ezekiel vision and the Revelation transformation of that vision, from the riders in the Chariot of Jewish mysticism and that strand of theophany that is known as Merkava.[119] Farrer writes: 'Those who explore the Jewish mystical tradition which lies behind

---

[117] Henry More, *Conjectura Cabbalistica* iii §3, p. 100.
[118] Christopher Rowland, *The Open Heaven* (New York: Crossroad, 1982), p. 222.
[119] See Guy G. Stroumsa, 'On the Early History of the *Visio Beatifica*', in *Mystical Approaches to God*, ed. P. Schäfer (Munich: Oldenbourg, 2006), pp. 67–80.

the ultimate emergence of the Cabbala, find a special place to be occupied in it by the Tetragrammaton, the first words of Genesis and the Chariot-vision of Ezekiel. The first words of Genesis are a staple of St Paul's more gnostical flights; Colossians 1.12-20 contains a multiple exposition of them. The Johannine Gospel springs out of the same text, as out of a well. We know that the Chariot vision of Ezekiel was mediated by Jews who wished to "ascend into heaven" by the Spirit: it was a technique of ecstasy. St John makes the meditation in Apocalypse 4, and into heaven he ascends. St Paul had ascended there before him, whether in Ezekiel's chariot or no, we cannot tell, for he refuses to write his vision.'[120]

The Tetragrammaton is the Divine name which is linked to Exodus 3.14 ('I am that I am'). Farrer understands this text in Johannine terms as also referring to the eternal Logos, to him who is the 'image of the invisible God, the firstborn of every creature', who is the creative plenitude of the Divine. Farrer argues that the Alpha and Omega claims refer back to Exodus 3.14 and it is significant that six 'I am' utterances in Revelation insist upon Christ's eternal being:

> Rev. 1.8: 'I am Alpha and Omega, the beginning and the ending.'
> Rev. 1.11: 'I am Alpha and Omega, the first and the last.'
> Rev. 1.17: 'Fear not; I am the first and the last.'
> Rev. 21.6: 'I am Alpha and Omega, the beginning and the end.'
> 'I am Alpha and Omega, the beginning and the end, the first and the last.'
> 22.16: 'I am the root and the offspring of David, and the bright and morning star.'

The book of Revelation brings the mythopoetic imaginative energy of Old Testament theophanies together with the monotheistic claim of Exodus 3.14. Farrer writes of the rebirth of images through the centrality of the sacrificial lamb: 'When St John's spirit flies up through the door of heaven, he sees a Lamb, standing as slaughtered: a symbol as pregnant for the new faith as that which Moses saw in the old, the flame of a bush, burning unconsumed.'[121] The sublime sense of transcendence in the image of the burning bush is deepened by the icon of the lamb triumphant.

---

[120] Austin Farrer, *The Rebirth of Images* (Westminster: Dacre, 1949), p. 262.
[121] Farrer, *The Rebirth of Images*, pp. 17–18.

Myth, Image and Recapitulation in Revelation

> Surely some revelation is at hand;
> Surely the Second Coming is at hand.
> The Second Coming! Hardly are those words out
> When a vast image out of *Spiritus Mundi*
> Troubles my sight: somewhere in sands of the desert
> A shape with lion body and the head of a man,
> A gaze blank and pitiless as the sun,
> Is moving its slow thighs, while all about it
> Reel shadows of the indignant desert birds.
> The darkness drops again; but now I know
> That twenty centuries of stony sleep
> Were vexed to nightmare by a rocking cradle,
> And what rough beast, its hour come round at last,
> Slouches towards Bethlehem to be born?

W. B. Yeats's oracular and yet trenchant lines from 'The Second Coming', written after the cataclysm of the First World War, are an apocalyptic vision of a perverted 'world soul', *anima mundi* or *spiritus mundi*, as a force of 'mere anarchy'. In Canto 33 of Dante's *Paradiso* God is the infinite sphere whose centre is everywhere and circumference is nowhere.[122] While the God of Western tradition is the principle of order and harmony, the surrogate Divine of Yeats's apocalyptic vision is not a principle of unity but disintegration, not of peace but violence. The beast's hour has 'come round at last', when it 'slouches towards Bethlehem'. This world soul is not the animating life force, a mediating aspect of the divine wisdom and creative power, but as the reference to Revelation 13 suggests, destruction and terror: the 'ceremony of innocence', the achievement of civilization so eloquently extolled by Burke, is drowned by bloody waters – the 'blood-dimmed tide' of cruel chaos.

The eschatological dimension of the book of Revelation is notorious for having enthralled and roused the Western Imagination with images of conflict and violence. The book of Revelation has a potent poetic dimension and unsurprisingly there is a strong literary dimension to our theme. The

---

[122] Second 'chapter' of the *Liber XXIV philosophorum*.

Apocalypse of John is full of vividly recognizable images: the Alpha and the Omega; Babylon, the great mother of harlots; the mark of the beast; the four horsemen; the seven seals; the blood of the Lamb; a new heaven and a new earth. John of Patmos also represents the model of a poet. The persecution, judgement and triumph of the Lamb employs the imagery of holy war but does it incite violence or does it refer to spiritual conflict and combat?

I wish to turn to Austin Farrer's construal of the book as a poetic-contemplative work of great beauty and power. Farrer writes of the book of Revelation: 'It is the one great poem which the first Christian age produced, it is a single and living unity from end to end, and it contains a whole world of spiritual imagery to be entered into and possessed.'[123] Rather than the *disjecta membra* of source criticism, a bit of apocalyptic here and touch of the prophets there, Farrer wishes to explore the poetic imagination of St John within the intelligible continuity of the text, as an integral part of the rebirth of images drawn from the Hebrew Scriptures.

'What sort of task was St John undertaking?'[124] These are visions. Not a product of 'simple lyrical inspiration' like Shelley on the skylark. The visions are 'seen with the mind' but constrained by the images of the tradition he has inherited. The 'final object' of his vision is the Kingdom of Heaven.[125] This inspired poetics rebirth of images is a Christocentric vision of 'the lamb slain from the foundation of the world'. It is the culminating point of a series of visions of Christ from his presentation in the Temple, his baptism, where the heavens open or his transfiguration.

> And there was war in heaven: Michael and his angels fought against the dragon; and the dragon fought and his angels,
> And prevailed not; neither was their place found any more in heaven.
> And the great dragon was cast out, that old serpent, called the Devil, and Satan, which deceiveth the whole world: he was cast out into the earth, and his angels were cast out with him.

Yet there are mythopoetic parallels with the Eastern Mediterranean–Middle Eastern world: the struggles between Marduk and Tiamat in Babylon, Horus

---

[123] Austin Farrer, *Rebirth of Images*, p. 306.
[124] Farrer, *Rebirth of Images*, p. 304..
[125] Farrer, *Rebirth of Images*, p. 307.

and Seth in Egypt, Apollo and Python, or Zeus and the Titans.[126] It is a theogonic drama in which Michael fights with the other angels against the host of Satan. This battle occurs between two visions: the seer is transported to the worship before the conflict and after the conclusion of the struggle there is a final liturgy of the new Jerusalem, as the meeting point of heaven and earth. A later Christian Neoplatonist could happily fuse the angels, powers and dominions of Christianity with pagan spirits:

> During Thy Ascension, Lord
> Th'aerial daemons trembled;
> The choir of deathless stars
> Was struck dumb with amaze.
> The laughing Aether, wise
> Engenderer of harmony,
> Struck its seven stringed lyre
> And played a tune of triumph.
> Lucifer, a day's herald
> Smiled at golden Hesperus,
> Evenstar of Venus.
> Her crescent filled with fire,
> There went ahead the Moon,
> The pasture of nocturnal gods.
> The Sun spread out his hair
> Flaming beneath thy feet.
> He knew the Son of God,
> The all-creating Spirit,
> His fire's archetype.[127]

It is not necessarily an either/or. As an educated Jew in the Graeco-Roman world, it is likely that John of Patmos should draw on themes and ideas that resonated throughout the civilized world, just as later Christians could depict the Madonna as Venus or David as a Greek God (cf. Michaelangelo's David in Florence). Bulgakov stresses the role of angels in the vision of Ezekiel: 'The image of sitting on cherubim (proper also to Ezekiel's vision of the chariot)

---

[126] Adela Yarbo Collins, *The Combat Myth in the Book of Revelation* (Missoula: Scholov's Press, 1976).
[127] Synesius, Quoted from Joscelyn Godwin, *Music, Mysticism and Magic: A Sourcebook* (London: Routledge & Kegan Paul, 1986), pp. 32–3.

contains the idea that God draws near to creation, is correlated with it through angels.[128] The angels would resonate with the polytheistic cults of the ancient Hellenistic world, a world in which intermediate powers were often combined in cults with a unique supreme principle.

Austin Farrer provides a particularly lucid and fertile account of the reworking of the stuff of ancient Hebraic materials into the contemplative imagination of the supersensible realm:

> The rebirth of images can be studied everywhere in the New Testament, but nowhere can we get so deep into the heart of the process as we can in St John's Apocalypse. For nowhere else have we a writing which is so simply devoted to the liberation of the image as this. The Evangelists clothe their history with the images, but they are restricted by the historical actuality upon which they fit them. The Epistles find their inspiration in the images, but they express them only in so far as serves the purpose of instruction or exhortation. But the Apocalypse writes of heaven and things to come, that is, of a realm which has no shape at all but that which the images give it. In this room, the image may grow to the fullness of its inborn nature, like a tree in a wide meadow.[129]

The poet-seer imagines through the 'flux of the senses' the 'permanent and self-circulating energies of the reason'. When speaking of the 'living educts of the Imagination' the mediating power that incorporates the ideas of reason into the images of sense, i.e. symbols, Coleridge speaks of these symbols as the 'Wheels which Ezekiel beheld … the truths and symbols that represent them move in conjunction and form the living chariot that bears up (for *us*) the throne of the Divine Humanity.'[130]

Farrer's mystical interpretation of the book of Revelation is very much in this Coleridgean mode. Farrer stresses the continuity between Ezekiel and John of Patmos: 'The image of the door has already appeared and re-appeared in the end of the Messages, a portent of what is to come. Inevitably St John falls into meditation of Ezekiel's Chariot vision, the traditional instrument of ecstasy, and passes through the heavenly door. The Chariot vision belongs to

---

[128] Bulgakov, *Jacob's Ladder*, p. 26.
[129] Farrer, *The Rebirth of Images*, p. 17. See also: 'To ask whether St John saw his visions by means of a mystical diagram or through the Holy Ghost, is like asking whether the flight of an eagle is sustained by his wings or on the airs', p. 304.
[130] Coleridge, *Lay Sermons*, p. 29.

Pentecost, not Passover, and so St John finds himself seeing the Passover-to-Pentecost period as one process, in which Pentecostal revelation is gradually made full by the breaking of the seals of the Book.'[131]

In the *Explanation of the Grand Mystery of Godliness* More claims that the writings of John of Patmos are 'nearest the Notions of the antient *Cabbala* of the *Jews*'.[132] One of the primary sources of the Cabbala is the throne vision of Ezekiel. The prophet Ezekiel is in every chapter of the book of Revelation. In Ezekiel we have his vision of the Divine throne on four wheels and four creatures. Art historians refer to this as the tetramorph, and it came into Christian iconography as the man, the lion, the ox and the eagle of the evangelists. In the Jewish tradition vision is the basis of the merkabah chariot.[133] Unlike Isaiah, Ezekiel is not quoted in the New Testament but his presence is ubiquitous (the good shepherd or Paul on the presence of God (Ezek. 37.27: 2 Cor. 6.16) the spirit of God softening stony hearts (Ezek. 36.26 and 2 Cor. 3.3)). This is especially true of the book of Revelation. In the cathedral of Chartres, in the celebrated rose window, St Mark is carried by Daniel and St John is carried by Ezekiel. Ezekiel's imagery is present in almost every chapter of the book of Revelation.[134]

Gregory saw the four wheels and the four elements of the Bible: Law, Prophets, Gospels and the Apostles. The wheels within the wheels for Gregory refers to the hidden New Testament meaning of passages in the Old Testament.[135] The other significant passage was 2.8–3.3 about the scroll that Ezekiel ate and which tasted sweet. Jerome viewed this as a passage about the scroll as a hermeneutical principle. The writing on the front and back of the surprisingly saccharine scroll became '*intus*' and '*foris*' of the literal and the spiritual reading.

The spiritual dimension of the text should not be forgotten when Dante, in the culmination of the pilgrim's ascent in the ineffable vision of *Paradiso*, describes the moment when his 'lofty fantasy' or imagination fails, and uses

---

[131] Coleridge, *Lay Sermons*, p. 312.
[132] Henry More, *Theological Works*, pp. 139–40
[133] G. Scholem, *Major Trends in Jewish Mysticism* (New York: Schocken, 1954), pp. 40–79.
[134] John Sawyer, 'Ezekiel in the History of Christianity', in *After Ezekiel*, ed. Andrew Mein and Paul M. Joyce (New York: T&T Clark, 2001), pp. 1–9, p. 2.
[135] Sawyer, p. 2.

the image of a wheel spinning in perfect motion: a power received from the Divine and returning to its transcendent source. Here at the extreme limit of his poetic powers, Dante uses the imagery of Ezekiel: the wheel of ascent to the throne of God.[136]

---

[136] John Frecero, 'The Final Image: Paradiso XXXIII, 144' in his collection of essays, *Dante, The Poetics of Conversion* (Cambridge: Mass.: Harvard University Press, 1986), pp. 245–57.

8

Imagination and Revelation

The religious imagination is possible without revelation but revelation is impossible without the religious imagination.[1]

And I saw a new heaven and a new earth: for the first heaven and the first earth were passed away; and there was no more sea.

And I John saw the holy city, new Jerusalem, coming down from God out of heaven, prepared as a bride adorned for her husband.

And I heard a great voice out of heaven saying, Behold, the tabernacle of God is with men, and he will dwell with them, and they shall be his people, and God himself shall be with them, and be their God. (*Revelation* 21.1)

This momentous passage in Revelation is used at Christian funerals as words of consolation to the bereaved. Does it, one may ask, exemplify wishful thinking? How can such an *imaginaire* stand up to the challenge of Feuerbach and Marx or Nietzsche's complaint that such a God is the enemy of life? Is it not obvious that belief in God and communion with the supreme Being is the projection of infantile needs for consolation, or worse as self-serving delusion and failure to recognize the suffering of the poor? Is it any more than a bizarre phantasy at best, and a dangerous psychosis at worst?[2] The book of Revelation constitutes for many cultured despisers of theology the embodiment of the worst of religion. It is, such critics aver, the obscure delirium of a fractious and twisted mind. Whitehead criticizes the violent God both of the Old and New Testaments and proposes the substitution of John's Apocalypse with Pericles' Funeral Oration.[3] Henry More in the preface to his *An Explanation of the*

---

[1] Richard Kroner, *The Religious Function of Imagination* (London: Oxford University Press, 1941), p. 47.
[2] John Gray, *Black Mass: Apocalyptic Religion and the Death of Utopia* (London: Allen Lane, 2007).
[3] Lucien Price, *Dialogues of A. N. Whitehead* (Boston: Atlantic-Little, Brown and Company, 1954), pp. 172f., 355f.

Grand Mystery of Godliness notes that it is a book that has been the cause of much strife: 'which Fanatick Hot-spurres so much abuse to the disturbance of the Church'.[4] No wonder, one might say, that precisely this text has been used to such effect, to incite violence and cruelty: 'violence can save the world'.[5] In this chapter I wish to present the book of Revelation as constituting a paradigmatic contemplative vision of the world transformed through the light of the supreme Being: the vision of creation restored through Christ. I shall follow the lead of Austin Farrer in accentuating the *poetic* or *imaginative* dimension of the work and its *metaphysical* implications. This is in no way to repudiate the importance of biblical scholarship proper. Indeed, I hope that the following chapter has profited from such scholarship.[6] Farrer remarks with his habitual felicity of expression: 'When St John's spirit flies up through the door of heaven, he sees a Lamb, standing slaughtered: a symbol as pregnant for the new faith as that which Moses saw in the old, the flame of the bush, burning unconsumed.'[7] It is a vision of the supreme Being centred upon the lamb sacrificed.[8] The absolute source of all being is identified with an image of tenderness, vulnerability and innocence.

St John of Patmos describes being shown a door to heaven and there encountering the intoxicating beauty and terrifying grandeur of the Divine throne and God himself, surrounded by a host of angels. The beauty experienced is that of precious stones and metals: jasper, gold and pearls, diamond and ruby. The throne is like an emerald rainbow and has four beings with six wings, many-eyed and with animal visages. We have the famous images of seven lamps, a glass sea and the great angel-messenger. God is still in his majesty while surrounded by a vibrant throng of angels and elders. Christ emerges as the sacrificed lamb. The liturgy of one of the readings, praise and song and the worship is described in terms of the harps, palm leaves, singing and incense upon the heavenly altar. The elements of the vision are derived from the Old Testament prophets. Yet the whole conveys the effect

---

[4] More, *An Explanation of the Grand Mystery of Godliness*, XIX.
[5] John Gray, *Black Mass*, p. 72.
[6] I will not, for example, speculate upon questions like authorship; even though I am inclined to follow my guides Farrer and Barker and accept the identity of the evangelist and John of Patmos.
[7] Austin Farrer, *The Rebirth of Images* (Westminster: Dacre, 1949), p. 17.
[8] See *Sacrifice Imagined: Violence, Atonement and the Sacred* (New York: Continuum, 2011).

of the paradoxical unity of intense life and stillness. The great Platonizing mystics of the West such as John Scot Eriugena or Nicholas of Cusa speak of this paradoxical coincidence of motion and rest as the *motus stabilis* or *status mobilis*.⁹ Cusa ingeniously uses the image of the spinning top, which seems *still* precisely when it is turning at its fastest.¹⁰ God in eternal motion is rest. Cusa is clear that these are images (with a preference for geometrical images) of the ineffable, or in his terminology 'conjectures'. The burning bush of Exodus 3.1-22 might constitute a biblical image of this paradoxical unity of stillness and life or power. The bush burns but is not exhausted or expended by the process of burning.

Ronald Hepburn notes that 'the aesthetic experience may keep alive some view of the world that the concepts of systematic metaphysical thought cannot precisely articulate, nor its arguments support'.¹¹ Sometimes, indeed, the aesthetic experience may precede a more explicit articulation. Coleridge's *Kubla Khan* is a good example of this. The poet has a vision of an oriental paradise, where opposites meet.¹² The poetry seems to have emerged out of the combined effect of Samuel Purchas and laudanum. Samuel Purchas (c. 1577–1626) in 1613 published *Purchas His Pilgrimage: or Relations of the World and the Religions observed in all Ages and Places discovered, from the Creation unto this Present*. The poem seems have been influenced by the effect of the luxuriant beauty of Culbone on the Somerset/Devon border upon the genius of the young poet. Holmes observes that the precise landscape of the poem can be detected in the poetic reverie.¹³ He writes:

> Any footwalker can still discover the most striking topographical 'source' for themselves: it lies in what might be called the erotic, magical geography of Culbone Combe seen from Ash Farm. Between the smooth curved flanks of the coastal hills, a thickly wooded gulley runs down to the sea (the 'romantic

---

⁹ Werner Beierwaltes, *Procliana, Spätantikes Denken und seine Spuren* (Frankfurt: Klostermann, 2007), p. 125; Eriugena, p. 89. See Kurt Flasch, *Die Metaphysik des Einen bei Nikolaus von Kues: Problemgeschichtliche Stellung und systematische Bedeutung* (Leiden: Brill, 1973), p. 10.

¹⁰ Nicholas of Cusa, *De possest*, §23-24, trs. Jasper Hopkins (Minneapolis: Arthur Banning Press, 1986), p. 923ff.

¹¹ R. W. Hepburn, 'Landscape and the Metaphysical Imagination', *Environmental Values* 5 (1996) 3: 191-204.

¹² See my article, 'Coleridge's Intellectual Intuition, the Vision of God, and the Walled Garden of "Kubla Khan"', *Journal of the History of Ideas*, vol. 59, no. 1, (January 1998): 115-34.

¹³ Margaret Barker suggested this to me in Borrowash many years ago.

chasm'), enclosing a hidden stream which gushes beneath the tiny medieval chapel of Culbone, a plague-Church and 'sacred site' since Anglo-Saxon and possibly pre-Christian times.[14]

In this chapter we shall explore the images of paradise, feast, contemplation and song. It is not immediately clear why these themes should be linked but in Christian culture, at least, they are fused in the idea of the heavenly city. Christian hymns will laud

> Jerusalem the golden,
> With milk and honey blest,
> Beneath they contemplation
> Sink heart and voice oppressed.

Within the 'halls of Sion, Conjubilant with song',

> There is the throne of David
> And there from care released,
> The song of them that triumph
> The shout of them that feast.[15]

Why should the communal meal, the vision of God and music be linked in this manner? What links feasting, music and the contemplation of the Divine in the occidental imaginary? The banquet might be an image of the fleeting pleasures and contingency of human life, as it is in the sparrow flying through the mead-hall on a winter night recounted by Bede in his description of the vision of the pagan English prior to their conversion: a view of life as a journey from darkness through the light of the hall and back into the bleak dark.[16] It need not necessarily be associated with any intellectual pleasures – a sort of don's delight or a celestial high table! Nor does the idea of the intellectual vision necessarily imply a community of viewers. It could be a highly individualistic salvation. Music fits with communal feasting, but its link with the vision Divine seems rather tenuous.

---

[14] Richard Holmes, *Coleridge, Early Vision*, p. 164.
[15] Bernard of Cluny, from *Hymns Ancient and Modern*, 1861, translated by John Mason Neale.
[16] Bede, *Ecclesiastical History* xiii.

Walking, Pilgrimage and Ecology

'I can only meditate when I am walking'
(Rousseau, *Confessions*)[17]

It seem'd like Omnipresence! God, methought
Had built him there a Temple: the whole World
Seem'd in its vast circumference
No profan'd my overwhelmed heart
Blest hour! It was a luxury, – to be!
(Coleridge, 'Reflections of Having Left a Place of Retirement')

Coleridge's great poem *Kubla Khan* was composed during a walking expedition in Somerset and he exemplifies an age of great enthusiasm for walking. He and Wordsworth covered vast swathes of the Quantocks and the Lakelands in their contemplation of the natural landscape and their iconic celebration of it. Obligate bipedalism, as has often been noted, is a distinctively human trait, and as we noted in Chapter Two, this facilitates a distinctively human experience of the world, enabling both a capacity for scrutiny and manipulation of the immediate environment denied to other intelligent primates. The Romantics popularized walking as a means of experiencing sublimity.[18] In a sense, they were drawing upon a more ancient tradition of pilgrimage.[19] Ronald Hepburn in his paper 'Contemporary Aesthetics and the Neglect of Natural Beauty' (1966) claimed that significant differences between the aesthetic grasp of nature and art should not generate a neglect of the former.[20] But Hepburn noted how our experiences of nature might be distinguished from our experiences of art. Awareness of the natural world is closer to immersion, the viewer is a part of what is being experienced. Secondly there are no obvious limits, like a frame or edges of an artistic object. Thus any aesthetic quality in the realm of nature 'is always provisional, correctable by reference to a different, perhaps wider context, or to a narrower

---

[17] Rousseau, *Confessions*, trans. J. Cohen (Harmondsworth: Penguin, 1973), p. 382.
[18] Robin Jarvis, *Romantic Writing and Pedestrian Travel* (London: Macmillan, 1997).
[19] Rebecca Solnit, *Wanderlust: A History of Walking* (London: Granta, 2014).
[20] R. Hepburn, 'Contemporary Aesthetics and the Neglect of Natural Beauty', in *British Analytic Philosophy*, eds B. Williams, and A. Montefiore (London: Routledge & Kegan Paul, 1966), pp. 206–309. Here quoted from *The Aesthetics of Natural Environments*, Allen Carlson and Arnold Berleant (Toronto: Broadview, 2004), pp. 43–62.

one realized in greater detail'.[21] Yet Hepburn was concerned to provide a realist or cognitivist dimension to the metaphysical imagination.

This set the course for the burgeoning of environmental aesthetics. Landscape has often been a source of contemplative awe. At the heart of Hepburn's work on environmental aesthetics was the Romantic speculative and metaphysical dimension of aesthetic experience. Hepburn believed that the metaphysical imagination has been undervalued – an imaginative grasp of reality *per se*, especially in those 'spots of time', experiences of 'sublimity' or 'joy', the aesthetic contemplation of nature which serves to renew inwardly our being and fosters a due respect and awe for the natural world.[22] Hepburn was worried that the fear of metaphysical dogmatism or the association of such elevated states with theism, not least the 'ineffable vision seen in ecstasy' of St Augustine[23] or *maraviglia, stupor* and *ammiratione* of Dante, might taint this tradition of metaphysical imagination for many contemporaries.[24]

Hepburn feared, furthermore, that resistance to this Neoplatonic-theistic strand might generate the opposing position – that of trivializing the aesthetics of nature.[25] The Romantics legitimately wanted to 'remove the film of familiarity'[26]: an instance of the more universal capacity of the human mind to heighten its awareness of its environment, to break out of an indolence induced and reinforced by habit or custom. Only then can one perceive the truth that 'Everything that lives is holy' (Blake).

Hepburn's re-introduction of the question of natural beauty into contemporary aesthetics is an example of a Romantic influence upon ecology. For the ancient Greeks, landscape was associated with the wild and threatening savagery outside the polis. When Petrarch climbed Mont Ventoux and took out his copy of St Augustine's *Confessions*, he started to reflect upon Augustinian mountains of the mind. For much of the early modern period, mountains were seen as great

---

[21] Hepburn, in *The Aesthetics of Natural Environments*, p. 47.
[22] Wordsworth, *Prelude* XI, 257–9.
[23] Augustine, *Ennarationes in Psalmos*, 37§12.
[24] Patrick Boyde, *Dante Philomythes and Philosopher: Man in the Cosmos* (Cambridge: Cambridge University Press, 1981), p. 50.
[25] See R. Hepburn, 'Trivial and Serious in the Aesthetic Appreciation of Nature', in *The Reach of the Aesthetic: Collected Essays on Art and Nature* (Aldershot: Ashgate, 2001), pp. 1–15.
[26] Coleridge, *Biographia Literaria* II, ed. W. Jackson Bate and James Engell (Princeton, NJ: Princeton University Press, 1985), p. 7.

landscape carbuncles, even evidence of the cosmic Fall.[27] John Muir (1838–1914), the great Scots-American environmentalist exemplifies the specifically Romantic estimation of the 'glory' of the natural world, especially the sublime, to elevate and renew the soul.[28] Muir's conservationism and activism, including the success in founding national parks like the Yosemite and the Sequoia in the USA was inspired by the Romantic vision of nature as an image of the Divine.[29]

The question of landscape is inextricably intertwined with the activity of imagination. As Simon Schama in his monumental *Landscape and Memory* notes, 'For although we are accustomed to separate nature and human perception into two realms, they are, in fact, indivisible. Before it can be a repose for the senses, landscape is the work of the mind. Its scenery is built up as much from strata of memory as from layers of rock.'[30] Schama stresses the importance of myths for the appreciation of landscape and in his book he explores the archetypal images of the sea, the mountain and the forest in the European imagination. Deep within the core of the Western psyche lies an archaic memory of the woodland as at once mysterious place and refuge, a terrifying challenging environment, a space of transformation and resource. He also explores the long history of human engagement with water. The need to control it as an essential prerequisite for life, to regulate its vagaries of supply and destructive forces, and to use it as a medium of movement have all resulted in a rich 'grammar of hydro-mythology'.[31]

Schama argues eloquently that it is human imagination that turns nature into landscape, and once this imagined nature becomes an inherited memory in the form of an idea, a belief, or a myth becomes attached to nature in the creation of a landscape. Schama considers wood, water, or rock, the three broad categories through which beliefs or myths in turn affect the interpretations and memories of later generations.

---

[27] Marjorie Hope Nicholson, *Mountain Gloom, Mountain Glory* (Ithaca: Cornell University Press, 1959).
[28] R. Dorman, *A Word for Nature* (Chapel Hill and London: University of North Carolina Press, 1998), pp. 105–71.
[29] R. Scruton, *Green Philosophy: How to Think Seriously about the Planet* (London: Atlantic, 2014), p. 277 – refers to figures like Wordsworth or Muir, 'all of whom urgently wished to convey their sense of being blessed by the land and by its spirit of renewal'.
[30] S. Schama, *Landscape and Memory* (New York: Alfred A. Knopf, 1995), pp. 6–7.
[31] Schama, *Landscape and Memory*, p. 277.

The following passage from Coleridge serves to illustrate Schama's point:

> That this is deep in our Nature, I felt when I was on Sca' fell –. I involuntarily poured forth a Hymn in the manner of the *Psalms*, tho' afterwards I thought the Ideas &c disproportionate to our humble mountains – & accidentally lighting on a short Note in some swiss Poems, concerning the Vale of Chamouny, & it's Mountain, I transferred myself thither, in the Spirit, & adapted my former feelings to these grander external objects ... It has struck [me] with great force lately, that the Psalms afford a most compleat answer to those, who state the Jehovah of the Jews, as a personal & national God – & the Jews, as differing from the Greeks, only in calling the minor Gods Cherubim & Seraphim – & confining the word God to their Jupiter.[32]

The deity that Coleridge has encountered in the Psalms is a cosmic presence. The God addressed in the Psalms is the same God that he encounters in his walks in the Lakelands, even if he recounts that the poem is to be set in the Alps. It is often assumed that this is pantheism. This, it seems, confuses a sense of the immanent presence of God in the cosmos, the theophanic dimension, with the identification of God as a purely immanent principle of the universe. It might be noted that many people who have no institutional religion and attend no formal worship still find a sense of the sacred in landscapes of great beauty and sublimity. It would be wrong to think that the scriptural inheritance has no resources for contemplating the natural realm as another book, and the great paeans to the creator in the Psalms are an important resource. In last three books of the *Confessions*, Augustine dwells on the Psalms in order to praise the glory of the Divine creation.[33] Referring to Psalm 104 in *Confessions* XI and XII, he writes:

> It is true that, Lord, that you made heaven and earth. It is true that the 'beginning' means your wisdom, in which you have made things.[34]

The image of the city is also an image of a garden.[35] In Revelation 22 there are features of the paradise garden with the river and the tree of life:

---

[32] S. T. Coleridge to William Sotheby, Friday 10 September, 1802.
[33] Augustine, Confessions XI, 9m 11. See also C. S. Lewis, *Reflections on the Psalms* (Orlando: Harcourt, 1986), pp. 76–89.
[34] On Augustine's extended and rich use of the Psalms, see Michael Fiedrowicz, *Psalmus Vox Totius Christi: Studien zu Augustins "Ennarationes in Psalmos"* (Freiburg Im Breisgau: Herder, 1997).
[35] The civic nature of Jerusalem is combined with the paradise imagery: i.e. it is not a pastoral arcadia.

> And he shewed me a pure river of water of life, clear as crystal, proceeding out of the throne of God and of the Lamb.
>
> In the midst of the street of it, and on either side of the river, *was there* the tree of life, which bare twelve *manner of* fruits, *and* yielded her fruit every month: and the leaves of the tree *were* for the healing of the nations. (Revelation 22.2)[36]

It is also viewed by the visionary John from a 'great high mountain' like his great predecessor Ezekiel, who was raised to a mountaintop and to whom was shown the Jerusalem Temple. Thus the image of the Temple contains within itself Schama's rock, tree and water motifs: Mount Zion contains a river and a tree!

There is an ecological dimension to the vision of the created order as a *image* of its source. Cudworth claims that 'The whole world is well called here the temple of God'.[37] Coleridge took this theme of nature as a Temple into the Romantic era in his *Reflections on Having Left a Place of Retirement* employs the Cudworthian language of the 'whole world' as a temple.

> it seem'd like Omnipresence! God, methought,
> Had built him there a temple: the whole World
> Seem'd imaged in its vast circumference:
> No wish profaned my overwhelmed heart
> Blest hour! It was a luxury, – to be (l. 27-31)

This is precisely not pantheism because the world is not identical with but the image of the omnipresence but transcendent God. The proper relationship is that of image to archetype. Nature is not itself divine but an *icon* of divinity. The spiritual world mirrored in nature is not a counterpart alien world, but rather, as the ground and archetype of the phenomenal world, it is *this* world in its most eminent form. The world as Temple provides access to its source. A non detached enjoyment and relish of the world and a deep gratitude for its existence and beauty is utterly opposed to the manipulation, plunder or economic desecration of the natural world. It is hardly surprising that environmentalists like Muir or more recent philosophers like Hepburn could draw upon this Platonic/Romantic tradition of nature as the Temple, a source of sacred value, and apply it to projects of revisioning and protecting the environment.

---

[36] See Margaret Barker, *The Revelation of Jesus Christ Which God Gave to Him to Show to His Servants What Must Soon Take Place* (Revelation 1.1) (London: T& T Clark, 2000), p. 279ff.

[37] Cudowrth, *The True Intellectual System of the Universe* (London: Royston, 1688), p. 538.

Pilgrimage and The Temple Image

The idea of the pilgrimage seems to have very ancient roots. Gobekli Tepe is located in south-eastern Turkey within the northern part of the Fertile Crescent, the very centre of the Neolithic or agricultural revolution. Hunter-gatherers would have been drawn to the mild climate and fertile terrain of the Persian Gulf to what is today Lebanon, Israel, Jordan and Egypt. The archeologist who discovered the site, Klaus Schmidt, could not find traces of human habitation and considers the hilltop 'Cathedral' as the first great site of Man's worship. Hunter-gatherers seem to have been on a pilgrimage to the site and human settlement only developed there much later.

The findings have deep implications for our view of culture and civilization. Whereas it was conventionally believed that agriculture generated religion and culture since religion could bind the larger communities facilitated by the emergence of agriculture, Gobekli Tepe suggests the opposite. The huge Temple constructed by hunter-gatherers on a hill overlooking the surrounding area suggests that the sense of the sacred and the drive to worship preceded the emergence of agriculture. Feasts were presumably a significant part of the holy Temple: stone basins have been adduced as evidence of such feasts and perhaps the creation of domestic cereals developed out of the rites and ceremonies held at the Temple site. One of the earliest instances of agriculture is to be found in walking distance of the site.[38]

Scholars have long believed that only after people learned to farm and live in settled communities did they have the time, organization and resources to construct temples and support complicated social structures. Schmidt, however, argues it was the other way around: the extensive, coordinated effort to build the monoliths literally laid the groundwork for the development of complex societies. One can imagine hunter-gatherers driven by a primordial sense of the sacred, the *mysterium tremendum et fascinans*, and thus seeking and constructing a place of worship. Six millennia older than Stonehenge, Gobekli Tepe is an imposing construction with theriomorphic designs carved into the monumental pillars.

---

[38] Charles C. Mann, 'The Birth of Religion', *National Geographic*, (June 2011), pp. 39–59.

If the construction of a Temple seems to be a primordial sacred occurrence in human experience and history, it remains immensely significant after the change from a hunter-gatherer to a pastoral life and the emergence of cities. Roger Scruton claims that the Temple provides a blueprint for much secular building. He notes that Moses obtains not merely the Ten Commandments from Mount Sinai but also the instructions for the building of a temple.[39] Scruton has developed a rich phenomenology of architecture based upon the relation between art, the sacred and the 'Lebenswelt'. The repeated use of the Temple motif in secular Western architecture is a hint of the presence of the sacred. Through architecture the indwelling of the Divine idea in human life is bodied forth through stones in the form of the Temple – the classical order is an exploration of the sacred, the intersection of the temporal with the timeless. Yet, for Scruton, it is the image of transcendence and not the representation of some sterile idealization. The trace of the Temple makes a building habitable: he insists, indeed, that the classical templates 'affirm what is sempiternal in the midst of change, and tell us that we *belong* where we are, and belong as a community'.[40]

John of Patmos describes his Revelation vision in terms of a temple. The problem is how to interpret this imagery of the 'temple'. In some respect the building seems more like a great gathering place, such as an imperial basilica.[41] The Temple was central for the religious life of the ancient Hebrews. Jerusalem was the place to worship God and its loss was a cataclysm that was marked by the Romans with the Arch of Titus and the construction of the Coliseum. Jan Assmann notes:

> It is one of the most remarkable coincidences in history that the Jewish temple was destroyed at precisely the moment when the inner development of the Jewish religion had rendered it superfluous. Scripture had already been installed in its place, and the meaning of the rites hollowed out from within, when Titus laid waste to the Temple in the year 70 CE. The Jesus movement was only one of many Jewish (and also Greek) movements that sought to abolish the basic idea of cult religion – namely blood sacrifice or ritual slaughter – through

---

[39] R. Scruton, *The Aesthetics of Architecture* (Princeton. NJ: Princeton University Press, 2013), p. x.
[40] Ibid., p. xi.
[41] McDannell and Lang, *Heaven: A History* (New Haven, CT: Yale Note Bene, 2001), p. 41.

sublimation, ethicization, and interiorization. Had Titus spared the Temple, it would have had to be shut down – either that, or Judaism, and thus Christianity and Islam as well, would never have arisen.[42]

The spiritualization noted by Assmann coincides with the power of the imagination in Jews, Christians and Muslims. The Temple of Jerusalem is still important throughout the centuries after its destruction, and yet is the Temple imagined. Long after the physical destruction, whether by the Babylonians or the Romans, the Temple continued to remain a presence.

The Sacred Feast

For human eating is more than consuming food. Indeed Claude Lévi-Strauss saw cooking at the basis of humanity's cultural development. The eminent Cambridge archaeologist of food Martin Jones shows how mankind treats food very differently from other animals. We share our food and we make eye contact with strangers, whereas for other animals eye contact is dangerous and threatening. Humans have a hearth or cooking fire; we have preferences and employ them to demonstrate rank and group. He explores these features of human ingestion through the image of the feast. Jones's book is composed of a series of vignettes based on particular archaeological sites, including remote ancestors and relatives of *homo sapiens* like Heidelberg man and Neanderthals. *Homo sapiens*, well adjusted to African savannah, moved into the more forbidding climes of Europe and Asia. But 400,000 to 300,000 years ago saw an increase in the brain size, smaller teeth and jaws as hominims developed into *homo sapiens*. Fire was a crucial prerequisite. We cannot consume wheat, potatoes and rice without cooking. Cooking also has the advantage of destroying parasites. *Homo erectus* was able to develop a small gut and a larger brain (both are the most significant drain on energy resources). Cooking also lessens the time required for the process of eating: chimps, for example, spend five hours each day feeding. Around 70,000 to 60,000 BC there seems to have been a cognitive revolution, one which saw the

---

[42] Assmann, *The Price of Monotheism* (Stanford, CA: Stanford University Press, 2010), p. 108.

development of the arts and religion but also of needles and boats seems to occur in this period.

The intense development of agriculture and the cultivation of livestock radically affected the consumption of food in different periods of human history. One might think, for example of the sourcing of exotic fish and fowl from various continents as part of a global food web. Whether looking at the trading links of the Roman Empire or the link between Benedict and white bread, Jones reflects upon the manifold ramifications of feasting for human culture. Though rarely a place of feasting, the European coffee house is an intriguing example of the meeting place of ideas, especially political change and revolution in Enlightenment Paris.

Randal Collins in his *Sociology of the Philosophies: A Global Theory of Intellectual Change* argues that, notwithstanding the invention of the printing press, face-to-face encounter is an essential aspect of the great periods of intellectual innovation. He repeatedly demonstrates that small platoons are the primary source of creativity. There may be a guru or sage figure at the core but one should not forget the importance of the group: 'The history of philosophy is to a considerable extent the history of groups'.[43] One might consider the image of philosophical dialogue or conversation and debate *as* the banquet or symposium.

Feast and Festival

Farrer considers the 'poem' of Revelation in terms of its festal patterns. The first is from the weekdays. The paradigm is the periodization of creation in Genesis: the repetition of various sevens being the pattern of the re-creation in Christ through the Holy Spirit. Alongside this structure, one finds a fourfold pattern of the yearly Hebrew feasts: and Farrer lays great stress on the 'liturgies of jubilant worship in heaven'. In Apocalypse 19 we are presented with the 'messianic supper and the heavenly singing'.[44] John of Patmos

---

[43] Randall Collins, *Sociology of the Philosophies: A Global Theory of Intellectual Change* (Belknap: Harvard University Press, 1998), p. 3.
[44] Farrer, *The Rebirth of Images*, p. 282.

beholds a heavenly feast. Whence this image of the celestial feast? We might begin by reflecting upon its earthly counterpart, the festival. In his slender but rich work on the topic, Josef Pieper notes that the feast is not just the antonym of work, nor is it play. Pieper is critical of Huizinga's suggestion that play is the key to the festival, perhaps somewhat unfairly. The role of imagination as invention and its kinship to playing games is an important aspect of imaginative activity. The feeling of delight associated with imaginary activity is clearly also an important part of human festivals, as Pieper himself stresses.

Art has its origins in the rituals and festivals of ancient culture, even if this fact has been obscured by the marginalization of the 'artistic' in contemporary utilitarian and commercially driven societies.[45] The festival is a celebration of existence. Pieper's *In Tune with the World* is well translated. The title, however, as *Zustimmung zur Welt* can be misleading. The English translation *In Tune with the World* only conveys one aspect of the title: the musical. In German to say '*Ich stimme zu*' denotes affirmation or avowal: 'I agree', or 'I can vote for that'. The festival, on Pieper's account rests upon the recognition and affirmation of the goodness of existence. For Pieper, such an affirmation of the world can only be compelling on the basis of theism. The capacity for joy invoked by the festival is incompatible with a belief in the radical contingency or meaninglessness of the cosmos. The origin of the festival is affirmation and praise in worship. When Romeo says of Juliet in the tomb 'her beauty makes / This vault a feasting presence full of light' (Act 5, Scene 3), we sense the dreadful irony that the tomb is transformed into a place of the feast! In Dante's *Commedia* the recurrent smile of Beatrice is an image of the goodness of the created order!

Festivity is linked, furthermore, to contemplation, by which Pieper means the loosing of the attention of the mind from proximate or utilitarian goals and the conscious awareness of the 'illimitable horizon of reality as a whole'.[46] It is also linked, he notes, to sacrifice. The lavish expenditure of the festival is a renouncing of utility and calculation. Pieper notes that antiquity from Plato to Augustine identified festivals with sacrifices: indeed Augustine sees

---

[45] Ellen Dissanayake, *Homo Aestheticus* (Seattle: Washington University Press, 1992).
[46] Josef Pieper, *In Tune with the World: A Theory of Festivity* (South Bend, IN: St. Augustine's Press, 1999), p. 17.

feriae as derived from *a feriendis victimis*.⁴⁷ Pieper quotes the great Oratorian Thomassin: 'The sacrifice is the soul of festivals.'⁴⁸

There is a striking parallel with Cudworth's 1642 *A Discourse Concerning the True Nature of the Lord's Supper*.⁴⁹ Here he explores what is right and wrong with the idea of the Christian views of sacrifice. According to Cudworth, the Eucharist is a 'federal rite' between God and his people, a meal, but it is also a symbolic continuation of Christ's sacrifice:

> The right notion of that Christian feast called the Lord's Supper, in which we eat and drink the body and blood of Christ that was once offered up to God for us, is to be derived, if I mistake not, from analogy to that ancient rite among the Jews of feasting upon things sacrificed and eating of those things which they had offered up to God.

Cudworth claims:

> Having thus shown that both amongst the Jews under the law, and the Gentiles in their pagan worship (for paganism is nothing but Judaism degenerate) it was ever a solemn rite to join feasting with sacrifice, and to eat of those things which had been offered up, the very concinnity and harmony of the thing itself leads me to conceive that that Christian feast under the Gospel called THE LORD'S SUPPER is the very same thing, and bears the same notion, in respect of the true Christian sacrifice of Christ upon the cross, that those did to the Jewish and heathenish sacrifices; and so is *EPULUM SACRIFICIALE*, a sacrificial feast, I mean, a feast upon sacrifice, or *EPULUM EX OBLATIS*, a feast upon things offered up to God. Only this difference arising in the parallel, that because those legal sacrifices were but types and shadows of the true Christian sacrifice, they were often repeated and renewed, as well as the feasts which were made upon them; but now, the true Christian sacrifice being come and offered up once for all, never to be repeated, we have therefore no more typical sacrifices left amongst us, but only the feasts upon the one true sacrifice still symbolically continued and often repeated in reference to that ONE GREAT SACRIFICE, which is always as present in God's sight and efficacious, as if it were but now offered up for us.⁵⁰

The Eucharist is the *feast* upon the body and blood of Christ! Because the Lord's Supper is a feast upon the sacrifice, it cannot be said to be a new

---

⁴⁷ Pieper, *In Tune with the World*, p. 36.
⁴⁸ Pieper, *In Tune with the World*, p. 37.
⁴⁹ Cf. *Sacrifice Imagined: Violence, Atonement and the Sacred* (New York: Continuum, 2011), pp. 203ff.
⁵⁰ Ralph Cudworth: *The Works Containing The True Intellectual System of the Universe*, Sermons by Ralph Cudworth, ed. Thomas Birch (Oxford: Talboys, 1829), IV, p. 231.

sacrifice. Yet note the emphasis upon the language of the image. Precursors of the Christian Eucharist are 'types and shadows' of 'the true Christian sacrifice'. Thus the feast is the symbolic continuation of the one great sacrifice on the cross. Catholics are thus right to insist upon the sacrificial nature of the Eucharist but the 'grand error of the papists concerning the Lord's Supper' is that they are wrong to see the mass as a repetition of the sacrifice of the cross. The Eucharist is an image of the celestial feast.[51]

The theme of the feast is important for Coleridge. The passage from Purchas's *The Pilgrimage* (1614), upon which Coleridge based his visionary poem *Kubla Khan*, recounts an opulent 'sacrificial drama':

> In *Xanada* did *Cublai Can* build a stately Pallace, encompassing sixteen miles of plaine ground with a wall, wherein are fertile Meddows, pleasant Springs, delightful Streames, and all sorts of beasts of chase and game, and in the midst thereof a sumptuous house of pleasure, which may be removed from place to place. Here he doth abide in the months of June, July and August, on the eighth and twentieth day thereof, he departeth thence to another place to do sacrifice in this manner: He hath a Herd or Drove of Horses and Mares, about ten thousand, as white as snow; of the milke whereof none may taste, except he be of the blood of Cingis Can. Yes, the Tartars do these beasts great reverence, nor dare any cross their way, or go before them. According to the directions of his Astrologers or Magicians, he on the eighth and twentieth day of the August aforesaid, spendeth and poureth forth with his owne hands the milke of these Mares in the aire, and on the earth, to give drink to the spirits and Idols which they worship, that they may preserve the men, women, beasts, birds, corne, and other things growing on the earth.[52]

Richard Holmes observes that this seems to refer to a 'fertility sacrifice'. The mythic dimension of the poem has long been noted, but the sacrificial dimension – the feast – has often been overlooked. This connection between the feast and the sacrifice has been a constant part of Christian iconography. One might reflect upon Van Eyck's monumental Ghent Altarpiece Lamb of God for the depiction of the Revelation vision of Eden and the New Jerusalem combined with the sacrificial lamb at its very centre.[53]

Nor does Kubla Khan alone have strong associations with the idea of the feast. The poem *The Rime of the Ancient Mariner* begins and ends with the

---

[51] *Sacrifice Imagined*, pp. 207ff.
[52] Quoted in Richard Holmes, *Coleridge, Early Visions*, p. 163.
[53] A. and N. O'Hear, *Picturing the Apocalypse*, pp. 59, 64.

theme of a Wedding Feast and the image of the 'kirk'. However dark and troubling the narrative of poem may seem, it unified by a feast that acknowledges and praises the goodness of Being. The seafarer shoots the albatross and suffers horrors but he is released from these torments after blessing the sea snakes. The redemptive aspect of the poem is symbolized through the feast. The Mariner descends, like Aeneas to the Underworld, into a domain of guilt and purgation, and returns 'a sadder and a wiser man' but recognizing the goodness of the created order.

> Farewell, farewell! but this I tell
> To thee, thou Wedding-Guest!
> He prayeth well, who loveth well
> Both man and bird and beast.
>
> He prayeth best, who loveth best
> All things both great and small;
> For the dear God who loveth us
> He made and loveth all.

The link between the heavenly city and the feast goes back to a passage in Exodus about Moses and the elders of Israel seeing God and feasting.

> [10] And they saw the God of Israel: and *there was* under his feet as it were a paved work of a sapphire stone, and as it were the body of heaven in *his* clearness.
> [11] And upon the nobles of the children of Israel he laid not his hand: also they saw God, and did eat and drink.
> And Melchizedek king of Salem brought forth bread and wine: and he *was* the priest of the most high God. (Gen. 14.18)

> Christ 'was designated by God to be high priest in the order of Melchizedek'. (Heb. 5.10)

Philo argues in the *Legum Allegoriarum* 3.79-82 that Melchizedek as high priest is the representation of reason and peace as opposed to tyranny and self indulgence. 'But Melchizedek shall bring forward wine instead of water, and shall give your souls to drink, and shall cheer them with unmixed wine, in order that they may be wholly occupied with a divine intoxication, more sober than sobriety itself.' Melchizedek is important for the lineage of Christ.[54]

---

[54] C. S. Lewis, *Reflections on the Psalms*, p. 122.

Ecology

There is also an *ecological* dimension to the feast. The meal is a sign of harmony. It is also an image of harmony with the created order. The prophets are eloquent in their critique of the great princes who abused their wisdom for the sake of profit and trade. Pieper notes that the muses accompany festivals and Plato designated them as 'festival companions'.[55] They enhance the festival but do not represent its essence. The substance of the festival lies in worship rather than art. This leads Pieper to another consideration: the bogus festivals that are evident in the modern world, from harmless commercialized trifles like Mother's Day to the sinister pseudo-sacred festivals of nihilistic and cynical totalitarian regimes. As De Maistre poured scorn on the absurdities of the French Revolution, so too Pieper derides the mock sacrality of the Bolshevik or National-Socialist festival, born not out of gratitude for the gift of creation but a cynical control, intimidation and subordination of the population to the state. Not the Goodness of Reality but a sham appeal to the will or weal of the people constitutes the purpose of these modern perversions of the festival from the ephemeral inventions of the French Revolution to the Nazi May Day festivities in the *Tempelhof* in Berlin.

Music and Contemplation

Jerusalem is a place of song, of praise. And David, of course, was a musician! Joseph de Maistre once wrote '*La raison ne peut que parler. C'est l'amour qui chante.*' Coleridge speaks of 'this strong music in the soul' in his *Dejection, An Ode*:

> O Thou pure of heart Thou need'st not ask of me
> What this strong music in the soul may be!
> What, and wherein it doth exist,
> This light, this glory, this fair luminous mist,
> This beautiful and beauty making power.

---

[55] Pieper, *In Tune with the World*, p. 52.

> Joy, virtuous Lady! Joy that ne'er was given,
> Save to the pure and in their purest hour,
> Life and life's effluence, cloud at once and shower,
> Joy, Lady! Is the spirit and power,
> Which, wedding Nature to us, gives in dower
> A new Earth and new Heaven,
> Undreamt of by the sensual and the proud:
> Joy is the sweet voice, Joy the luminous cloud.

Raphael's *The Ecstasy of St Cecilia* (1515) can be seen in the Pinacoteca Nazionale in Bologna, where it has been since 1815.[56] Cecilia is depicted with St Paul, John the Evangelist, St Augustine and Mary Magdalene. St John, with his eagle peering out of his robes, is probably standing upon the book of Revelation. The picture is an image of conversion from sorrow to joy. The image is also an interesting demonstration of the wider connotations of music within Renaissance Platonism, especially the influence of Marsilio Ficino. A key biblical text is *Wisdom X, 21* 'Thou hast ordered all things in measure, and number, and weight' was interpreted in a deeply philosophical mode. *Omnia in mensura, et numero et pondere disposuisti.* God is the creative and determining measure or *mensura* of all things. He is also *numerus* as the mathematic harmony of the cosmos. Finally, He is also the source of the teleological 'gravity' of the universe, as its highest good.[57] The vision of God is at the same time the contemplation of the *summum bonum*.[58] Vasari describes the painting in detail.[59] In it, he says, 'a St Cecilia who stands enraptured by a choir of angels on high and listens to their singing, is wholly absorbed by the music'. The great Romantic poet Shelley noted:

> The central figure, St. Cecilia, seems rapt in such inspiration as produced her image in the painter's mind; her deep, dark, eloquent eyes lifted up; her chestnut hair flung back from her forehead – she holds an organ in her hands – her countenance, as it were, calmed by the depth of its passion and rapture, and penetrated throughout with the warm and radiant light of life. She is listening

---

[56] I am very grateful to Hans Jakob Meier for his suggestion that I visit Bologna to see the painting.
[57] Beierwaltes, 'Augustins Interpretation von Sapientia' 11, 21, *Revue d'études augustiniennes et patristiques*15 (1969), pp. 51–61.
[58] S. Mossakowski, 'S'Raphael's "St Cecilia": An Iconographical Study', *Zeitschrift fuer Kunstgeschichte* 31 (1968): 1–26.
[59] Vasari, *Lives of the Artists* (Harmondsworth: Penguin, 1979), p. 304.

to the music of heaven, and, as I imagine, has just ceased to sing, for the four figures that surround her evidently point, by their attitudes, towards her; particularly St. John, who, with a tender yet impassioned gesture, bends his countenance towards her, languid with the depth of emotion. At her feet lie various instruments of music, broken and unstrung.[60]

As Shelley notes, the Platonic-Pythagorean dimension of the painting is striking.[61] Cecilia is looking up to the heavens, while the broken instruments are at her feet. Paul and John, the latter with the book of Revelation under his feet, are the visionaries of the NT. Augustine was associated in the Middle Ages with the possibility of the vision divine.[62] There is also the intriguing figure of Mary Magdalene who gazes at the viewer with such candour. Mossakowski notes that Mary represents the shift from profane to sacred love, while inviting the spectator to engage in the *amor divino* depicted in the painting. Hence she has a mediating position in the painting.

The Romantics loved this picture.[63] Raphael represented for Romantics like Wackenroder the ideal fusion of personal creativity and pious reception of Divine inspiration. In Wackenroder's *Herzergiessungen eines kunstliebenden Klosterbruders* (1796–7) (*Cordial effusions of an art loving Monk*), the fictional monk declares that '*sein Inneres war durchbohrt*' ('his soul was thoroughly penetrated') by the painting.[64] And Raphael is depicted as the great patron saint of music Cecilia. Music is the most immaterial and spiritual of the arts.

Wackenroder's work is a panegyric to the spiritual supremacy of music among the arts: 'I consider music to be the most marvellous of these inventions (sc. the fine arts), because it portrays human feelings in a superhuman way, because it shows us all the emotions of our soul above our heads in incorporeal form, clothed in golden clouds of airy harmonies ... the language

---

[60] Esther Singleton, *Great Pictures as Seen and Described by Famous Writers* (New York, Dodd, Mead and Company, 1899), p. 288.
[61] Joscelin Godwin, *Harmonies of Heaven and Earth, Mysticism in Music from Antiquity to the Avant-garde* (London: Thames and Hudson, 1987).
[62] Cf. Olivier Boulnois, *Au-delà de L'image: Une archéologie du visuel au moyen âge, ve-XVIe siècle* (Paris: Seuil, 2008), pp. 133ff.
[63] Brad Prager, *Aesthetic Vision and German Romanticism* (Rochester, NY: Camden House, 2007), pp. 44ff.
[64] The translation is mine. Mary Hurst Schubert translates it as 'His soul was pierced through'. Wilhelm Heinrich Wackenroder, *Confessions and Fantasies*, translated and annotated by Mary Hurst Schubert (University Park: Penn State, 1971), p. 89.

of angels.'⁶⁵ 'Let all the world in every corner sing/ My God and King'; so begins the much-loved George Herbert hymn. The connection between music and celebration is too obvious to dwell upon. David is a musician and the author of the Psalms for the early Church – for Augustine the psalms are at the centre of Christian worship (*Confessions*, xix, 28). 'Let my song give joy to God who is a joy to me' (Ps. 104.34).⁶⁶ The link between spiritual healing and music is, perhaps, less apparent. Plato thought music has an effect upon the soul, whether good or bad.⁶⁷ Music clearly has an impact upon our emotions, but it is less obvious that the whole organism can be helped by music.⁶⁸ Mothers sing to their babies throughout the world and serious medical research shows that music can reduce stress and blood pressure, even stabilize the heart rate. For the adult music gives expression to deep and powerful emotions.⁶⁹ As Wackenroder lyrically observed: 'The human heart becomes acquainted with itself in the mirror of musical sounds; it is they through which we learn to feel emotion; to many spirits, dreaming in hidden crannies of the mind, they give living consciousness, and they enrich our souls with entirely new, bewitching essences of feeling.'⁷⁰ Roger Scruton's view that music is a 'repository for emotional knowledge' (it teaches us how to feel and act) is related to the familiar distinction between 'emotions felt' and 'emotions perceived'.⁷¹ This is a distinction between emotion expressed in music and that which is actually felt by a listener, internal and external locus of emotion. Recent psychological research supports Scruton's position. It reveals a strong relation between listening to sorrowful or joyful music and the heightened capacity to recognize the mood of facial expressions in photographs. Music enhances

---

[65] Wilhelm Heinrich Wackenroder, p. 180.
[66] For use of the Psalms within the Church of England, see Nicholas Temperley, *The Music of the English Parish Church*, vol. 1 (Cambridge: Cambridge University Press, 1979).
[67] *The Republic*, Book IV, *The Laws*, II, 655a-b.
[68] Joscelin Godwin, *Harmonies of Heaven and Earth*, pp. 11–44, esp. 36–9.
[69] Godwin, *Harmonies of Heaven and Earth*.
[70] Wackenroder, *Confessions and Fantasies*, p. 191. 'What other power doth solder and glue that spirituall strength, which is indued with an intellect to a mortall and earthly frame, than that Musicke which every man that descends into himselfe finds in himselfe? Hence it is, that we loath and abhorre discords, and are delighted when we hear harmonicall concords, because we know there is in our selves the like concord.' John Dowland, translating Ornithoparcus, in Micrologus (1609), p. 1, quoted in Christopher R. Wilson, *Shakespeare's Musical Imagery* (London: Bloomsbury, 2011), p. 20.
[71] Roger Scruton, *Understanding Music, Philosophy and Interpretation* (Continuum, 2009).

the ability to recognize emotions in others, and this deepening understanding and sympathy with the emotions furnished by music would seem to support Wynn's claims about salience and the issues of value. Nor is this an exclusively 'Western' phenomenon. Ramanuja refers to the company of the blessed, where souls commune to sing the praises of the Lord.[72]

Thus music can be associated with knowledge of objective features of the world, the music of the spheres, but also with the knowledge of the more obscure dimensions of the self. Indeed, Shakespeare is eloquent on the healing dimension of music: 'The man that hath no music in himself, Nor is not moved with concord of sweet sounds, Is fit for treasons, stratagems, and spoils; The motions of his spirit are dull as night, And his affections dark as Erebus. Let no such man be trusted. Mark the music' (*Merchant of Venice*, V act 1).[73]

In Shakespeare's late romances the healing power of music is a central theme. In *Pericles*, upon the resuscitation of Thaisa through the medic Cerimon Pericles says:

'The music of the spheres! List, my Marina … Rarest sounds! Do ye not hear?
… I hear/Most heavenly music!' (5.1. 229–233)

In *The Winter's Tale*, while reconciling Hermione to her husband Leontes, Paulina calls upon the help of music:

Music! awake her! strike!
'Tis time; descend; be stone no more; approach;
Strike all that look upon with marvel. Come …
Bequeath to death your numbness; for from him
Dear life redeems you. You perceive she stirs (5.3. 98–103)

Ironically referring to the sense of magical healing power of music Leontes exclaims: 'O, she's warm!/If this be magic, let it be an art/Lawful as eating' (5.3 11.111).

In *The Tempest*, Prospero employs celestial music to control the raging Storm and to console Ferdinand for the apparent loss of his father. Ariel's songs, especially 'Full fathom five thy father lies' affect Ferdinand's distraught

---

[72] Lipner, *The Face of Truth: A Study of Meaning and Metaphysics in the Vedantic Theology of Ramanuja* (Albany, NY: State University of New York, 1976), p. 118.
[73] I am grateful to Anthony Esolen for pointing out the importance of music for Shakespeare.

emotions, 'Allaying both their fury and my passion/With its sweet air' (*The Tempest*, Act 1, Scene 2). Prospero invokes music when he confronts the shipwrecked lords, the ship's crew and their followers with their guilt and forgives them. The link between healing, forgiveness and reconciliation and the power of music is very evident in the romance plays.

Coleridge was developing the same idea in the *Rime of the Ancient Mariner*:

And now 'twas like all instruments,
Now like a lonely flute;
And now it is an angel's song
That makes the heavens be mute. (*Rime of the Ancient Mariner*, Part 5)

By way of contrast, in Thomas Mann's great novel, *Doctor Faustus*, the protagonist, who is the musician Adrian Leverkühn, modelled in part on the figure of Friedrich Nietzsche, is a modern Faust figure re-imagined in the era from Imperial Germany to the Nazi regime.[74] This life is recounted by the classicist, schoolteacher and resolute anti-Nazi, Serenus Zeitblom. He notes the affinity of Leverkühn's oratorio *Apocalypsis cum Figuris* to the Kridwiss circle of fascist thinkers in Munich. The figure of Serenus Zeitblom, observing and narrating the descent into madness of his brilliant musician friend, is an image of the collapse of the German mind into a cruel irrationalism in the twentieth century. The atonal and dissonant music of Leverkühn is meant to be a disturbing 'score'. Schoenberg was incensed by being portrayed as syphilitic and in league with the devil. His response may have been an instance of Teutonic humourlessness but the satanic mood in the novel is deliberate.[75] The oratorio is said to have been performed (in the fictional narrative) in Frankurt in 1926, directed by Otto Klemperer.[76] Zeitblom describes the work as 'Sehnsucht ohne Hoffnung' (longing without hope).[77]

---

[74] Cf. *Sacrifice Imagined*, pp. 138f.
[75] Natasha O'Hear and Anthony O'Hear *Picturing the Apocalypse: The Book of Revelation in the Arts over Two Millennia* (Oxford: OUP, 2015), p. 256.
[76] Thomas Mann, *Dr Faustus* (Frankfurt: Fischer Verlag, 2003) p. 500.
[77] Ibid., p. 502.

Gratitude

Attributed to Eckhart. If the only prayer you said was thank you, that would be enough.
Meister Eckhart
Denken ist Danken[78]

In his *Reflections on the Psalms*, which he dedicated to Austin Farrer, C. S. Lewis asks the question, why does God require praise in the Psalms? What *kind* of God demands grovelling obeisance?[79] Lewis is fully aware that giving thanks for the gift of life is a basic theme and tenet of many religious traditions.[80] Throughout Christendom before the Sanctus, the priest or minister says in preparation for the Eucharist: 'Let us give thanks unto our Lord God', the congregation responds: 'It is meet and right so to do.' The Psalms, in particular, are full of giving thanks and sacrificial practice in the Jerusalem Temple, and indeed all the temples of the ancient world, was bound to some idea of thankfulness, however crude or implicit.

The emphasis in the vision of Revelation is, as Natasha and Anthony O'Hear point out, upon the universalism and the gift: 'The New Jerusalem descending from Heaven underlines the idea that this is not something that can be built up by humans ... the heavenly city comes down from above, a gift of God at the time of his choosing.'[81]

Recent theology has been deeply concerned with the question of the 'gift'.[82] Such theological reflections often begin with the perceived problem with the 'gift'. Traditional societies are grounded upon reciprocal obligations and these obligations have been historically momentous for European culture. From Seneca and Aquinas to Shakespeare, *gratitude* has been seen as a key virtue with a context of gift-reciprocity. Gratitude to a patron or donor is thus an essential cement of the commonweal. Gifts and gratitude for those gifts helped forge and sustain the common life of society.

---

[78] Heidegger, *Was Heisst Denken*, (Frankfurt a.M.: Klustermann, 1952).
[79] Lewis, *Reflections on the Psalms*, p. 90.
[80] For a touching account of how Lewis and T. S. Eliot became friends while working on the revision of Coverdale's magnificent rendering of Psalms, see George Musacchio, 'C. S. Lewis, T. S. Eliot and the Anglican Psalter', *An Anglo-American Literary Review*, 22 (2005), pp. 45–55.
[81] O'Hear and O'Hear, *Picturing the Apocalypse*, p. 216.
[82] Risto Saarinen, *God and the Gift: An Ecumenical Theology of Giving* (Collegeville, MN: Liturgical Press, 2005), pp. 15–35.

Blow, blow, thou winter wind,
Thou art not so unkind
    As man's ingratitude;
Thy tooth is not so keen,
Because thou art not seen,
    Although thy breath be rude.
Heigh-ho! sing, heigh-ho! unto the green holly:
Most friendship is feigning, most loving mere folly:
Then, heigh-ho, the holly!
    This life is most jolly.

Freeze, freeze, thou bitter sky,
That does not bite so nigh
    As benefits forgot:
Though thou the waters warp,
Thy sting is not so sharp
    As friend remembered not. (*As You Like It* Act 2, Scene 7)

The Elizabethan English culture of Shakespeare, however, is essentially hierarchical and reinforces dependence. The rise of modernity and the free market economies of the Western world have displaced this culture of 'gratitude'.[83] In the modern period, Leithart notes, European thinkers seemed to envisage a political economy divested of the burdens of gratitude within the parameters of the asymmetrical reciprocity of traditional cultures. Leithart notes the peculiar role of Christianity within the history of Western thought.[84]

On Leithart's account, Jesus and Paul revolutionized this by preaching the unconditional gift of God: the debts of Christians are simply to love one another and to give thanks and praise to God. The alternative, for Leithart, is that we are grateful to other human beings and thus bound to reciprocity and the limits of a society constituted by rank and competition and return. Or we are only grateful to God for the gifts of other persons to us and so are liberated from the vicious reciprocity of societies of rank. Leithart's stress is upon the revolutionary role of Christianity with its message of freely given and unilateral grace. The erasing of the debts of Christians was reinforced in the

---

[83] E. J. Harpham, 'Gratitude in the History of Ideas', in *The Psychology of Gratitude,* eds R. A. Emmons and M. E. McCullough, (Oxford: Oxford University Press, 2004), pp. 20–36.
[84] Peter Leithart, *Gratitude: An Intellectual History* (Waco: Baylor, 2014).

Reformation with Luther's insistence that the mass is not an exchange but the unmerited bestowal of grace. Yet the Christian drive to unilateral grace was always threatened by attenuation into mere *altruism*. This occurred, according to Leithart, in Enlightenment ethics.

Leithart's account over-emphasizes the iconoclastic dimension of Christianity's contribution to the idea of thankfulness, a tendency linked to his Reformed/Barthian agenda. The figure of Job and the perennial problem of evil pose problems for any theistic account of thankfulness, including the Christian. Moreover, the idea of gratitude has always had its critics. The great-souled man of Aristotle is not given to demeaning feelings of gratitude, just as he has a poor estimate of modesty. This sentiment is close to Churchill's notorious quip while being assured of the 'modesty' of his rival, Clement Attlee, when Churchill replied: 'He has a lot to be modest about!' Epicurus viewed some forms of gratitude as evidence of servile weakness and to be avoided, like anger. Certainly he denies that gratitude is owed to the gods. The gods feel neither anger nor gratitude.[85]

There is a common and universal aspect of human nature involved. The psychological impact of abusive parents is well documented, and the impact of deep bitterness and resentment towards an abusive parent or carer is palpable. The positive impact of gratitude towards a generous, concerned and constructive parent is equally evident. Such an upbringing may not produce positive, compassionate and humble persons, but the likelihood is much greater. It is very hard, indeed, to imagine a *society* (even one composed of resolute egoists) as opposed to a mere aggregation of individuals, without gratitude, loyalty and a sense of belonging.[86] The relative decline of the idea of gratitude in modern ethics may well be closely associated with a prevailing rationalistic psychology in which emotions have little or no cognitive component.[87]

---

[85] Epicurus, *Kuriai Doxai*, see Diogenes Laertius, *Life of Epicurus*, X.139.
[86] Mark Wynn, *Emotional Experience and Religious Understanding: Integrating Perception, Conception and Feeling* (Cambridge: Cambridge University Press, 2005),
[87] See McGilchrist, pp. 428–62.

Contemplation

The Eucharist is etymologically a thanksgiving. The Latin cognates of communion and communication also have an etymological link with 'gift' or *munus*. One could construe the etymology of the English 'communication' as the sharing of gifts (cum-munus). The God of Christianity is a God of self-communication. The doctrine of the Logos is a theory of the self-communicative power of the Divine. The spirit is the indwelling response to the original gift.

In his great spiritual and contemplative work, *De Visione Dei* (*On the Vision of God*), written specifically for the monks of Tegernsee, Nicholas of Cusa uses the term '*cena*' or meal for Eucharist and *visio beatifica*.[88] The connection between the heavenly banquet and the contemplative vision may not be immediately obvious, but it has pivotal pagan precedents. The *locus classicus* in antique philosophy is the 'heavenly feast and banquet' of Plato's *Phaedrus* with its 'blessed sights'.[89]

The decisive contribution of Plotinus to the Western concept of contemplation is often overlooked.[90] The dual tenets of his transformation of Platonism are:

1. The procession of all reality potential and actual from the transcendent Good
2. Creative contemplation of the source.

In his seminal Ennead III 8, which is quoted enthusiastically in Coleridge's *Biographia Literaria* and is a key text for the Cambridge Platonists, he radicalizes the idea of contemplation inherited from Plato and Aristotle. Contemplation is the ontological motor of being. Everything is striving to contemplate – from the superhuman to the sub-human, from the noetic world

---

[88] See Werner Beierwaltes, *Fußnoten zu Plato* (Frankfurt: Vittorio Klostermann, 2011), pp. 143–229. Also Jacob Sherman, *Partakers of the Divine: Contemplation and the Practice of Philosophy* (Fortress Press, 2014). Peter Cheyne, *Ars biographica poetica: Coleridgean Imagination and the Practical Value of Contemplation*. Doctoral thesis, Durham University, 2014. See also, Alfons Fürst and Christian Hengstermann, *Origines: Die Homilien zum Buch Jesajas,* (Berlin: de Gruyter, 2009), pp. 111ff.

[89] (247a) ὅταν δὲ δὴ πρὸς δαῖτα καὶ ἐπὶ θοίνην ἴωσιν.

[90] A. H. Armstrong, *Gottesschau (Visio beatifica)* in *Das Reallexikon für Antike und Christentum* 12 (1983): 1–19. See also John Peter Kenney, *The Mysticism of Saint Augustine: Rereading the Confessions* (London: Routledge, 2005).

to the material stuff of the world. Coleridge designates as Pythagorean the view that 'the very powers which in men reflect and contemplate are in their essence the same as those powers which in nature produce the objects contemplated'[91] or 'philosophical imagination, the sacred power of self-intuition'.[92]

Only through its return to its source, the Good, does the Intellect emerge. And the drama of the soul's conversion and return to Intellect and the One is a repetition of this pattern of *exitus* and *reditus*. Contemplation, for Plotinus, is connected to Gift. Contemplation is always a return to the 'Giving' of the One (rooted in Plato's 'unbegrudging' Goodness of the demiurge in the *Timaeus* 29).

> When anyone, therefore, sees this light, then truly he is also moved to the Forms, and longs for the lights which play upon them and delights in it, just as with the bodies here below our desire is not for the underlying material things but for the beauty imaged upon them. For each is what it is by itself; but it becomes desirable when the Good colours it, giving a kind of grace to them and passionate love to the desirers. Then the soul, receiving into itself an outflow from thence, is moved and dances wildly and is all stung with longing and becomes love. Before this it is not moved even towards Intellect, for all its beauty; the beauty of intellect is inactive till it catches a light from the Good and the soul by itself 'falls flat on its back' and is completely inactive and, though Intellect is present, is unenthusiastic about it. But when a kind of warmth from thence comes upon it yet all the same it rises higher to something greater which it seems to remember. And as long as there is anything higher than that which is present to it, it naturally goes on upwards, lifted by the giver of its love.[93]

This process of gift and return is mirrored throughout different levels of reality. The soul (which suffuses organic and inorganic nature) contemplates the intellect and thereby animates the material cosmos. We should note the idea that contemplation is a component of human happiness. It is Plotinus who is the first Hellenic philosopher to insist upon the vision of God as contemplation and unification as the highest happiness and goal of mankind.[94]

---

[91] *Lectures 1818–1819: On the History of Philosophy* Edited by J. R. de J. Jackson, I, p. 111.
[92] Coleridge, *Biographia Literaria* I 167.
[93] Plotinus, *Ennead*, VI.7[38].22, 1-20.
[94] Plotinus, *Ennead*, I.[6].7, 33

> The man who attains this is blessed in seeing that blessed sight, and he who fails to attain it has failed utterly. A man has not failed if he fails to win beauty of colours or bodies, or power or office or kingship even, but if he fails to win this and only this. For this he should give up the attainment of kingship and of rule over all earth and sea and sky, if only by leaving and overlooking them that he can turn to that and see. [95]

Here we have not just the notion of soul as distinct from the body but his doctrine of a transcendental self (we ourselves) which is capable of the vision of God.

A recent Christian Platonist writes of Genesis 1:

> The generally accepted understanding of this sacred text, in which the most general outline of the whole creaturely world appears, is that the text speaks here about the creation of a noetic heaven, or the angelic world of bodiless spirits and of the earth as the prime substance and simultaneously the universal substance of our world, which has as its head and focus the human being ... It also seems to be the most natural on the basis of the general correlation between the spiritual and human world, expressed in the significant word *and*.[96]

The Christian beatific vision is within the company of the heavenly city. The Plotinian vision of the Divine intellect as a 'community of living intelligences' is a helpful model of that state. Indeed, the Christian doctrine of angels reinforced the Plotinian paradigm of the noetic cosmos as a vibrant commonwealth. As Farrer notes:

> The many eyes of the Ezekiel cherubim are interpreted as the organs of unceasing wakefulness, like the hundred eyes of Argus. 'Outwards and inwards they are full of eyes, and have no rest day or night, saying, Holy, holy, holy.'[97]

For all the individualism and impersonal monism of the crude caricatures of Plotinus, in the magnificent treatise Ennead VI.7[38].15, 26 Plotinus uses the perplexing term 'wholly face' παμπρόσωπος (*pamprosopos*) precisely to express this communion of intelligences at the level of the Divine mind, a realm of noetic intersubjective exchange:

---

[95] *Ennead* 1. 6[1].7, 33.
[96] Sergei Bulgakov, *Jacob's Ladder* (Grand Rapids: Eerdmans, 2010), p. 22.
[97] Farrer, *The Rebirth of Images*, p. 276.

> And so, if one likens it to a living richly varied sphere, or imagines it as a thing all faces, shining with living faces, or as all the pure souls running together into the same place, with no deficiencies but having all that is their own, and universal Intellect seated on their summits so that the region is illuminated by intellectual light – if one imagined it like this one would be seeing it somehow as one sees another from outside; but one must become that, and make oneself the contemplation.[98]

Armstrong even speculates about the possible Alexandrian links with 'Indian many-faced representations of the gods'.[99] The imagery is connected to the idea in Plotinus that finite subjects are most themselves in this bustling and vibrant world of the ideas or intelligibles as a unity of inter-related intelligences.

Farrer may be thinking of Dante's comparison of the hundred eyed giant Argus Panoptes to the four beasts of the Ezekiel-Revelation vision (derived from to Ezekiel 1.4-14 and Revelation 4.6-8) in the dramatic allegorical procession of the triumphant Church in Purgatorio 29.

The model of the exchange and mutual interdependence of the spiritual life as presented by Plotinus in his model of the noetic cosmos or the Christian representation of the celestial Jerusalem with 'Angels and Archangels and with all the company of heaven' finds emphatic affirmation in the thought of Charles Williams. In acts of exchange, sacrifice and substitution the fragmented and fallen realm of man and nature is restored, however imperfectly: 'The divine reciprocity is everywhere in love.'[100] This is Williams's doctrine of co-inherence:

> The feast of Christ the King is also the feast of Christ the City. The Principle of that City, and the gates of it, are the nature of Christ as the Holy Ghost exhibits it and inducts us into it. It is the doctrine that no man lives to himself or indeed *from* himself. This is the doctrine common to nature and grace.[101]

The capacity of human beings to transcend kith and kin and tribe and to live peaceably with strangers is an important aspect of the city as a feature of

---

[98] Διὸ καὶ εἴ τις αὐτὸν ἀπεικάζει σφαίρᾳ ζώσῃ ποικίλῃ, εἴτε παμπρόσωπόν τι χρῆμα λάμπον ζῶσι προσώποις εἴτε ψυχὰς τὰς καθαρὰς πάσας εἰς τὸ αὐτὸ συνδραμούσας φαντάζοιτο οὐκ ἐνδεεῖς, ἀλλὰ πάντα τὰ αὑτῶν ἐχούσας, καὶ νοῦν τὸν πάντα ἐπ' ἄκραις αὐταῖς ἱδρυμένον, ὡς φέγγει νοερῷ καταλάμπεσθαι τὸν τόπον — φανταζόμενος μὲν οὕτως ἔξω πως ἄλλος ὢν ὁρῴη ἄλλον·δεῖ δὲ ἑαυτὸν ἐκεῖνο γενόμενον τὴν θέαν [ἑαυτὸν] ποιήσασθαι.
[99] Armstrong in Plotinus (Cambridge, Mass.: Loeb, 1988), VII, p. 137.
[100] Charles Williams, *The Figure of Beatrice: A Study in Dante* (New York: Noonday Press, 1961), p. 169.
[101] Williams, *The Image of the City*, p. 104.

man. The city, moreover, as an image of mutual indwelling, rather than the competing models in Williams's age of class or race, provides the key image of humanity in the vision of Charles Williams. The city is a biblical image and correspondingly Williams thinks that human beings should be viewed as the image of Christ. If the whole of the created order is an inter-related sphere, even if discord and disruption is a feature of the world experienced, then the mutual interdependence of all, humans, beasts and environment is represented as the heavenly city. Free agents can recognize and avow this often occluded unity through love. The process of 'union' is through 'free exchange'.[102] 'The unexclusive life of the City, then, is everywhere vicarious life, up to the level of each capacity. It is as much the instinct of the gentleman as the climax of the saints'. The 'bear one another's burdens' runs through all.[103] Unlike commercial exchange, the sharing in the celestial city does not mean loss or diminishing of the goods. Just as a teacher gives but does not lose in the process, in spiritual matters, sharing is the process of enlargement of self. In heaven, as Dante notes, the goods shared make all wealthier: 'and the more souls that are enamoured there above the more there are to be rightly loved and the more love there is and like a mirror the one returns it to the other'.[104]

Jerusalem as the Cathedral

The foundational Christian Platonist Origen fused the antique idea of contemplation with the image of Jerusalem in a powerful and nuanced manner. Origen never wrote a commentary of Revelation but we do possess fragments and scholia. He viewed it as scriptural and as authored by John of Patmos (*De Principiis*, 2, 11, 2-3). Origen is scathing about Jewish literalism about the eating and drinking in heaven, or the notion that the city is literally made of jewels. These are images of a *civitas sanctorum*. In book four of his

---

[102] Williams, *The Image of the City*, p. 103.
[103] Williams, *The Image of the City*, p. 107.
[104] Dante, *Purgatorio*, XV, 'e come specchio l'uno all'altro rende', Sinclair, *Dante the Divine Comedy: Purgatorio*, (Oxford): OUP, 1961, pp. 200-1.

Commentary on John, Origen says that prophecies about Jerusalem are in fact about the heavenly city 4.3.8.[105] The 'living precious stones' are rational beings after their purification. The violence in the book of Apocalypse is part of a soteriology (for the sake of salvation) since it refers to the destruction of thraldom of evil. The heavenly Jerusalem is built upon the rooting out of evil and the planting of paradise. The ousting of evil and putting good in its stead is the real message of the book of Revelation.[106] The heavenly Jerusalem is identified with the Temple and gates of City of God symbolizing the return of the souls to the vision of God (*dia symbolon*).

The New Jerusalem is itself an *image* or *mirror* of the Divine, 'having the glory of God. Her light *was* like a most precious stone, like a jasper stone, clear as crystal', (Revelation 21.11). This translucence was the foundational principle of the Gothic cathedral. Anthony and Natasha O'Hear underline that one of the most dynamic and pervasive images of Jerusalem was the medieval cathedral. They note Chaucer speaks of the pilgrims seeing Canterbury Cathedral as an image of the heavenly city:

> Of thilke parfit glorious pilgrimage
> That highte Jerusalem celestial[107]

To such medieval pilgrims the height and apparent transparency of the walls would have conveyed the impression of the transcendent heavenly realm and encouraged the vision of heavenly truths.[108] To John Scot Eriugena *Omnia quae sunt lumina sunt* (all that are, are lights) – the world is theophany of its hidden source.[109] Drawing upon the great Neoplatonic aesthetic, perhaps modified by the Byzantine distinction between the unknowable Divine Essence and the Divine Energies, Eriugena provided the Neoplatonic paradigm for the work of Abbot Suger of St Denis, the man traditionally Suger

---

[105] Robert J. Daly, *Apocalyptic Thought in Early Christianity*, p. 97.
[106] Ilaria L. E. Ramelli, 'Origen's Interpretation of Violence in the Apocalypse: Destruction of Evil and Purification of Sinners'. In *Ancient Christian Interpretations of "Violent Texts" in the Apocalypse*, Joseph Verheyden, Tobias Nicklas and Andreas Merkt, with Mark Grundeken (Göttingen: Vandenhoeck & Ruprecht, 2011).
[107] O'Hear, *Picturing the Apocalypse*, p. 221ff. See also *Envisaging Heaven in the Middle Ages*, eds C. Muessig and Ad Putter (London: Routledge, 2007).
[108] Andrew Martingale, *Gothic Art* (London: Thames and Hudson, 1986).
[109] *In Ierarchiam Caelestiam* I.1, in J. Barbet (ed.) *Iohannis Scoti Eriugenae. Expositiones in Ierarchiam Caelestem* (Turnhout: Brepols, 1975), p. 3.

was considered the *spiritus rector* of European Gothic.¹¹⁰ Abbot between 1122 and 1151, and this was a period of rebuilding the abbey. Deeply influenced by Christian Neoplatonic theory of the image, the point of the beauty of the cathedral was not the denial of aesthetic appreciation but the perception of physical beauty as a trace and image of its transcendent source – as a *porta coeli* (gate of heaven):

> God interposes images between Him and us. Holy Writ as well as nature are such 'screens'; they present us with images of God, designed to be imperfect, distorted, even contradictory. This imperfection and mutual contradiction, apparent even to our minds, is to kindle in us the desire to ascend from a world of mere shadows and images to the contemplation of the Divine Light itself.¹¹¹

In his impressive account, von Simson writes, 'This metaphysical and theological vista that light and the luminous opened up to medieval man is closed to us.'¹¹²

Von Simson's view that the medieval vista is 'closed to us' seems to me a failure of imagination. (We employ light to calculate the time of the Big Bang, the point of creation itself?) Consider the example of the influence of Westminster Abbey upon the mind of William Blake. The revival of Gothic emerged with the eccentric figure of Horace Walpole and his neo-Gothic 'cabinet of curiosities' at Strawberry Hill in Richmond, built in 1747. William Blake was open to the force of this early English Romantic movement that exerted such an influence upon later Romanticism, especially in Germany. While an apprentice in Westminster Abbey, Blake's mind seems to have been profoundly inspired by the images he encountered and their spiritual power: 'his earliest and most sacred recollections [visions] were from his days in Westminster Abbey.'¹¹³ 'Blake's brain and imagination became another abbey.'¹¹⁴ It has been observed that Blake's 'imagination was Gothicised'. Within Westminster Abbey Blake 'found in stone monuments not only form

---

[110] Dominique Poirel, 'Symbolice et anagogice: l'école de Saint-Victor et la naissance du style gothique', in *L'abbé Suger, La manifeste gothique de Saint-Denis et la pensée victorine* (Turnhout: Brepols, 2001), pp. 141–70.
[111] Von Simson, *The Gothic Cathedral*, p. 53.
[112] Von Simson, *The Gothic Cathedral*, p. 54.
[113] Michael Davies, *William Blake: A New Kind of Man* (Berkeley: University of California Press), p. 17.
[114] Osbert Burdett, *William Blake* (New York: Parkstone Press, 2009), p. 26.

and outlines for his art, but also a mythic English history, a symbolic language and the place that colour once had played in architectural structure.[115] Davies notes that during long periods of his apprenticeship with Westminster Abbey 'the inward eye of the visionary artist in his late teens perceived, in his dim, vaunted solitude, a great procession of monks and priests, choristers and censer-bearers; entranced he heard the chant of plainsong and chorale'. Once he saw a vision of Christ and the apostles.

> No bleached skeleton such as his contemporaries saw, but a brilliantly painted, gilded temple, made radiant again by the light of his imagination shining on faint traces of paint which he found as he climbed and sketched among the tombs.[116]

The contemporary German neo-expressionist artist Anselm Kiefer (b. 1945) has employed images drawn from Lurianic Cabbala, those of the breaking of vessels – light dispersed as sparks and as reflections in evil splinters or fragments waiting to return to the source of light. Initially famous, indeed notorious, for his themes from twentieth-century German history, during the 1980s, Kiefer turned especially to biblical and mystical themes. In the Walker Museum of Minneapolis two works in particular, *The Hierarchy of Angels* of 1985–7 and *Emanation* (1984–6) are fine expressions of this phase in his work. His sober, melancholy and austere intimations of both holiness and destruction are visible in his depiction of *Jerusalem* (1986), with its gold leaf and lead, a work that emerges from this period. Apart from the mourning of the loss of German-Jewish culture, Jerusalem is significant as the point of joining of Heaven and Earth. This is a motif that Kiefer often expresses through wings or ladders (Seraphim).[117] His work is permeated with the sense of a tension between the horizontal and the vertical, immanence and transcendence.[118] The visual images of Fludd abound in his work, and especially the coincidence of opposites. The pillar of fire (Exodus 13.21), Jerusalem and the snake-encircled tree of paradise

---

[115] Burdett, *William Blake*, p. 23. I am grateful to Freya Gibbs for this reference.
[116] Davies, *William Blake*, p. 17.
[117] See Werner Beierwaltes, 'Some Remarks about the Difficulties in Realizing Neoplatonic Thought in Contemporary Philosophy and Art', in *Neoplatonism and Contemporary Thought vol. II*, edited by R. Baine Harris (Albany, NY: State University of New York, 2001), 269–84.
[118] Lily Fürstenow-Khositashvili, *Anselm Kiefer – Myth versus History*. Dissertation of the Humboldt University of Berlin, 2011.

are prominent themes in the bizarre Neoplatonic/Apocalyptic imaginary of Kiefer.[119]

Kiefer and Blake share many common influences, particularly through Neoplatonism. Rather than marginal eccentrics, they both constitute examples of the continuing power of this tradition to affect and shape the modern imagination.

Confusion of Eschatology and Revelation: Revelation is Consoling

When Beatrice dies Dante quotes Jeremiah's lament: *Quomodo sedet sola civitas*! How lonely stands the city![120] The desolation of the city points to Baudelaire's melancholic sense of the ruins of the modern city and the ancient Jerusalem of the Hebrew prophets. Modern readers are inclined to associate the book of Revelation with some grim eschatological nightmare: images such as the four horseman or the Babylonian whore. Yet the word apocalypse means 'revelation' and that revelation can be seen as a feature of the reality now as much as any predictions of future woe. Indeed, 'For the premoderns, the images of plagues and judgement were but a necessary precursor to the longed-for eternal New Jerusalem that would surely follow.'[121]

> Behold the Tabernacle of God is with men
> And he will tabernacle with them
> And they shall be his people
> And God – with – them shall be their God. (*Revelation* 21.3)

The Book of Common Prayer expresses the idea of communing with the heavenly host in the words before the Eucharist:

> Therefore with angels and archangels,
> with all the company of heaven,

---

[119] *Anselm Kiefer* (London: Royal Academy, 2014). See Beierwaltes, 'Some Remarks about the Difficulties in Realizing Neoplatonic Thought in Contemporary Philosophy and Art'.
[120] Charles Williams, *The Figure of Beatrice*, p. 86.
[121] A. and N. O'Hear, *Picturing the Apocalypse*, p. 220.

> It would seem that prior to the event of the eucharist, the worshippers join the heavenly host
> And heaven and earth are fused.

Augustine's two cities are not straightforwardly opposed to each other. The life of the Christian, he thinks, is not simply the preparation for the 'after'-life but also the participation in the eternal city now: to live with you is joy, to praise you and never stop.[122]

We saw in Chapter Six that Mark Wynn has recently argued that our experience of the sensory world need not be seen in crass opposition to the religious view of the world. His starting point is the kind of conversion experience that one finds discussed in William James's classic *Varieties of Religious Experience*. Yet concepts can also shape perception. Wynn offers a way of showing how the imagination (in my sense of the word) can furnish ways of thinking about an ideal realm through a spatio-temporal entity. Wynn uses Scruton's example of the Gothic Church and the heavenly city. If our perceptual experience is shaped by the idea of the heavenly Jerusalem as an example of how ideas can suffuse the perception of a sensory object or domain. The relevant religious thought informs the mind's image of building. Thus there is no inference from the image to the idea or vice versa: the image of the cathedral is *shot through* by the idea of the celestial city. Scruton in his work on architecture employs the example of the heavenly city: 'Once our experience is organized according to the concept of the heavenly city, once the concept of the heavenly city comes to inhabit the appearance of the building, then the building is capable of functioning as an image of the heavenly city.'[123] The conceptual can prompt a perceptual shift. Yet this is not Humean projectivism – that 'we should allow that when we find a religiously significant thought or image can be inscribed in the sensory appearances, this can, on occasion, be a reason for supposing that the world really, and not just in the imagination, conforms to that thought or image.'[124] Wynn claims that 'we can allow that ideas can be encountered, and can be assimilated and more deeply understood, in our experience of the sensory world, insofar as the

---

[122] (Ps. 85.5) Mary T. Clark, 'St Augustine's Use of the Psalms', *The Way Supplement* 87 (1996), 91–101.
[123] Mark Wynn, *Renewing the Senses* (Oxford: Oxford University Press, 2013), p. 47.
[124] Wynn, *Renewing the Senses*, p. 197.

sensory appearances have been penetrated by those ideas'. There can be a real mirroring of reality through such 'Thought-infused seeing'.¹²⁵

> The non observable can structure our experience of the sensory world. And … the sensory appearances will be able to image the non observables … rather in the way that the appearance of the Gothic Church can image the heavenly city.¹²⁶

This link between the emotional state and the phenomenal experience is part of Wynn's concern to deny that a two world view of reality (as in Platonism or Christian theology) diminishes or 'demeans' the significance of the sensory world. He is trying to address the criticisms of the supposed antiquated 'two-storey' Christianity by feminists:

> a focus upon the divine world need not after all imply any neglect in our relationship to the world of sensory forms; and it may even be that it is in our encounter with the realm of sensory forms that certain religious insights are presented to us most vividly.¹²⁷

Religion detracting from the enjoyment of the world and reinforcing what Hume called 'monkish virtues'. Wynn wishes to argue that the assumption of a set of non-empirical goods can trigger a sense of value in the here and now. Plotinus writes:

> We cannot get there on foot; for our feet only carry us everywhere in this world, from one country to another. You must not get ready a carriage, either, or a boat. Let all these things go. And do not look. Shut your eyes, and change to and wake another way of seeing, which everyone has but few use.¹²⁸

Indeed these goods can enhance what Traherne calls 'enjoyment' of the world and real felicity:

> You never enjoy the world aright, till the Sea itself floweth in your veins, till you are clothed with the heavens, and crowned with the stars: and perceive yourself to be the sole heir of the whole world, and more than so, because men are in it who are every one sole heirs as well as you. Till you can sing and

---

¹²⁵ Wynn, *Renewing the Senses*, p. 54.
¹²⁶ Wynn, *Renewing the Senses*, p. 54.
¹²⁷ Wynn, *Renewing the Senses*, p. 15.
¹²⁸ Plotinus, *Ennead*, I.6[1].8, 16-28.

rejoice in God, as misers do in gold, and Kings in scepters, you never enjoy the world.[129]

On the view we have been exploring, this is fundamentally because a transformation in the person, as they approach the condition of enlightenment, or as they develop spiritually, will make for a reciprocal transformation in the appearance of the sensory world – and accordingly far from being simply a movement 'upwards' or 'inwards, enlightenment, or spiritual awakening can also be an opportunity for, and will be partly constituted by, a movement 'outwards' and into the realm of the senses.[130] As the Cambridge Platonist John Smith notes: 'When reason once is raised by the mighty force of the Divine Spirit into a converse with God, it is turned into sense'.[131]

Wynn's main concern is with positive visions of the world. He wants to present the transfiguration of the face of nature, not just an isolated region of experience but the whole world, as a way whereby everyday objects and ordinary human beings acquire a new dimension of significance. Drawing upon the use of 'appearance' in spiritual writers like Jonathan Edwards or John of the Cross, Wynn suggests that disclosure of the divine should not be thought as mere understanding of a putative divine object but rather is to be mediated by the sensory experience of the world and a changed relation – a conversion – in the perceiver stance towards the sensory world. A person so 'awakened', one might say knows creatures *in* God.

Caspar David Friedrich's Teschen altarpiece presents the crucified Christ as the window into the Divine nature.[132] It is often, though certainly not always, the prerogative of the artist to awaken and help renew the human sense of the world. Is the world just the backdrop for human interests or locus of the breaking through of the Kingdom of God? The great central image of the Book of Revelation alongside the seals, the trumpets, the bowls, is the slain lamb. Handel's remarkable double fugue chorus – 'Worthy is the lamb that was slain'

---

[129] Thomas Traherne, *Centuries of Meditations* §29, edited by Bertram Dobell (London: P. J. and A. E. Dobell, 1927), p. 19.
[130] Wynn, *Renewing the Senses*, p. 41.
[131] John Smith, *Select Discourses*, 15-16.
[132] Besançon's interpretation of the mystical atheism of Friedrich in his *The Forbidden Image*, p. 290, strikes me as implausible and in conflict with Friedrich's own words. See *Caspar David Friedrich in Briefen und Bekenntnissen*, edited by Sigrid Hinz (Munich: Rogner and Bernhard, 1968). See further Werner Busch, *Caspar David Friedrich: Aesthetik und Religion* (Munich: C. H. Beck, 2003).

gives great musical and imaginative expression to the claim that light will prevail over darkness. Goodness, imaged through John's distinctive, and prima vista bewildering, symbol of the sacrificial lamb presented with such power by John of Patmos. Such a vision builds on but does not invalidate everyday objects and the quotidian existence of human beings. There is, however, a radically novel dimension of significance and a renewal of the perception of the sensory world as a whole. The appearance and the emotional weight of the material cosmos unveils the divinely charged significance of things.

Few poets have expressed the vision of the world as divulging its sacred and transcendent source with such stark animation as Thomas Traherne. The opening of the heavens to the spiritual eye is one of his recurring themes. In the following passage we find our themes of the celestial vision and the celebration feast in his praise of the holy days of the Church:

> Why should we not spend som time upon Holy Days in Con-Templating the
> Beauty of Holy Dais in themselves?
> They are the ornaments of Time, and the Beauty of the World.
> The Days of Heaven seen upon Earth,
> The Seasons of Melody, Joy and Thanksgiving.
> The Lucid Intervals and Lights of the Year,
> The Relicks of Eden, and superadded Treasures,
> A gratefull Relaxation from Cares and Labors.
> The very Cream and Crown and Repose of our Lives ...
> Wherein we Antedate the Resurrection of the Dead
> And come from our shops to our Saviour's Throne,
> From plowing our fields to Manna in the Wilderness
> From Dressing our Vineyards to the Wine of Angels
> From caring for our Children to be the Sons of God.
> They are Heavenly Perspectivs wherein behold the Mystery of
> The Ages.
> Spiritual Regions, wherein we Walk in the paths of GOD.
> Market Days of Heaven,
> Appointed Seasons, wherein GOD keepeth Open House
> And Blessed Opportunities wherein we com from our solitary
> Closets and see ourselves in Solemn Assemblies.
> Single Devotions are weak in comparison of these; here is the Joy
> And the Strength of Union.

> A Privat Person is but Half Himself, and naturally magnified in
> Others.
> He is enlarged and Multiplied, when he sees Himself in so many
> Faces in Divine Assemblies.
> The Difference between Earth and Heaven is, that here we are
> Dispersed, there we shall ever be united together.
> These Days are Tastes and Earnests of our Eternal Rest,
> Wherein we enter the Temple, as the Schole of Christ
> And like Angels are adorned with Wings
> That we light flie unto heaven.[133]

The holy days, for Traherne, serve as an image of the end: the contemplation of the eternal rest in great heavenly city, the Kingdom of God and the Temple of celestial co-inherence, where 'each sees Himself in so many Faces', and each is greater in the whole.

---

[133] The Church's Year Book. Quoted from A. M. Allchin, 'The Sacrifice of Praise and Thanksgiving' in *Profitable Wonders: Aspects of Thomas Traherne*, eds A. M. Allchin, Anne Ridler, Julia Smith (Oxford: Amate, 1989), pp. 22–37, p. 29.

Epilogue

Here power failed the high phantasy; but now my desire and will, like a wheel that spins with even motion, were revolved by the love that moves the sun and the other stars.

(Dante, *Paradiso*, Canto XXXIII).[1]

The seeds of the present trilogy originate in my earlier research on the later thought of Samuel Taylor Coleridge. The great Victorian Utilitarian and social reformer John Stuart Mill visited the Romantic seer in Highgate and wrote one of the most penetrating and sagacious accounts of Coleridge in the English language, presenting him as the font of the 'Germano-Coleridgean' doctrine of British Romanticism. Unlike Bentham, whose concern was with a narrowly conceived truth of belief or opinion, Coleridge wanted to explore the 'meaning' of beliefs.[2] In contrast to Carlyle's mordant depiction of Coleridge as the magus of Highgate, 'girt in mystery', Mill was aware of the depth and seminal power of Coleridge's shaping imagination. One can think of the young Lakeland poet and the author of *Aids to Reflection* in the last phase of his life in Highgate as rather distinct figures. Yet perhaps the earliest poetry is proleptic, if not prophetic, of the interests and obsessions of the philosopher-theologian. The paradise garden of Kubla Khan foreshadows the 'hunger for eternity' of the sage of Highgate and Coleridge came to identify himself explicitly with the Mariner. This prophetic power of his shaping imagination continues to exert its sway today. The tale of the shooting of the Albatross, for example, and the curse upon the crew and the mariner, has come to have meaning in the early 21st century as an image of the ecological havoc created by the man-made debris in the north Pacific, where the albatrosses are poisoned by the plastic pollution in the Midway Atoll.

All three works were written with the intense conviction that these are 'living' forms of the imagination that shape our world, regardless of the

---

[1] John D. Sinclair *Paradiso* (Oxford: OUP, 1961) pp. 484-5.
[2] See my *Coleridge, Philosophy and Religion: Aids to Reflection and the Mirror of the Spirit* (Cambridge: CUP, 2000).

pervasive and dominant materialism of the age that seeks to erase the proper distinction between philosophy and science. Rather than adduce a simple role call of champions of the imagination, we have set out to oppose the hidden and mysterious power of the soul revealed in the imagination in opposition to programmatic physicalism. We have opposed the ideology of a scientism that views consciousness as the epiphenomenon of brain activity, freedom as an illusion, and God a delusion. Coleridge is probably the source of the English term 'scientist'.[3] He was concerned to distinguish the activity of experimental science from the contemplation of ideas that he regarded as properly philosophical. Coleridge, friend of Humphry Davy and admirer of Michael Faraday, was certainly not hostile to experimental science. Yet he was troubled by the conviction that only 'science', in this immensely important but limited sense of knowledge derived from the laboratory and experiment, constitutes knowledge.[4] The Faustian identification of 'science' and knowledge and the corresponding demotion of the humanities to forms of ornament, rhetoric or crypto-politics, has generated its passionate advocates and its grave critics. This is hardly surprising given the threat to the environment presented by the most advanced technology and weaponry, dangers recognised by leading scientists. The British Astronomer Royal and President of the Royal Society in the Twenty First century has written an eschatological Jeremiad against the misuse of scientific technology called ominously 'Our Final Century'.[5] Yet it was Mary Shelley in *Frankenstein, or the Modern Prometheus* who imagined the most startling image of the potential terrors of the human conquest of nature in the modern period – inspired, amongst other things, by Byron's dramatic recital from an early version of Coleridge's eerie poem *Christabel*.[6]

Living Forms of the Imagination was founded upon a conviction that the Coleridgean insistence upon the shaping power of the imagination deserves renewed attention, not least in a culture where a truncated utilitarian and economic model of humanity enjoys such ascendancy. Coleridge viewed his

---

[3] Richard Holmes, *The Age of Wonder* (London: HarperPress, 2009), p. 449.
[4] For an eloquent defence of Coleridge see Thomas Pfau, *Minding the Modern: Human Agency, Intellectual Traditions, and Responsible Knowledge* (South Bend: Notre Dame, 2013).
[5] Martin Rees, *Our Final Century: Will the Human Race Survive the Twenty-first Century?* (London: William Heinemann, 2003)
[6] The origins of the Frankenstein story lie in a recounting of horror tales in the Genevan house party with her lover Shelley, Lord Byron and Polidori.

own childhood sense of the transcendent in fairy tales as the spring of his later metaphysics and he was a forerunner of the later attempts of C. S. Lewis and the Inklings to fuse imagination with reason as part of a defence of Christian theism. We proposed a middle way between the rationalist view of religious belief as an inference to best explanation and the fideistic alternative of religious belief as incontrovertible immediacy. Indeed, man is amphibious. The imagination in its deepest sense is the mediating power of the intellectual world in the physical cosmos and the presence of the transcendent ideal in the world of senses. Belief in God is neither a purely intellectual exercise nor is it a brute given of human awareness. The idea of God on our account is rather mediated through the human imagination, somewhat akin to the imagination of other minds or moral facts. Building on this account of the mediating function of the religious imagination, we developed an account of myth, story and revealed images.

In *Sacrifice Imagined* we explored the indispensable but troubling language and imagery of the sacrificial. We rejected the widespread dismissal of sacrifice as barbaric and obsolete by recommending the continuing relevance of the 'making sacred' of sacrifice in the aesthetic domain – especially tragedy – and the ethical. Far from the simplistic portrayal of religion being simply the barbaric motor of pointless cruelty, we developed a version of the religious phenomenon as rooted in the legitimate desire to find atonement in the transformation of suffering and loss into love and reconciliation.

In this concluding volume we dwell upon the connection between image and imagination. Is it merely an accident of English etymology that 'imagination' is cognate with image? Here we plead for a metaphysics of the image as the bearer of transcendence. There is a cosmic as well as an artistic dimension to this experience of transcendence *through* the image. Only if the world bears an image-like resemblance to its transcendent source can a sacramental imagination be intelligible and defensible. In this way, the image becomes a source of world affirmation. Rather than a path to abstraction and cold asceticism, it is the vision of the eternal through the visible and in the temporal. The endorsement of transcendence is not the denial but the affirmation of the world.

The greatest philosopher of the Western tradition was a poet. He gave us the cave of his *Republic* and wrote in the *Phaedrus* about the super-celestial place of which none of the earthly poets have sung. *Living Forms of the Imagination* started with the Phaedran chariot as an image of the power of the imagination to bridge Becoming and Being. The imagination is needed in art to reconcile the eternal with the characteristics of one's own age. Transcendence is requisite for the operation of the religious imagination, with its sense of the enigmatic, symbolic and yet 'complex and indivisible totality' (Baudelaire) of the world. As the chariot of Plato and Ezekiel was the primary image used in the first volume, the Temple of Jerusalem acts as the core symbol for *Sacrifice Imagined*. That volume is concerned not primarily with the anthropological or sociological phenomenon of sacrifice, but with sacrifice as the substitution (or even sublimation) of a desire for a higher value or principle. Though the physical Temple has been destroyed, it remains conceptually as the meeting place between the spiritual and the physical; though sacrifice has become spiritualized, its cultural impact and metaphysical importance remain. The core of image of *The Iconic Imagination* is the city as an image of paradise. Jerusalem overlaps with the paradise garden. As *Living Forms of the Imagination* invoked John of Patmos and his vision bridging Athens and Jerusalem, *The Iconic Imagination* concludes with John's vision, with its balance between familiar and strange.

The eminent twentieth century Russian poet Boris Pasternak presents the eponymous hero of his novel *Dr Zhivago* contemplating the question of art:

> He realised, more vividly than ever before, that art has two constant, two unending preoccupations: it is always meditating upon death and it is always creating life. He realised that this was true of all great art; it was true of that work of art which is called the Revelation of St. John, and of all those works which have been completing it through the ages.[7]

The vision of John is not, we have argued, some ancient Middle Eastern product of a Nietzschean ressentiment. Why is the book of Revelation paradigmatic? In the Ezekiel image, we observed the ambivalence of the chariot: is it moving up or down? Is it imagination or revelation? In Revelation 4 and 21 we have the divine theophany as both an upward and a downward movement. The image of the heavenly door to the lamb is an image of ascent. The image of the bride or city is one of descent. In the fusion of the images of ascent and descent, the imaginative theophany of revelation is a unity of upward and downward movement. And the content of the vision is motion and rest, life and stillness: feast, contemplation and song.

---

[7] Pasternak, Boris, *Doctor Zhivago*, (London: Random House, 2002), p. 89.

Bibliography

Abrahamson, Robert L., 'Est in re veritas: Models for Sacramental Reading in the Place of the Lion'. In *Charles Williams and His Contemporaries*, eds Suzanne Bray and Richard Sturch, 130–44. Newcastle upon Tyne: Cambridge Scholars, 2009.

Aelian, Claudius, *Varia Historia, or Historical Miscellany*, ed. and trans. N. G. Wilson. Cambridge: Loeb, 1997.

Albanese, Catherine L., *A Republic of Mind and Spirit: A Cultural History of American Metaphysical Religion*. New Haven, CT: Yale University Press, 2007.

Allchin, A. M., *Participation in God: A Forgotten Strand in Anglican Tradition*. Wilton, CT: Morehouse-Barlow, 1988.

Allchin, A. M., Anne Ridler and Julia Smith, eds, *Profitable Wonders: Aspects of Thomas Traherne*. Oxford: Amate, 1989.

Alston, A. J., *The Devotional Poems of Mirabai*. Delhi: Motilal Banarsidass, 1980.

Anselm, *The Major Works*, ed. Brian Davies. Harmondsworth: Penguin, 2008.

Aquinas, Thomas, *Summa theologiae*, 5 vols. Ottawa: Medieval Institute, 1948.

Aquinas, Thomas, *A Commentary on Aristotle's De anima*, trs. R. Pasnau, New Haven: Yale University Press, 1999.

Archibald, Elizabeth, 'Ancient Romance'. In *A Companion to Romance from Classical to Contemporary*, ed. C. Saunders, 1–25. Oxford: Blackwell, 2004.

Aristotle, *Categories, On Interpretation, Prior Analytics*, trans. H. P. Cooke and Hugh Tredennick. Cambridge: Loeb, 1939.

Aristotle, *Posterior Analytics Topica*, trans. Hugh Tredennick and E. S. Forster Cambridge: Loeb, 1976.

Armstrong, A. H., *The Architecture of the Intelligible Universe in the Philosophy of Plotinus: An Analytical and Historical Study*. Amsterdam: A. M. Hakkert, 1967.

Armstrong, A. H., 'Negative Theology'. *Downside Review* 95 (1977): 176-89, repr., *Plotinian and Christian Studies*, XXIV. London: Variorum, 1979.

Armstrong, A. H., 'Gottesschau (Visio beatifica)'. *Reallexikon für Antike und Christentum* 12 (1983): 1–19.

Armstrong, A. H., 'Platonic Mirrors'. *Eranos Yearbook* 55 (1988): 147–81.

Armstrong, D. M., *Sketch for a Systematic Metaphysics*. Oxford: Clarendon, 2010.

Arnold, Thomas, *Painting in Islam: A Study of the Place of Pictorial Art in Muslim Culture*. Oxford: Clarendon, 1928.

Assmann, Jan, *Moses the Egyptian: The Memory of Egypt in Western Monotheism*. Cambridge, MA: Harvard University Press, 1997.
Assmann, Jan, *The Price of Monotheism*. Stanford, CA: Stanford University Press, 2010.
St Augustine, *The City of God*, trans. Henry Bettenson. Harmondsworth: Penguin, 2003.
St Augustine, *Enarrationes in Psalmos Brepols*, eds E. Dekkers and J. Fraipont. Turnhout: Brepols, 2013.
Bachelard, Gaston I., *Water and Dreams*. Dallas: Dallas Institute Publications, 1994.
Bacon, Francis, *Advancement of Learning, book II, Works*, eds James Spedding, Robert Leslie Ellis and Douglas Denon Heath. London: Longman, 1857-74.
Balthasar, Hans Urs von, *Theologik*. Einsiedeln: Johannes Verlag, 1985.
Balthasar, Hans Urs von, *Presence and Thought: Essay on the Religious Philosophy of Gregory of Nyssa*. San Francisco, CA: Ignatius Press, 1995.
Balthasar, Hans Urs von, Joseph Fessio and John Kenneth Riches, *The Glory of the Lord: A Theological Aesthetics*. Edinburgh: T&T Clark, 1991.
Barasch, Moshe, *Icon: Studies in the History of an Idea*. New York: New York University Press, 1992.
Barfield, Owen, *Saving the Appearances: A Study in Idolatry*. New York: Harcourt, Brace & World, 1965.
Barfield, Owen, *Romanticism Comes of Age*. Middletown, CT: Wesleyan University Press, 1966.
Barfield, Raymond, *The Ancient Quarrel between Philosophy and Poetry*. Cambridge: Cambridge University Press, 2011.
Barker, Margaret, *The Older Testament*. London: SPCK, 1987.
Barker, Margaret, *The Gate of Heaven: The History and Symbolism of the Temple in Jerusalem*. London: SPCK, 1991.
Barker, Margaret, *The Revelation of Jesus Christ Which God Gave to Him to Show to His Servants What Must Soon Take Place (Revelation 1.1)*. London: T& T Clark, 2000.
Barth, Bernhard, *Schellings Philosophie der Kunst Göttliche Imagination und aesthetische Einbildungskraft*. Freiburg: Alber, 1991.
Barton, Stephen, *Where Shall Wisdom Be Found?: Wisdom in the Bible, the Church and the Contemporary World*. Edinburgh: T&T Clark, 1999.
Barua, Ankur, *Debating Conversion in Hinduism and Christianity*. London: Routledge, 2015.
Barua, Ankur, 'God's Body at Work: Ramanuja and Panentheism'. *International Journal of Hindu Studies* 14 (2010): 1-30.

Bates, Jennifer Ann, *Hegel and Shakespeare on Moral Imagination*. Albany, NY: State University of New York Press, 2010.

Bateson, Gregory, *Mind and Nature: A Necessary Unity*. New York: Dutton, 1979.

Baudelaire, Charles, 'Salon de 1859', in *Critique d'Art*, ed. Claude Pichois, 2 vols, Paris: Armand Colin, 1965, vol. 2, pp. 295–378. (Originally published in four instalments, *Revue Française*, between 10 June and 20 July 1859; published posthumously and abbrev. in the first edn of Baudelaire's collected works, *Curiosité esthétiques*, vol. 2, Paris: Michel Lévy Frères, 1868; published as, 'The Salon of 1859', in *Art in Paris 1845–1862*, ed. and trans. Jonathan Mayne. London: Phaidon, 1965, pp. 144–216.)

Baudelaire, Charles, *Selected Writings on Art and Artists*, trans. P. E. Charvet. Cambridge: Cambridge University Press, 1972.

Bauer, Bruno, *Christianity Exposed*, trans. by Esther Ziegler and Jutta Hamm, ed. Paul Trejo, Lewiston: Mellen, 2002.

Bede, *Ecclesiastical History*, 1–3, trans. J. E. King. Cambridge, MA: Loeb, 1930.

Beierwaltes, Werner, 'Augustins Interpretation von Sapientia 11:21'. *Revue d'études augustiniennes et patristiques* 15 (1969): 51–61.

Beierwaltes, Werner, 'Subjektivitat, Freiheit: Die Philosophie der Renaissance zwishen Tradition und neuzeitlichen Bewusstsein'. In *Der Übergang zur Neuzeit und die Wirkung von Traditionen: Vorträge gehalten auf der Tagung der Joachim Jungius-Gesellschaft der Wissenschaften, … Hamburg Der Ubergang der Neuzeit*, 15–31. Göttingen: Vandenhoeck & Ruprecht, 1978.

Beierwaltes, Werner, 'Some Remarks about the Difficulties in Realizing Neoplatonic Thought in Contemporary Philosophy and Art'. In *Neoplatonism and Contemporary Thought vol. II*, ed. R. Baine Harris, 269–84. Albany, NY: State University of New York, 2001.

Beierwaltes, Werner, *Das Wahre Selbst Studien zu Plotins Begriff des Geistes und des Einen*, Frankfurt: Klostermann 2001.

Beierwaltes, Werner, *Procliana, Spätantikes Denken und seine Spuren*. Frankfurt: Klostermann, 2007.

Beierwaltes, Werner, *Fußnoten zu Platon*. Frankfurt: Klostermann, 2010.

Belting, Hans, *Likeness and Presence, A History of the Image before the Era of Art*. Chicago, IL: University of Chicago Press, 1994.

Belting, Hans, *Das Echte Bild: Bildfragen als Glaubenfragen*. Munich: Beck, 2006.

Benedict, Ruth, *The Chrysanthemum and the Sword*. Boston: Houghton Mifflin Harcourt, 1946.

Bentley Hart, David, *The Experience of God: Being, Consciousness, Bliss*. New Haven, CT: Yale University Press, 2013.

Benz, Ernst, 'Theogonie und Wandlung des Menschen bei Friedrich Wilhelm Joseph Schelling'. In *Urbild und Abbild: Der Mensch und die mythische Welt*. (Gesmmelte Eranos-Beiträge), 69–130. Leiden: Brill, 1974. (English translation: 'Theogony and Transformation in Friedrich Wilhelm Schelling'. In *Man and Transformation: Papers from the Eranos Yearbooks*, ed. Joseph Campbell, 203–49. Princeton, NJ: Princeton University Press, 1964.

Benz, Ernst, *Augustins Lehre der Kirche*. Wiebaden: Steiner, 1954.

Bergman, M. and J. E. Brower, 'A Theistic Argument against Platonism'. *Oxford Studies in Metaphysics* 2 (2006): 357–86.

Berleant, Arnold, 2004. *Re-thinking Aesthetics: Rogue Essays on Aesthetics and the Arts*. Aldershot: Ashgate, 2004.

Berlekamp, Persis, *Wonder, Image, and Cosmos in Medieval Islam*. New Haven, CT: Yale University Press, 2011.

Berman, Morris, *The Reenchantment of the World*. Ithaca, NY: Cornell University Press, 1981.

Besançon, Alain, *The Forbidden Image*. Chicago, IL: Chicago University Press, 2009.

Betram, Georg, *Philosophische Gedankenexperimente*. Stuttgart: Reclam, 2012.

Biemann, Asher, 'Art and Aesthetics'. In *The Cambridge History of Jewish Philosophy: The Modern Era*, ed. Martin Kavka, Zachary Braiterman and David Novak, 759–79. Cambridge: Cambridge University Press, 2012.

Bigger, Charles P., *Participation: Platonic Inquiry*. Baton Rouge, LA: Louisiana State University Press, 1968.

Blackburn, Simon, *Spreading the Word: Groundings in the Philosophy of Language*. Oxford: Oxford University Press, 1984.

Blumenberg, Hans, *Legitimacy of the Modern World*, trans. Robert Wallace. Cambridge, MA: MIT, 1985.

Blumenberg, Hans, *Paradigmen zu einer Metaphorologie*. Frankfurt am Main: Surkamp, 1997.

Boehm, Gottfried, 'Die Wiederkehr der Bilder'. In *Was ist ein Bild*, ed. Gottfried Boehm, 11–38. Munich: Fink, 1994.

Boehm, Gottfried, 'Die Bilderfrage'. In *Was ist ein Bild*, ed. Gottfried Boehm, 325–43. Munich: Fink, 1994.

Bonin, Thérèse, *Creation as Emanation: The Origin of Diversity in Albert the Great's On the Causes and the Procession of the Universe*. South Bend, IN: Notre Dame University Press, 2001.

Bouyer, Louis, *Le trône de la sagesse*. Paris: Éditions du Cerf, 1987.
Blake, William, *A Vision of the Last Judgement*. The Complete Poetry and Prose of William Blake, ed. David V. Erdman. Garden City: Anchor Books, 1982.
Bloom, Harold, *The Anatomy of Influence*. Garden City: Doubleday, 1982.
Blunt, Anthony, *Artistic Theory in Italy 1450–1600*. Oxford: Oxford University Press, 1962.
Boland, Vivian, *Ideas in God According to Saint Thomas Aquinas: Sources and Synthesis*. Leiden: Brill, 1996.
Bonnemann, Jens, *Der Spielraum des Imaginären*. Sartres Theorie der Imagination und ihre Bedeutung für seine phänomenologische Ontologie, Ästhetik und und Intersubjektivitätskonzeption. Hamburg. Meiner, 2007.
Boulding, Kenneth E., *The Image: Knowledge in Life and Society*. Ann Arbor, MI: University of Michigan Press, 1961.
Boulnois, Olivier, *Être et représentation: Une généalogie de la métaphysique moderne à l'époque de Duns Scot*. Paris: Presses Universitaires de France, 1999.
Boulnois, Olivier, *Au-delà de l'image: Une archéologie du visuel au moyen âge, ve-XVIe siècle*. Paris: Seuil, 2008.
Bowie, Ewen and Jaś Elsner, *Philostratus*. Cambridge: Cambridge University Press, 2009.
Boyde, Patrick, *Dante Philomythes and Philosopher: Man in the Cosmos*. Cambridge: Cambridge University Press, 1983.
Brand, Dennis J., *The Book of Causes: Liber de Causis*. Milwaukee, WI: Marquette University Press, 1984.
Brann, Eva, *The World of the Imagination: Sum and Substance*. Lanham, MD: Rowman & Littlefield, 1991.
Bravo, Benedetto, 'F. Creuzer et F. G. Welcker'. In *L'impensable Polytheisme: Etudes D'historigraphie religieuse*, ed. Francis Schmidt, 375–424. Chippenham: Editions des archives contemporaines, 1988.
Bredekamp, Horst, 'Götterdämmerung des Neuplatonismus', *Kritische Berichte* 14 (1986): 39–48.
Bredekamp, Horst, *Darwins Koralle: Frühe Evolutionsmodelle und die Tradition der Naturgeschichte*. Berlin: Klaus Wagenbach, 2005.
Brochard, Victor and Victor Delbos, *Études de philosophie ancienne et de philosophie modern*. Paris: J. Vrin, 1954.
Bulgakov, Sergei, *Jacob's Ladder*. Grand Rapids: Eerdmans, 2010.
Bulger, Thomas, 'Platonism in Spenser's Mutabilitie Cantos'. In *Platonism and the*

English Imagination, ed. Anna Baldwin and Sarah Hutton, 126-38. Cambridge: Cambridge University Press, 1994.

Bultmann, Christoph, *Die biblische Urgeschichte in der Aufklärung*. Tübingen: Mohr-Siebeck, 1999.

Bundy, Murray Wright, *The Theory of Imagination in Classical and Mediaeval Thought*. Urbana, IL: The University of Illinois, 1927.

Burckhardt, Titus, *Art of Islam: Language and Meaning*. Bloomington, IN: World Wisdom, 2009.

Burdett, Osbert, *William Blake*. New York: Parkstone Press, 2009.

Bussanich, J., 'Socrates' Religious Experience'. In *The Bloomsbury Companion to Socrates*, ed. J. Bussanich and N. Smith, 276-300. London: Continuum, 2012.

Butler, John F., 'Creation, Art and Lila'. *Philosophy East and West* 10 (1960): 3-12.

Bychkov, O. V., *Aesthetic Revelation: Reading Ancient and Medieval Texts after Hans Urs von Balthasar*. Washington, DC: Catholic University of America Press, 2010.

Bychkov, V. V., *The Aesthetic Face of Being: Art in the Theology of Pavel Florensky*. Crestwood, NY: St. Vladimir's Seminary Press, 1993.

Calasso, Roberto, *The Marriage of Cadmus and Harmony*. New York: Knopf, 1993.

Calasso, Roberto, *KA*, trans. Tim Parks. London: Jonathan Cape, 1998.

Calasso, Roberto, *La letteratura e gli dèi*. Milano: Adelphi, 2001.

The Cambridge History of Jewish Philosophy: The Modern Era, vol 2, eds. Martin Kavka, Zachery Braiterman, David Novak, vol 2 Aesthetics and Art 759-79

Carman Rose, Mary, 'The Christian Platonism of C. S. Lewis, J. R. R. Tolkien, and Charles Williams'. In *Neoplatonism and Christian Thought*, ed. D. J. O'Meara, 203-22. Norfolk, VA: International Society for Neoplatonic Studies, 1982.

Cassirer, Ernst, *Essay on Man: An Introduction to a History of Human Culture*. New Haven, CT: Yale University Press, 1944.

Cassius Dio Cocceianus, *Dio's Roman History*, eds Earnest Cary, Herbert Baldwin Foster and William Heinemann. New York: Harvard University Press, 1914.

Cavaliero, Glen, *Charles Williams, Poet of Theology*. London: Macmillan, 1983.

Cheney, Liana and John Hendrix, *Neoplatonic Aesthetics: Music, Literature & the Visual Arts*. New York: Peter Lang, 2004.

Chesterton, *The Collected Works of G. K Chesterton*, San Francisco: Ignatius Press, 1987, Rutler Azar and George Marlin (eds).

Clark, Mary T., 'St Augustine's Use of the Psalms'. *The Way Supplement* 87 (1996): 91-101.

Clark, Maudemarie, 'On the Rejection of Morality: Bernard Williams's Debt to

Nietzsche'. In *Nietzsche's Postmoralism: Essays on Nietzsche's Prelude to Philosophy's Future*, ed. Richard Schacht. Cambridge: Cambridge University Press, 2001.

Clark, Stephen R. L., *How to Think about the Earth, Philosophical and Theological Models for Ecology*. London: Mowbray, 1993.

Clooney, Francis X., *His Hiding Place is Darkness: A Hindu-Catholic Theopoetics of Divine Absence*. Stanford, CA: Stanford University Press, 2014.

Cocking, J. M. and Penelope Murray, *Imagination: A Study in the History of Ideas*. London: Routledge, 1991.

Cohen, Marc, Patricia Curd and C. D. C. Reeve, *Readings in Ancient Greek Philosophy*, 2nd edn. Indianapolis: Hackett Publishing, 2000.

Cohn, Norman, *Europe's Inner Demons: An Enquiry Inspired by the Great Witch-Hunt*. London: Sussex University Press, 1975.

Coleridge, Samuel T., *Collected Letters of Samuel Taylor Coleridge*, vols 1–6, ed. Earl Leslie Griggs. Oxford: Oxford University Press, 1956–71.

Coleridge, Samuel T., *The Collected Works of Samuel Taylor Coleridge* vols 1–16, ed. Kathleen Coburn. Princeton, NJ: Princeton University Press, 1971–2001.

Coleridge, Samuel T., *Lay Sermons*, ed. R. T. White. Princeton, NJ: Princeton University Press, 1973.

Coleridge, Samuel T., *Poems*, ed. John Beer. Dent: Everyman 1974.

Coleridge, Samuel T., *Biographia Literaria*, ed. W. Jackson Bate and James Engell, Princeton, NJ: Princeton University Press, 1985.

Coleridge, Samuel T., *Aids to Reflection*, ed. John Beer. Princeton, NJ: Princeton University Press, 1994.

Coleridge, Samuel T., *Opus Maximum*, ed. Thomas MacFarland. Princeton, NJ: Princeton University Press 2002.

Collingwood, Robin G., *The Principles of Art*. Oxford: Oxford University Press, 1938.

Collins, Randall, *Sociology of the Philosophies: A Global Theory of Intellectual Change*. Belknap: Harvard University Press, 1998.

Connolly, Thomas, *Mourning into Joy: Music, Raphael, and Saint Cecilia*. New Haven, CT: Yale University Press, 1994.

Coomaraswamy, A. K., *Door in the Sky*. Princeton, NJ: Princeton University Press, 1998.

Coomaraswamy, A. K., *Dance of Shiva*. New Delhi: M. Manoharlel, 1974.

Corbin, Henry, *Alone with the Alone: Creative Imagination in the Sūfism of Ibn 'Arabī*. Trans. Ralph Manheim (Princeton: Princeton University Press, 1998).

Cornford, Francis Macdonald, *From Religion to Philosophy*. New York: Longmans, Green and Co., 1912.

Cornford, Francis Macdonald, *Plato's Theory of Knowledge: The Theaetetus and the Sophist of Plato Translated with a Running Commentary.* New York: Harcourt, Brace and Company, 1935.

Cox, Murray and Alice Theilgaard, *Mutative Metaphors in Psychotherapy: The Aeolian Mode.* New York: Tavistock Publications, 1987.

Craig, Edward, *The Mind of God and the Works of Man.* Oxford: Oxford University Press, 1987.

Creuzer, Friedrich, *Idee und Probe alter Symbolik* (Stuttgart: Friedrich Fromann, 1969).

Creuzer, Friedrich, *Symbolik und Mythologie der alten Völker* (Leipzig and Darmstadt: 1843).

Crocker, R., 'The Cupri-cosmits and the Latitude-Men'. In *Henry More: 1614–1687*, ed. Sarah Hutton, 79–92. Dortrecht: Springer, 1989.

Cudworth, Ralph, *The True Intellectual System of the Universe.* London: Royston, 1678.

Cudworth, Ralph, *The Works Containing The True Intellectual System of the Universe, Sermons* by Ralph Cudworth, ed. Thomas Birch. Oxford: Talboys, 1829.

Cusa, Nicholas of, *Idota de mente.* In *Nicholas of Cusa's Dialectical Mysticism*, trans. Jasper Hopkins. Minneapolis: Banning, 1996.

Cutsinger, James S., *Paths to the Heart: Sufism and the Christian East.* Bloomington, IN: World Wisdom, 2002.

Daniélou, Alain, *Shiva and Dionysus: The Religion of Nature and Eros.* New York: Inner Traditions International, 1984.

Darwin, Charles, *Descent of Man.* Amherst, NY: Prometheus Books, 1998.

Davies, Brian, *An Introduction to the Philosophy of Religion.* Oxford: Oxford University Press, 1993.

Davies, Michael, *William Blake: A New Kind of Man.* Berkeley: University of California Press, 1977.

Day, Jerry, *Voegelin, Schelling and the Philosophy of Historical Existence.* Columbia: University of Missouri Press, 2003.

Dennett, Daniel, *The Intentional Stance.* London: MIT Press, 1989.

Derrida, Jacques, *Of Grammatology*, trans. Gayatri Chakravorty Spivak. Baltimore: Johns Hopkins University Press, 1997.

Dewick, E. C., *The Indwelling God.* Mysore: Oxford University Press, 1938.

Dickie, G., *Aesthetics, An Introduction.* Cambridge: Pegasus, 1971.

Didi-Huberman, Georges, *Confronting Images Questioning the Ends of a Certain History of Art.* University Park, PA: Pennsylvania State University Press, 2005.

Dillenberger, Jane and Diane Apostolos-Cappadona, *Image and Spirit in Sacred and Secular Art.* New York: Crossroad, 1990.
Dillon, John M., 'Image, Symbol and Analogy: Three Basic Concepts of Neoplatonic Allegorical Exegesis'. In *The Significance of Neoplatonism*, ed. R. Baine Harris, 247–62. Albany, NY: State University of New York Press, 1976.
Dillon, John M., *The Middle Platonists, 80 B.C. to A.D. 220.* Ithaca, NY: Cornell University Press, 1977.
Dillon, John M., 'Aisthêsis noêtê: A Doctrine of Spiritual Senses in Origen and in Plotinus'. In *Hellenica and Judaica*, eds André Caquot, Mireille Hadas-Lebel and Jean Riaud, 443–55. Leuven: Peeters, 1986.
Dillon, John M. and A. A. Long, *The Question of 'Eclecticism': Studies in Later Greek Philosophy.* Berkeley: University of California Press, 1988.
Dillon, John M. and Sarah Klitenic Wear, *Dionysius the Areopagite and the Neoplatonist Tradition: Despoiling the Hellenes.* Aldershot: Ashgate, 2007.
Dissanayake, Ellen, *Homo Aestheticus.* Seattle: Washington University Press, 1992.
Dodds, Eric R., 'From Shame Culture to Guilt-Culture'. In Dodds, *The Greeks and the Irrational*, 28–63. Berkeley, CA: University of California Press, 1951.
Dooley, M., *Roger Scruton: The Philosopher on Dover Beach.* London: Bloomsbury, 2009.
Dorman, Robert, *A Word for Nature.* Chapel Hill and London: University of North Carolina Press, 1998.
Duclow, Donald F., '"Whose Image is this?" in Eckhart's Sermones'. In *Masters of Learned Ignorance: Eriugena, Eckhart, Cusanus.* Ashgate: Aldershot, 2006.
Duhem, Pierre, *The Aim and Structure of Physical Theory.* Princeton, NJ: Princeton University Press, 1954.
Eck, Diana L., *Darśán, Seeing the Divine Image in India.* Chambersburg, PA: Anima Books, 1981.
Eckhart, Meister, *Lectura Eckhardi, Predigten Meister Eckharts von Fachgelehrten gelesen und gedeutet*, eds Georg Steer and Loris Sturlese. Stuttgart: Kohlhammer, 1998.
Eckhart, Meister, *The Complete Mystical Works of Meister Eckhart*, trans. and ed. Maurice O'C. Walshe; revised with a foreword by Bernard McGinn. New York: Crossroads, 2001.
Eckhart, Meister, Bernard McGinn, Frank J. Tobin, Elvira Borgstädt and Frank J. Tobin, *Meister Eckhart, Teacher and Preacher.* New York: Paulist Press, 1986.
Edinger, Edward F., Dianne D. Cordic, and Charles Yates, *The New God-image: A Study of Jung's Key Letters Concerning the Evolution of the Western God-image.* Wilmette, IL: Chiron Publications, 1996.

Edmonds, Radcliffe G., *Myths of the Underworld Journey: Plato, Aristophanes, and the 'orphic' Gold Tablets*. Cambridge: Cambridge University Press, 2004.

Edwards, Mark J., 'The Tale of Cupid and Psyche'. *Zeitschrift fuer Papyrologie und Epigraphik* 94 (1992): 77–94.

Edwards, Mark J., *Image, Word, and God in the Early Christian Centuries*. Farnham: Ashgate, 2013.

Elgood, Heather, *Hinduism and the Religious Arts*. London: Cassell, 1999.

Eliade, Mircea, *Images and Symbols: Studies in Religious Symbolism*. Princeton: New Jersey, Princeton University Press, 1961.

Eliade, Mircea, *Shamanism: Archaic Techniques of Ecstasy*. New York: Bollingen Foundation, 1964.

Eliade, Mircea, *Yoga, Immortality and Freedom*. Princeton, NJ: Bollingen, 2009.

Elias, Jamal J., *Aisha's Cushion Religious Art, Perception, and Practice in Islam*. Cambridge, MA: Harvard University Press, 2012.

Elkins, James and David Morgan, *Re-Enchantment*. London: Routledge, 2008.

Embry, Charles, *The Philosopher and the Storyteller: Eric Voegelin and Twentieth Century Literature*. Columbia: University of Missouri, 2008.

Emerson, Ralph Waldo, *Works*. Cambridge, MA: Harvard University Press, 1980.

Empson, William, *Milton's God*. New York: New Directions, 1961.

Eriugena, J. Barbet, ed., *Iohannis Scoti Eriugenae. Expositiones in Ierarchiam Caelestem*. Turnhout: Brepols, 1975.

Erlewine, Robert, *Monotheism and Tolerance: Recovering a Religion of Reason*. Bloomington: Indiana University Press, 2010.

Faivre, Antoine, *Theosophy, Imagination, Tradition: Studies in Western Esotericism*. Albany, NY: State University of New York Press, 2000.

Farrer, Austin, *The Rebirth of Images*. Westminster: Dacre, 1949.

Ficino, Marsilio and Jayne Sears Reynolds, *Commentary on Plato's Symposium on Love*. Dallas, TX: Spring Publications, 1985.

Fiedrowicz, Michael, *Psalmus Vox Totius Christi: Studien zu Augustins "Ennarationes in Psalmos"*. Freiburg Im Breisgau: Herder, 1997.

Findlay, John N., *Plato. The Written and Unwritten Doctrines*. London: Routledge & Kegan Paul, 1974.

Flasch, Kurt, *Metaphysik des Einen. Problemgeschichtliche Stellung und systematische Bedeutung*. Leiden: Brill, 1973.

Flasch, Kurt, 'Procedere ut imago: Das Hervorgehen des Intellekts aus seinem göttlichen Grund bei Meister Dietrich, Meister Eckhart und Berthold von

Moosburg'. In *Abendländischen Mystik im Mittelalter*, ed. Kurt Ruh, 125–34. Stuttgart: Metzler, 1986.

Flasch, Kurt, 'Converti ut imago – Ruckhehr als Bild. Eine Studie zur Theorie des Intellekts bei Dietrich von Freiburg und Meister Eckhart'. In *Albert le Grand et sa reception au moyen age: Freiburger Zeitschrift für Philosophie und Theologie*, 45 (1998): 130–50.

Flasch, Kurt, *Dietrich von Freiburg, Philosophie, Theologie, Naturforschung um 1300*. Frankfurt: Klostermann, 2007.

Florensky, Pavel, *Iconostasis*. Crestwood, NY: St Vladimir's Seminary Press, 1996.

Florensky, Pavel, Nicoletta Misler, and Wendy R. Salmond. *Beyond Vision: Essays on the Perception of Art*. London: Reaktion, 2002.

Fost, Frederic F., 'Playful Illusion: The Making of Worlds in Advaita Vedanta'. *Philosophy East and West* 3 (1998): 387–405.

Fowden, Garth, *Empire to Commonwealth: Consequences of Monotheism in Late Antiquity*. Princeton, NJ: Princeton University Press, 1993.

Frecero, John, 'The Final Image: Paradiso XXXIII, 144' in *Dante, The Poetics of Conversion*. Cambridge: Mass.:Harvard University Press, 1986, pp. 245–57.

Freud, Sigmund, 'Animism, Magic and the Omnipotence of Thought'. In *Totem and Taboo*, trans. and ed. James Strachey. London: W. W. Norton, 1989.

Fuchs, Thomas, 'Fragmented Selves: Temporality and Identity in Borderline Personality Disorder', *Psychopathology* 40 (2007): 379–87.

Fürstenow-Khositashvili, Lily, *Anselm Kiefer – Myth versus History*. Dissertation of the Humboldt University of Berlin, 2011.

Gadamer, Hans Georg and Robert Bernasconi, *The Relevance of the Beautiful and other Essays*. Cambridge: Cambridge University Press, 1986.

Ganeri, Jonardon, *Philosophy in Classical India: The Proper Work of Reason*. London: Routledge, 2001.

Gersh, Stephen E., *From Iamblichus to Eriugena*. Leiden: Brill, 1977.

Gerson, Lloyd P., *Knowing Persons: A Study in Plato*. Oxford: Oxford University Press, 2003.

Gerson, Lloyd P., *Aristotle and other Platonists*. Ithaca, NY: Cornell University Press, 2005.

Gerson, Lloyd P., *From Plato to Platonism*.Ithaca, NY: Cornell University Press, 2013.

Gibbon, Edward, *The History of the Decline and Fall of the Roman Empire*. 3 vols. ed. Womersley, David. London and New York: Penguin, 1994.

Gilson, Etienne, *Painting and Reality*. New York, Meridian Books, 1957.
Godwin, Joscelin, *Harmonies of Heaven and Earth: Mysticism in Music from Antiquity to the Avant-garde*. London: Thames and Hudson, 1987.
Godwin, Joscelyn, *Music, Mysticism and Magic: A Sourcebook*. London: Routledge & Kegan Paul, 1986.
Gombrich, Ernst, 'Icones Symbolicae: The Visual Image in Neo-Platonic Thought'. *Journal of the Warburg and Courtauld Institutes* 11 (1948): 163–92.
Gombrich, Ernst, *Art and Illusion*. New York: Phaidron, 1960.
Graevenitz, Gerhart von, *Mythos: Zur Geschichte einer Denkgewohnheit*. Stuttgart: J. B. Metzler, 1987.
Grafton, Anthony, *Defenders of the Text. The Traditions of Scholarship in an Age of Science, 1450–1800*. Cambridge, MA: Harvard University Press, 1994.
Granoff, Phyllis and Koichi Shinohara, *Images in Asian Religions. Texts and Contexts*. Vancouver: UBC Press, 2004.
Gray, John, *Black Mass: Apocalyptic Religion and the Death of Utopia*. London: Allen Lane, 2007.
Griffiths, Bede, *The Marriage of East and West*. London: Harper Collins, 1982.
Guénon, René, *Etudes sur le Hinduisme*. Paris: Editions Traditionnelles, 1989.
Gutmann, Joseph, *The Image and the Word: Confrontations in Judaism, Christianity and Islam*. Missoula, MT: Scholars Press for the American Academy of Religion, 1977.
Gutting, Gary, *Thinking the Impossible*. Oxford: Oxford University Press, 2011.
Haas, Alois, 'Meister Eckharts mystische Bildlehre'. In *Der Begriff der Repraesentatio im Mittelalter*, ed. Albert Zimmermann, 113–38. Berlin: Walter de Gruyter, 1971.
Hadot, Pierre, 'Conversion'. In *Encyclopaedia Universalis* 4, 979–81. Paris: Encyclopedia universalis France, 1968.
Hall, Peter, *Exposed by the Mask: Form and Language in Drama*. New York: Theatre Communications Group/Saint Paul, MN 2000.
Hamann, Johann Georg, *Sämtliche Werke*, ed. Josef Nadler. Vienna: Verlag Herder, 1949–57.
Hardy, Friedhelm, *Viraha-bhakti: The Early History of Krishna Devotion in South India*. New Delhi: Oxford University Press, 2001.
Harper, Kyle, *From Shame to Sin: The Christian Transformation of Sexual Morality in Late Antiquity*. Cambridge, MA: Harvard University Press, 2013.
Harpham, Edward J., 'Gratitude in the History of Ideas'. In *The Psychology of Gratitude,* eds Robert A. Emmons and Mike E. McCullough, 20–36. Oxford: Oxford University Press, 2004.

Harris, Baine, *The Significance of Neoplatonism*. Norfolk, VA: International Society for Neoplatonic Studies, Old Dominion University, Albany; distributed by State University of New York Press, 1976.

Harris, Erdman, *God's Image and Man's Imagination*. New York: Scribner, 1959.

Harvey, John, *Image of the Invisible: The Visualization of Religion in the Welsh Nonconformist Tradition*. Cardiff: University of Wales Press, 1999.

Haugbolle, Sune and Christiane J. Gruber, *Visual Culture in the Modern Middle East Rhetoric of the Image*. Bloomington, IN: Indiana University Press, 2013.

Hedley, Douglas, 'Pantheism, Trinitarian Theism and the Idea of Unity: Reflections on the Christian Concept of God'. *Religious Studies* 32 (1996): 61–77.

Hedley, Douglas, *Coleridge, Philosophy and Religion: Aids to Reflection and the Mirror of the Spirit*. Cambridge: Cambridge University Press, 2000.

Hedley, Douglas, *Living Forms of the Imagination*. London: T&T Clark, 2008.

Hedley, Douglas, *Sacrifice Imagined: Violence, Atonement and the Sacred*. New York: Continuum, 2011.

Hegel, Georg W. F., *Mythologie der Vernunft. Hegels ältestes Systemprogramm des deutschen Idealismus*, eds Christoph Jamme and Helmut Schneider. Frankfurt am Main: Suhrkamp, 1988.

Heidegger, Martin, *Platons Lehre der Wahrheit*. Bern: Francke, 1947.

Heidegger, Martin, *Was Heisst Denken*. Frankfurt am Main: Klostermann, 1952.

Heidegger, Martin, *Identity and Difference*. New York: Harper & Row, 1969.Heine, Hilde, "Play as an Aesthetic Concept." *The Journal of Aesthetics and Art Criticism* 27 (1968): 67–71.

Hepburn, Ronald W., 'Contemporary Aesthetics and the Neglect of Natural Beauty'. In *British Analytic Philosophy*, eds Bernard Williams and Hugh Montefiore, 206–309. London: Routledge & Kegan Paul, 1966.

Hepburn, Ronald W., 'Landscape and the Metaphysical Imagination'. *Environmental Values* 5 (1996): 191–204.

Hepburn, Ronald W., 'Trivial and Serious in the Aesthetic Appreciation of Nature'. In *The Reach of the Aesthetic: Collected Essays on Art and Nature*, ed. R. Hepburn, 1–15. Aldershot: Ashgate, 2001.

Herder, Johann G. von, *Werke*. Gaier et al. Frankfurt am Main: Surkamp, 1985.

Herling, Bradley L., *The German Gita: Hermeutics and Discipline in the German Reception of Indian Thought*. London: Routledge, 2006.

Hesson, Elizabeth, *Twentieth Century Odyssey: A Study of Heimito von Doderer's Die Dämonen*. Columbia: Camden House, 1982.

Hick, John, 'The Copernican Revolution in Theology'. In *God and the Universe of Faiths*, ed. J. Hick, 120–32. London: Collins, 1977.

Hick, John, *An Interpretation of Religion: Human Responses to the Transcendent*. London: Macmillan, 1989.

Hillegas, Mark, *Shadows of Imagination*. Carbondale: Southern Illinois University Press, 1969.

Hillman, James, *Re-visioning Psychology*. New York: Harper & Row, 1975.

Hillman, James, *The Dream and the Underworld*. New York: Harper & Row, 1979.

Höfling, Helmut and Wilhelm Szilasi, *Beiträge zu Philosophie und Wissenschaft*. München: Francke, 1960.

Hooper, Walter, ed. *The Collected Letters of C. S. Lewis*, Volume II: Books, Broadcasts, and the War 1931–1949. HarperOne 2004.

Hope, Nicholson, Marjorie, *Mountain Gloom, Mountain Glory*. Ithaca, NY: Cornell University Press, 1959.

Hopkins, Gerard M., 'No Worst, There is None. Pitched Past Pitch of Grief' and 'Carrion Comfort'. In *The Poems of Gerard Manley Hopkins*. London: Oxford University Press, 1967.

Hopkins, Robert, *Picture, Image and Experience: A Philosophical Inquiry*. Cambridge: Cambridge University Press, 1998.

Howells, Christina, *Sartre's Theory of Literature*. London: Modern Humanities Research Association, 1979.

Hughes, Christopher, *On a Complex Theory of a Simple God: An Investigation in Aquinas' Philosophical Theology*. Ithaca, NY: Cornell University Press, 1989.

Hughes, Glenn, *Mystery and Myth in the Philosophy of Eric Voegelin*. Columbia: University of Missouri Press, 1993.

Hume, David and Richard H. Popkin, *Dialogues Concerning Natural Religion and the Posthumous Essays, of the Immortality of the Soul and of Suicide*, ed. Richard H. Popkin. Indianapolis: Hackett Publishing, 1980.

Hume, David, *Treatise of Human Nature* 2nd ed. Nidditch. Oxford: OUP, 1981.

Hume, David, *Principal Writings on Religion*, ed. J. C. A Gaskin. Oxford: OUP, 1993.

Hüppauf, Bernd-Rüdiger and Christoph Wulf, *Dynamics and Performativity of Imagination: The Image between the Visible and the Invisible*. New York: Routledge, 2009.

Husserl, Edmund, *Phenomenology and the Crisis of Philosophy*, Translated with Notes and an Introduction by Quentin Lauer. Harper Torchbooks, 1965.

Hyde, Thomas, *The Poetic Theology of Love: Cupid in Renaissance Literature*. Newark: University of Delaware Press, 1986.
Ibn Arabi, *The Bezels of Wisdom*, trans. R. W. J. Austin. Mahwah, NJ: Paulist Press, 1980.
Ingelo, Nathaniel, *Bentivolio and Urania, in Four Books*. London: J. Grismond, 1660.
Ingelo, Nathaniel, *Bentivolio and Urania, the Second Part*. London: J. Grismond, 1664.
Jackson, Frank, 'What Mary Didn't Know'. *Journal of Philosophy* 83 (1986): 291–5.
James, Sue, *Spinoza on Philosophy, Religion, and Politics: The Theologico-Political Treatise*. Oxford: Oxford University Press, 2012.
Janaway, Christopher, *Self and World in Schopenhauer's Philosophy*. Oxford: Oxford University Press, 1999.
Jarvis, Robin, *Romantic Writing and Pedestrian Travel*. London: Macmillan, 1997.
Johnston, Mark, *Saving God: Religion after Idolatry*. Princeton, NJ: Princeton University Press, 2009.
Johnston, Mark, *Surviving Death*. Princeton, NJ: Princeton University Press, 2010.
Jonas, Hans, 'Tool, Image and Grave: On What is Beyond the Animal in Man'. In *Mortality and Morality, A Search for the Good After Auschwitz*, ed. Laurence Vogel, 75–86. Evanston, IL: Northwestern University Press, 1996.
Jonas, Hans, 'Image Making and the Freedom of Man'. In *The Phenomenon of Life: Towards a Philosophical Biology*, ed. Hans Jonas, 157–75. Evanston, IL: Northwestern University Press, 2001.
Jonas, Hans, 'The Nobility of Sight: A Study in the Phenomenology of the Senses'. In *The Phenomenon of Life: Towards a Philosophical Biology*, ed. Hans Jonas, 135–56. Evanston, IL: Northwestern University Press, 2001.
Joy, Morny, *Imagination*. 'Image and Imagination'. In *Encyclopedia of Religion*. Vol. 7, ed. Mircea Eliade. New York: Macmillan Publishing Company, 1987, 104–9.
Jung, Werner, *Von der Mimesis zur Simulation: Eine Einführung in die Geschichte der ästhetik*. Hamburg: Junius, 1995.
Kant, Immanuel, *Critique of Pure Reason*, trans. Norman Kemp Smith. London: Macmillan, 1933.
Kant, Immanuel, *Religion within the Boundaries of Mere Reason And Other Writings*, trs. Allen Wood and George di Giovanni. Cambridge: CUP, 2004, §6:192, p. 184.
Kavka, Martin, 'Judaism and the Visual Image: A Jewish Theology of Art (book-review)'. *Journal of Religion* 91 (2011): 278–80.
Kennedy, Helena, *Justice and Human Rights*. London: The Athenaeum, 2014.
Kenney, John, *Mystical Monotheism*. Wipf & Stock Publishing, 2010.

Kenney, John, *The Mysticism of Saint Augustine: Rereading the Confessions*. London: Routledge, 2005.

Kenny, Anthony and John Patrick, *Aquinas on Being*. Oxford: Clarendon Press 2002.

Kiefer, Anselm, *Exhibition Catalogue*. London: Royal Academy, 2014.

King, Evan, 'Robert Crouse on Meister Eckhart'. *Dionysius* 30 (2012): 101–16.

King-Farlow, John, *The Challenge of Religion Today: Essays on the Philosophy of Religion*. New York: Science History Publications, 1976.

Knowles, Dudley, *Explanation and its Limits*. Cambridge: Cambridge University Press, 1990.

Koerner, Joseph Leo, *The Reformation of the Image*. Chicago IL: University of Chicago Press, 2004.

Kolakowski, Leszek, *The Presence of Myth*, trans. by Adam Czerniawski, 138 pp. Chicago, IL: University of Chicago Press, 1989.

Koslowski, Peter, *The Concept of God, the Origin of the World, and the Image of the Human in the World Religions*. Dordrecht: Kluwer Academic Publishers, 2001.

Kroner, Richard, *The Religious Function of Imagination*. London: Oxford University Press, 1941.

Kuhn, Annette, *The Power of the Image: Essays on Representation and Sexuality*. London: Routledge & Kegan Paul, 1985.

Lakoff, George and Johnson, Mark, *Metaphors We Live By*. Chicago: University of Chicago, 1980.

Lakoff and Johnson, *Metaphors We Live By*, Chicago: University of Chicago, 1980.

Lamarche, Paul et al., eds, 'Image et ressemblance', *Dictionnaire de spiritualité*, vol. 7 (1969): 1401–72.

Lauster, Jörg, *Die Verzauberung der Welt. Eine Kuturgeschichte des Christentums*. Munich: Beck, 2014.

Lavelle, Louis, *The Dilemma of Narcissus*. London: Allen & Unwin, 1973.

Layard, John, *The Lady of the Hare; Being a Study in the Healing Power of Dreams*. London: Faber & Faber, 1944.

Lear, Jonathan, *Love and its Place in Nature: A Philosophical Interpretation of Freudian Psychoanalysis*. New York: Farrar Straus Giroux, 1990.

Lee, Rensselaer Wright, 'Ut Pictura Poesis: The Humanistic Theory of Painting', *Art Bulletin* 22 (1940): 197–269.

Leff, Gordon, *Medieval Thought: St Augustine to Ockham*. London: Merlin Press, 1958.

Leithart, Peter, *Gratitude: An Intellectual History*. Waco, TX: Baylor, 2014.

Lessing, Gotthold E., *Gesammelte Werke*, 10 vols, ed. Paul Rilla. Berlin: Aufbau Verlag, 1954–58.

Lessing, Gotthold E., *Werke and Briefe*, ed. Wilfried Barner. Frankfurt a.M.: Deutscher Klassiker, 1990.

Lévy-Bruhl, Lucien and Lilian A. Clare, *The 'Soul' of the Primitive*. London: G. Allen & Unwin Ltd, 1928.

Lewis, Clive S., *The Four Loves*. London: Geoffrey Bles, 1960.

Lewis, Clive S., *Experiment in Criticism*. Cambridge: Cambridge University Press, 1961.

Lewis, Clive S., *Preface to George Macdonald*. New York: Macmillan Publishing Co., Inc., 1978.

Lewis, Clive S., *Reflections on the Psalms*. Orlando: Harcourt, 1986.

Liber XXIV philosophorum. In *Le livre des XXIV philosophes: résurgence d'un texte du IVe siècle*, trans. Françoise Hudry. Paris: Vrin, 2009.

Lincoln, Bruce, *Theorising Myth: Narrative, Ideology and Scholarship*. Chicago, IL: Chicago University Press, 1999.

Lings, Martin, *Symbol and Archetype: A Study of the Meaning of Existence*. Louisville, KY: Fons Vitae, 2006.

Lipner, Julius, *The Face of Truth: A Study of Meaning and Metaphysics in the Vedantic Theology of Ramanuja*. Albany: State University of New York, 1976.

Lobsien, Verena Olejniczak and Claudia Olk, *Neuplatonismus und Ästhetik: Zur Transformationsgeschichte des Schönen*. Berlin: De Gruyter, 2007.

Lopez, C., P. Halje and O. Blanke, 'Body Ownership and Embodiment: Vestibular and Multisensory Mechanisms'. *Clinical Neurophysiology* 38 (2008): 149–61.

Lucretius, *De Rerum Natura*, trans. W. H. D. Rouse. Revised with new text, introduction, notes, and index by Martin Ferguson Smith. London: Heinemann, 1975.

Luft, David, *Eros and Inwardness*. Chicago, IL: University of Chicago Press, 2003.

Lyons, John D., *Before Imagination Embodied Thought from Montaigne to Rousseau*. Stanford, CA: Stanford University Press, 2005.

MacDonald, Scott Charles, *Being and Goodness: The Concept of the Good in Metaphysics and Philosophical Theology*. Ithaca, NY: Cornell University Press, 1991.

Mackey, James P., *Religious Imagination*. Edinburgh: Edinburgh University Press 1986.

MacQueen, Graeme, 'Inspired Speech in Early Mahāyāna Buddhism I'. *Religion* 11 (1981): 303–19.

MacQueen, Graeme, 'Inspired Speech in Early Mahāyāna Buddhism II'. *Religion* 12 (1982): 49–65.

MacSwain, Robert and Michael Ward, *The Cambridge Companion to C. S. Lewis* Cambridge: Cambridge University Press, 2010.
Magnard, Pierre, 'Imago Dei, Imago Mundi'. *Miroirs et reflets, Cahier du centre de recherche sur l'image, le symbole, le mythe*, 4 (1989): 47–64.
Maimonides, Moses, *The Guide for the Perplexed*, ed. M. Friedländer. New York: Dover Publications, 1956.
Mann, Charles C., 'The Birth of Religion'. *National Geographic* (June 2011): 39–59.
Mann, Thomas, *Doktor Faustus*. Frankfurt a.M.: Fischer Verlag, 2003.
Marback, Richard, *Plato's Dream of Sophistry*. Columbia: University of South Carolina Press, 1999.
Marchand, Suzanne L., *German Orientalism in the Age of Empire: Religion, Race, and Scholarship*. Cambridge: Cambridge University Press, 2009.
Marenbon, John, *Pagans and Philosophers. The Problem of Paganism from Augustine to Leibniz*. Princeton, NJ: Princeton University Press, 2015.
Marinus, *Vita Procli*. In *Neoplatonic Saints. The Lives of Plotinus and Proclus by their Students*, trans. Mark Edwards. Liverpool: Liverpool University Press, 2000, pp. 58–115.
Marion, Jean-Luc, *L'idole et la distance: Cinq études*. Paris: B. Grasset, 1977.
Marion, Jean-Luc, *Réduction et donation: Recherches sur husserl, heidegger et la phénoménologie*. Paris: Presses Universitaires de France, 1989.
Marion, Jean-Luc, *La croisée du visible*. Paris: Presses Universitaires de France, 1996.
Marion, Jean-Luc, *Reduction and Givenness: Investigations of Husserl, Heidegger, and Phenomenology*. Evanston, IL: Northwestern University Press, 1998.
Marion, Jean-Luc, *The Idol and Distance: Five Studies*. New York: Fordham University Press, 2001.
Marion, Jean-Luc, *Dieu sans l'être*. Paris: Presses Universitaires de France, 2002.
Marion, Jean-Luc, *The Crossing of the Visible*. Stanford, CA: Stanford University Press, 2004.
Marion, Jean-Luc, *Le visible et le révélé*. Paris: Cerf, 2005.
Marion, Jean-Luc, *The Erotic Phenomenon*. Chicago, IL: University of Chicago Press, 2007.
Marion, Jean-Luc, *Au lieu de soi L'approche de St Augustin*. Paris: Presses Universitaires de France, 2008. Translated as *In the Self's Place: The Approach of St Augustine*, trans. J. Kosky. Stanford, CA: Stanford University Press, 2012.
Marion, Jean-Luc, *God Without Being: Hors-texte*, trans. and ed. Thomas A. Carlson and David Tracy. Chicago IL: University of Chicago Press, 2012.

Marion, Jean-Luc and Dan Arbib, *La rigueur des choses*. Paris: Flammarion, 2012.

Marion, Jean-Luc and Stephen E. Lewis, *The Reason of the Gift*. Charlottesville: University of Virginia Press, 2011.

Marks, Jonathan, *What It Means to Be 98% Chimpanzee: Apes, People, and Their Genes*. Berkeley: University of California, 2003.

Marks, Jonathan, *The Alternative Introduction to Biological Anthropology*. New York: Oxford University Press, 2012.

Marks, Jonathan, *Tales of the Ex-Apes: How We Think about Human Evolution*. Oakland: University of California Press, 2015.

Martin, David, *Art and the Religious Experience: The 'Language' of the Sacred*. Lewisburg, PA: Bucknell University Press, 1972.

Martingale, Andrew, *Gothic Art*. London: Thames and Hudson, 1986.

Marvell, Andrew, 'The Garden'. In *Andrew Marvell*, eds Frank Kermode and Keith Walker, 48. Oxford: Oxford University Press, 1990.

Masson, J. L., 'Imagination vs. effort'. *Journal of Indian Philosophy* 1 (1971): 296–9.

Matsuzawa, Tetsuro, *Primate Origins of Human Cognition and Behaviour*. Hong Kong: Springer, 2008.

McCall, Thomas H. and Michael C. Rea, *Philosophical and Theological Essays on the Trinity*. Oxford: Oxford University Press, 2009.

McCoull, Leslie S. B., 'A Woman Named Damaris: Pseudo-Dionysius' Celestial Hierarchy in The Place of the Lion'. In *Charles Williams and his Contemporaries*, eds Suzanne Bray and Richard Sturch. Newcastle: Cambridge Scholars, 2009.

McDannell, Colleen and Bernhard Lang, *Heaven, A History*. New Haven, CT: Yale Note Bene 2001.

McFarland, Ian A., *The Divine Image: Envisioning the Invisible God*. Minneapolis: Fortress Press, 2005.

McGilchrist, Iain, *The Master and his Emissary: The Divided Brain and the Making of the Western World*. New Haven, CT: Yale University Press, 2010.

McGinn, Bernard, *The Harvest of Mysticism in Medieval Germany: Volume IV in the Presence of God Series*. New York: The Crossroad Publishing Company, 2005.

McGinn, Colin, *The Power of Movies: How Screen and Mind Interact*. New York: Pantheon Books, 2005.

Medcalf, Stephen, 'The Athanasian Principle in Williams's use of Images'. In *The Rhetoric of Vision: Essays on Charles Williams*, eds Charles A. Huttar and Peter J. Schakel, 27–43. Bucknell: Lewisburg, 1996.

Merricks, Trenton, *Truth and Ontology*. Oxford: Clarendon Press, 2007.
Metzler, Dieter, *Porträt und Gesellschaft: über die Entstehung des griechischen Portraets in der Klassik*. Münster: Wasmuth, 1971.
Middleton, J. Richard, *The Liberating Image*. Grand Rapids: Baker, 2005.
Millington, Constance, *Whether We be Many or Few*: a history of the Cambridge/Delhi Brotherhood. Bangalore: Asian Trading Corporation, 1999.
Milton, John, *Paradise Lost*, ed. Alasdair Fowler. London: Longman, 1971.
Mirandola, Pico della, *Pico della Mirandola: Oration on the Dignity of Man, A New Translation and Commentary*, eds Francesco Borghesi, Michael Papio and Massimo Riva. Cambridge: Cambridge University Press, 2012.
Mitchell, William J. T., *Iconology. Image, Text, Ideology*. Chicago, IL: University of Chicago, 1986.
Mitchell, William J. T., *Picture Theory: Essays on Verbal and Visual Interpretation*. Chicago, IL: University of Chicago, 1994.
Mithen, Steven, *The Prehistory of the Mind: A Search for the Origins of Art, Religion and Science*. London: Thames and Hudson, 1996.
Mitter, Partha, *Much Maligned Monsters: A History of European Reactions to Indian Art*. Chicago, IL: University of Chicago Press, 1992.
Mitter, Partha, 'Rammohun Roy et le nouveau language du monotheisme'. In *L'impensable Polytheisme: Etudes d'historiographie religieuse*, ed. Francis Schmidt, 257–97. Chippenham: Anthony Rowe, 1988.
Mojsisch, Burkhard, *Meister Eckhart: Analogie, Univozität und Einheit*. Hamburg: Felix Meiner, 1983.
Monk, William Henry, ed., *Hymns Ancient and Modern*. London: J. Alfred Novello, 1861.
Monti, Martino Rossi, *Il cielo in terra: La grazi fra teologia ed estetica*. Turin: Libreria, 2008.
Moog-Grünewald, Maria, *Eros – zur Ästhetisierung eines (neu)platonischen Philosophems in Neuzeit und Moderne*. Heidelberg: Winter, 2006.
Mooney, Hilary Anne-Marie, *Theophany: The Appearing of God According to the Writings of Johannes Scottus Eriugena*. Tubingen: Mohr-Siebeck, 2009.
Moosa, Ebrahim, *Ghazālī and the Poetics of Imagination*. Chapel Hill, NC: University of North Carolina Press, 2005.
More, Henry, *Conjectura Cabbalistica*. London: Flesher, 1653.
More, Henry, *Discourses on Several Texts of Scripture*. London: JR, 1692.
More, Henry, *Divine Dialogues*. London: James Flesher, 1668.

More, Henry, *Apocalypsis Apocalypseos*. London: J. Martyn, and W. Kettilby, at the Bell, and the Bishops-Head in St Paul's Church-yard, 1680.

Moreland, James Porter, *Recalcitrant imago Dei: Human Persons and the Failure of Naturalism*. London: SCM in association with the Center of Theology and Philosophy, University of Nottingham 2009.

Morris, Thomas V., *Anselmian Explorations: Essays in Philosophical Theology*. Notre Dame, IN: University of Notre Dame Press, 1986.

Mossakowski, Stanislaw, 'S. Raphael's "St Cecilia": An Iconographical Study'. *Zeitschrift fuer Kunstgeschichte* 31 (1968): 1–26.

Moyn, Samuel, 'Personalism, Community and the Origin of Human Rights'. In *Human Rights in the Twentieth Century*, ed. Stephan Ludwig Hoffman, 85–106. Cambridge: Cambridge University Press, 2011.

Mueller, Max, *The Six Systems of Indian Philosophy*. London: Longmans, Green & Co., 1919.

Muessig, Caroline and Putter Ad, eds, *Envisaging Heaven in the Middle Ages*. London: Routledge, 2007.

Musacchio, George, 'C. S. Lewis, T. S. Eliot and the Anglican Psalter', *An Anglo-American Literary Review* 22 (2005): 45–55.

Myers, Doris T., *Bareface: A Guide to C. S. Lewis's Last Novel*. Columbia: University of Missouri Press, 2004.

Nahm, Milton Charles and Milton C. Nahm, *Genius and Creativity; An Essay in the History of Ideas*. New York, Harper & Row, 1965.

Narbonne, Jean-Marc, *Hénologie, Ontologie et Ereignis (Plotin- Proclus-Heidegger)*. Paris: Les Belles Lettres, 2001.

Narbonne, Jean-Marc, *Plotinus in Dialogue with the Gnostics*. Leiden: Brill, 2011.

Nasr, Sayyed Hossein, 'The World of Imagination and the Concept of Space in the Persian Miniature'. *Islamic Quarterly* 13 (1969): 129–34.

Nassar, Dalia, *The Romantic Absolute: Being and Knowing in Early German Romantic Philosophy, 1795–1804*. Chicago, IL: University of Chicago Press, 2014.

Nehamas, Alexander, *Only a Promise of Happiness: The Place of Beauty in a World of Art*. Princeton, NJ: Princeton University Press, 2007.

Nelson, Charles, Nathan A. Fox and Charles H. Zeanah, *Romania's Abandoned Children, Brain Development, and the Struggle for Recovery*. Cambridge, MA: Harvard University Press, 2014.

Nichols, Angus, *Myth and the Human Sciences: Hans Blumenberg's Theory of Myth*. London: Routledge, 2015.

Nichols, Shaun, *The Architecture of the Imagination: New Essays on Pretence, Possibility, and Fiction.* Oxford: Clarendon, 2006.

Nicolson, Marjorie Hope, *Mountain Gloom and Mountain Glory: The Development of the Aesthetics of the Infinite.* Seattle, WA: University of Washington Press, 1997.

Nietzsche, Friedrich, *The Anti-Christ. The Twilight of the Idols and the Anti-Christ: or How to Philosophize with a Hammer*, trans. R. J. Hollindale. Harmondsworth: Penguin, 1990.

Nietzsche, Friedrich, *Kritische Gesamtausgabe.* 40 vols, Giorgio Colli, Mazzino Montinari, Wolfgang Muller-Lauter, Karl Pestalozzi, De Gruyter, 1996–.

Norris Clarke, William, 'The Problem of the Reality and Multiplicity of Divine Ideas in Christian Neoplatonism'. In *Neoplatonism and Christian Thought*, ed. Dominic J. O'Meara, 109–27. Albany, NY: State University of New York Press, 1982.

Noyes, James, *The Politics of Iconoclasm: Religion, Violence and the Culture of Image-breaking in Christianity and Islam.* London: I. B. Tauris & Co. Ltd, 2013.

O'Hear, Anthony, *Beyond Evolution, Human Nature and the Limits of Evolutionary Explanation.* Oxford: Oxford University Press, 1997.

O'Hear, Anthony and O'Hear, Natasha, *Picturing the Apocalypse: The Book of Revelation in the Arts over Two Millennia.* Oxford: OUP, 2015.

Olivelle, Patrick, trans., *The Upanishads.* Oxford: Oxford University Press, 1996.

O'Meara, Thomas F., *Romantic Idealism and Roman Catholicism: Schelling and the Theologians.* Notre Dame, IN: University of Notre Dame Press, 1982.

Origen, *Commentary on Romans*, trans. Thomas P. Sheck. Washington: Catholic University of America, 2001.

Oster, Patricia, *Der Schleier im Text. Funktionsgeschichte eines Bildes für die neuzeitliche Erfahrung des Imaginären*, Munich: Fink, 2002.

Otto, Rudolf, *Gnadenreligion: Indiens und das Christentum.* Gotha: Klotz, 1930.

Owen, Huw Parri, *Concepts of Deity.* New York: Herder and Herder, 1971.

Palmer, John A., *Plato's Reception of Parmenides.* Oxford: Oxford University Press, 1999.

Panofsky, Erwin, *Studies in Iconology, Humanistic Themes in the Art of the Renaissance.* New York: Harper Row, 1962.

Panofsky, Erwin, *Idea: A Concept in Art Theory.* New York: Harper Row, 1968.

Parker, Robert, 'Greek Religion'. In *The Oxford History of the Classical World*, eds John Boardman, Jasper Griffin and Oswyn Murray, 254–74. Oxford: Oxford University Press, 1986.

Parkin, Jon, *Taming the Leviathan*. Cambridge: Cambridge University Press, 2007.
Pasnau, Robert, *Metaphysical Themes 1274-1671*. Oxford: Oxford University Press, 2011.
Pausanias, *Pausanias' Description of Greece with an English Translation* 1-4, eds W. H. S. Jones and H. A. Ormerod. Cambridge, MA: Harvard University Press, 1918.
Pears, David, *Paradox and Platitude in Wittgenstein's Philosophy*. Oxford: Oxford University Press, 2006.
Peers, Glen, *Subtle Bodies: Representing Angels in Byzantium*. Berkeley: University of California Press, 2001.
Pender, Elizabeth E., *Images of Persons Unseen: Plato's Metaphors for the Gods and the Soul*. Sankt Augustin: Academia, 2000.
Pendergrast, Mark, *Mirror Mirror: A History of the Human Love Affair with Reflection*. New York: Basic Books, 2003.
Perl, Eric D., *Theophany: The Neoplatonic Philosophy of Dionysius the Areopagite*. Albany, NY: State University of New York Press, 2007.
Philostratus, *Apollonius of Tyana*, VIII, 22, 5ff, trans. Christopher Jones. Cambridge: Loeb, 2005.
Pieper, Josef, *Happiness and Contemplation*. South Bend, IN: Notre Dame, 1998.
Pieper, Josef, *In Tune with the World: A Theory of Festivity*, South Bend, IN: St. Augustine's Press, 1999.
Pippin, Robert B., *After the Beautiful: Hegel and the Philosophy of Pictorial Modernism*, Chicago, IL: University of Chicago Press, 2014.
Plato, and Francis Macdonald Cornford, *Plato's Theory of Knowledge; The Theaetetus and the Sophist of Plato*. London: Routledge & Kegan Paul, 1935.
Plautus, Amphitryon, trans., Wolfgang de Melo. Cambridge: Loeb, 2011.
Poirel, Dominique, 'Symbolice et anagogice: l'école de Saint-Victor et la naissance du style gothique'. In *L'abbé Suger, La manifest gothique ed Saint Deis et las pensée victorine*, ed. Dominique Poirel. Paris: Brepols, 2001.
Pollock, Sheldon I., *The Language of the Gods in the World of Men: Sanskrit, Culture, and Power in Premodern India*. Berkeley: University of California Press, 2006.
Prager, Brad, *Aesthetic Vision and German Romanticism: Writing Images*. Rochester, NY: Camden House, 2007.
Pretila, Noel, *Re-appropriating 'Marvellous Fables': Justin Martyr's Strategic Retrieval Myth in I Apology*. Eugene: Pickwick, 2014.

Probst, Jorg and Klenner, Jost Philipp, *Ideengeschichte der Bildwissenschaft*. Frankfurt am Main: Surkamp, 2009.

Prosad Sil, Narasingha, *Swami Vivekananda: A Reassessment*. London: Associated Universities Presses, 1997.

Proust Marcel, Jean Santeuil trs. Gerard Hopkins. Norwich, Jarrold & Sons.

Pseudo-Dionysius the Areopagite, *The Works of Dionysius the Areopagite*, trans. and ed. John Parker. Merrick, NY: Richwood Publishing Co., 1976.

Pseudo-Dionysius the Areopagite, *Dionysius the Areopagite: On the Divine Names and Mystical Theology*, trans. Clarence E. Rolt. New York, Macmillan Co., 1940.

Radhakrishnan, Sarvapali, *East and West and the End of their Separation*. New York: Harper and Brothers, 1956.

Radhakrishnan, S. and A. Moore, *Sourcebook in Indian Philosophy*. Princeton, NJ: Princeton University Press, 1967.

Raphael, Melissa, *Judaism and the Visual Image: a Jewish Theology of Art*. New York: Continuum, 2009.

Read, Herbert, *The Forms of Things Unknown*. London: Faber & Faber, 1960.

Rees, Valery, *From Gabriel to Lucifer: A Cultural History of Angels*. London: I B Tauris, 2013.

Reilly, Robert James, *Romantic Religion: A Study of Barfield, Lewis, Williams and Tolkien*. Athens: University of Georgia Press, 1971.

Renfrew, Colin and Iain Morley, *Image and Imagination: A Global Prehistory of Figurative Representation*. Cambridge: McDonald Institute of Archeological Research, University of Cambridge, 2007.

Riem Natale, Antonella, *The One Life, Coleridge and Hinduism*. Jaipur: Rawat, 2005.

Rorty, Richard, *Philosophy and the Mirror of Nature*. Princeton, NJ. Princeton University Press, 1979.

Rosenblum, Robert, *Modern Painting and the Northern Romantic Tradition*. London: Thames and Hudson, 1975.

Rousseau, Jean-Jacques, *Confessions*, trans. J. Cohen. Harmondsworth: Penguin, 1973.

Rowland, Christopher, *The Open Heaven*. New York: Crossroad, 1982.

Roxburgh, David J., *Prefacing the Image: The Writing of Art. History in Sixteenth-Century Iran*. Leiden: Brill, 2001

Rudd, Anthony, 'In Defence of Narrative'. *European Journal of Philosophy* 17.1 (2009): 60–75.

Rudman, Stanley, *Concepts of Person and Christian Ethics*. Cambridge: Cambridge University Press, 1997.

Ruh, Kurt, *Abendländische Mystik im Mittelalter: Symposion Kloster Engelberg 1984*. Stuttgart: J. B. Metzler, 1986.

Ryan, Christopher, *Schopenhauer's Philosophy of Religion: The Death of God and the Oriental Renaissance*. Leuven: Peeters, 2010.

Saarinen, Risto, *God and the Gift: An Ecumenical Theology of Giving*. Collegeville, MN: Liturgical Press, 2005.

Safranski, Rüdiger, *Heidegger. Ein Meister aus Deutschland: Heidegger und seine Zeit*. Frankfurt am Main: Fischer Taschenbuch, 1997.

Saïd, Suzanne, Deux noms de l'image en grec ancient: idole et icône *Comptes rendus des séances de l'Academie des Inscriptions et Belles-Lettres*, v. 131, v. 2 (1987), 309–30.

Sartre, Jean-Paul, *L'imaginaire: psychologie phenomenologique de l'imagination*. Paris: Gallimard, 1940.

Sartre, Jean-Paul, *L'Être et le Néant*. Paris: Gallimard, 1948.

Sartre, Jean-Paul, *Qu'est que c'est la literature?* Paris: Gallimard, 1948.

Scarry, Elaine, *On Beauty and Being Just*, Princeton, NJ: Princeton University Press, 1999.

Schakel, Peter J., *Reason and Imagination in C. S. Lewis: A Study of Till We Have Faces*. Grand Rapids, MI: W. B. Eerdmans Publishing Co., 1984.

Schama, Simon, *Landscape and Memory*. New York: Knopf, 1995.

Schefer, Christina, *Platon und Apollon: Vom Logos zurück zum Mythos*. Sankt Augustin: Academia Verlag, 1996.

Schefold, Karl, 'Statuen auf Vasenbildern', *Jahrbuch des deutschen archäologischen Instituts* 52 (1937): 30–75.

Schelling, Andrew, *The Oxford Anthology of Bhakti Literature*, xvi. Oxford: Clarendon, 2011.

Schelling, Friedrich W. J., *Werke 1–6*, ed. Manfred Schröter. Munich: Beck, 1959.

Schelling, Friedrich W. J., *Über das Wesen der Menschlichen Freiheit*. Stuttgart: Reclam, 1964.

Schelling, Friedrich W. J., *Philosophie der Offenbarung*. Darmstadt: Wissenschaftliche Buchgesellschaft, 1974.

Schelling, Friedrich W. J., *The Philosophy of Art*. Minneapolis: University of Minnesota, 1995.

Schier, Flint, *Deeper into Pictures: An Essay on Pictorial Representation*. Cambridge: Cambridge University Press, 1986.

Schlegel, Friedrich von, *Ueber die Sprache und Weisheit der Indier. Ein Beitrag zur Begründung der Alterthumskunde; Nebst metrischen Übersetzungen Indischer Gedichte*. Heidelberg: Mohr und Zimmer, 1808.

Schlutz, Alexander M., *Mind's World, Imagination, and Subjectivity from Descartes to Romanticism*. Seattle, WA: University of Washington Press, 2009.

Scholz, Oliver R., *Bild, Darstellung, Zeichen: Philosophische theorien bildlicher darstellung*. Frankfurt am Main: Klostermann, 2004.

Schopenhauer, Arthur, *Die Welt als Wille und Vorstellung* (Zurich: Diogenes, 1977), vol. 1, p. 29.

Schroeder, Frederic M., *Apperception und Vorurteil: Untersuchungen zur Reflexion Heimito von Doderers*. Heidelberg: Winter, 1976.

Schroeder, Frederic M., *Form and Transformation: A Study in the Philosophy of Plotinus*. Montreal and Buffalo: McGill-Queen's University Press, 1992.

Scruton, Roger, *Art and Imagination: A Study in the Philosophy of Mind*. London: Methuen, 1974.

Scruton, Roger, 'Fantasy, Imagination, and the Screen', *Grazer Philosophische Studien 19 (1983), 35–46*.

Scruton, Roger, *Modern Philosophy: An Introduction and Survey*. New York: Penguin Press, 1995.

Scruton, Roger, *The Aesthetic Understanding: Essays in the Philosophy of Art and Culture* South Bend, IN: St. Augustine's Press, 1998.

Scruton, Roger, *Modern Culture*. London: Continuum, 2005.

Scruton, Roger, *Sexual Desire: A Philosophical Investigation*. London: Phoenix, 1994.

Scruton, Roger, *Beauty*. New York: OUP, 2009.

Scruton, Roger, *I Drink Therefore I Am*. London: Continuum, 2009.

Scruton, Roger, *The Face of God: The Gifford Lectures 2010*. London: Continuum, 2012.

Scruton, Roger, *The Aesthetics of Architecture*. Princeton, NJ: Princeton University Press, 2013.

Scruton, Roger, *The Soul of the World*. Princeton, NJ: Princeton University Press, 2014.

Scruton, Roger, *Green Philosophy: How to Think Seriously about the Planet*. London: Atlantic, 2014.

Seaford, Richard, *Money and the Early Greek Mind: Homer, Philosophy, Tragedy*. Cambridge: Cambridge University Press, 2004.

Sen, Ramendra K., 'Imagination in Coleridge and Abhinavagupta: A Critical Analysis of Christian and Saiva Standpoints'. *Journal of Aesthetics and Art Criticism* 24 (1965): 97–107.

Seneca, *Tragedies*, vol. 1, ed. and trans. John G. Fitch. Cambridge, MA: Loeb, 2002.

Seznec, Jean, *The Survival of the Pagan Gods: The Mythological Tradition and its*

Place in Renaissance Humanism and Art, trans. Barbara F. Sessions. New York: Pantheon Books for the Bollingen Foundation, 1953.

Shakespeare, William, *The Winter's Tale*, by Anthony David Nuttall. London: Arnold, 1996.

Sharma, B. N. Krishnamurti, *Philosophy of Sri Madhvacarya*. Delhi: Motilal Banarsidass, 1991.

Shelley, Percy Bysshe, *The Major Works*, eds Zachary Leader and Michael O'Neill, Oxford: Oxford University Press, 2009.

Sherman, Jacob, *Partakers of the Divine: Contemplation and the Practice of Philosophy*. Minneapolis: Fortress Press, 2014.

Shulman, David, 'Illumination, imagination, creativity: Rājaśekhara, kuntaka, and jagannātha on pratibhā'. *Journal of Indian Philosophy* 36 (2008): 481–505.

Simonds, P. Munoz, *Myth, Emblem, and Music in Shakespeare's Cymbeline: An Iconographic Reconstruction*. Newark: University of Delaware Press, 1992.

Singleton, Esther, *Great Pictures as Seen and Described by Famous Writers*. New York, Dodd, Mead and Company, 1899.

Sklar, Jonathan, *Landscapes of the Dark: History, Trauma and Psychoanalysis* London: Karnac Books, 2011.

Smith, John E., *Select Dicourses*. London and Cambridge: Flesher, 1660.

Smith, John E., *Select Discourses*. Royston: Flesher, 1660.

Smith, John E., *Reason and God; Encounters of Philosophy with Religion*. New Haven, CT: Yale University Press, 1961.

Solnit, Rebecca, *Wanderlust: A History of Walking*. London: Granta, 2014.

Sreekantaiya, T. Nanjundaiya, *Imagination in Indian Poetics and other Literary Studies*. Mysore: Geetha Book House, 1980.

Stafford, Emma, *Worshipping Virtues: Personification and the Divine in Ancient Greece*. London: Duckworth, 2000.

Stanford, William Bedell, *The Ulysses Theme; A Study in the Adaptability of a Traditional Hero*. New York, Barnes and Noble, 1964.

Strawson, Galen, 'Against Narrativity', *Ratio* 2004, 17, pp. 428–54.

Stroumsa, Guy G., 'On the Early History of the *Visio Beatifica*'. In *Mystical Approaches to God*, ed. Peter Schäfer, 67–80. Munich: Oldenbourg, 2006.

Sturlese, Loris, 'Von der Wuerde des unwurdigen Menschen'. In Loris Sturlese, *Homo divinus Philosophische Projekte in Deutschland zwischen Meister Eckhart und Heinrich Seuse*, 35–45. Stuttgart: Kohlhammer, 2007.

Sullivan, Kevin P., *Wrestling with Angels: A Study of the Relationship between Angels and Humans in Ancient Jewish Literature and the New Testament*. Leiden: Brill, 2003.

Synesius of Cyrene, *The Essays and Hymns of Synesisus of Cyrene*, trans. A. Fitzgerald, 2 vols, Oxford: Oxford University Press, 1930.

Taliaferro, Charles and Chad V. Meister, *The Cambridge Companion to Christian Philosophical Theology*. Cambridge: Cambridge University Press, 2010.

Tanner, Jeremy, *The Invention of Art History in Ancient Greece: Religion, Society and Artistic Rationalisation*. Cambridge: Cambridge University Press, 2006.

Tanner, Sonja, *In Praise of Plato's Poetic Imagination*. Lanham, MD: Lexington Books, 2010.

Tattershall, Ian, *Becoming Human: Evolution and Human Uniqueness*. Oxford: Oxford University Press, 1998.

Taylor, T. K. and Giles Waller, *Christian Theology and Tragedy: Theologians, Tragic Literature and Tragic Theory*. Farnham: Ashgate, 2011.

Te Velde, Rudi A., *Participation and Substantiality in Thomas Aquinas*. Leiden: Brill, 1995.

Thomas, Alan, *Bernard Williams*. Cambridge: Cambridge University Press, 2007.

Thomas, Keith, *Religion and the Decline of Magic*. New York: Charles Schribner, 1973.

Tighe, Richard, *A Short Account of the Life and Writings of the Late Rev. William Law*. London: Harvey and Darton, 1828.

Tillich, Paul, *Shaking the Foundations*, Harmondsworth: Penguin, 1969.

Tillich, Paul, *Philosophical Writings*. Berlin and New York: De Gruyter, 1989.

Tola, Fernando and Carmen Dragonetti, 'Some Remarks on Bhartrhari's concept of Pratibha', *Journal of Indian Philosophy* 18/2 (1990): 95-112.

Too, Yun Lee, *Education in Greek and Roman Antiquity*. Leiden: Brill, 2001.

Torrance, Alan, 'Is There a Distinctive Human Nature? Approaching the Question from a Christian Epistemic Base'. *Zygon*, 47 (2012): 903–17.

Traherne, Thomas, *Centuries of Mediations*. London: P. J. and A. E. Dobell, 1927.

Traherne, Thomas, *Selected Poems and Prose*, ed. Alan Bradford. Harmondsworth: Penquin, 1991.

Tuve, Rosemond, *Elizabethan and Metaphysical Imagery: Renaissance Poetic and Twentieth-century Critics*. Chicago, IL: University of Chicago Press, 1947.

Tuveson, Ernest Lee, *The Imagination as a Means of Grace; Locke and the Aesthetics of Romanticism*. Berkeley: University of California Press, 1960.

Ustinova, Yulia, *Caves and the Ancient Greek Mind. Descending Underground in the Search for Ultimate Truth*. Oxford: Oxford University Press, 2009.

Van der Toorn, Karel, *The Image and the Book: Iconic Cults, Aniconism, and the Rise of Book Religion in Israel and the Ancient Near East*. Leuven: Uitgeverij Peeters, 1997.

Van Huyssteen, J. Wentzel, *Alone in the World: Human Uniqueness in Science and Theology.* Grand Rapids, MI: William B. Eerdmans Publishing Co., 2006.

Vasari, *Lives of the Artists.* Harmondsworth: Penguin, 1979.

Versluis, Arthur, *The Esoteric Origins of the American Renaissance.* Oxford: Oxford University Press, 2001.

Vickery, John B., *The Literary Impact of The Golden Bough.* Princeton, NJ: Princeton University Press, 1973.

Voegelin, Erich, *Order and History 4, The Ecumenic Age.* Columbia: University of Missouri Press, 2000.

Voegelin, Eric and Ellis Sandoz, *Published Essays, 1966-1985.* Baton Rouge: Louisiana State University Press, 1990.

Vogel, Cornelia J. de, *Rethinking Plato and Platonism.* Leiden: Brill, 1986.

Voss Roberts, Michelle, *Tastes of the Divine: Hindu and Christian Theologies of Emotion.* New York: Fordham, 2014.

Wackenroder, Wilhelm Heinrich, *Confessions and Fantasies*, trans. Mary Hurst Schubert. University Park, PA: Pennsylvania State University Press, 1971.

Walbridge, John, *The Wisdom of the Mystic East.* Albany: State University of New York, 1981.

Waldron, Jeremy, *God, Locke, and Equality: Christian Foundations in Locke's Political Thought.* Cambridge: Cambridge University Press, 2002.

Walker, D. P., *Ancient Theology.* Ithaca, NY: Cornell, 1972.

Walton, Brad, *Jonathan Edwards, Religious Affections, and the Puritan Analysis of True Piety, Spiritual Sensation, and Heart Religion.* Lewiston: E. Mellen Press, 2002.

Watson, Daniel, 'Images of Unlikeness: Proclus on Homeric σύμβολον and the Perfection of the Rational Soul'. *Dionysius* 31 (2013): 57-78.

Weber, Dietrich, *Heimito von Doderer.* Munich: Beck, 1987.

Weber, M. Andreas, *David Hume und Edward Gibbon: Religionssoziologie in der Aufklärung.* Frankfurt am Main: Anton Hain, 1990.

Weddle, Polly, 'Touching the Gods: Physical Interaction with Cult Statues in the Roman World'. PhD thesis, University of Durham, 2010.

Weeks, Dennis, L., *Steps Toward Salvation: An Examination of Coinherence and Substitution in the Seven Novels of Charles Williams.* New York: Peter Lang, 1991.

Weigel, Peter, *Aquinas on Simplicity: An Investigation into the Foundations of his Philosophical Theology.* Bern: Peter Lang, 2008.

Weil, Simone, *First and Last Notebooks.* Oxford: Oxford University Press, 1970.

Werkgartner-Ryan, Ingrid, *Zufall und Freiheit in Heimito von Doderers 'Dämonen'*. Vienna: Hermann Böhlhaus, 1986.
Westcott, Brook Foss, *Essays in the History of Religious Thought in the West*. London: Macmillan, 1891.
Whichcote, Benjamin, *The Sermons of Benjamin Whichcote 1–4*, ed. William Wishart. Edinburgh: Printed by T. W. And T. Ruddimans, 1742.
Wierenga, Edward R., *The Nature of God: An Inquiry into Divine Attributes*. Ithaca, NY: Cornell University Press, 1989.
Williams, Bernard, *Ethics and the Limits of Philosophy*. London: Fontana, 1993.
Williams, Bernard, *Shame and Necessity*. Berkeley: University of California, 2008.
Williams, Charles, *Witchcraft*. London: Faber, 1941.
Williams, Charles, *The Figure of Beatrice: A Study in Dante*. New York: Noonday Press, 1961.
Williams, Christopher J. F., *Being, Identity, and Truth*. Oxford: Clarendon, 1992.
Williams, Rowan, *The Edge of Words*. London: Bloomsbury, 2014.
Williamson, George, *The Longing for Myth in Germany: Religion and Aesthetic Culture from Romanticism to Nietzsche*. Chicago: University of Chicago Press, 2004.
Willson, Leslie, *A Mythical Image*. Durham: Duke, 1964.
Wind, Edgar, *Pagan Mysteries of the Renaissance*. London: W. W. Norton, 1968.
Winship, George P., 'The Novels of Charles Williams'. In Mark Hillegas, *Shadows of Imagination*, 111–24. Carbondale: Southern Illinois University Press, 1969.
Wittgenstein, Ludwig, *Philosophical Investigations*. Oxford: Blackwell, 1981.
Wittgenstein, Ludwig, *The Blue and Brown Books: Preliminary Studies for the Philosophical Investigations*. Oxford: Blackwell, 1980.
Wollheim, Richard, *The Thread of Life*. Cambridge, MA: Harvard University Press, 1984.
Wolterstorff, Nicholas, *On Universals; An Essay in Ontology*. Chicago, IL: University of Chicago Press, 1970.
Woods, Richard, *Understanding Mysticism*. Garden City, NY: Image Books, 1980.
Wordsworth, William, *Prelude*, ed. Ernest de Selincourt and corrected by Stephen Gill, Oxford: Oxford University Press, 1984.
Wordsworth, William, *Complete Poetical Works, A New Edition*, revised by Ernest de Selincourt. Oxford: Oxford University Press, 1936.
Wynn, Mark, *Emotional Experience and Religious Understanding: Integrating*

Perception, Conception and Feeling. Cambridge: Cambridge University Press, 2005.
Wynn, Mark, *Renewing the Senses.* Oxford: Oxford University Press, 2013.
Yarbo Collins, Adela, *The Combat Myth in the Book of Revelation.* Missoula: Scholar's Press, 1976.
Yeats, William Butler, *Poems.*
Zanker, Paul and Björn Christian Ewald, *Mit Mythen leben: Die Bilderwelt der römischen Sarkophage.* München: Hirmer, 2004.

Index of Subjects

Abhasa 197
absolute 28, 77, 136, 139, 143–4, 168, 186, 188, 194
abstraction
    in art 166, 194, 259
    in philosophy 50, 126, 128, 132, 259
aesthetics xiv, 25, 29, 60, 63–4, 68, 71, 73, 85, 163, 166, 197, 203, 221–2 227
Agalma, 17–25
albatross 233
ambiguity xiii
    of apparitions 172
    living with 180
analogia entis 177
anarchy 95
angels 79, 120, 135, 212ff., 218, 235 *see also* Bulgakov
anthropology xiv, 3–4, 30, 32ff.
anthropomorphism 153
apes xii, xvii
    glabrous 41, 46
    higher 33–4
Apocalypse of St John the Divine 210, 212, 214, 217, 229, 248, 251ff.
apocalyptic 163, 207, 211, 251
apophaticism 136
archetypes 16, 73, 121, 131, 201
art
    Belting on 4
    and Benjamin 3
    in the cave 56
    Chesterton on 55
    Goethe on 28
    Gomrich 28
    Hegel's definition of 61
    historians of 8
    historians and Platonism 29
    Jonas on 45
    Lessing on 27
    and magic 170
    and metaphysics
    as mirror 62
    and Neoplatonism 15
    organ of contemplation 71
    Plotinus on 20
    Schelling on 28
    Scruton on 62ff., 201ff.
    Shakespeare on 7
    and theology xiv
ascent of the soul 76
aseity, divine 132–3
atheism 24, 163, 170, 174
    in Antiquity xvi
    Buddhism 168, 170
    modern 183ff.
atman 195 *see also* soul
attunement xv, 145, 205–6
autonomy
    ethical 94
    of the image 1, 8, 29
    see also Kant
avatar 197

banquet
    eucharistic 243
    heavenly xv, 243ff.
    platonic 220, 243
Banyan Tree 193
Barzakh 10
beauty xiv, 15–29, 43, 59, 62–87, 98, 105–6, 117, 124, 132, 135, 144
    absolute 140
    of the divine intellect 203, 218, 244
    Gothic 249ff.
    Indian 155
    natural 219ff.
    Somerset 219
becoming 18, 44ff., 139, 260
Begriff 46, 167ff.
being 11ff., 16ff., 44, 68, 73–4, 77, 123,

127, 132ff., 184ff., 196–7, 205–6,
243 see also esse
community of 181, 205 see also
Voegelin
divine 163, 177, 198, 210, 260
perfect 139ff., 188ff., 207, 217ff., 233, 260
Bhakti 193–4
Bidepalism, obligate 41–2, 221
Bild 4, 7–8, 12ff., 21–2, 27–8, 48–9, 71, 200
borderline personality disorder 93, 181
Brahman 170, 191, 193, 195
brain, large human xii, 180, 228, 258
Buddhi 207

cathedral
Gobekli Tepe as proto cathedral 226
gothic 60, 215, 226, 247ff., 252
image of Jerusalem 247
causae primordiales 126 see also Eriugena
causal nexus, human removal from 39 see
also determinism
cause 54, 144
final 140
Neoplatonic 72, 132, 137, 139
cave, Platonic
Byzantine 56
Chauvet and other Palaeolithic
painting 55
chakra 192
character, ethical 91, 93, 109
in Shakespeare 172
chariot
divine xi
Ezekiel 209, 214
merkabah 215
Parmenides 207
platonic 260
Upanishads 207
Chauvet 37, 55–6
co-inherence 125, 246, 256 see also
Williams, C.
cognitive science 36–7, 183
commands, divine 127
commodification 2
communion
of atman with Brahman 195
as eucharist 106, 172

with God as personal encounter 35,
71, 106, 172, 245
concepts
empiricist account of inadequate 131
infused with feeling 179
Marion on 149
conjectures 219
conscience 111
consciousness
historical 202, 204ff.
illusion of 43, 191, 258
consensus gentium 185ff.
contemplation 220ff.
conversion, not substitution of self 151
Cosmos, as mirror 140ff.
Noetic 24, 135, 245
creatio ex nihilo, ambiguity of 140–1,
189
culture 31–46 see also nature

darshana 11
Darwinism xiv, xvii, 7, 32ff., 41, 131, 145
deception 167, 184
Deification 103–4
demonology 173 see also Doderer
demons 37, 152, 154ff., 160ff., 175
determinism incoherence of 35, 95, 258
Spinoza's 169
disenchantment 3, 13 see also Weber
distinction vs division 138
dualism, cognitive 70ff. see also Scruton

ecology 221ff.
Egyptians, the wisdom of, 1–2, 23ff.
ekphrasis 2
emanation 16, 79, 140ff., 165, 189, 196,
250 see also divine ideas
emotion 46, 67, 84, 86, 93, 106, 169,
179–80, 194ff.
enjoyment 18, 99, 253 see also Traherne
escapism 174
eschatology 251ff.
esse 125, 144 see also God; Being
ens necessarium 144
esse ipsum 125
ethics 91ff., 169, 242
eucharist 101, 231, 251–2, 243

Index of Subjects

evil 96, 116, 134, 155, 160, 167, 178, 242, 248, 259
experience, religious xv, xvii, 16, 25ff., 60, 68, 76, 112 *see also* Plotinus
expression, in art 1, 75, 84–5, 237
expressivism 79, 163, 250

face 96ff.
fact, spiritual 147
faith, religious 56, 71, 117, 187, 210
feast, days of xv, 220–56, 260
festival 229ff.
fiction xii, 42, 85, 89, 102, 109, 120
food 228ff.
forma 48
forms, Platonic xvii, 12, 16, 21, 25, 76, 95, 120, 122–48, 165, 244
  of the imagination 257
  sensory 253
freedom 32, 44–5, 63, 89–118, 167, 176, 183, 198, 258
  as illusion 97

Gegenbild 28, 71, 107
genus 51
ghosts 154
gift 244ff.
Gobekli Tepe 38, 226
God
  as immaterial 50
  love of 104, 169
  as personal 117, 138ff., 194ff., 244–5
  as spiritual 47, 49, 52–3, 106, 118, 135, 255, 260
  violent 217
good, the 15, 19, 43, 50, 56, 71ff., 127, 134ff., 177, 186, 199, 205, 225, 233ff., 243–4, 255 *see also* One, the
Goodness 19ff, 50, 71–2, 85, 134–5, 141–2, 230–4
gratitude 240ff.
guilt, of humanity 170
  contrasted with shame 94ff.

hedonism 193
hell, 107, 112, 117, 177–8
  spiritual nature of 104
Hinduism, definition of 193
  of the gods 199ff.
  history
  link with idolatry 188
  sacred 205ff.
homo
  ludens 107
  necans 107
  sapiens xii, 33, 35ff., 38, 41, 46, 54, 131, 228
hunter-gather 226–7

icon 3-10, 74, 149ff., 215, 225
iconic turn 4ff.
iconoclasm, myths of 163ff.
iconography, Christian xiv, 1, 215, 232
ideas
  divine 119ff., 214, 246
  of God 146ff. *see also* symbol
  living powers 21, 73, 121ff.
  not opposed to universals 130
identity
  divine 137
  personal 93
ideology, reassuring narratives of 171
idolatry 149–81
idols 18, 149–81
illusion 41, 169, 174, 197
  of immanence 65 *see also* Sartre
  of myth 97
images
  and archetypes 73ff., 131, 201
  of Christ 195
  and freedom 32, 89ff.
  Hindu 154ff., 188ff.
  indeterminate 46ff.
  Islamic 60, 164ff.
  Jewish 163ff.
  in language 4, 10–11
  to live by 15
  living 7
  ontology of 99
  opposed to concepts 15ff.
  Plotinian 17ff.
  prohibitions against 166ff.
  revealed 210ff., 259 *see also* Farrer

symbolic xvii, 10, 37, 55, 81, 123, 147, 231–2, 250, 260
imaginatio vera 77
imagination
  anagogic 59ff.
  and deception 167
  platonic 72
Imago Dei 31ff.
immanence, divine 175, 250
incarnation xii–xiii, 71, 125, 204
inspiration
  artistic 60, 235
  critique of 167
  divine 29, 83, 86, 208, 212–13, 235
instantiation 144
intellect
  divine 144
  feeling 125
Interpretatio Graeca 98
Isvara 197

Jivanmukta 197
joy, of the feast 230
judgement 54, 66, 80
  last 114, 212, 251
justice 54, 94–5, 100, 207
justification, epistemic 27, 185

knowledge
  by acquaintance 5, 16, 89ff.
  of God 244ff.
  and imagination 116ff., 244–5, 249

language xii
  animal language 34ff.
  apophatic 69–70
  of the Egyptians 26ff., 221
  mythic dimension of 200
  picturing the world 11ff.
  of stone 207
law
  moral 94, 96, 111, 139, 152, 157
  of nature 70, 90, 98, 143–4
  of revelation 166, 215, 231
light, symbol of 13, 19, 21–2, 25, 47, 53, 73, 101, 105ff., 142, 165, 198, 218, 220, 230, 234–5, 244–56

Lila 195–6
literature
  apocalyptic 163
  English Renaissance 172
  Greek 109
  and philosophy 90ff.
logos
  divine xiv, 6, 28, 75, 126, 132, 135, 189, 210, 243
  spermatic 199
love, various forms of 100, 115ff.
  Christian 96, 101–4, 111, 143, 241, 247, 257
  courtly 75
  and the demonic 177
  Hindu theology of 194–6
  Islamic account of 73
  Neoplatonic theory of 71, 141
  Platonic 236
  Plotinus on 16, 198, 244ff.
  Scruton on 63
  Spinoza on 169
loyalty 70, 242
luck, moral 109ff. *see also* Williams, B.

madness 81, 239
magic, perversion of sacramental 178
mankind
  deficit creature 41
  Palaeolithic 39, 55ff.
materialism 21 *see also* composition
materialism, crudity of 1, 116, 132, 191ff., 257
  supernatural 18
maya 169, 196–7
meals, distinctively human 220, 225, 231, 234, 243
melancholy 179, 181, 250
menagerie, Platonic 134
merkabah 215 *see also* chariot
metaphorics 13 *see also* Blumenberg
metaphors xii, 2, 9ff.
  absolute 13ff. *see also* Blumenberg
  not symbols xv
metaphysics, critique of 13
metaxy 145, 175, 181 *see also* Voegelin
mind xiv, 32, 40ff.

and brain 179-80
chariot image 207ff., 175
divine 21, 51, 72, 126ff., 131, 140, 202, 243
unity 21-2, 135
visual paradigm defended 43ff., 73-4
monism vs mystical theism 138
monotheism, its price 161
mystical and monarchical 162
mood 125
morality xv, 94ff., 101, 109, 146
morality system 95
music 234ff.
mysteries 202ff.
myths 200ff.

narcissism 116
naturalism, failure of 36ff.
nature, aesthetics of 221ff., 234ff.
book of 222-3
divine 127ff.
Neanderthals 36ff.
necessity, Divine 127ff.
Nirvana 136
nominalism, in medieval thought 10
incoherence of 132
novel, the 101

objects, abstract 141, 205
obligation, moral 95, 127, 240
oblivion, imaginative 181
ontology, of the image 99
Orthodoxy, persecution by the Soviets 174

padma 192
paradise xv, 77, 219ff., 248ff., 257ff., 260
participation
divine ideas 139ff.
mysteries 148
right brain hemisphere 180
perception 46, 8, 11, 26ff., 43, 45, 65ff., 75-7, 82, 174, 179, 242
persecution 174
persons, divine 117, 128-38
and narrative 91ff.
not things 51
poets, lies of 99

polytheism 153-62, 183-206
Hume and Gibbon on 157, 202
positivism
scientific 126, 146
theological 32, 46
predication 128-9, 195
presence, Divine 52, 57, 60, 79, 125, 139, 145, 148, 150, 162, 186, 195ff., 205
projectivism 41, 252
prophecy 123, 162
Psalms 137, 209, 224, 237, 240
psychoanalysis 167
psychology, evolutionary, bogus nature of 56-7
puja 153

qualities, primary and secondary 75, 173

reality, secondary 175
apprehended through imagination 91
reality, transcendent xiii, 20, 151, 174ff., 208
redemption 71, 178
reductionism 10
reification 2, 13, 134
relativism 35
religion
and artistic imagination 60, 82, 85ff.
cultured despisers of 32
Durkheim view of 70ff.
Greek 18
of love 73, 153
Lucretius on 106, 167
Palaeolithic 55
political 170-1
revelation
and imagination 57, 83, 145
and mythology 211ff.
philosophy of 199ff.
of St John 197, 209ff.
rights, human, grounded in theology 31, 53-4
ritual, pointlessness 172
romanticism 83, 189, 200, 257

sacrifice 69-70, 104-3, 108ff., 142, 151ff.,

160, 167, 189, 210, 218, 230ff., 239–40, 246, 255
salience, perceptual 179–80, 238
scepticism 131, 146
scientism 64, 258
scientist, word coined by Coleridge 258
secularism xvi, xvii, 30, 54, 90, 118, 173, 180, 200, 227, 268
seeing, thought infused 178–80, 253
self
    divided 112
    episodic 93ff.
    narrative 92ff.
semen religionis 202
senses, spiritual 26, 86, 254
sensus divinitatis 37, 185, 202
Seraphim 124, 224, 250
simplicity, divine, not a property 132–8
soul, as image 74, 76, 99, 105
species, biological 33, 39, 43
    philosophical 48–51, 126, 130-1, 143
spirit, divine 243
stoicism 106
summum bonum 235
superstition 153
sympathy 238

Tao 94, 205
temple
    Jerusalem 213, 217ff., 225–56
    Konarak 207
Tetragrammaton 210 *see also* God
theatre, Cartesian, advantage of 43ff.
theogony, drama of 204ff.
theology, ancient 161, 190ff.
theophany 71, 77–8, 139, 145, 192, 205–6, 209, 248, 260
tragedy 94, 109

transcendence xiv, xvii, 1, 26, 29, 68, 76, 79, 113, 138–9, 175–6, 200, 202, 205, 210, 227, 233, 250, 259ff. *see also* immanence
truth
    of imagination 76, 78, 83, 89ff., 105 109, 146, 191, 203, 208, 214
    non propositional 13, 15, 24, 26ff., 86, 97, 106, 207, 248

uniqueness, human, defended 32ff., 41, 51, 55ff.
unity, opposed to composition 21, 138
Upanishads 184, 193, 205
utilitarianism 230, 257–8

value xiii, 63, 66, 72, 92ff., 110, 144, 179, 225
violence, theism accused of 33, 156-7, 161, 173, 218
vision
    artistic 82
    apocalyptic 163, 173, 209-60
    beatific 115, 243
    contemplation 22ff., 86, 103, 144ff., 151, 191, 205, 220ff., 234ff., 243ff.
    Neoplatonic 15, 19, 24
    pre-eminence of 43ff.
voluntarism, Platonic opposition to 142, 196

Whiggism 95
White Rose 113–14
will 186–7 *see also* Schopenhauer, A.
witches 172–3, 178
world, of imagination as *mundus imaginalis* see Corbin, H.
    intelligible 10, 20ff. 74, 86

Index of Names

Adkins 110
Adorno 9
Aelian 186, 261
Akhenaton 159
Al Baruni 187
Alexander 23
Amor 98, 111
Apuleius 96, 98, 105
Aquinas xiii, 32, 40, 48–9, 126, 130, 137, 140–1, 198, 240, 261, 263, 273, 275, 286, 288
Argus 245–6
Aristotle 5, 9, 22, 40, 43, 83, 89, 129ff., 140, 206, 242–3, 262, 272
Armstrong, A. H. 18, 59, 149, 188, 243, 246, 261
Augustine of Canterbury 2
Augustine of Hippo 4, 19, 40, 46, 48–9, 68–9, 117, 126ff., 135, 139, 142, 150ff., 190, 222, 224, 230, 235–6, 243, 252, 262, 266, 274

Bachelard, G. 19, 97
Bacon, Lord F. xvi, 47, 54
Balthasar, H. U. von xvi, 149–50, 262, 266
Barker, M. x, 162–3, 218–19, 225, 262
Barnett Newman 29, 163
Barth, B. 28, 262
Barth, K. 149, 242
Baudelaire, C. 66, 68, 89, 145, 251, 260, 263
Bede, The venerable 2–3, 171, 263
Beierwaltes, W. v, 53, 79, 149, 151, 171, 219, 235, 243, 250–1, 263
Belting, H. 3–4, 263
Benjamin, W. 3
Bentham, J. 3, 257
Berlekamp, P. 164–5, 264
Berlin, I. xvii
Bescancon, A. xiii, 166, 169, 254, 264
Blackburn, S. 6, 264

Blake, W. xvii, 207, 222, 249–50, 264, 265, 268
Bloom, H. 172, 264
Blumenberg, H. 13ff., 202, 264, 280
Bossuet 60
Botticelli 27
Boulding, K. 6, 10, 43, 80, 265
Brooke, R. 107–8
Bulgakov, S. 213–14, 245, 265
Burke, E. 63, 91, 107, 211
Byron, Lord 258

Carlyle, T. 257
Cassio Dio 17
Ceausescu 36
Cecilia 235–6, 267, 279
Chagall 163
Chaucer 248
Chesterton, G. K. 54, 101
Cicero 40, 102, 183
Clark, S. R. L. 233
Clement of Alexandria 39
Cleopatra 23
Coleridge, S. T. xvii, 5, 14–15, 45, 63–4, 73, 76–7, 80, 83–4, 91, 97, 100, 118–19, 125, 138–9, 142, 144, 188, 214–15, 221–2, 232, 234, 239, 243–4, 257–8, 266–7
Collingwood, R. G. 80, 82, 84, 85, 267
Conway Morris, S. 143
Coomaraswamy, A. 191–2, 208, 267
Copernicus 33
Corbin, H. 10, 73, 106, 165, 200
Cornford, F. M. 129, 148, 267, 282
Craig, E. 31–2, 267
Creuzer, G. F. 25–6, 186, 191, 203–4, 265
Cupid 96ff., 100, 114
Cusa, N. (Cusanus) 46, 48, 137, 147, 152, 186–7, 200, 219, 243, 267, 269

Dante viii, xi, 19–20, 27, 43, 73ff., 107–8,

120–1, 135, 211, 222, 246–7, 251, 257, 265, 288
Darwin, C. xiv, xvii, 7, 32ff., 41, 131, 145, 268
Davies, B. 136–7, 261
Derrida, J. 4, 268
Dickie, G. 61
Didi-Huberman 8
Dietrich of Freiburg 47ff., 137, 176, 270
Dionysius the Areopagite 15, 71, 79, 105, 120, 135, 141, 268, 275, 278, 281, 282, 287
Dionysus 120, 189, 195, 204, 268
Dodds, E. R. 110, 268
Doderer, H. von 173ff., 273, 284
Donne, J. 74
Duchamp, M. 61
Durkheim, E. 70–1, 171

Edwards, J. 141
Edwards, M. 16, 97
Eliade, M. 41, 97, 191, 195
Erasmus, D. 60
Eriugena, Johannes, Scotus 48, 69, 71–2, 77, 126, 219, 248, 269
Ethelbert (King of Kent) 2
Ezekiel xi, 123, 145, 208ff., 213ff., 225–6, 245–6, 260

Farrer, A. x, xi, xv, xvi, 163, 209–10, 212, 214, 218, 229, 240, 245–6, 270
Ficino, M. 63, 72, 76–7, 98, 235, 270
Field, H. 133
Flaubert, G. 67
Frankfurt, H. 93
Frege 64, 133
Freud, S. xvii, 8, 33, 41, 82, 84, 97, 116, 129, 145, 159, 161–2, 166, 171

Gandhi 143
Gehlen, A. 41–2
Gibbon, E. 125, 132–3, 156
Girard, R. 151
Goethe, J. H. von 28, 38, 77, 178
Gombrich, Sir E. 1, 8, 28, 154, 271
Gray, J. 170–1, 217–18, 271
Gregory (the Great) 215

Harari, Y. xii
Hegel xv, 1, 9–10, 13, 28–9, 61, 94, 146, 162, 166, 168, 183, 188, 189, 200–1
Heidegger, M. 4, 9, 12–13, 29, 32, 45, 69, 85, 134, 149–50, 184, 240, 272
Hepburn, R. 219ff.
Heraclitus 17–18, 21
Herder, J. G. xvii
Hick, J. 187
Hobbes, T. xvi, 5, 83, 162, 202
Hölderlin, F. 183–4
Holmes, R. 219–20, 232, 258
Homer 2, 15, 17, 74, 96, 185
Hosea 145
Huber, K. 113–14
Hume, D. 43, 65, 67, 92, 128, 156–7, 202, 252
Husserl, E. 65, 184, 193

Ibn Arabi 10, 73–4, 153, 185
Ingelo, N. 101ff.
Isaiah xvii, 145, 156, 206, 215

Jackson, F. 90
Johnson, M. 9–10
Johnson, S. 60
Jonas, H. 32, 42, 44–5, 55
Jones, M. 228
Jones, Sir W. 191
Justin Martyr 162

Kandinsky, W. xvii
Kant xvii, 28, 42–3, 65, 67, 94ff., 150, 166, 168, 169
Keats, J. 45, 85
Kenney, J. 162, 188
Kierkegaard 69, 116, 142
Krushchev 174

Lakoff, G. 9–10, 134
Lane Craig, W. 134
Law, W. 122, 178
Leithart, P. 241–2, 275, 298
Lessing, G. E. 27
Lewis, C. S. xiv, 33, 89ff., 94ff., 104ff., 114ff., 177, 233

Lipner, J. 193
Locke, J. 5, 11, 29, 31, 92
Lucretius 101, 153, 167, 202
Luther 32, 117, 242
Lynceus 75

MacDonald, G. 97
MacIntyre, A. 92–3
Madhva 195
Magritte, R. 27
Maimonides 140, 163–4
Maistre, J. de 225, 234
Mann, T. 239
Marion, J.-L. 149ff.
Marks, J. 34, 37
Matsuzawa 54
McGilchrist 180ff., 242
Mill, J. S. 257
Milton, J. 31, 139, 152ff.
Mirabai 194
Mirandola, Pico 52
Mitchell, W. G. T. 8–9
Mithen, S. xi
Mondrian, P. 29
More, H. xvi, 53, 101ff., 115, 209, 215, 217–18
Muir, J. 223, 225

Narcissus 2
Nietzsche, F. 9–10, 32, 94, 109, 149, 167, 217, 239, 260
Nussbaum, M. 89

Ockham, W. 128ff.
Orff, C. 113ff.
Origen of Alexandria 26, 39, 152, 247–8

Panofsky, E. xiv, 1, 8, 29
Parfit, D. 92
Parmenides 184, 207–8
Pascal, B. 69
Pasternak, B. 73, 260
Pausanias 17
Pieper, J. 225, 230ff.
Pheidias 16
Philo 233
Pinker, S. 36

Plato 56, 96, 98, 110, 120, 123, 126–49, 184, 203, 206ff.
Plotinus xiv, xvii, 1–2, 15ff., 232–4, 63, 72ff., 84ff., 102, 115, 120, 134ff., 151, 185, 198, 203, 244–5, 253
Plutarch 21, 24, 154
Powell, A. 175
Prager, B. 27–8, 236
Prinz, J. 36
Proclus 15–16, 120, 137, 141, 149
psyche 96ff., 111ff., 114
Purchas, S. 232
Putnam, H. 133

Quine, W. V. O. 129, 133

Ramanuja 186, 194–5, 238
Rappaport, R. 171
Rorty, R. 10ff., 15
Rothko, M. 29, 163
Roy, Ram Mohan 190
Ruskin, J. 155
Russell, Lord B. 183ff.

Sassoon, S. 125
Schama, S. 223ff.
Schlegel, F. 189
Schelling, F. W. J. von 9, 28, 71, 116ff., 141, 145, 168, 174, 183, 189, 194, 199ff.
Scholl, Sophie and Hans 113–14
Schonberg, A. 239
Schopenhauer, A. 166–70, 189
Scruton, R. 60–83, 201, 223, 227, 237, 252, 268
Shakespeare 7, 27, 33, 52, 75, 83, 85–6, 100–11, 172, 237–41, 241, 262
Shelley, P. B. 7 6, 212, 235ff., 258
Shiva 154, 189, 191–2, 195, 197, 204
Simson, von 249
Smith, J. 26, 46–7, 53, 141, 151, 153–4, 166–7, 254, 256
Spenser, E. 73, 75, 96, 98ff.
Spinoza 136, 166ff., 189, 202
Stillingfleet, E. 53
Strawson, G. 92–3

Suger, Abbot 248–9
Suhrawardi 73
Suk-Yong Chwe 171
Synesius 213

Tagore, R. 190, 207
Tattershall, I. 37–8
Tavener, J. xvii
Taylor, C. xvii, 92–3
Thamos 23
Theut 23
Tillich, P. 116–17, 146–7, 184–5
Tolkien, J. R. R. 100, 108, 125
Tolstoy, L. xiv, 81, 90, 143, 179
Traherne 199, 253ff., 261

Van der Leeuw 60
Van Gogh 29
Van Huyssteen, W. 40, 55–6
Voegelin, E. 145–6, 173ff., 181, 199, 205–6

Voltaire 60, 145

Walbridge, J. 186–7
Walpole, H. 249
Warburg, A. 8, 159
Warnock, M. 65
Watson, J. 32, 145
Weber, M. 3
Westcott, B. F. 188–9
Wells, H. G. 119
Whichcote, B. 43, 151, 177
Whitehead 217
Williams, B. 90, 94ff., 110–11
Williams, C. 75, 119–25, 177–8, 246ff.
Williams, R. 1
Willson 192, 203
Wittgenstein, L. 4–5, 6, 12, 64–5, 77
Wordsworth, W. xii, 23, 78, 116, 124, 190, 221ff.
Wynn, M. x, 178–81, 238, 242, 252ff.

www.ingramcontent.com/pod-product-compliance
Ingram Content Group UK Ltd.
Pitfield, Milton Keynes, MK11 3LW, UK
UKHW020414060225
454752UK00010B/240

9 781441 194633